THE

Dark Side

OF THE

Enlightenment

THE

Dark Side

OF THE

Enlightenment

WIZARDS, ALCHEMISTS, AND SPIRITUAL
SEEKERS IN THE AGE OF REASON

JOHN V. FLEMING

W. W. NORTON & COMPANY

New York · London

[Frontispiece] The widely consulted *Collectanea Chemica Leidensia*, or *Leiden Chemical Anthology*, was principally the work of two seventeenth-century physicians: the Dutchman Theodorus Muykens and the Englishman Christopher Love Morley. It contained several cuts (including this classic of alchemical iconography, taken from the 1693 edition) that united occult and sacred emblems to suggest the moral and scientific unity of the alchemical quest. The Latin title page described it as a work "necessary and of utmost usefulness" to every doctor, chemist, and pharmacist.

For information about permission to reproduce selections from this book, write to Permissions, W. W. Norton & Company, Inc., 500 Fifth Avenue, New York, NY 10110

For information about special discounts for bulk purchases, please contact W. W. Norton Special Sales at specialsales@wwnorton.com or 800-233-4830

Manufacturing by RR Donnelley, Harrisonburg, VA
Book design by Ellen Cipriano
Production manager: Anna Oler

ISBN 978-0-393-07946-3

W. W. Norton & Company, Inc.
500 Fifth Avenue, New York, N.Y. 10110
www.wwnorton.com

W. W. Norton & Company Ltd.
Castle House, 75/76 Wells Street, London W1T 3QT

1 2 3 4 5 6 7 8 9 0

for Luke, Melanie,
and, of course,
John Henry

Contents

List of Illustrations

A Brief Word to the Reader
on How the Book Was Made
and Who Helped Me Make It

I GIVE AN ACCOUNT OF the genesis of *The Dark Side of the Enlightenment* in the introduction, which also attempts to lay out its principal subject matter. A long-standing interest in the English and French literature of the eighteenth century led me to its chief subjects. The reading of any work of literature becomes richer and more intelligible when conducted against the background of the intellectual climate in which it was created, but for the period of the Enlightenment the historical "background" is often indispensable. First in preparing to write the book and then again while actually writing it, I spent several years pursuing such apparently disparate topics as alchemy, epistolary culture, Renaissance Egyptology, Jansenism, Pietism, the spread of Freemasonry in France, and the rise and decline of the literary *salon*. I say "apparently" disparate because one at length discovers in the period of the Enlightenment, as of course in other historical periods, some convincing overarching unities.

This book, though necessarily founded in a wide reading of scholarly literature over many years, is intended for the educated general reader rather than the specialist. Accordingly, I do not supply the footnote citations and extensive bibliography appropriate for the genre of the academic monograph. However, I have appended to each chapter a brief bibliography. It gives the details of works on which I have chiefly relied and identifies most from which I have actually quoted. Some of the sources appear in specialized journals found only in research libraries. In the hopes that *The Dark Side* may stimulate the reader's interest in this or that aspect of its materials, I also offer some general suggestions for possible further reading. I have tried whenever possible to direct the reader to materials written in the English language or available in English translation. I have also tried to exercise an option for the readable. Inevitably the best sources on European topics and persons are sometimes written in European languages, and I cite such foreign-language scholarship as has significantly shaped my book.

With a few rare exceptions, such as perhaps St. John the Divine on the isle of Patmos, authors rarely really write books on their own. Certainly I could never have written this one without the help of many family members, friends, colleagues, and professional collaborators in the publishing business. I want to acknowledge some of them by name here:

Most of the preparation of this book was done in the Firestone Library of Princeton University, but I also enjoyed the facilities of the American Library in Paris. My first debt of gratitude, as always, is to the librarians who work so effectively to preserve and make accessible the materials of humanistic study. Without the stimulating conversations of many professional friends and colleagues over the decades I would never have undertaken the project. Stimulation in genesis is not the same thing as approbation in result, and my sincere gratitude for the former comes entirely without any spurious claim of the latter. My family, typified by the young scholars to whom I have dedicated the book, have tolerated my foibles and indulged my enthusiasms for a long time, in some instances for more than half a century. I *am* aware of my great good fortune.

I have been fortunate, too, in the professionals I have worked with in the publishing world. The cheerful optimism of my delightful literary agent, Julia Lord, is an unfailing tonic. At W. W. Norton I enjoyed once again the expert help of Starling Lawrence, this time aided by his young associate Ryan Harrington. If I think of them as the Batman and Robin of New York literary editors, Ann Adelman, my copy editor, is beyond question the Wonder Woman. My wife Joan and my friend Eli Schwartz shared with me the inglorious labors of proofreading. Thank you.

THE

Dark Side

OF THE

Enlightenment

Introduction:
The Light and the Dark

THE DARK SIDE OF THE ENLIGHTENMENT is a work of cultural and literary history. Its subjects include certain historical phenomena of the Enlightenment period (the awkward persistence of miracles, learned occultism, Rosicrucianism and Freemasonry, among them) and certain personages (Cagliostro and Julie de Krüdener most prominently) presenting challenges to the generally held views of what the Enlightenment was, and what it did. My book does not pretend to present a sequential argument, let alone a new definition of Enlightenment or a fresh interpretation of it. It does, however, argue for a more capacious examination of what was "enlightened."

One of the first things that strikes the interested reader who approaches the large literature of eighteenth-century intellectual history is that the very term "Enlightenment" as used by scholars is elastic if not protean. Thus we have political Enlightenment, radical Enlightenment, classical Enlightenment, scientific Enlightenment, and many more. We have local Enlightenments galore: the Scottish, the French, the Baltic, and the Bavarian. They are joined by Counter-Enlightenment, an anti-Enlightenment, enemies of Enlightenment.

It is not going too far to say that many scholarly definitions of the

Enlightenment have been designed in part to exclude important phenomena uncongenial to the definer. Thus historians of the Age of Reason have often taken a more restrictive definition of "reason" than did the thinkers and writers of the seventeenth and eighteenth centuries. Henry Stubbe was, in his view, a scientist. His defense of the "miracles" wrought by Valentine Greatrakes was based in a rational and scientific mentality, though one of a different sort than that exhibited by some of his antagonists in the Royal Society. It was likewise an increasingly augmented and "enlightened" confidence in the power and potential of "natural philosophy" that encouraged the "natural" magicians and the alchemists—alchemy being, indeed, the Queen of Enlightenment Science.

Each of the chapters of this book deals with topics or personages enabled and defined by the Enlightenment context. Sorcerers had existed since the time of the Bible and before. But a sorcerer like Count Cagliostro was made possible only by an essentially new social context, the features of which included extensive and rapid international communication of ideas in a functioning "Republic of Letters," and a self-conscious and well-organized international intellectual elite of Rosicrucians and Freemasons. There seems to me no good reason to divorce from the Enlightenment the focus on personal emotion and artistic sentiment of a Julie de Krüdener. Romanticism was not always the rejection of Enlightenment, but often—at least in the minds of the "Romantics"—its expansion and refinement. The origins of Romanticism are intimately connected with hermetic and occult traditions nurtured by an Enlightenment elite.

I CHOSE THE TITLE *The Dark Side of the Enlightenment*, which is meant to be good-humored as well as lighthearted, for probably obvious reasons. It seems rather catchy. It plays against the flattering idea of intellectual and spiritual illumination that gave birth to the word

"Enlightenment," as well as its principal European equivalents, the French *Lumières* and the German *Aufklärung*. Since the period of the Enlightenment witnessed, among other things, a remarkable efflorescence of occultism and mysticism, and since such topics occupy much of my attention, the title seemed to me not merely appropriate but inevitable. Only when I was well into my researches did I come across a German book (Thomas Freller's *Cagliostro: Die dunkle Seite der Aufklärung,* 2001) that anticipates it in its subtitle.

The author of an odd book about odd people perhaps owes his readers an explanation. Of old the troubadours sometimes called their art the "gay saber," the "happy" science or knowledge. "Saber" is a Romance derivative of the Latin *sapere*, "to know"; and the poets meant by "happy" knowing or science, I believe, that form of intellectual activity that was delightful both in its practice and in its product. Thomas Carlyle perhaps had this phrase in mind when he coined the derisive term "the dismal science" to denote the discipline of economics, or political economy, ever rising in prestige in Victorian England.

Carlyle was hardly the first to note or deplore the progress of the dismal science in its broadest sense. Edmund Burke, perhaps less appalled by the decapitation of Queen Marie-Antoinette than by the social changes that could make it seem for thinking men an acceptable or tolerable act, let alone a just or virtuous one, saw in it the end of an era. "But the age of chivalry is gone," he famously wrote in his *Reflections on the French Revolution.* "That of sophisters, economists, and calculators has succeeded; and the glory of Europe is extinguished forever." Was the change lamented by Burke indeed so dramatic and ominous as he thought?

The province of humanistic "knowing" is a mixed terrain. It has its dark valleys as well as its bright, shining peaks, not to mention its vast stretches that are flatter than Flanders and drier than the Gobi Desert. But it is the troubadours' concept of *saber* that has defined my own ambition in *The Dark Side of the Enlightenment*. The first half of their concept (pleasure in the practice of *saber*) I can fairly claim to have achieved.

I am a professional medievalist, and specifically one who has pursued a career investigating various aspects of the Christian thought, literature, and pictorial art of Europe in the long period between Augustine and Erasmus. The book I now present deals with very different materials from a very different historical period—namely, the period usually called the European Enlightenment, and usually dated, approximately, between about 1650 and, say, 1815, with most of its principal salient achievements falling within the eighteenth century. (The precise span of my own study runs from 1662, when an Irish squire awoke with the "impulse" that he had the power to cure scrofula, to the date uncertain, but early in the post-Napoleonic period, when Julie de Krüdener disappeared in the Crimea. One iconic emblem of the Enlightenment was the great French *Encyclopédie*, which appeared over the course of the third quarter of the eighteenth century. Scholarly experts in this field are forever tinkering with dates. Harold Nicolson is probably right in his elegant study *The Age of Reason* in saying that it would be unwise to seek some spurious chronological precision, though he himself points to two great intellectual landmarks that might suggest a beginning.

These are Isaac Newton's *Principia* (1687) and John Locke's *Essay Concerning Human Understanding* (1690). In very general terms these enormously influential books mark a decisive shift in the way thinkers regarded the natural world around them, and the way they thought about thinking itself. What they proposed between them was no small innovation. It would after all be difficult to find a sphere larger than that of the human mind and all possible objects of its attention. I came up with the pseudo-terminal date of 1815, the year of Waterloo, myself. I am not alone in regarding Napoleon Bonaparte as at the very least an *implication* of Enlightenment. Among the most famous and ghoulish of the etchings in Goya's *Los caprichos* is the one entitled *El sueño de la razón produce monstruos*. This is usually translated *The Sleep of Reason Breeds Monsters*. So also and in another sense, as I hope to suggest in this book, did the Dream of Reason.

In truth I have been drawn to my project by both positive and negative stimuli, in part by inclination and in part by provocation. Under the heading of "inclination" I would list, in addition to the nearly inexhaustible riches of eighteenth-century literature and the attractive monuments of eighteenth-century thought, a distinct element of patriotism. Really, all Americans ought to be interested in the Enlightenment as our nation is Enlightenment's child—a thought that should lead us to view the parental abuse of our quotidian political life with an augmented sense of irony or embarrassment. In addition to this I have a more local and personal reason. I spent my long career teaching at Princeton University. Most of our oldest academies were founded at least in part on Enlightenment concepts, but Princeton, as a monument to the Presbyterian Reform in the eighteenth century, had particular connections with that most interesting seat of Enlightenment in the Anglophone world: Scotland. Two Scottish-American Princeton presidents, John Witherspoon (1723–1794) and James McCosh (1811–1894), were in differing ways living emblems of the Enlightenment. Witherspoon, a learned clergyman, was the only signer of the Declaration of Independence who was a college professor. James McCosh continued on to the very threshold of the twentieth century the Enlightenment's conception of "moral philosophy."

As for the provocation, it is related to my vocation of Medieval Studies. Early in my career as a medievalist I became aware of and annoyed by a certain historical "narrative," of nearly ubiquitous credit among the semi-educated, that might be called Gibbon's canard. The reference, of course, is to the great English historian Edward Gibbon, author of *The Decline and Fall of the Roman Empire*. It goes roughly like this. There was once a great Western Civilization in which people

walked around in their bathrobes writing epic poems, building Parthe-
nons and Coliseums and civilizing known worlds by imperial domina-
tion. That beautiful world came to an end when a cultural disaster
(Christianity) and something called the *Völkerwanderung* (barbarian
hordes running hither and thither) joined forces to create the Middle
Ages, aka the Dark Ages, a bleak millennium of brutality, disease,
ignorance, and superstition. Things began to get a little better eventually when one day in the fourteenth century Petrarch walked into a
cave, found a pile of long-neglected manuscripts, and decided to start
a Renaissance. But they only got good again when toward the end of
the seventeenth century Newton published the *Principia* and only
really good in the eighteenth century when Jean-Jacques Rousseau
arrived on the scene and taught his friends and relations (many of
whom in Rousseau's case were his abandoned bastard children) how
to have a New Sensibility.

But this is to subject to travesty an author who subjected the European Middle Ages to nothing stronger than caricature, perhaps.
Unfortunately, the Gibbonesque view of the matter has become permanent in our lexicon. In 1984, at the annual meeting of the Medieval
Academy of America in Atlanta, Professor Fred Robinson of Yale, who
was in that year the president of the academy, delivered the annual
presidential address on the topic "*Medieval, the Middle Ages*," italicizing
the words in such a fashion as to make clear that his business was to
be with "the terms *medieval* and *Middle Ages*, not with the period itself."
Fred Robinson is a learned philologist, but also a very witty fellow, and
his talk had a sparkle not always to be associated with the phrase
"presidential address."

He surveyed a wide sampling of occurrences of the adjective "medieval" in our contemporary discourse. Using the *Computational Analysis
of Present-Day English* of Kucera and Francis, one of the early gifts of
computer technology to humanistic study, Robinson was able to confirm that the adjective "medieval" as used in contemporary English

refers to the actual Middle Ages only infrequently. Medieval "is most often used in Modern English simply as a vague pejorative term meaning 'outmoded,' 'hopelessly antiquated,' or even simply 'bad.'"

A typical anecdote had to do with the meaning of the word as imagined by *NBC Nightly News*. In 1983 the Dutch beer baron, Freddy Heineken, along with his driver, was kidnapped and held for ransom by a gang of desperadoes. During the time the kidnappers were successfully negotiating a huge tribute, the victims were held prisoner, unharmed, in a cement-block room. They were fed, amply but monotonously, with Chinese take-out packaged in Styrofoam. This treatment, according to Tom Brokaw, was "medieval." Fast-food restaurants are a cultural feature of modernity, and General Tso's Chicken is a delicacy unknown even to such ancient baronial sybarites as are imagined to have feasted on larks' tongues.

WHEREAS THE NAMES OF other historical periods have been invented by their friends, the poor medieval period has been left, onomastically speaking, naked before its enemies. The Middle Ages, obviously, must be medial, in the middle of something. What they were medial between, of course, was on one side "the glory that was Greece and the grandeur that was Rome" and on the other side "the Renaissance," the period in which the glory that was Greece and the grandeur that was Rome became "born again." The Middle Ages are perhaps the eighteen-and-a-half-minute gap in the cultural tape of Western culture. This is too widespread and common a notion to be attributed to a single "source." Gibbon simply gave particularly forceful and witty expression to attitudes endemic to the Enlightenment.

Think for a moment of the terminology historians use to denote other remote objects of their interests and attention. "Antiquity," for instance, has a nice positive ring about it, even when it is not yet further dignified as "*Classical* Antiquity." Needless to say, the "Classical

Period" itself has an even nicer ring to it, as do its more localized subdivisions, such as the "Greco-Roman" and the "Hellenistic." One might suppose that historians would be kinder to submissive and cooperative vassals than those rebellious and unyielding, but such is not the case. Even "prehistory," a term used by historians to denote those vast eons forever lost to their ministrations in the thick fogs of their pre-alphabetic remoteness, is at least a neutral term. Think for a moment of the origins of the English word "Gothic." Better yet, try the following experiment. Go onto the eBay Web site and search for items under the heading "Gothic." You will find lots of very interesting stuff, but not many postcards of the Sainte-Chapelle.

Renaissance is a French word meaning "rebirth." As a term of historical periodization, it complements itself at the expense of what it has replaced, namely, the Middle Ages. The Middle Ages are indeed medial precisely in terms of the European "classical" period in its first and second iterations, a re-emergence after long, dull hibernation of highly desirable cultural habits and achievements. Of course, if you have spent a lifetime with such shadows of that dark night as the subtle mind of Augustine or the magnificent Latin of John of Salisbury or the poetic genius of Dante Alighieri, you are more likely to view the matter in terms of continuities and modulations of emphasis rather than intellectual revolution, root and branch.

There were some Renaissance figures who self-consciously enjoyed a sense of superiority with regard to the centuries immediately earlier. There was widespread revulsion at the sterilities of the Scholastic method. Our English word "dunce" derives from the personal name of one of the most subtle of the Scholastic doctors, John Duns Scotus. But the anti-Scholastic attitude long antedated Scholasticism's decay. There is a beautiful passage in Rabelais (2.8) in which Gargantua, writing to his son Pantagruel away at college, exults in advances in culture since the day of his own father Grangousier, who lived when the "time was still dark, and smacking of the infelicity and calamity of the Goths, who had brought all good literature to destruction." But it was really the thinkers and writers of the Enlightenment who dogmatized the historical concept of the "Dark Ages"; it was in response to their goading that, many years ago, I began to collect the materials that would eventually become the subject matter of this book. I did this in a casual and amateur way, around the edges of my general interest reading. I soon discovered that a scholar seeking to study "medieval" witchcraft or "medieval" alchemy would find but comparatively slim pickings before the centuries of Renaissance and Enlightenment. There is something droll in this perception, and in exploring it I have allowed myself to be guided by an assumption that has informed my entire scholarly life. It is this: although cultural history is a serious business, cultural historians do well to try to honor in their own work those elements of the lighthearted, the absurd, the comic, and the ironic that are a part of the lived experience of even the grimmest of historical periods.

The medieval theme is serious in this book to the following extent. There are numerous aspects of the intellectual life of the Enlightenment in which the medieval continuities are as conspicuous as the medieval rejections. The machinery of medieval Christianity was easier to jettison than the appetite for transcendental experience, and long traditions of medieval religious practice seemed to offer natural conduits to it.

Although everybody knows what the Enlightenment was (is) in a very general sense, the consensus crumbles with every step toward specificity. Immanuel Kant was one of the greatest of Enlightenment philosophers, perhaps *the* greatest. He wrote a famous essay entitled "What is Enlightenment?" He certainly ought to know, if anybody knows, and we must in a moment consider his noble answer to the question he put to himself. Suffice it for the moment to say that Kant's answer does little to delimit our conception of the chronological period of the Enlightenment, its principal intellectual characteristics, or the subject matter of its characteristic preoccupations.

The general meaning of "Enlightenment" is perhaps self-evident. In one standard reference work, Chisick's *Historical Dictionary of the Enlightenment*, we find the following definition: "the process of spreading certain kinds of information, knowledge, understanding and attitudes." The editor adds the following gloss: "The name of the movement is its own key metaphor: light spreading and driving out the darknesses of ignorance, superstition and fanaticism." The enlightened is the obverse of the benighted, as day is the obverse of night. But of course images of enlightenment in this sense will be found in all the major religions and secular philosophies of the world. Perhaps the most famous Christian convert of the post-biblical period was St. Augustine, just as Paul was the most famous convert of the biblical period. It was thematically appropriate, therefore, that Augustine's moment of conversion should come through a fortuitous reading of a passage in Paul in which the Apostle admonishes his hearers to move from metaphoric night to metaphoric day, to put off the works of darkness and to don the armor of light. "The night is far spent, the day is at hand: let us therefore cast off the works of darkness, and let us put on the armour of light." That text became, and remains to this day, an appointed reading for the first Sunday in Advent, at the very beginning of each new year of the Christian calendar.

In this book there will inevitably—and at least superficially, *surprisingly*—be numerous references to the Bible. Whatever their preconceptions, candid students of the European Enlightenment must soon discover that it had a great deal to do with religion. Indeed, I am tempted to write that it was *all about* religion—salvaging it in some way, or finding a suitable replacement. "Nature and Nature's laws lay hid in night," wrote the English poet Alexander Pope in the early eighteenth century; "God said, *Let Newton be!* and all was light." That is an obvious and for its time rather daring play on the cosmogony in the first chapter of the Book of Genesis. "God said, 'Let there be light!' and there was light." Pope himself was a lifelong Roman Catholic sufficiently steadfast in his paternal religion to absorb the considerable personal indignities and social disadvantages of Anglican prejudice for a lifetime. Sir Isaac Newton, whom he inserted into the text of Holy Writ, was a religious enthusiast who almost certainly regarded his investigations into the prophetical meaning of the Book of Daniel as of equal importance to his articulation of the law of gravity. They are both "Enlightenment figures," and even in certain respects "typical" ones.

Many philosophers and writers have sought to give a more precise or pointed definition of Enlightenment. I have already mentioned one of the earliest and most famous: the German philosopher Immanuel Kant. In 1784, Kant wrote an essay entitled "Answering the Question: What is Enlightenment?" It is a brilliant essay, studded with perceptions and suggestions of permanent value. For Kant, Enlightenment was a liberation from a self-imposed or at least tolerated childishness.

"Enlightenment is man's emergence from his self-imposed immaturity. Immaturity is the inability to use one's understanding without guidance from another. This immaturity is self-imposed when its cause lies not in lack of understanding, but in lack of resolve and courage to use it without guidance from another. *Sapere aude!* 'Have courage to use your own understanding!'—that is the motto of enlightenment." The more literal translation of Kant's Latin motto *Sapere aude* is "Dare to know." Kant, that is, proclaimed the audacity of knowledge.

Kant believed in a universalized human capacity of independent reason. The great impediment to human progress (which Kant imagined principally in ethical terms) was not incapacity but mental timidity or cowardice, the *fear* of independent thinking and fear's vicious sibling, the comfortable habit of settling for secondhand authority. There can be no doubt that one of the principal achievements of the European Enlightenment was to encourage thinking about things in radically new ways, and in seeking knowledge that for long centuries had been judged by the arbiters of the sacred and secular realms alike as at best unattainable if not forbidden. The overthrow of the great edifice of medieval thought was inevitable.

Yet the view of many, perhaps even most, students of the European Enlightenment is that Enlightenment has failed us, or at least remains radically imperfect. It certainly failed to inoculate us against the two great cultural pathologies of the twentieth century, Bolshevism and Nazism. In 1944, two eminent German philosophers who had the most poignant reasons to deplore the latter, Max Horkheimer and Theodor Adorno, published their *Dialectic of Enlightenment*. This is a very famous book, far more famous than comprehensible, in my opinion. It is more theoretical and speculative than historical and analytical. It is not precisely a critique of the *historical period* of the Enlightenment, but of a certain concept of Enlightenment. One line of its argument that for me approaches clarity posits the collapse of Enlightenment rationality into "myth" of the sort that rationality was meant to replace. A more global claim is that "the program of the Enlightenment was the disenchantment of the world."

I myself would never want to seem to speak *against* enlightenment, with or without its capital letter. Better than most, perhaps, a medievalist might know with concrete specificity the meaning for the progress of human felicity of the political, material, and medical advances associated with the Enlightenment and the ideas and attitudes to which it gave birth. But I perhaps am inclined to view the matter in a rather different light.

How could rationality unadorned possibly compensate for the loss of the mythic world? It seems to me that to understand the "problem" of Enlightenment rationality we need search no further than the opening sentence of the most famous of books by the most famous of Enlightenment philosophers—the *Critique of Pure Reason*, by Immanuel Kant (1781, rev. 1787). "Human reason," Kant wrote, "has this peculiar fate, that in one species of its knowledge it is burdened by questions which, as prescribed by the very nature of reason itself, it is not able to ignore, but which, as transcending all its powers, it is also not able to answer."

Surely no human heart can be deaf to what Kant is saying here. He is talking about the mystery of life: the God question, the soul question, the questions of the origin of the earth and the origin of species, man among the animals, the truth or the illusion of the freedom of the will, the conundrums of time and space. Reason cannot ignore these questions, yet it cannot answer them either. The implication is that if such questions *were* to be answered, it would require something more than reason to answer them. The old world had found that something more in "revelation." In the period of the Enlightenment, revelation became a highly contested category. There were many who, though they could not accept in their usual and conventional form the usual and conventional claims, were unable to dispense altogether with "transcendence." This book is about some of those people.

One of the fouler libels smearing the Middle Ages is that it was "irrational." On the contrary, medieval thinkers insisted that reason was the deiform faculty which raised human beings far above the beasts and placed them near the angels, in relation to whom they were in the biblical phrase "a little lower" only on account of the inconvenience of their materiality. Unfortunately it was no small inconvenience. O, that this too, too solid flesh would melt. Human indenture to appetite, human morbidity, above all human mortality were all badges of a fallen nature strictly limited in its rational horizons.

Think for a moment of the pilgrim Dante's two guides in the *Divine Comedy*: Virgil and Beatrice. They are much more than simple ciphers for Reason and Revelation, but they do exemplify the special capacities of those two realms. Virgil is the greatest poet of Latinity, and in the tradition Dante inherited one of the world's greatest intellects. He might rightly be regarded by the Latin Middle Ages as the exemplar of the highest achievements of human thought. Beatrice was a young girl Dante saw a couple of times in Florence. Yet Beatrice leads Dante where Virgil cannot tread. She has the answers to those questions Virgil can only ask.

The general tendency of the Enlightenment was to constrain if not abolish the realm of Revelation, with the ground lost to Revelation quickly annexed to the realm of Reason. Among the famous and highly influential books of the Enlightenment is one by the Irish philosopher John Toland. Its title is eloquent: *Christianity not Mysterious* (1696). The first recorded appearance of the English word "free-thinker," found in the writings of the philosopher Berkeley, is applied by him to Toland. Toland was not an atheist, nor were most other "free-thinkers." Atheism is the exception rather than the rule among the enlightened. But their "theology," such as it was, was of a distinctly minimalist character.

The minimalism had an ancient ancestry in the medieval doctrine of *invisibilia per visibilia*. That was the Latin phrase of a passage in Paul's Epistle to the Romans (1:20): "For since the creation of the world [God's] invisible attributes are clearly seen—his everlasting power also and divinity—being understood through the things that are made." The idea in the passage is a commonplace of "natural" theology and became the basis for the "argument by design." It is very frequently found in Enlightenment texts, one memorable appearance being that in Daniel Defoe's *Robinson Crusoe* (1719). One day Crusoe finds on the sandy beach of his island the imprint of an unshod human foot. He reasons that if there is a footprint, there had to be a foot that made it, and it will turn out that the foot belongs to his man Friday, the second most important character in the novel. But the discovery leads Crusoe to contemplate the marvelous workings of Providence, and the manner in which the uncreated Creator manifests Himself through His creatures.

In medieval theology knowledge of God gained through Nature, while valid and convincing, was of a primitive sort compared with the knowledge of God given by Revelation. "Natural" religion was a kind of spiritual first aid, or the lowest rung on a ladder of spiritual ascent. "And this our life, exempt from public haunt," says the Duke in the Forest of Arden,

> *Finds tongues in trees, books in the running brooks,*
> *Sermons in stones, and good in every thing.*

What happened in the eighteenth and nineteenth centuries was that what for many had been the minimal theology of the Old World became the maximal of the New. Here the English Romantic poets have much to teach us. Not a single one of the major Romantics (with the possible exception of Wordsworth as he approached his dotage) had much truck with traditional Christianity. Shelley was expelled from Oxford for, among other things, his atheism. Byron was as much of a mocker in his way as Voltaire. Yet few men more valiantly worried over those Kantian questions raised by a mind capable of posing, but not of resolving them. In particular Coleridge was a genius deeply versed in Enlightenment learning, including contemporary trends, at that time so threatening, in biblical interpretation. He could not accept in any simple or literal way the traditional supernatural and mythic claims of Christianity, but he and his friend the young Wordsworth strove mightily to preserve some realm of transcendence.

They found it in the world of *Nature.*

TO DEMYSTIFY CHRISTIANITY WAS to reject its two most mysterious ancient doctrines: the doctrine of the Incarnation (that Jesus Christ was God in human flesh) and the doctrine of the Trinity (that God is manifested in three "persons," Father, Son, and Holy Ghost). Neither doctrine, according to the freethinkers, was reasonable, nor was either even to be found in the Bible. The empirical fact of the material universe was a sufficient evidence for the existence of its almighty Creator, but not evidence at all for the presumptuous belief that the Creator continued to meddle in its operations or those of the human beings who inhabited the earth's crust. This minimalist theology was termed "Deism" and its proponents "Deists."

What Immanuel Kant called the "peculiar fate" of human reason to propose and worry over questions it cannot seem to answer or dismiss might be called, metaphorically, "the religious gene." In good eighteenth-century fashion, Kant regarded the doomed search after mysteries as an aspect of the very *nature* of human reason. Nature may be deflected, but it will not finally be denied. In this regard it is useful to invoke a well-known apothegm of Horace, perhaps the eighteenth century's favorite Latin poet: *Naturam expellas furca, tamen usque revenit* ("You may drive Nature out with a pitchfork; she will nevertheless return").

It is meet that the Enlightenment, as an age of bold thought and great advances in human intellection, should have attracted the penetrating erudition of so many able historians. In the manner of historians they have been energetic in defining peculiarities and in drawing distinctions. To some of these I have already referred. We have national Enlightenments in their significant variations—German, French, Scottish. We have Enlightenment of varying political shades—"moderate" Enlightenment, "radical" Enlightenment. We have a "Counter-Enlightenment" asserted, debunked, and reaffirmed. We have prominent "enemies of Enlightenment." In this book, however, I am taking a more tolerant and Latitudinarian approach to Enlightenment. How would it be possible not to see Count Cagliostro, for example, as a quintessentially Enlightenment figure? Most of the materials dealt with here are the sometimes whimsical evidences of the operations of the religious gene resisting its expulsion and seeking new temporary habitations to replace those from which it had been evicted.

Large social and intellectual changes of the kind I want to suggest are seldom immediate or complete. The American Constitution, a noble monument of enlightened liberal democracy, accommodated certain Aristotelian ideas that must seem to contemporary Americans simply fantastic. The very peculiar way the document dances around the subject of chattel slavery shows at least that the subject was troublesome in the minds of the framers, but there is scant evidence of any serious thought about women's suffrage. Despite such peculiarities, few would deny that the American Constitution evidenced a very dramatic change in the way people imagined their political arrangements. Many would argue that the Thirteenth and Nineteenth amendments to the Constitution (the first abolishing slavery, the second enfranchising women) were simply the inevitable and logical implications of the document, awaiting only certain "game-changing" circumstances for their implementation. In the year 2000, a well-received book by Malcolm Gladwell popularized the idea of the "tipping point" in the process of change. His argument is Aesop's old fable of the straw that broke the camel's back expanded to book length, and exemplified by such phenomena as the amazing commercial success of Hush Puppy shoes. The realm of ideas, which are frequently no less fashion accessories than handbags or footwear, is the realm of the tipping point par excellence. The Enlightenment was a huge tipping point in our cultural history, the aggregate of dozens of smaller mental tipping points reached at different times and in different places.

Stasis and Change

All history must necessarily be concerned either with change or with stasis, and often enough it is a record of the struggle between the two. It is safe to say that on the whole historians, particularly modern historians, prefer change. For this reason, many famous historical titles include such words as "evolution," "emergence," "development," "rise," "fall," "decline," "expansion," "triumph," "eclipse," and so forth. *The Decline and Fall of the Roman Empire* is a terrific title. *Four Centuries of*

Stasis in Burgundian Agriculture would be less terrific. Much of the subject matter of this book has to do with the often unanticipated possibilities brought about by change—one of which is an important shift in attitudes toward change itself.

One of the great founders of the discipline of anthropology, Edward Burnett Tylor, proclaimed with elegance and economy a radical principle of cultural conservatism. According to Tylor, most things that exist in the world exist for the reason that they once existed. "When a custom, an art, or an opinion is fairly started in the world, disturbing influences may long affect it so slightly that it may keep its course from generation to generation, as a stream once settled in its bed will flow on for ages. . . . This is the permanence of culture; and the special wonder about it is that the change and revolution of human affairs should have left so many of its feeblest rivulets to run so long."

In his first campaign for the presidency, Barack Obama chose to express one of his major themes in the catchy motto "Change You Can Believe In." Without subjecting this curious phrase to the kind of serious examination that no political slogan could sustain, it is worth noting one or two things about it. The assumption, in the first place, is that such change would be change *for the good*. Indeed, one could go further. Perhaps change, in and of itself, *is* a terminal good.

Mr. Obama's adversaries and rivals were not against change. Although it is in the nature of conservatism to be wary of change, the conservative objections to his proposals appeared to be based in the belief that they were not "change" at all, but rather covert stasis, "the same old failed policies." Since much of the specific "change" Obama advocated had also been proposed by others in the past and by some competitors in the present, in one of the candidates' debates Hillary Clinton in effect accused Obama of plagiarism or, as she put it, "change you can Xerox." This criticism was not well received by the debate audience or by those who commented upon it afterwards, though the generally negative reaction implied no displeasure with change itself.

There are other points of view. One of the great men of the English seventeenth century, Lord Falkland, famously stated that "when it is not necessary to change, it is necessary not to change." He was apparently talking about the episcopal form of ecclesiastical governance, but his dictum has become a watchword for certain ideological conservatives, who have applied it widely. It is an idea that contrasts sharply with another—namely, the necessity of change under all circumstances. Such was the concept of the "permanent revolution" advocated by certain modern Marxists and others.

The term "progressive" comes of course from progress. In Latin *pro* + *gradior*, with its participle *gressus*, meant to walk in a forward direction (as opposed to *retro* + *gradior*, moving backwards). Formerly one could make literal progress in any activity involving movement with a definite end (walking to the Coliseum) or metaphoric progress in many others (painting a fence, reading a book, learning a language, etc.). The literal meaning has virtually disappeared from modern English, though it is preserved in the title of John Bunyan's once famous *Pilgrim's Progress*. Today "progress," at least as an item in the political lexicon, always implies amelioration—in other words, *change for the better, improvement*. This usage definitely dates from the Enlightenment. It is preserved in the titles of numerous European learned societies established for the *progress* of knowledge or the *improvement* of the arts. Among the most famous of these was the British Royal Society—the founding title of which is the Royal Society of London for Improving Natural Knowledge.

Certain strains of "progressive" political thought, such as political Marxism, posit a more or less definite goal, upon reaching which progress presumably ceases, as the man ceases walking once he reaches the Coliseum. On the whole, however, modern progress is open-ended, directed toward an indefinite perfection that by a kind of metaphysical Zeno's Paradox it will never achieve, a circumstance that, far from being depressing, actually allows indefinite progress. We may regard this as a sort of political Couéism, after the French self-help guru Emile Coué, who counseled his followers to improve their lives through autosuggestion by frequently repeating the mantra: *Tous les jours à tous points de vue je vais de mieux en mieux* ("Every day in every way, I am getting better and better").

THE TOPIC OF THE PROPER boundaries of optimism is one that has frequently been raised in relationship to the Enlightenment, as for example in the intellectually influential book by Horkheimer and Adorno. Critics have raised a metaphysical version of the old accusation—*If you're so smart, why aren't you rich?* Of course the question was perhaps most interestingly raised by the enlightened themselves. Here the important exemplary text is Voltaire's *Candide*, subtitled "Optimism," which appeared in 1759. Voltaire was too much of a scoffer not to scoff even at scoffing; hence the ironies of the work are nearly endless. Nonetheless it still has a clear enough Enlightenment drift. The meaning of the word "candid" in the eighteenth century had not yet strayed far from the Latin. It meant generous, ingenuous, innocent, straightforward—untouched by the cynicism that is often the diploma granted by the school of sophistication and worldly experience.

The character Candide, a young man of *candor* in this sense, has been taught by his tutor Pangloss to believe that "this is the best of all possible worlds." When cast out into the cruel world as a result of an innocent sexual appetite, he has ample opportunity to test his mentor's maxim. After experiencing a jolly *auto-da-fé* ostensibly organized to prevent a repetition of the Lisbon earthquake, the hero is forced to ponder: "If this is the best of all possible worlds, what can the others be like?" In other words, Pangloss's bromide is more convincing as pessimism than as optimism.

This fact by no means suggests that Voltaire himself was mired in gloom, however. The chief source of obscurantism in *Candide*, revealed religion, was in the form of Roman Catholicism—the "infamous thing" it was his life's work to "crush." He and his like-minded enthusiasts of Enlightenment had every reason to rejoice in their progress. By the time he died an old man in 1778, France was no longer simply on a pathway toward a revolution largely prepared by the kind of Enlightenment thought he so brilliantly exemplified, but in its very vestibule.

Thus modern optimism reaches the threshold of parody, where it has been long awaited, perhaps, by the more excessive expressions of ancient pessimism. In the old poetic pre-Copernican astronomy, mutability reigned everywhere beneath the moon. Hence the invariably negative metaphoric sense of the adjective "sublunary"—meaning mortal, fickle, changeable, material, temporal, impermanent, imperfect. The moon itself was an emblem of mutability. When Romeo would swear upon the moon his undying love of Juliet, she responds in alarm:

> *O swear not by the moon, th'inconstant moon,*
> *That monthly changes in her circled orb . . .*

Mutability—the slow decay of the human body, the crumbling of stone buildings, the brevity of fleshly pleasures—all these things seemed to confirm the wisdom of the world-denying asceticism that shaped so much of the cultural life of the Old World. Of all unstable creatures, none were more unstable that human beings. "I will show you a great wonder" says Lady Philosophy to Boethius: "a man happy and despairing within the space of a single hour."

THE "DARKER" ENLIGHTENMENT PHENOMENA touched upon in this book—the reluctance of the miraculous to capitulate and leave the field, the esoteric enthusiasms of eighteenth-century Rosicrucians and Freemasons, the extraordinary careers of a Cagliostro or a Julie de

Krüdener—are to be found lodged in the crevices of the rocky and uneven landscape of major cultural change. When we think of decisive epochs of Western history, we are likely to point to the collapse of the Roman Empire in late Antiquity, or to the renaissance of the twelfth century or its greater and capitalized sibling, *the* Renaissance. Yet no century constitutes a more emphatic punctuation point in European history than the eighteenth. The world of the year 1700 differed from that of the year 1800 in many profound ways—intellectual, spiritual, economic, political, demographic. Most change is gradual, but intellectual change supremely so. The French Revolution could impose by force the abolition of titles of social rank and the fraternity of all citizens. Such changes in the direction of democracy gained the assent of actual individuals at very different tempos.

The Crevices of History

What I mean by the crevices of history can perhaps be exemplified by briefly considering one or two large and consequential developments in the history of European thought in the Enlightenment period, developments that appeared and flourished at different rates of speed in different places and contexts, and that gained the adherence of some more easily than of others.

There is a family of allegorical tableaux painted by Lucas Cranach the Elder and some of his followers called *Law and Grace* or *Justice and Grace*. Cranach was a personal friend of Martin Luther, of whom he painted portraits, and his pictorial theology is often didactic Protestantism. *Law and Grace*, the most famous example of which is the painting housed in Prague Castle, is a telling exemplification of Luther's doctrine of "justification by faith." As the gloomy German friar brooded over the fourth chapter of Paul's Epistle to the Romans, a light flashed within his mind. "Abraham believed God, and it was reckoned to him as righteousness." You cannot *do* anything to be saved except believe that you cannot do anything. Giving up the pleasures of the flesh and disciplining bodily appetite won't save you. Certainly building a huge cathedral in Rome won't. The only channel of salvation is divine grace, absolutely arbitrary and unmerited, indeed unmeritable.

In Cranach's pictorial scheme there are within a single frame two starkly contrasting landscapes separated by a central tree. The tree itself is allegorical, divided along its vertical axis into two halves, one dead and blasted, the other green and flourishing. In the left-hand scene, death reigns. There is a corpse in its coffin, Adam and Eve beside the fatal tree, Hebrews attacked by fiery serpents in the background, and above it all the Tables of the Law against murky clouds. The right half is the realm of grace. Here the chief elements are John the Baptist pointing to the Lamb of God, and the Lamb himself first on the Cross, then exiting his tomb. High above on a peak Grace, allegorized as a beautiful woman, looks over the scene. The meaning is very clear. Grace, not justice, is the only hope of salvation. Indeed to hope for *justice* is to ask for death. In the left ("Law") side of Cranach's image death is everywhere, including the left half of the tree that divides it. Only the gratuitous *grace* of Christ's sacrifice offers hope.

We argue still about what things are rights and what things are privileges. The great French historian Jules Michelet (1798–1874) began what is perhaps his most famous single work, *The History of the French Revolution*, with an introductory essay entitled "Concerning the Religion of the Middle Ages." He sought, he said, to answer *the* indispensable question concerning the French Revolution: Was the French Revolution Christian or anti-Christian? That may strike one as an odd question, since most of us are likely to call to mind such famous revolutionary episodes as the mass murder of Carmelites, or such widespread phenomena as the desecration and demolition of churches, or such legislative initiatives as the Civil Constitution of the Clergy.

Michelet was a determined secularist. He was, furthermore, genuinely appalled at the Christian history of his own country, which included such horrors as the Albigensian crusade and the massacre of St. Bartholomew's Day. But he was not an anti-Catholic bigot or a crude propagandist. He was trying to look deeper, to the very philosophical foundations of revolution. He finally concluded that the Revolution was founded in the concept of *justice*, whereas the Christian economy was founded in the concept of *grace*. Man had sinned. Man had been saved by the sacrifice of Jesus Christ. No merit of his own had gained his salvation; all flowed from divine grace, a gift that could never be earned. Man had no right to salvation.

Two unfortunate implications flowed from this doctrine, and both encouraged the arbitrary at the expense of the just. The first was that human political arrangements were founded in a nexus of grace and favor. The relationships of feudalism were anything but lawless, but they sounded everywhere with echoes of the divine condescension. There was an ideological thread, however finely spun, between the great Lord of the Heavens and the local "lord of the manor."

The foundation of the Old World was a supposed divine order, everywhere exhibited by the world of nature and sought after, however imperfectly, in human institutions. The "divine right of kings" did not mean that any particular king was divinely right, but that kingship itself was. Human monarchy echoed the divine order. The principal word for "God" in the Bible was *Dominus* (Lord). In the vocabulary of Old Europe that was a *political* term, denoting one who has possession, claims authority, and exercises power. Its English descendants—"domain," "dominion," "dominate," and so forth—preserve its sense. Don Quixote, an Oxford don, or for that matter a Mafia one, are its distant echoes.

Thus in *Hamlet*, Claudius (though himself a king-killer) at least imagines himself invulnerable:

> *There's such divinity doth hedge a king*
> *That treason can but peep to what it would,*
> *Acts little of his will.*

The second baneful implication related to the clergy who, in Michelet's opinion, could hardly avoid, under such a theological system, claiming for themselves the arbitrary powers of semi-divine dispensers of sacramental grace.

The Revolution, on the contrary, was legal and contractual. It claimed its basis in *droit*—a word that in French bears the burden of two English words, "law" and "right." The primary document of the French Revolution, the moral equivalent of the American Declaration of Independence, which indeed influenced it, is *The Declaration of the Rights of Man as Citizen*. The American Declaration of Independence speaks of "certain inalienable rights" which have been "endowed" by man's Creator. This is, however, about as untheological as a theological commonplace can be.

THE PRESUMPTION OF A political order at least *theoretically* based in the democratic dogma approaches the status of an innate idea in America and the rest of the "enlightened" world. We need to remind ourselves how *new* the idea is. The opening paragraphs of the *Politics* of Aristotle come as a shock to most contemporary undergraduates who, knowing in advance that Aristotle's is a name great in the annals of human thought, suppose also that his thought will be generally attuned to their own. Instead, Aristotle starts with several alarming suppositions presumed by him to be natural truths: the authority exercised by masters over slaves and the superiority of men to women. Very right, he says, is that line in Hesiod: "It is meet that Hellenes should rule over Barbarians."

The apparently abstract question—"Justice *or* grace?"—has concrete implications of the very greatest moment. There are numerous other weighty abstractions that were in flux in the period of the Enlightenment. They may encourage us to put to the Enlightenment the same question Michelet put to the Revolution: was the Enlightenment Christian or anti-Christian? The materials dealt with in this book show how difficult it is to give a decisive, clear-cut answer. The medievalist D. W. Robertson invoked the concepts of "hierarchy" and "dynamically interacting polarities" to identify one of the most consequential contrasts between the older and the newer mental worlds. A great deal of modern thought has been founded in one form or another on belief in the progressive power of dynamically interacting polarities. This may be described as the Hegelian paradigm. Thesis *A* encounters Antithesis *B*, resulting in something new and different from both, Synthesis *C*. The Marxist analysis, which in a variety of manifestations has been enormously influential for the better part of two centuries, is founded in the belief that "all previous history is the history of class struggle."

The dynamic idea is congenial to the Darwinian theory of evolutionary adaptation and of the "survival of the fittest." It accords with Freud's theories of subconscious struggle as a mainspring of human action.

Here the inevitable metaphor has been that of the *body*. So pervasive is the image in ancient literature that it has attracted more than one learned study. For our purposes, we can safely fast-forward to the Apostolic age and the letters of St. Paul, and in particular to his repeated descriptions of the Church as "the body of Christ," and especially in the extended metaphor in the First Letter to the Corinthians (I Cor. 12: 12–31).

The salient point, perhaps, is that Paul combines the ideas of organic unity and hierarchical subordination. All the members of the body are "worthy"; all have useful functions. But the image is anything but "democratic," let alone anarchic. Christ is the "head" of the Church in precisely the way that someone is the head of General Motors or the head of the Bureau of Indian Affairs.

There developed in medieval Europe a tripartite pattern of social organization, often invoked in pictorial form by the image of a group of three men: one an armed knight; one a tonsured cleric; one identifiable as a peasant by some attribute of his agricultural labor. These were the "three Estates." "I fight for you," said the knight. "I pray for you," said the cleric. "I work for you," said the peasant. The Assembly of the Estates-General called by Louis XVI in the hopes of securing tax revenues from them was structured around this ossified social structure; the Revolution to which the Estates-General acted as midwife suggests how obsolete it had in reality become.

Paradise Lost

The same phenomena viewed from opposite ends of a period of dramatic intellectual change may look very different. *The Dark Side of the Enlightenment* begins with an obscure Anglo-Irish squire, Valentine Greatrakes, in the 1660s. This man's moment of greatest fame almost exactly coincided with the publication of the first edition of John Milton's *Paradise Lost* in 1667. *Paradise Lost* is an epic poem based in the history of Adam and Eve as recounted in the first two chapters of the Book of Genesis. Milton's poem treats the subject in a baroque and learned style that mingles, in the classical style of Christian humanism, the Hebrew Scriptures with the literary and mythological opulence of ancient Greece and Rome. The subject of *Paradise Lost* is "the Fall of Man," the "original sin" of ancient Christian theological orthodoxy.

The results of the primal transgression were catastrophic, for sin "brought death into the World, and all our woe, with loss of Eden." Our human ancestors, now rendered mortal by their own disobedience, were banished into the harsh world of labor and necessity—*our* world. This myth was universally understood among Christian thinkers both as an historical account of the primal fall and an allegory of every act of sin in which sensuality masters reason and willfulness conquers a required obedience.

John Milton, an actual revolutionary both in politics and in art, very clearly grounded his poem in a strictly static hierarchy of the Great Chain of Being. There was a metaphysical pyramid with God at its apex. Just below that were the hierarchically ordered angels. A "little lower than the angels" were human beings, with man the superior to woman. Below that were all the animals and birds, all of vegetative life from the mighty oak to the lichen scabrous upon the stone, then the stones and minerals themselves, down to the meanest clods of the earth. "A place for everything and everything in its place." Sin at its core was the overthrow of divinely established hierarchies, turning things upside down. The woman/sensuality controlled the man/reason. Sin at its core was the manifestation of things not staying in their proper places.

IN 1793—NEAR THE endpoint of the period dealt with in this book— the proto-Romantic English poet and artist William Blake created a work called *The Marriage of Heaven and Hell*. If ever there was a title that dramatized the notion of dynamically interacting polarities, it was this title. The *Marriage* takes *Paradise Lost* as its point of departure, and it makes the following criticism of it: "Note: The reason Milton wrote in fetters when he wrote of Angels & God, and at liberty when of Devils & Hell, is because he was a true Poet and of the Devils party without knowing it."

The idea that Milton was subconsciously "of the Devils party"—or putting it in more forceful terms that Satan is the true hero of *Paradise Lost* and God Almighty its true villain—has become one of the orthodoxies of modern literary history. It seems to accord with our sense of what is good and true, and it seems confirmed by the nature of the verse. Milton's God is arbitrary and autocratic, and His words, when compared with Satan's fiery speeches, are boring. According to one famous interpretation, by the literary critic William Empson, Milton's God is actively evil. Satan, on the other hand, is dynamic. Pandemonium—the parliament of all the devils—is less like a royal court than a democratic senate. There is verbal thrust and verbal parry, the most fundamental challenging of authority. *Non serviam*, cries Satan. *I shall not serve.* His most memorable line may be "Better to reign in hell than serve in heaven!"

Despite tortured attempts to attribute this "reading" to Milton's *conscious* intention, it seems impossible that a seventeenth-century English Puritan would write a biblical epic in which God is the villain and Satan the hero, or that it would be received by nearly the entire Protestant eighteenth century as the greatest Christian poem ever written. Slightly more plausible, but only slightly, is the notion that such an interpretation reveals a *subconscious* irresolution within John Milton. It is much more likely that what seemed manifestly clear to the twentieth-century literary critic Empson never occurred to anybody for a century or more after the poem's publication. When, however, the Old World view of the Great Chain of Being and the rightness of fixed hierarchies gives way to a very different view—of the generative power of dynamically interacting polarities—the phenomena may look very different. Yet unless we are willing to turn all of cultural history into a vast Rorschach test that can tell us only what is already in our own minds, we need to make a strenuous effort to grasp something very different from what may already be there. "A perfect judge will read each work of wit," says Alexander Pope, "With the same spirit that its author writ."

Scholars must cooperate with their publishers and their readers in honoring an imperative of originality, but they can surrender to it entirely only at some risk. Some topics—as for example the French Revolution—have been written about for so long, in such depth, and by so many historians writing from so many differing "perspectives" that it is actually not plausible to claim that one's own ideas are "original." *The Dark Side of the Enlightenment* hopes to offer some fresh perspectives, but hardly pretends to break new ground on every page. Some of the materials in this book have been frequently studied, such as various aspects of eighteenth-century esotericism. There are numerous English-language books about Count Cagliostro. Most of them take a very different view from the one I have come to credit; but he is, in any event, far too compelling and complicating a figure to omit from such a study. Valentine Greatrakes and Madame de Krüdener, on the other hand, are scarcely known at all outside the world of specialized scholarship.

The anxious scholar may gain some comfort in subscribing to Alexander Pope's definition of "wit." True wit, he wrote,

> *is Nature to advantage dress'd,*
> *What oft was thought, but ne'er so well express'd.*

Put in other terms, the reinvention of the wheel remains a sacred duty of every generation of scholars. What one hopes to avoid is the reinvention of the flat tire.

The reinvention of the wheel, indeed, turns out to have a good deal to do with the extraordinary intellectual ferment of the Enlightenment period, which in Europe witnessed a dramatic increase in international travel and communication. The word "coach" (meaning the wheeled conveyance) is a rare example of an English word of Hungarian (Magyar) origin. It derives from a place name, Kocs, an Hungarian village that at the end of the Middle Ages was already a famous center of wheelmaking. Improved wheel technology gradually moved westward across Europe. Lázló Tarr, the definitive historian of the coach (*The History of the Carriage*, 1969, translated from the Hungarian), documents the gradual improvements in the ancient invention of wheeled conveyances that had led, by the beginning of the eighteenth century, to a considerable elevation in the status of the wheelwright. Improvements included several features of body design and suspension, but the wheel itself was also improved through more accurate lathing of the barrel hub, more precise auguring of the spoke holes, and more effective smithing of the rims. These were all small technical increments, yet their effects enabled significant social change. Creating roads worthy of the new and improved vehicles often lagged behind, but John Loudon McAdam, inventor of the macadam or metaled road, was as pure a product of the Scottish Enlightenment as David Hume or Dugald Stewart.

Bibliographical

The bibliography for the vast topic of the Enlightenment might well be as long as this entire book. The general reader seeking to explore the topic will not want for elegant and illuminating general studies. Among the classics available in English are Ernst Cassirer, *The Philosophy of the Enlightenment* (Princeton, 1951), and Peter Gay, *The Enlightenment: An Interpretation*, 2 vols. (New York, 1997). Two books I find particularly readable are Harold Nicolson's *The Age of Reason, the Eighteenth Century* (New York, 1961) and Daniel Roche's *France in the Enlightenment* (Cambridge, MA, 1998, first publ. in French in 1993). Somewhat more traditionally academic, but invaluable for its literary breadth, is Ira Wade, *The Intellectual Origins of the French Enlightenment* (Princeton, 1971).

One of the most prominent of modern intellectual historians, Jonathan Israel, has devoted many of his books to topics relevant to the period, and especially two magisterial volumes—*Radical Enlightenment: Philosophy and the Making of Modernity, 1650–1750* (Oxford, 2001) and *Enlightenment Contested: Philosophy, Modernity, and the Emancipation of Man, 1670–1752* (Oxford, 2006).

There are also a number of valuable specialized reference works, especially the *Encyclopedia of the Enlightenment,* 4 vols., ed. Alan Charles Kors (Oxford, 2003). Less ambitious but highly useful is Harvey Chisick, *Historical Dictionary of the Enlightenment* (Lanham, MD, 2005).

Of more specialized academic books I am obliged to mention two that were instrumental in exciting my interest in the topics of this book. The first is the two-volume work of Auguste Viatte, *Les sources occultes du Romantisme* (Paris, 1928, with subsequent editions). The other is Giovanna Summerfield, *Credere aude: Mystifying Enlightenment* (Tübingen, 2008), dealing principally with figures not specifically covered in this book.

Books specifically cited or alluded to in this chapter:
Edmund Burke, *Reflections on the French Revolution* (1790).
D. W. Robertson, *A Preface to Chaucer: Studies in Medieval Perspectives* (1962).
Edward B. Tylor, *Primitive Culture: Researches into the Development of Mythology, Philosophy, Religion, Language, Art, and Custom,* 4th ed. (1903).

The true and lively Pourtraicture of Valentine Greatrakes Esq.ͬ
of Affane in y.ͤ County of Waterford, in y.ͤ Kingdome of Ireland.
famous for curing several Deseases and distempers
by the stroak of his Hand only.

1   *Valentine Greatrakes, the Stroker*

THERE IS A PASSAGE IN Alexander Pope's *Essay on Man* of the early 1730s in which the poet attempts a brief poetic theodicy—that is, a defense of the goodness and justice of Providence in the light of the world's manifest evils.

> *But errs not Nature from this gracious end,*
> *From burning suns when livid deaths descend,*
> *When earthquakes swallow, or when tempests sweep*
> *Towns to one grave, whole nations to the deep?*
> *"No" ('tis replied) "the first Almighty Cause*
> *Acts not by partial, but by gen'ral laws . . ."*

Pope was actually a Roman Catholic, but the theological vocabulary he uses, and the argument he advances, could be agreed to by any

---

The classic "portrait" of Greatrakes the Stroker first appeared in his apologetic *Brief Account* of his life (1666), dedicated to the famous chemist Robert Boyle. It was many times copied, and sold on the streets from the chapman's cart. It shows the wonder-worker, clad in severe, quasi-ecclesiastical garb, gazing toward the viewer as he works at healing a young boy suffering from scrofula. The window opens onto a bucolic landscape.

Deist. The Almighty works by "general laws"—what we would call *natural* laws—not by an arbitrary or "partial" interference in human affairs. This might be called the Retired Watchmaker theory. Having once established the magnificent mechanism of the universe, its Creator has withdrawn, allowing it to operate on its own sufficient and unwavering regularity.

A miracle is an interference with or abrogation of "general laws." One important aspect of radical Enlightenment thought was its denial of the miraculous. Enlightened scientists said that miracles were impossible in the world they observed. Enlightened historians and scriptural scholars struggled with the question of whether the miracles reported in the Bible *ever* could have occurred as described. That was a debate that continued throughout the Enlightenment, and so must recur throughout this book. What concerns us here are two episodes of the dramatic intrusion of contemporary miracles upon an evolving intellectual world in which they were distinctly unwelcome.

I. An Anglo-Irish Country Gentleman

Affane is a rural place in County Wexford in the south of Ireland, about midway between the county towns of Wexford and Cork. At the time of the Restoration of King Charles II in 1660 there was living at Affane an obscure country squire with the imposing name of Valentine Greatrakes, a surname still surviving in a number of orthographic variants such as Gretorex, Gretraches, etc. He had been born in 1628, and thus achieved his majority in the year of the execution of Charles I. Though he was of an old Irish family, the political disquiets of his time had made an exile of him, and he grew up in Devon in southern England. He had been a "Parliament man" in his first youth and a commissioned officer of the Roundhead army. In religion he had been a latter-day Puritan and an enemy of episcopacy. However, he had otherwise shown

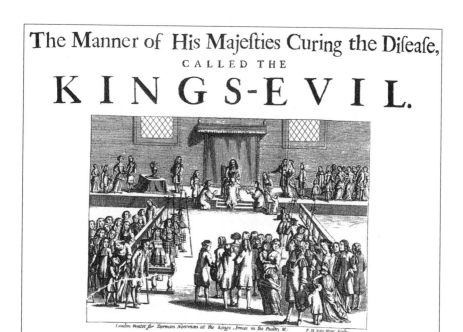

The Manner of His Majefties Curing the Difeafe,
CALLED THE
KINGS-EVIL.

"The Manner of His Majesties Curing the Disease, called the King's-Evil." The restored monarch, Charles II, was eager to revive such ideas of sacred kingship as were still alive after Cromwell. This broadsheet from the 1660s described the ceremony in detail, including the proper liturgical readings. (Note the two priests with liturgical books kneeling at either side of the "patient.")

few signs of unusual religiosity, except that he had been an admirer of the Lutheran mystic Jakob Boehme (d. 1624). This was not particularly remarkable, since Boehme's influence was strong in many places throughout Protestant Europe. Furthermore, Greatrakes had as a youth in Devon studied under the guidance of a German tutor.

The re-establishment of monarchy in Britain was relatively irenic. Grotesque punishments were visited upon the still living regicides and gross indignities on the corpses of the dead ones. But formal and informal amnesties let bygones be bygones for the large mass of the old republican aristocracy and army veterans. Greatrakes had accepted the re-established order and had made a formal act of conformity to re-established Anglicanism. He left the army in 1656. He was living comfortably though not idly on his remote farm when, one morning in

1662, he awoke with a strange notion. To comprehend it, insofar as it was comprehensible at all, requires a little medical and social history.

The disease called scrofula was common in premodern Europe. Scrofula was a tubercular inflammation of the lymph nodes (cervical lymphodenitis) in the neck. Its external manifestations, which were often prominent and revolting, included large, angry-looking protuberances on the neck, shoulders, arms, and face. Scrofula was a highly visible ailment, which could not be hidden or disguised. The neck swelling was not painful but it could lead to the opening of lesions and invite other infection. With the general conquest of tuberculosis, scrofula virtually disappeared in the West, though it made something of a comeback in the AIDS epidemic.

Another name for scrofula in England was the "King's evil." That name preserved an ancient belief in the thaumaturgical powers of royalty, a bit of medieval superstition that survived the Reformation. It was believed by many that a reigning monarch could, with the touch of his hand, cure scrofula. Since medieval times in England there had been formal occasions on which the reigning monarch "touched" sufferers from scrofula, or those seeking inoculation against it, just as there were formal ceremonies for other ritual acts of charity, such as the distribution of the Maundy monies. It is of possible relevance to the history of Greatrakes that Charles II had begun "touching" almost immediately upon his placement on the throne. The diarist John Evelyn was present at a session in July 1660: "The chirurgeons caused the sick to be brought or led, up to the throne, where they kneeling, the King strokes their faces or cheeks with both his hands at once, at which instant a chaplain in his formalities says, 'He put his hands upon them, and he healed them.' [Luke 4:40] This is said to every one in particular." Since the biblical reference is of course to the healing miracles of Jesus Christ, the suggestion of such divinity as doth hedge a king was hardly subtle. There was also a close parallel with the words uttered by the priest when administering Holy Communion. This practice of regal "touching" actually continued up until the Georgian period. Queen Anne "touched" the infant Samuel Johnson.

The idea that had entered the mind of Valentine Greatrakes was that he, too, could cure the King's evil. The idea apparently simply appeared in his mind, suddenly and fully grown, in the manner that a sense of religious assurance had once come upon Blaise Pascal and would later come upon John Wesley. "I had an impulse or a strange persuasion in my own mind (of which I am not able to give any rational account to another) which did very frequently suggest to me, that there was bestowed on me the gift of curing the King's evil."

Greatrakes's experience—the inner conviction of a suddenly appearing miraculous grace—has many general parallels in religious history, and it will be found in different forms in William James's *Varieties of Religious Experience.* His reaction was, compared with that of many of his mystical peers, cautious and contained. He rather diffidently told his wife Ruth of his "strange persuasion"; she found it more strange than persuasive. He spoke to no one else of it, but it continued to occupy his mind.

A fortuitous opportunity to test his intuition shortly presented itself. A country man named Maher, from the nearby settlement of Salterbridge, appeared at the manor house at Affane on business of some sort. He was accompanied by his young son, who was terribly afflicted with visible scrofula eruptions on his neck, shoulders, and face. He seemed in danger of losing an eye to the rampaging blisters. We have only Greatrakes's own account of what happened, and it is spare. His motive in attempting a cure seems in the first instance to have been to prove himself in the face of his wife's stinging skepticism. He walked up to the boy, put his hands upon him, and said a prayer.

Nothing dramatic happened immediately, but a few days later the Mahers returned in some excitement. Now there was a dramatic physical improvement. The scabrous lumps had retreated from the area of the eye. The throat and neck areas were almost clear. Within a few weeks all signs of scrofula had completely disappeared from the body of young Maher.

Scrofula is not necessarily a fatal disease, and people do recover from it. Its horrible stigmata appear, but they can also in time go away. Still, the noise of the Maher affair reverberated through the local parishes. Now one Margaret McShane of Ballinecly, apparently a poor cottager, appeared at Greatrakes's gate. She had a horrible case of scrofula. "She looked so dreadfully and stunk so exceedingly, that she would have affrighted and poisoned anyone almost that saw or came near her."

There is in this story a "hagiographic topos," a theme recurrent in the old literature of sanctity, according to which the saint himself must overcome a strong initial revulsion to the maladies he cures. It is in serving that we are served, in healing that we are healed. "When I was still in my sins," said Francis of Assisi, "lepers were hateful to me." A cardinal stage in his conversion was ratified when he forced himself to embrace and kiss a leper. Greatrakes approached the hideous McShane. "My hands suppurated the nodes, and drew and healed the sores, which formerly I could not have endured the sight of, nor smell, nor touched without vomiting, so great an aversion had I naturally to all wounds and sores."

The McShane healing was once again one of delayed action. At the end of a six-week period of steady improvement, the woman found herself entirely cured. Gathering her widow's mite in the form of a basket of hazelnuts, she returned, like the lone Samaritan leper, to give thanks to her healer.

This second healing was crucial for Greatrakes. By chance a local physician, a neighborhood acquaintance, had been visiting the manor at the very time McShane appeared. Greatrakes had first asked this man, Anthony, to treat the woman. Anthony demurred, ostensibly on the grounds that the disease was too far advanced to be curable. Greatrakes suspected, however, that the real reason was that the doctor saw no prospect of a fee from this peasant woman. The avarice of medical men is a recurrent theme of the old social satire. It is already in classical Latin literature. It is in Petrarch's "Invective Against a Doctor." It is in Chaucer's portrait of his "Doctour of Phisik":

And yet he was but esy of dispence;
He kepte that he wan in pestilence.

Greatrakes's *lack* of cupidity became a major theme in his career. He may have accepted the gift of McShane's hazelnuts, but he was scrupulous about refusing all other payment. There may be little difference between the Healing Hand and the Midas Touch. At the height of his fame Greatrakes could have made a large fortune out of his cures. He refused to take a penny, and he punished some servants who had accepted from grateful beneficiaries the medical equivalent of finder's fees for facilitating access to their master.

In reprimanding Dr. Anthony for his presumed materialism, Greatrakes had blurted out that he would cure McShane himself. Anthony had replied with indignation that if Greatrakes could cure McShane, he could cure any ailment on earth. As he certainly did not believe that Greatrakes could cure any ailment on earth, we here anticipate one of the important themes of Greatrakes's history: the natural hostility of the official medical profession to unconventional and uncredentialed "practitioners." It is a theme that appears again with Cagliostro, and no doubt in many other places. The medical profession on the whole distrusted Greatrakes because he was healing people. The Church would on the whole distrust Greatrakes because he appeared in the eyes of many to be performing miracles in the name of the founder of Christianity, who was after all reported to have said that faith the size of a mustard seed would be sufficient to move a mountain.

Greatrakes did not document the next three years of his life in detail, but it is clear that he healed "many" sufferers from the King's evil in County Wexford. His reputation as a healer was growing, but as yet it remained local. Another development familiar in the careers of medieval wonder-workers now appeared: Greatrakes experienced a gradual increment in the understanding of his gift, which impelled him from specialization in scrofula to what we might call general practice. Before following him there, however, it is necessary to say a few words about his therapeutic method.

He was called "the Stroker" because of the peculiar method with which he "touched" his patients. The ritual of regal touching observed by John Evelyn makes it clear that belief in the efficacy of the King's touch had a literary basis in the scriptural accounts of the healing miracles of Christ. Ordinarily, Jesus healed the sick simply by touching or "laying hands" on them. On one occasion he made an effective opthalmological ointment by mixing his spittle with dust (John 9:6–7). On another (Luke 8:37–48), a woman tried to heal herself by touching the extreme fringe of Jesus's garment as he passed through a crowd. Though Jesus did not see her do this, he *felt* it. "Someone did touch me, for I felt that power had gone out from me." This comes closer to the language of ancient magic than any other account of Christ's healing miracles. It seems to suggest on the part of the wonder-worker a finite store of "power" that can decrease and that is not entirely within his own volitional control. All these are themes finding an echo in the history of Valentine Greatrakes.

Over the long course of his career as a healer Greatrakes sometimes succeeded entirely, sometimes partially, and sometimes not at all. Certain remarks he made suggest that he may have believed that his access to "the power" was variable or intermittent, and subject to factors outside his control. His method of "stroking" was often described by patients or observers. It usually involved rubbing and pressing the afflicted areas with considerable pressure, directing the force in the direction of a bodily extremity. The patient often had the sense of the illness being expelled through fingers, toes, or capital orifices. In his account of McShane he says he "suppurated the nodes," using a technical medical term meaning to expel the pus from a wound, swelling, or infection. A skeptical doctor friend of my acquaintance, who has interested herself in my account of Greatrakes, suggests that such a method might have indeed provided a very *temporary appearance* of amelioration in scrofula symptoms by breaking up the forming fistulae.

It seems apparent that Greatrakes at first regarded his "gift" as an equivalent of the King's touch—that is, something specifically and exclusively directed toward scrofula. This would leave room for the exploration of a possible subconscious *political* dimension to this history, but one that falls outside our task. It is not infrequent in the old hagiographic literature to find that the nascent saint misunderstands or only partially understands his divine calling. The crucifix still hanging in the ruined church of Damiano spoke to the young Francis saying, "Francis, rebuild my church." His first response was to turn stonemason. Only later did he understand this command in a more metaphorical and spiritual sense. We find something similar here.

One morning in 1664 Greatrakes awoke to the sense of an augmented medical mission. He already knew he could cure scrofula. He now felt that "there was bestowed upon me the gift of curing the ague." Though he seems to speak of "the ague" as some definite malady, the term actually covered many if not a multitude of feverish ailments. In fact, the word is an English version of the Romance form of "acute" in the medical term "acute fever," usually meaning malaria. His wife proved to be a serial skeptic, but the very next day saw his vindication. Mrs. Bateman of Fallow Bridge appeared at his door trembling and sweating with the ague. Though it is not clear how one could stroke the ague, Greatrakes cured the woman completely and instantly. She returned the next day with several ague-stricken members of her family. He cured all of them completely and instantly.

Greatrakes, had he lived long enough, might have worked his way slowly through the library of the Royal College of Pathology; but on Low Sunday, April 2, 1665, he received a general revelation that God had granted him plenary therapeutical powers. Once again he found an early opportunity for confirmation. Business soon took him to Lismore, a market town some few miles from the neighborhood that had become his therapeutic arena. There he would discover that his reputation had preceded him. He took the occasion to visit his old friend Cornet Dean, one of whose neighbors, having heard rumor of his visit, rushed over to meet him. Actually "rushed" is hardly the right word. The man was suffering from a badly ulcerated leg, which according to Greatrakes had turned completely black. He could barely walk with the aid of stick supports. He reported that the doctors were advising amputation—a report rendered credible by the frequency with which early surgeons wielded their hideous tools. They did not get their ghoulish sobriquet "sawbones" idly. Greatrakes touched the afflicted leg, with an instantaneous positive effect. Further touching transformed the ghastly color of the leg, which now glowed with a healthier red. Three of five ulcers immediately healed, "and the rest within a few hours afterward." Soon the amazed man walked out of the house with a spring in his step and a story on his lips.

There is no plausible medical explanation for the "instant" disappearance of gaping lesions, but of course all the evidence so far considered has been offered by Greatrakes himself. While nothing in the man's history suggests that he was a liar or a conscious fraud, we still feel the force of Hume's criterion that it is more probable that he was mistaken or deluded than that he actually cured with his touch a gangrened limb ripe for amputation. What created his reputation as a miracle worker was the testimony of others. And while God is no respecter of persons, persons themselves usually are, and in the seventeenth century were even more likely to be. The testimony of Irish plowboys and old wives might impress other plowboys and other old wives, but it was unlikely to become the buzz of the London coffeehouses.

The healing of Robert Phayre was something else again. In the Civil War, Greatrakes had served under the regimental command of this man—who later, as one of the three military officers to whom the warrant for the execution of King Charles was addressed, became one of the technical regicides. He nonetheless escaped the selective retribution at the Restoration and, after a time, gained the liberty to return to the life of the squirearchy in southern Ireland. In 1665, his old subordinate Greatrakes visited him at Cahemore in County Cork. At the moment of Greatrakes's arrival, Phayre was suffering acutely from an ague. There is documentary eyewitness testimony in the form of a letter later written by one of Phayre's sons that Greatrakes immediately stroked the illness away in a matter of moments. It is from the second half of 1665 that the Stroker's wonder-working reputation "went viral."

II. The Royal Society and the Cambridge Platonists

So long as Greatrakes stayed in rural Ireland, his fame was likely to remain both geographically and sociologically local. He was more than the obscure "village Hampden" of Gray's "Elegy," a "flower born to blush unseen." Boatloads of English medical pilgrims were, after all, making their way up the Blackwater to seek him out. But he was not yet an international phenomenon. His true celebrity, and therefore the nature of his complicating role for the formation of our notion of the Enlightenment, was naturally related to his interactions with important men and intellectual tendencies of the age. His history requires the brief introduction of two groups in particular: the members of the Royal Society of London for Improving Natural Knowledge, and the "Cambridge Platonists."

The Royal Society was founded in 1660 and granted a formal royal charter in 1662. It was the fruit of a gradual maturation of associations among modern-minded scientists animated by the spirit of Francis Bacon's *New Atlantis*, a utopian novel in which advances in scientific knowledge move in harmony with the purification of religion and the moral improvement of the human race. As we shall soon see when we consider some of the important roles played by Rosicrucianism and Freemasonry in creating the spiritual vocabulary of the Enlightenment, the concept of "the advancement of learning" typically implied that the augmentation of scientific knowledge consisted of both material and spiritual aspects. The setting of Bacon's novel is an imaginary island, the name of which (Bensalem) means "Son of Peace." Its central educational institution, Solomon's House, invokes a proto-Masonic concept of wisdom.

A predecessor of the Royal Society had been called the "Invisible College," where the word "Invisible" bore the general force of the contemporary cybernetic "virtual." It was not a college of stone and mortar, matriculations and graduations, but a sociable intellectual community like the later "Republic of Letters."

From the start, one of the hallmarks of the Royal Society had been its passion for scientific experiments and the experimental sensibility. It immediately became prominent and also controversial. One of its founders and most influential members was the chemist Robert Boyle, the Boyle of Boyle's Law concerning the relationship between volume and pressure in contained gases. Boyle plays an important role in the history of Greatrakes the Stroker.

If the members of the Royal Society consisted of the cutting edge of British science in the period of the Restoration, the so-called Cambridge Platonists aspired to be the cutting edge among humanists. They were an informal group of men who took their name from the fact that most of them were prominent in Cambridge University and most of them were knowledgeable about and admiring of ancient Greek idealist philosophy. The two most important were Ralph Cudworth, author of *The True Intellectual System of the Universe*, and Henry More, a major Anglican theologian and an impressive philosopher. These men rejected the arid chop-logic of the old Scholastic thinking with the humanistic vigor of Erasmus and Rabelais, if not quite their wit. They kept up with the latest developments in British and Continental philosophy alike, reading Descartes and Spinoza as well as Hobbes and Bacon. Naturally they were interested in the Royal Society, with whose members they had many intellectual and personal connections.

The intermediary through whom Greatrakes would come into intimate commerce with the greatest names in British secular and sacred science was an enlightened English nobleman named Edward Conway. In the 1660s, not yet come into his earldom, he was a wealthy landed aristocrat notable for his many amateur intellectual and cultural accomplishments and connections. Lord Conway was a true patron of learning. Not infrequently he opened his house to the adepts of the "new learning," and the "virtuosi" of the new society. His seat was at Ragley Hall, a great house set in the Warwickshire countryside a few miles west of Stratford-on-Avon, and no very great distance from the dreaming spires of Oxford University. Conway's private library was among the largest in England, and also among the most "modern." He had a book agent charged with keeping abreast of European erudition.

Conway was an important man. Beyond that the historical record suggests that he was a thoroughly decent and admirable man, a corollary that did not inevitably accompany importance among the British aristocracy. Even so, he claims a place in this history primarily by marriage. His beloved wife Anne was *truly* remarkable.

Lady Anne Conway was born in 1631 and died in 1679. She was the posthumous daughter of Sir Heneage Finch, at one time the Speaker of the House of Commons. It is perhaps relevant to her later remarkable achievements that the Finch family included several learned and independent-minded men interested in strange religious speculations. For example, her uncle, Sir Henry, was an erudite jurist whose intellectual eccentricities included the writing of a scandalous work of Christian Zionism (*The World's Great Restoration*), for which he was briefly imprisoned. His prediction of the imminent restoration of a temporal empire of the Jews, whether or not such a development might seem necessary to theologians of history, had rather offended King James.

In an age in which the intellectual subordination of women was as a law of the Persians and the Medes, when women were neither expected to be well educated nor offered serious opportunities for intellectual self-improvement, at a time when there were no women at all in the universities, in the clergy, or in the "learned" professions, Lady Anne Conway became a savant and a philosopher whose abilities were publicly recognized by some of the great minds of her time—*male* minds, of course. Despite the fact that her sex barred her from the halls and cloisters of Academe, she became by correspondence the special and prized pupil of Henry More, the most renowned theologian and philosopher in the faculties of Cambridge University. Her brother, who had studied under More in a more conventional setting, had introduced his master to his sister. The history of Anne Conway's triumphs happily allows us to applaud the uncommon liberality of both those men, no less than that of her husband. It is obvious, given the social realities of the period, that Edward Conway at the very least tolerated and almost certainly encouraged his wife's career as an intellectual adventuress.

The tender marital love of Lord and Lady Conway is illustrated by a real-life macabre episode worthy of the poetic imagination of an Ovid or a Chrétien de Troyes. The viscount possessed important properties in County Antrim in Ireland, and he was absent on business there when Anne's illness took a fatal turn and she died. He had lived in fear of losing her for most of his married life, and he appears to have left instructions with the live-in Rosicrucian physician Francis Mercury van Helmont. Helmont had prepared a special leakproof casket in which he could preserve the woman's body in a clear liquid spirit.

There was a glass window on its top just above the place where the corpse's head would rest, so that upon his return the grieving husband was able to gaze for a final time upon the face of his beloved.

Though Greatrakes was to encounter Lady Conway for medical treatment rather than for philosophical discussion, several factors of her intellectual physiognomy are relevant to the history of their association. Eamon Duffy, a prominent ecclesiastical historian who has written brilliantly about the Greatrakes episode, points out one of the curious implications of the Anglican *via media* in the Restoration period. The extremes between which the "middle way" was thought to pick its safe and sensible path were the twin enthusiasms of Catholicism on the one hand and radical Dissent on the other. The Roman Catholics believed in the living continuity of a miraculous tradition. The able Jesuit controversialist Robert Bellarmine had pointed to the continuity of miracles as a badge of divine approbation. Even among Protestants, writes Duffy, "The relentless reduction of the supernatural in Christianity in favour of 'good morality' was not unresisted." Many of the more radical sects believed in faith healing. In particular the Quakers did so: George Fox, the Quaker founder, not infrequently healed people.

The surprising conclusion of Anne Conway's lifelong spiritual quest was her embrace of Quakerism. Surprising is one word; scandalous would be another. Her old mentor and friend Henry More was horrified, and he no doubt was representative of most people in their shared circles. But there was more than one path that might lead to Platonic "transcendence." Anne Conway had mastered the learned tongues. She knew Greek in great depth, and she knew enough Hebrew to handle the learned Scriptural exegesis of the university theologians. Her studies with More, which included wide readings in Plato and Plotinus, would have inevitably led her to ancient esotericism, even had she not included Philo Judaeus as a "special topics" author. But she did read Philo, and read him with fascination.

Here if not before she became interested in classical and modern kabbala, gematria, and other occult features of the old Christian exegesis of the Scriptures. The early parts of the *Kabbala denudata* of Christian Knorr von Rosenroth, a serious Hebraist who had concluded that the three highest circles of the *sephiroth* were actually the three persons of the Holy Trinity, appeared near the end of her life. Only the most erudite dared open their pages; she devoured them with enthusiasm. It is possible, though uncertain, that she may even have met Rosenroth during the period of his scholarly wanderings in Britain.

She was in daily contact for many years with the aforementioned family physician, Francis Mercury van Helmont, who became her close friend as well as her doctor. The career of this important man has been considerably illuminated in a recent study by Allison Coudert. He was a good friend of Knorr von Rosenroth, and an avid kabbalist himself. Like many linguists of his time he was obsessed with the idea of the "original language," and with the supposed special properties of Hebrew and the Hebrew alphabet. He was rightly regarded by his enlightened colleagues as a kind of hero of science, for he had fallen into the clutches of the Inquisition in Italy and emerged from its torments alive and with his intellectual honor intact. If it seems odd to you that a Dutchman should be named "Mercury," you may be on the right track. Helmont's father was a "iatrochemist" noted in his day, iatrochemistry (the "higher" chemistry) being, so to speak, the medical side of alchemy, or medicine along the Paracelsan model. The word has disappeared. We now have "chemotherapy." Quite apart from the exalted role of mercury in the alchemical universe, the liquid metal was a common medical "specific" down through the eighteenth century. One of the great medical adventurers of that age, Thomas Dover, reveled in the name "Doctor Quicksilver." He was much in demand. Mercury could be an effective remedy for syphilis, provided that it did not kill the patient first. But of course the same could be said of other forms of chemotherapy. Helmont was an occultist and a kabbalist and, like Anne Conway herself, much taken with Quaker spirituality. In any event, Lady Conway's Enlightenment credentials, crowned by occult expertise, were impeccable.

She wrote a good deal, though only one book went through the press. That was a posthumous publication in Latin translation. Modern British philosophers have been conspicuous for the verbal economy of the titles of their books and essays, with an apparent preference for the free-standing gerundive: "Becoming," "Hesitating," "Beginning or Ending," that sort of thing. Lady Anne Conway was limited by no such constraints. The title of her posthumous work is *The Principles of the Most Ancient and Modern Philosophy, Concerning God, Christ, and the Creatures, viz., of Spirit and Matter in General: Whereby May Be Resolved All Those Problems or Difficulties, Which Neither by the School, nor by Common Modern Philosophy, nor by the Cartesian, Hobbesian, or Spinosian Could Be Discussed.* That is its *short* title.

Anne Conway had a serious medical condition: chronic migraine headaches. According to her report, she was never without a headache, though serious and incapacitating attacks of the *megrim* were only intermittent. The achievement of her erudition must have required a most courageous spirit as well as brilliance and unrelenting labor. When traditional medicine failed, she submitted to various experimental regimes, many of them nasty. On one occasion she traveled to France to consult with some surgeons supposedly expert in curing migraine by trepanning. In the end, they declined to break into her skull, probably out of a sensible caution prompted by her high social station, though according to the *DNB* "they are said to have made incisions in the jugular arteries." Such were the advanced medical techniques of the second half of the seventeenth century.

In the summer of 1665 Greatrakes was in Dublin, where he caused a good deal of stir, as he did everywhere he went. Here he ran into religious opposition. The (Anglican) archbishop of Dublin at this time was Michael Boyle, a stout Protestant of the modern school. William

Edward Hartpole Lecky, the great Irish historian of the nineteenth century, somewhere describes the common Tory attitude to the Church of England in the post-Restoration period. The Church's theology was, in this view, "an admirable auxiliary to the police force" in which religion should play as small a part as possible, and ostentatious religion no part at all. Archbishop Boyle appears to have exemplified this school of thought.

He was horrified to discover that a churchman was going about laying his hands on sick people and rubbing their ulcerations, praying all the while in a loud and confident voice. He was even more horrified that the objects of these attentions were in many cases declaring themselves cured *by miracle*. He instituted his own private Protestant Inquisition, which soon revealed to his yet further discomfort the technicality that in actual fact there was no Anglican canon against performing miracles in the name of Jesus Christ. He was reduced to charging Greatrakes with practicing medicine without a license. And as the Protestant Inquisition was much less practiced than its Catholic analogue in colluding with the secular arm, nothing whatsoever happened. Greatrakes greeted the proceedings with the amused contempt they so richly deserved. He simply ignored Archbishop Boyle, though the business about licensed and unlicensed medicine did in a general way adumbrate the contours of the controversy still ahead.

As the holder of important estates in Ireland requiring frequent attention, Lord Conway had naturally heard of Greatrakes the Irish wonder-worker. Now he learned that he was in Dublin. He wrote to Greatrakes there through a noble intermediary, asking him to come to Ragley Hall to treat Lady Anne for the *megrim*. Naturally, all expenses would be handsomely covered. It was very characteristic of the diffident Greatrakes that he at first showed no interest in an invitation that could hardly fail to work for his aggrandizement. It is possible also that his reluctance betrayed a political attitude. He was a reformed rebel, but he remained a lay ascetic committed to plain living and high thinking. He did not know Lord and Lady Conway, and he probably had a stereotypical notion of the life of a country magnate. The prospect of sumptuous meals in a stately home in Warwickshire was not in and of itself a powerful inducement.

However, Conway continued to press the invitation, and after several months of hesitation Greatrakes acceded. He took ship for Bristol in January 1666. Both on shipboard and especially in the English port city itself, eager petitioners sought his ministrations. He effected "many" cures. It is about seventy miles from Bristol to Alcester, the town nearest to Ragley Hall. He claims to have been solicited "at every milepost." Perhaps a little awkwardly he arrived at Ragley on January 24, a week before the annual solemnities remembering the execution of Charles Stuart, King and Martyr.

All this was being played out, of course, against the backdrop of a huge national medical disaster. The year 1665–66 was the infamous "Plague Year," permanently memorialized in Daniel Defoe's powerful book. The mortality in London, especially in the second half of 1665, was appalling. The king and the court had retired to the country. Many wealthy burghers had also fled.

Valentine Greatrakes was at Ragley Hall for about three weeks. In his ostensible mission he failed utterly. He could not cure Lady Anne's headaches, and after several attempts he frankly confessed his defeat. He left no detailed account of the efforts. It is in any case difficult to imagine how his usual method of applying repeated, hard "strokes" upon the afflicted bodily part could have been employed against headache. Neither on this occasion nor on any other did he apologize for his failure. He always prefaced his therapeutic sessions with a clear announcement of failure's possibility. From the time of first receiving Conway's invitation, he had expressed to Conway's intermediary, Sir George Rawdon, his inexperience with migraine and his frank doubts that he could cure it. He had come to believe he was a mere vessel of the divine grace, and that the success of his cures could not be guaranteed by the intensity of his own intentions. On the frequent occasions when there was evidence of instant improvement, he appeared as delighted and grateful as his patients themselves. The relatively high incidence of his failures, the frankness with which he anticipated their possibility, and the equanimity with which he acknowledged them after the fact—all these things argued for the man's sincerity and his honesty. A charlatan might seek for alibis in some external circumstance or atmospheric detail peculiar to the venue of the therapeutic attempt. Greatrakes never did. Though they must have been disappointed, neither Lord nor Lady Conway expressed any sense of grievance.

Besides, the failure was soon overtaken by success. The news that Greatrakes was at Ragley had brought a dozen or more scrofula victims to the gates of the estate. The loudly reported accounts of his sensational cures in this field soon drowned out further speculation concerning his inability to remove the migraines of Lady Conway. For a fortnight he went on a virtual medical rampage, dealing with dozens of importunate sufferers each day. These were mostly, but not exclusively, cases of the King's evil. All of Greatrakes's cures remain mysterious, but particularly mysterious are the reports of the instant reparation of serious bodily injury from accidents—broken bones, deep lacerations, crushed and brutalized tissue.

While all this was going on in public and in broad daylight, various great men were at or passing through Ragley. These included Boyle (the chemist, not the archbishop), Cudworth, George Rust, and Henry More. These men met Greatrakes personally and, without exception, formed a positive opinion of his candor and character. Several of them witnessed actual episodes of apparently inexplicable successful healing. Rust and More later described the method as very like a religious ceremony. It always involved "the laying on of hands" (to use the biblical expression) and a set prayer. Greatrakes always invoked the name of Jesus. He prayed: "God Almighty heal thee for His mercy's sake."

He invariably deflected attempts to thank him, saying that all thanks were due to God alone.

At Ragley Hall, Valentine Greatrakes had entered a cultural world, rare if not unique in all of England, that would guarantee a public and consequential debate concerning miracles among leading men of science and leading philosophers and theologians. The subject was uncongenial to them, but its discussion now became unavoidable. The "Ragley wonders" became the occasion for a pamphlet war that provides most of the comparatively rich documentation on which this and all other accounts of Valentine Greatrakes have depended. What Valentine Greatrakes had actually done remains mysterious after more than three centuries. What his contemporaries *thought* or *said* he had done is another matter, and to that we shall shortly return, after briefly concluding a survey of his sojourn in England in 1666. The nearest big place to Ragley was Worcester. The town fathers sent emissaries to Greatrakes with importunate invitations to visit their ancient town, and in the middle of February he did so, arriving there on or near his thirty-seventh birthday. (He had been born on St. Valentine's Day, accounting for his uncommon given name.) His stay there is not well documented, but once again there were "many" cures.

By now, Greatrakes and his marvels were being talked about throughout the land wherever cosmopolitan gossip was to be heard, and especially in the London coffeehouses. The plague having considerably abated, the capital was reanimating. The king himself, recently returned to the city, had taken an interest in the news of Greatrakes. The secretary of state, Lord Arlington, wanted him to visit the capital, and sought a way to persuade him. This time the intermediary was Edmund Bury Godfrey, with whom Greatrakes may already have been in correspondence. Godfrey was a prosperous businessman and one of the heroes of the Plague Year, having courageously stayed at his London post (he was a justice of the peace) throughout. He was later rewarded with a knighthood. His mysterious violent death in 1678, at the time supposed to be the work of Roman Catholic conspirators, was a kind of distant, jarring echo of the Gunpowder Plot of 1605.

Greatrakes accepted and moved on immediately to London, where commodious quarters had been made ready for him in Lincoln's Inn. He stayed there until June, treating "many scores" of supplicants, always on a scrupulously gratuitous basis. The Stroker always gave the appearance of an intense application in his efforts, and several successive "sessions" appeared to leave him exhausted, as from heavy manual labor. The results were, as usual, mixed. Some he appeared to cure; others showed no improvement. The number in the former category, however, was sufficiently large to keep his fame alive. What might be called a "command surgery" was arranged for the king and the court at Whitehall. On this occasion Greatrakes failed entirely, leaving the monarch with as dim a view of Greatrakes's supposed medical powers as he must at least secretly have had of his own. The royal skepticism did not long remain private.

In June, Greatrakes returned to Ireland, and in September 1666 a good deal of old London burned to a crisp. So far as I know nobody ever suggested a connection between the two events, but the Great Fire definitely changed the subject of conversation. He did make two more visits to England—in 1668 and 1672—but they were not the occasions of publicized medical events. Mainly he simply relapsed into his quiet and comfortable life of rural obscurity. When his skeptical wife Ruth died, he married a local widow. Valentine Greatrakes, the Stroker, died at his estate at Affane on November 29, 1683, at the age of fifty-four.

III. A Preemptive Defense: Henry Stubbe

Under any circumstances the history of Valentine Greatrakes would remain an historical curiosity. It became a significant episode in the history of Enlightenment thought once it was the occasion of debate among the enlightened. And that debate had become inevitable when Greatrakes entered the circle of public intellectual prominence surrounding Lord Conway. One of his first great public champions was Henry Stubbe (1621–1676). Stubbe is one of those minor figures beloved by intellectual historians because they are so often "more representative" than the major ones. What Stubbe principally represented was the "old science" in confrontation with the "new philosophy"—that is, the experimental sensibility of the recently founded Royal Society.

Stubbe was a meritocrat, of whom the number in seventeenth-century England was perhaps larger than is sometimes imagined. He overcame early difficulties to gain entry to the Westminster School in London, where his precocity as a Greek student won him attention, admiration, and eventually a place at Christ Church, Oxford. The republican tendencies of his youth lapsed into an accommodating royalism in middle age. Stubbe was a pamphleteer of ability, but his splenetic essays were never favorable to his political career. He was for a time the sublibrarian of the Bodleian, but he was forced out of Oxford at the Restoration and took up the full-time practice of medicine. Good connections procured for him the possibly sour plum of an appointment as King's Physician in Jamaica.

The literary product of this appointment, which proved to be brief, was a pamphlet entitled *The Indian Nectar or a Discourse Concerning Chocolata*. Upon returning to England, Stubbe took up the full-time practice of medicine in Warwickshire, centered in Stratford-on-Avon. It was in this connection that he came to know, and to be befriended by, Lord Conway of Ragley Hall, a man who loved his nectar.

Stubbe's little book about the Irish wonder-worker is entitled *The Miraculous Conformist: or, An Account of Severall Marvailous Cures Performed by the Stroaking of the Hands of Mr. Valentine Greatarick*. It was published in Oxford by Hall, the University printer, in 1666. It bears the Latin *sententia* "One ought not to deny what is manifest because one cannot understand what is hidden [*occultum*]." His attack on the

Royal Society began formally only in 1669, but the Latin motto adumbrates one of its central attitudes. Are the empirical claims of the "new science" comprehensive and global? Is there still room within the new "scientific" universe for the supernatural?

Here it is necessary to draw attention to the implications of the word "conformist," as Stubbe himself did in his prefatory letter. It meant that Greatrakes was a member of the Church of England. "It may seem equitable that I tell you why I call the Gentleman the Miraculous Conformist: many strange reports have and do runne of him; but he is reclaimed from all that is fanatique; and this gift of Healing was bestowed on him, since the Restoration of his Sacred Majesty, and the restitution of the Doctrine and Discipline of the English Church."

There is a certain amount here that may need unpacking. The English Civil War had been in equal parts about politics and religion, and politics and religion packaged in a certain way. Ever since the Elizabethan settlement many Anglicans regarded the Church as a *via media* between two destructive extremes, identified by Duffy as unreformed Roman Catholicism on the one hand and on the other the radical Protestants called Dissenters or Nonconformists. Both of these groups were often characterized by Anglicans as *fanatic*—meaning utterly and unreasonably unyielding in their loyalty to extravagant belief and practice. As for the Nonconformists, what they were in dissent against and refused to conform to was the Anglican polity of Church governance: episcopacy. Charles I, now called Charles the Martyr in the Anglican Church, was primarily a martyr to episcopal polity, which even under extreme duress he would not abandon in favor of the Presbyterianism demanded by the radicals. Needless to say, there was the political dimension famously captured in a statement made by his father, James I: "No bishop, no king!" The Restoration of the monarchy in 1660 had been also the ratification of the Anglican episcopal polity—what Stubbe calls the "Discipline of the English Church." Those who did not dissent against Anglican polity were said to *conform* to it and, hence, were conformists. Stubbe was one of those himself, and an affinity of political trajectory perhaps attracted him to Greatrakes.

Stubbe's pamphlet is in the form of a long letter addressed to Robert Boyle, whose fame as a scientist, already very great, would come to rival that of Isaac Newton himself. The printed version contains a brief preface of dedication to Thomas Willis, "Doctor of Physique, and Professor of Natural Philosophy in Oxford." Stubbe attempted to forgive the irregularity of such an arrangement with ponderous wit. "It may seem improper to Dedicate that to one which is sent to another: but whether it be that I am too busy, or too lazy to write more: or that I manage my friendships with lesse of ceremony and formality than usual, I have resolved upon this course." It was after all a course that bagged two birds with a single stone, or in this instance two famous natural philosophers with a single pamphlet.

Stubbe was not a great writer. His baroque rhetorical periods, which occasionally seem like travesties of Thomas Browne, are made yet less prepossessing by an unctuous tone. Nonetheless, his little book is full of ideas. He makes an historical survey of the healing touch from biblical and classical sources, and brings it down to the contemporary monarchs of England and France. "Queen Elizabeth did, for some time, discontinue the Touching for the Kings Evil, doubting either the Success, or Lawfulnesse of that way of Curing. But she soon quitted that Fitt of Puritanisme, when the Papists defamed her, as if God had withdrawn from her the gift of Healing in that manner because she had withdrawn herself from the Roman Church." Here he alludes to a recurrent theme. The apparent significance of Greatrakes's cures for Stubbe is that they are the first known instance of God performing miracles *among the Protestants*. His view is surprisingly liberal. He doubts not that Catholics and Muslims have indeed had their miracles. "Undoubtedly God hath permitted all Religions (though not the Protestants, till now) to have their real miracles, that men may learne to trye Miracles by the Truth, and the Truth by Miracles."

Though he knows he is writing to a great man of science, he makes so bold as to attempt various *scientific* explanations of his own. Since disease can be spread by contagion, why might it not also be cured by contagion? This may have been a common speculation among the "Ragley group," as it had already appeared in More's *Enthusiasmus Triumphatus* (1656): "there may be very well a sanative and healing contagion, as well as a morbid and venomous."

It was only natural that the reports of the miraculous healings would be greeted with suspicion by one who had not been present, and Stubbe is concerned to dispel all suggestions of chicanery or fraud. He does this partly by relating his own empirical observations and partly by repeating the testimony of men more intimate with the Stroker than he. Stubbe has observed Greatrakes closely. He watched his hands closely, and *smelled* them, assuring himself "that his Hands had no manner of Medicaments upon them." He noted also that the man washed his hands frequently—a detail reassuring to anyone who had ever seen a scrofula boil. Here Stubbe himself acted in the experimental spirit of the Royal Society.

He is entirely prepared to entertain the possibility of magic, but only to reject it in this instance. "I observed that he used no manner of Charmes or unlawful words; sometimes he Ejaculated a short Prayer before he cured any, and always, after he had done, he bad them give God the Praise."

Most interesting, perhaps, is his account of the more intimate observations of Greatrakes's daily companions. On one occasion Greatrakes came into Lord Conway's bedroom. His lordship smelled a pleasant odor, as of a flowery bouquet. He asked the attendant servant "what sweet water he had brought into the room"? (The sanitary arrangements of the Old World, even in the great houses of the one percent, encouraged the lavish use of what we would today call deodorants.) None, he answered. "Whereupon his Lordship smelled on the hand of Mr. Greatarick, and found the fragrancy to issue thence; and examining his Bosome, he found the like scent there."

An evidence more intimate yet came from George Rust, a member of the Royal Society and a friend of the Cambridge Platonists and of Joseph Glanville. This man, who had been the rector of the church at Lord Conway's Irish seat and who would soon succeed Jeremy Taylor as bishop of Dromore, was among the "natural philosophers" attempting to save a small preserve of the supernatural in their increasingly scientific universe. He had been present at Ragley during Greatrakes's charitable rampage. "Dean Rust observed [Greatrakes's] Urine to smell like Violets, though he had eat nothing that might give it that scent." Here is testimony, perhaps, not to be cross-examined. But we must remember that the close examination of urine had been fundamental to medical science since ancient times. The most conspicuous attribute in the iconography of the medical saints Cosmas and Damian (third century) is the *jordan*, or urine flask.

The modern reader may find equally startling Stubbe's further report. "Sir Amos Meredith who had been his Bedfellow said that in the Night he had observed the like agreeablenesse of the smell in Mr. Greataricks Body, at some hours." Here, once again, the history of material culture impinges upon metaphysical speculation. In the Old World there were often more travelers than there were hotel beds to accommodate them: a fact attested to with equal force by the opening chapters of the Gospel of Matthew and *Moby-Dick*.

What strikes one from the longer historical perspective is the *medieval* character of this testimony. For us, the phrase "odor of sanctity" has only a metaphoric meaning, if it has any meaning at all. But the odor of sanctity was a real odor, sweet and floral, and in the old hagiographic texts, whether emanating from the living or the dead, was among the more common physical manifestations of divine spiritual approval. Herbert Thurston in his classic study of *The Physical Phenom-*

ena of Mysticism devotes an entire chapter to the odor of sanctity. "The vast majority of cases have to do with the fragrance proceeding after death from the mortal remains of some of God's specially devoted servants . . . but there are also many instances of Saints whose person, dress, and cell have diffused sweet odours during life in such a way as to attract the general attention of their intimates and visitors."

Stubbe thus seems to belong to the retrograde school of the "old" science. Yet his championing of Greatrakes, from another point of view, associates him with some fashionable tendencies of his day. The search for unifying themes often leads us to fascinating but somewhat obscure individuals, of the sort normally classed among the "minor figures" of their age. One such figure, yet more obscure than Stubbe himself, is the Londoner Ezekiel Foxcroft, born in 1633, Fellow of King's College, Cambridge, from 1652 to 1674, the year of his death.

Even the laundry lists of great geniuses may be honored by scholarly editions, and among the eagerly studied informal writings of Sir Isaac Newton are the flyleaf doodles and marginal notations to be found in many of the books once in his private library. One graffito of 1675 is recorded in a book entitled *Manna—a disquisition of the nature of alchemy:* "This philosophy, both speculative and active, is not only to be found in the volume of nature, but also in the sacred scriptures, as in Genesis, Job, Psalms, Isaiah and others. In the knowledge of this philosophy, God made Solomon the greatest philosopher in the world." The book had been a gift from Newton's erudite friend Ezekiel Foxcroft.

Foxcroft was the very able translator of the first known English version of the German Johann Valentin Andreae's *Chemical Wedding of Christian Rosecross.* I say "first known" translation because so many works continued to circulate in erudite circles in manuscript form, and especially, perhaps, "esoteric" works. It is probable that Andreae's book had been known and discussed in England much earlier. Foxcroft's translation itself found its way into print only fourteen years after his death.

There is another connection—that with Greatrakes the Stroker. Foxcroft had been an intimate in the "Ragley group." He knew Henry More and Ralph Cudworth well. When Henry Stubbe sought to get a "blurb" for his *Miraculous Conformist*, it was to Foxcroft that he turned. The lengthy title of Stubbe's pamphlet ends thus: "With a Letter Relating some other of his Miraculous Cures, attested by E. Foxcroft M.A. and Fellow of Kings Colledge in Cambridge." But if Greatrakes had his public defenders, he no less had public detractors.

IV. A Bitter Attack: David Lloyd

Throughout the periods of the Restoration and eighteenth centuries, job printing was *relatively* inexpensive in England. For this reason, among others, it was the Golden Age of the Pamphlet. It did not cost very much to get a few of your ideas into print in a few dozen copies, and this could often be done in an amazingly short period of time. It was also the period of the rise of the periodical. Serious legal risk attended certain subjects, but for many others the sole editorial constraint was the author's pocketbook. The fact that some few of the brightest jewels of English literature first appeared as pamphlets still read today, while some few others introduced ideas destined for celebrity, might easily cause one to forget that much pamphlet literature was dross read by practically nobody even then. Much of it had a distinctly hurried, temporary, "time-sensitive" character rather like that of our electronic mail. That the "learned" pamphlet by convention required a certain amount of citation in the learned languages, together with frequently errant or incomprehensible footnote citation, does not much alter this characterization. The *desiderata* were speed of writing and speed of delivery.

The immediate circumstances of Stubbe's *Miraculous Conformist* are not known, but at times it suggests a tone of preemptive defense. He may very well have heard some of the less complimentary gossip from London. But we are obliged to recognize that Stubbe regarded himself primarily as a scientist defending data derived from his own empirical observation at Ragley. That there is a fixed rule concerning the ratio between volume and pressure in compressed gases was a scientific discovery. That blood circulates through the human body impelled by the pumping action of the heart was a scientific discovery. So far as Stubbe was concerned, it was a scientific discovery that God was now working miracles *through Protestants.*

An anonymous pamphlet attacking Greatrakes is entitled *Wonders No Miracles, or Mr. Valentine Greatrakes Gift of Healing Examined.* This is a work much more in the older theological mode—remembering always that theologians frequently exemplified their materials with "scientific" matter. It dates from the middle of March 1666, as an immediate response to Stubbe's *Miraculous Conformist* of a month earlier.

Its author was an eccentric Welsh clergyman named David Lloyd, the hack author of more than one strange work. The most famous perhaps was a long martyrology of Royalist victims of the Civil War, beginning of course with King Charles himself. According to Anthony à Wood, the book made Lloyd's reputation as "not only the character of a most impudent plagiary but a false writer and meer scribbler." It may have been Greatrakes's undisguised Roundhead past that offended Lloyd's extravagant Caroline royalism.

The haste of its accomplishment is perhaps suggested by a serious error in its title page. The immediate occasion for Lloyd's "examination" of Greatrakes was an episode on March 7, when according to Lloyd the Stroker very nearly killed a man in Charter-House Yard, in London, with his futile and most untender mercies. This could not have happened in 1665, as the title page asserts, when Greatrakes was still pondering the breadth of his medical mandate back on his Irish farm. Yet though the organization of *Wonders No Miracles* is badly confused, the author practically assaults his reader with an appearance of a scholastic rigor of organization. The man has a wonderfully taxonomic mind. He likes to make numbered lists. He cites classical authority for fifteen causes of the corruption of the imagination. (It may be corrupted "by windy Meats, and want of due Evacuations," among other things.)

Once he has fired off a barrage of gross libels in his opening pages, he rarely succumbs to mere personal vituperation, though one easily enough deduces he must have hated Greatrakes. His concern is not that the Stroker's supposed miracles are an insult to *science*. They are an insult to *religion*. Greatrakes frequently used the word "impulse" when speaking of his inner apprehension of his healing gift. That word is to Lloyd as a red rag is to a bull. Impulses have impelled most of the great frauds and madmen of history (more detailed lists). The impulsive is the very negation of the rational.

He accuses Greatrakes of *enthusiasm*, and derides as dishonest his claim to be a "Latitude-Man," a Latitudinarian, or Broad Churchman. He was after all formerly of the rebel party. Enthusiasm was the great fear of the Anglican Establishment. It meant an excessively emotional ("impulsive," perhaps) investment in religion, indecorous tears, obscene shouts of "Halleluia," any sort of Holy-Rolling. Enthusiasm was on a par with superstition, of which it was sometimes reckoned a subspecies or a sign. In general, though, Anglicans imputed superstition to the Roman Catholics and enthusiasm to the Protestant sectaries. The charge of enthusiasm was a predictable one to level against a former Roundhead, and Stubbe had anticipated it with a firm denial.

Lloyd's attack on Greatrakes's supposed miracles is partly based in observed specifics, but mainly in a priori general principles. That Greatrakes did not always succeed, and that some of his supposed successes were at best only *partial* cures, is for Lloyd a sufficient refutation of any claim to the miraculous. Greatrakes himself invariably faced his failures with equanimity. He had never claimed to be able to cure all ill-nesses all the time. Lloyd also chastises the Stroker for the physical violence of his technique. He speaks not only of the vigorous manhan-dling of various bodily parts but of frequent "cutting." This is the only place in the contemporary literature in which I find such an imputa-tion. One doesn't know quite what to make of it. It seems obvious that Lloyd himself never personally witnessed one of the sessions. He is relying on secondary reports, including some probably indignant ones. It is entirely credible that a severely ill person with badly inflamed sores, limbs, or joints would experience considerable pain from Great-rakes's ministrations, and that if they did not make him feel better they might well make him feel worse.

Mainly, however, Lloyd objects to the miraculous claims on theo-retical grounds. He is forced to believe in the miracles recorded in the Bible, but assumes, rather than argues, that any miracle whatsoever must conform to biblical type. Jesus' miracles had been under discus-sion for fifteen hundred years. Surprisingly little of the large clerical commentary suggested that Jesus had healed the sick out of compas-sion or to relieve suffering. The two-fold purpose of Jesus' miracles was generally held to be (1) to demonstrate his divine powers; and (2) to confirm the authenticity of his religious revelation. So also were the underlying purposes of the biblically warranted Apostolic miracles. Greatrakes, who always insisted he was a mere instrument or conduit, claimed no divine power, let alone any new revelation. Hence the cures, *even if authentic*, would not be miraculous by Lloyd's standard.

But he is far from believing them to be authentic. One very modern aspect of *Wonders No Miracles* is the confidence with which he dis-missed a large body of first-person testimony as superstition or delu-sion. History is replete with delusions of the grossest sort, and he lists a fair number of them—the man who thought he could live on air alone, the Jew sufficiently convinced of immediate resurrection to kill himself, and so on. He makes one powerful point not always considered in the "literature": the dangerous potential of religious enthusiasm in this particular year. Here he clearly alludes to the Plague of 1666, a general catastrophe perhaps capable of infecting even sane minds with delusions. This was, after all, the year of the millennium plus the number of the Beast (1,000 + 666). And although Lloyd heaps scorn upon the popular apocalypticism of the enthusiasts, his own framework is in fact apocalyptic. Greatrakes is yet another of the false prophets of the last days.

V. Greatrakes Strikes Back

In April 1666, Greatrakes met Robert Boyle in London. They were very near contemporaries and in childhood had been very near neighbors. The distance between Lismore Castle, where Boyle was born on January 25, 1627, and Affane manor house, where Greatrakes was born on February 14, 1628, is perhaps six miles. As Greatrakes points out, he had his early education in the free school of Lismore, which had been established by Boyle's grandfather. In the sixteenth and seventeenth centuries England had pursued a policy of "Plantation"—the encouragement of large-scale Protestant emigration from England and Scotland to confiscated lands in Ireland. The two families were members of the Plantation colonists, of "Scotch Irish," as they are sometimes called, a group from which derived an astonishing number of Nature's aristocrats, including several presidents of the United States. Both men were more conventional aristocrats as well, though Boyle of a degree considerably higher than Greatrakes. Greatrakes would certainly have been aware of the recent publication of *Wonders No Miracles* at the time of their meeting; and Boyle, too, may have been. It was undoubtedly with the prior permission of the recipient that the Stroker structured his autobiographical rebuttal in the form of a letter to Boyle.

It is called *A Brief Account of Mr. Valentine Greatraks, and Divers of the Strange Cures by Him Lately Performed,* and it was licensed on May 10, 1666, shortly before Greatrakes returned to Ireland. It crackles with outrage. Greatrakes was pretty sure who the author of *Wonders No Miracles* was—namely, the convicted libelist of *The Countess of Bridgewater's Ghost,* which had cost Lloyd six months in the clink—but he simply treats him as an anonymous scoundrel motivated by an unexplained malice. He begins by denying, vehemently, a number of Lloyd's untruths that had particularly stung him. First he never told the bishop of Chichester that he had heard the voice of God speaking to him from the heavens. He includes a letter from His Grace testifying to the fact that Greatrakes told him no such thing. Secondly, he places upon the record a letter from Mr. Cresset, proprietor of the house in Charter-House Yard where Greatrakes is supposed to have carried out some of his worst depradations, to the effect that Mr. Greatrakes did not at that time and place utter a blasphemous oath, taking the name of the Lord in vain. Next the anonymous author of *No Miracles* had charged that although the pretended healer never actually charged for his services, he did *borrow* money from his patients. Greatrakes was that kind of Protestant who thinks that debt is probably more criminal than theft. He had never borrowed a farthing in his life! A second point of particular pique is that the author of *Wonders No Miracles* had called him a "Good Fellow"—a phrase meaning something along the spectrum between "good ole boy" and "goodfella," an old drinking buddy with possibly criminal tendencies. Greatrakes is emphatic concerning his moderation in food and drink. As for "having to do with women," there has been in his whole lifetime only the skeptical Ruth.

Having relieved himself of a certain weight of righteous indignation, Greatrakes settles into a more conventional autobiographical mode, giving Boyle an economical but detailed sketch of his life and, in particular, of that part of it having to do with his religious views in relation to his stroking activities. It is a dignified document, and I regard it as credible and veracious. It must be pointed out, however, that almost everything that has appeared in print about the life of Greatrakes derives from his own authority alone.

He himself was conscious of the potential difficulty. That is why he concluded it with a lengthy dossier of testimonials written by friends, acquaintances, and former patients. The aggregate effect of these documents is most impressive. Among his witnesses is Andrew Marvell, poet and prominent politician, and the philosopher Ralph Cudworth. Benjamin Whitecote, the provost of King's College, Cambridge, and famous preacher of the time, was actually one of his patients and gives his affidavit of miraculous healing. There are several others. Furthermore, from this testimony and from that of all others made by people who actually knew him, such as Lord and Lady Conway, one gets the picture of a kind, sincere, level-headed, socially "normal" sort of a fellow. Many commentators seem to be as admiring of the eleemosynary nature of his medical practice as of its inexplicable efficacy.

Robert Boyle himself was perhaps one of those. He was cautious, and he was puzzled. We have some of his autograph notes in which he began a first attempt to account for the apparently "miraculous" phenomena in scientific and materialistic terms. But he did not get very far, and apparently dropped the matter, as Greatrakes himself appears to have done. Miracles that were an embarrassment to the bishops of the Church of Ireland and the members of the Royal Society alike were probably, after all, better left unmentioned.

Bibliographical

The only recent monograph study of Greatrakes the Stroker known to me is Leonard Pitt, *A Small Moment of Great Illumination: Searching for Valentine Greatrakes, the Master Healer* (Emeryville, CA, 2006). This is a rather slight work, but it does have an extensive bibliography. Most of the relevant primary sources are now available in print-on-demand format or on the Internet. These include Henry Stubbe's *The Miraculous Conformist* (1666), David Lloyd's anonymously published *Wonders No Miracles* (1666), and Greatrakes's own *Brief Account* (1666).

The most important contribution to historical analysis is the scholarly essay by Eamon Duffy, "Valentine Greatrakes, the Irish Stroker: Miracle, Science, and Orthodoxy in Restoration England," in *Religion and Humanism, Papers Read at the Eighteenth Summer Meeting and the Nineteenth Winter Meeting of the Ecclesiastical History Society*, edited by Keith Robbins (Oxford, 1981), pp. 251–72. Additional scholarly studies include A. B. Laver, "Miracles No Wonders: The Mesmeric Phenomena and Organic Cures of Valentine Greatrakes," *Journal of the History of Medicine*, 33 (1978): 35–46, and Caoimhghin S. Breathnach, "Robert Boyle's Approach to the Ministrations of Valentine Greatrakes," in *History of Psychiatry*, Vol. 10 (1999), pp. 87–107.

There is a good book on *The Cambridge Platonists* by C. A. Patrides (1969; 2nd ed. 1980). *Conway Letters: The Correspondence of Anne Viscountess Conway, Henry More, and Their Friends, 1643–1684*, edited by Marjorie Hope Nicolson (Oxford, 1930; expanded and renovated 1992), is a collection replete with fascinating information concerning personages involved in the major phase of the Greatrakes affair.

Books specifically cited or alluded to in this chapter:

Allison Coudert, *The Impact of the Kabbalah in the Seventeenth Century: The Life and Thought of Francis Mercury Helmont, 1614–1698* (Leiden, 1999).

W. E. H. Lecky, *History of the Rise and Influence of the Spirit of Rationalism in Europe* (1875).

Herbert Thurston, S.J., *The Physical Phenomena of Mysticism* (1952).

2 | *The Convulsionists*

I N   T H E   W E E   H O U R S of a morning at the end of January in the year
1732, there was a dramatic police raid on the church of Saint-
Médard in Paris. The church is no longer there, but tourists who have
taken in the street market in the rue Mouffetard have been very near
its former site. Large numbers of Louis XV's finest were present,
including the chief of the Metropolitan Police himself. Many were on
their expertly trained combat horses, weapons gleaming in their
hands. It must have looked like an elite special ops force tasked with
capturing a well-defended redoubt. Yet both the church itself and its
small contiguous graveyard were silent and empty in the cold winter
dawn. The actual task of the police commandos was to chain shut the
gates of the Saint-Médard churchyard and to affix upon them a sign
announcing that, by order of the king himself, entry to the cemetery
was strictly forbidden.

Deacon François de Pâris, who rapidly became the object of a popular cult, was celebrated in
numerous popular prints and "holy cards." Thus he soon enjoyed a burgeoning iconography. This
imaginary scene of the saint in private prayer derives from a familiar medieval stereotype of St.
Jerome. The image was produced by an artist of some reputation, Jean Restout, for inclusion in
the influential apologetic book by magistrate Louis-Basile Carré de Montgeron, *La Vérité des Miracles* (1737). Carré de Montgeron, having come to Saint-Médard to scoff, remained to pray.

Such a show of force might have seemed disproportionate to the threat addressed: the long dead bones of one of the occupants of the small graveyard. The authorities, however, had their reasons. That skeleton had proved to be at least as lively as the one encountered by Ezekiel in the Valley of Dry Bones, and had proved a cause of serious civil disturbance and a potential threat to altar and throne alike. Sometime the following morning a satirical wit added his own version of the royal "No Trespassing" sign in the form of the following distych:

> *De par le Roi, Défense à Dieu*
> *De faire miracle en ce lieu.*

This might be roughly translated as follows:

> *By order of the King: God may not*
> *Perform any miracles on this spot!*

Such was the first of many contributions to what would in time become the rich literature devoted to the odd doings at Saint-Médard Church, usually called "the Affair of the Convulsionists."

Men and women sometimes act upon the basis of ideas and convictions that, while sufficiently clear and compelling to themselves, cannot be grasped intelligently even by their contemporary adversaries. In the long view of history it often occurs that little more is remembered of their motives than that they lost. Any honest attempt to understand the Convulsionists of Saint-Médard requires at least a momentary consideration of certain "background" matters of which many of the Convulsionists themselves would have been innocent. The essential background for the episode of Parisian Convulsionism begins with the contest between the Jesuits and the Jansenists. The Jesuits define a major topic in the history of modern Roman Catholicism, the Jansenists a kind of historical blip. But that is a judgment of the long run. We must try to reimagine things from the perspective of the seventeenth century.

I. The Jesuits

Jesuits are members of the Society of Jesus, a religious order founded in 1534 by an old soldier, Ignatius of Loyola, and a few of his friends. By 1540 it had already "caught on," and had gained papal approbation. Specific features of the founder's biography combined with major historical developments in western Europe to define the nature and mission of the new religious order. From his military background Ignatius had taken not merely a vocation of militancy but a strong sense of discipline and the chain of command. The metaphor of religious life as "warfare" was a hoary one, and there were already a number of orders of actual military monks dating from the time of the medieval Crusades. Even so, the military structure of the Society of Jesus was of novel conception. The Jesuits thought of themselves as the shock troops of the Church. They were the Society of Jesus, but their supreme earthly commander was the "Vicar of Christ," the Pope.

Two particular historical stimuli animated Jesuit activity. The first was the Protestant Reformation. What was seen as a divinely inspired achievement by the Reformers was to the old Catholic hierarchy and its political adherents a prodigious disaster. The Jesuits were genuine reformers, but their Reformation would be carried out within the Church. They would be the spearhead of a *Counter*-Reformation. But of course Counter-Reformation, no less than Reformation itself, implies change. The question was: would the change be restoration or innovation? The first might be good, but the latter, especially in the context of an intrinsically conservative religious institution, was necessarily bad. In breaking with Rome, Luther, Calvin, and the others had, in the opinion of the Counter-Reformers, thrown out the baby with the bathwater. They themselves would get rid of the scum, but keep the babe.

This part of the Jesuit vocation might be described as a kind of spiritual damage control. It manifested itself in a remarkable intellectual efflorescence that redefined for several centuries such fundamental cultural phenomena as the shape of Christian education and the shape of lay piety. A second strand, no less decisive, was evangelical and missionary. Less than half a century had passed since Columbus had completed his first voyage to the New World. Columbus had discovered the West by mistake. Before the fifteenth century was out Vasco da Gama had discovered the East on purpose. The vision of vast new lands, many of them as rich in souls as in spices or precious metals, now captured the European consciousness. The theory developed among Catholic providentialists that there was a connection between the newly lost Protestants and the newly found pagans of the Americas and Asia. On the great exchequer of history the Jesuits would replenish the Church's spiritual balance through missionary activity.

The distinction between restoration and innovation, though prominent in the polemics of the Reformation period, is a subtle one that may baffle the historian. In all social institutions we shall find a commerce between continuity and change, ebb and flow. Religious difference is much less about *belief* than often meets the eye. At issue between Jansenists and Jesuits were certain doctrines concerning divine grace that proved, for some of them, literally worth dying for. But the conflict between Jesuits and Jansenists was about much more than academic theology. The Jansensists were not members of a particular religious order, but a coalition of like-minded theological conservatives who shared many traditional beliefs concerning the proper nature of religious life. Shared attitudes made of them a quasi-order, and one can speak of a Jansenist *style*, just as one can speak of a Bene-

Libre ou prisonnier il est le triomphe de la verité des miracles.

FRONTISPICE POUR LES NOUVELLES Ecclesiastiques, DE L'ANNÉE 1738

The journal *Nouvelles ecclésiastiques* (*Church News*), which catered to the Jansenist clergy and their concerns about the papal bull *Unigenitus Dei Filius*, widely proclaimed and defended the miracles at the shrine of the Deacon Pâris at Saint-Médard Church. This etched vignette (1738) suggests the futility of the royal persecution of the true believers. A pious youth stands reading in the courtyard of a Bastille-like prison: "Whether free or a prisoner, he is the triumphant demonstration of the truth of the miracles."

dictine or a Franciscan style. In truth, there is abundant evidence in the history of Christianity to demonstrate that there are fashions and styles of spiritual life just as there are fashions and styles of painting or of architecture. The stylistic element in the battle between Jesuits and Jansenists should not be minimized.

Everything about the Jesuit style was "modern." The military metaphor might have been hoary with age, but the "army" upon which the Society of Jesus was modeled was not that of St. Louis but that of the emperor Charles V, an army of gunpowder rather than arrowheads.

The phrase "the religious life" is likely to call to mind an image of a monk laboring tediously with stylus and parchment at his inclined desk in a cold *scriptorium*. The Jesuits were par excellence the order of the new printing press. Their prodigious learning was on a scale of which the Middle Ages had been technologically incapable; their prodigious literary production was the new Renaissance learning of print culture.

That the early Jesuits should find themselves in conflict with the Church conservatives of their day should not upon reflection surprise us. The history of institutional Christianity is a history of tension between a supposedly fixed and unchanging body of doctrine and practice and the irresistible innovations brought about by political, social, and material change. There is a clear medieval parallel to the seventeenth- and eighteenth-century contest between Jesuits and Jansenists in the conflict between the secular clergy (the parish priests "in the field," so to speak) and the members of the new mendicant orders, the Franciscan and Dominican friars, in the thirteenth and fourteenth centuries. Since like the Jesuits the friars "won," we have long forgotten that in their early centuries many considered them the practitioners of dangerous and inadmissible innovations.

These strands came together dramatically at the Council of Trent (1545–63), the workshop of the Counter-Reformation. In this reforming council the members of the new Society of Jesus played prominent roles, and from it the Jesuits emerged with considerably augmented prestige and reputation. Among the actions of the Council of Trent was the formal adoption of Thomist Scholasticism as the "official" theology of the Church. The Jesuits, who would increasingly dominate the theology faculties of Catholic Europe over the next several decades, became the prominent proponents of an updated Scholasticism. They became, in short, the friars of the new age.

II. Jansenism

By and large, Newton's third law applies to the exertions of religious reformers: for every action there is an equal and opposite reaction. There was a Protestant Reformation. In reaction to it there occurred within the Roman Church what is called the Counter-Reformation. As we have just seen, a prominent feature of the Counter-Reformation was the extraordinary efflorescence of the newly founded Society of Jesus, whose members, for a time, seemed destined to command a near monopoly on the intellectual and moral lives of Catholicism. But no conservatism, perhaps, is more rigid than religious conservatism. For religious conservatives, changes that may seem insignificant in the eyes of the distant historical observer may take on all the weight of a *causus belli*. The large and consequential schism of the Old Believers within the Russian Orthodox Church was triggered in part by an orthographic adjustment to the spelling of the name of Jesus in the Bible. Thus it was that the Counter-Reformation itself was countered in various ways by men ever wary of the powers of discernment of all reformers and revolutionaries to distinguish between the dirty bath-water and the baby within it.

Jansenism takes its name from a seventeenth-century theologian, Cornelius Otto Jansen (1585–1638)—often called Jansen the Younger, to distinguish him from a like-named ecclesiastical uncle. The Jansenists themselves did not of course speak of "Jansenism." Most *isms* are pejorative, and Jansenism is no exception. It was a term used by others who believed it to be a heresy. Of course anyone who has spent much time studying the development of Christian doctrine is likely to adopt a certain wit's definition of heresy: "Heresy is the side that loses." By this definition, if no other, Jansenism was a heresy. Young Jansen was brilliant, pious, indefatigably studious, and of a gloomy frame of mind. He by no means approved of all the tendencies of Counter-

Reform. In particular he viewed with alarm and distaste the modes of neo-Scholastic philosophy now fashionable in the Faculty of Theology and much in vogue among the Jesuits.

So thorough was the subsequent triumph of Scholasticism that today it is difficult to realize that there was nothing novel in Jansen's attitude, that indeed he was in many ways a typical theological conservative. There had been vigorous opposition to the Schoolmen of the thirteenth and fourteenth centuries, who had taken it as their task to "reconcile" so far as was possible biblical spirituality and Aristotelian moral philosophy. According to a conservative critic of that age, "All true divinity has yielded to sophistry, and Paul to Aristotle." But the Scholastic method of the great thirteenth-century Dominican theologian Thomas Aquinas ("Thomism") had received the official approbation of the Church in conclave at the reforming Council of Trent.

Together with a like-minded friend, Jean Du Vergier de Hauranne (aka the abbé de Saint-Cyran, or simply Saint-Cyran), with whom he for several years shared an intimate friendship based in strict ascetic practice and shared intellectual affinity, Jansen conducted an intense program of reading in the Fathers of the Church, and particularly in Augustine. The two friends greatly preferred the old biblically oriented patristic theology to what they considered the sterile procedures of the Scholastic academics. They studied Augustine with an almost preternatural intensity. They were men who knew their Augustine. Cornelius Jansen read through the doctor's complete works, which are vast, ten times in their entirety. The polemical works dealing with the theological questions that most troubled him he read *thirty* times.

Those questions had to do with reconciling divine grace—that is, the help or favor afforded to men and women directly by God—with the possibilities and limitations of human moral merit, and with the nature of God's justice. These questions had of course been prominent in the minds of the Protestant reformers, including the two most important ones, Martin Luther and John Calvin. Both men were considerable Augustinians. Luther had actually been a brother of the Order of the Hermits of St. Augustine. So close are Augustine's and Calvin's teachings on grace that some scholars have spoken of "Augustinianism" and "Calvinism" almost interchangeably.

The Protestant critique of the late medieval Church was that it had become a machine that promised salvation by mechanical means. Sinful human nature meant that everyone was a debtor, but there were ways to pay off the debt, or at least to cancel it, through penance. Various penitential good works, ascetic disciplines, private devotions, pilgrimages—all these things were "meritorious." It was also possible, through good works, to effect merit vicariously, on the behalf of others, such as a dead parent or spouse. Finally, it might be possible to make withdrawals from the great treasury of merit built up by the saints, and especially by the Blessed Virgin. Among the most charming miracle stories of late medieval popular literature is the well-known tale of the "Jongleur de Notre Dame." A *jongleur* (juggler, common street musician, a practitioner of an officially despised profession) is to be hanged for crimes committed. He has led a conspicuously reprobate life, his sole act of piety being his unfailing habit of saying a daily *Ave* to the Virgin. That proves to be enough, for when the support is removed from beneath his feet, the Virgin herself reaches out her hand to uphold the falling body and frustrate the lethal work of gravity. So great a grace might so little meritorious action gain.

The Church never said that one could buy forgiveness of sins with money. You might, however, buy a piece of paper declaring that sins had been forgiven or were in a state of progressive remission. That is what an *indulgence* was. Some minds considered that a distinction without a difference. Everyone knows that a precipitating event in Luther's career was the preaching of the Dominican pardoner John Tetzel.

Jansen was an academic theologian, a scholar. From one perspective, he was simply working in the well-established Augustinian tradition of the theology faculty at Louvain. Saint-Cyran, on the other hand, clearly was interested in current topics of ecclesiology, and especially in what he regarded as some dangerous novelties introduced by the Counter-Reformers at the Council of Trent. In particular he developed a studied hostility to the Jesuits, the most conspicuous champions of "cheap grace." In order to justify the ways of God to man, John Milton wrote *Paradise Lost.* Though reading it has seemed to many a student a heavy burden, it is as child's play to the work produced from the same motive a couple of decades earlier by Cornelius Jansen. Jansen's book was called *Augustinus*, the Latin form of the name of St. Augustine of Hippo (354–430), the greatest and most influential of the Fathers of the Church.

I said earlier that Jansen and Saint-Cyran knew *their* Augustine. There were other Augustines to be known. It is perhaps to be regretted that one of the greatest thinkers—and writers—the world has ever known so often felt himself constrained to write in a polemical, sometimes violently polemical style. That is because he was forever writing against "heretics." He knew the power of false ideas personally, and he had for a time embraced the gross dualism of the Manichaeans. In Augustine, anti-heretical polemic sometimes clouds over the sunny sky of an attractive teaching. Many people know that Augustine said, "Love God, and do as you please." Fewer know the context: a license to do as one pleases in the extirpation of the Donatist heresy.

IT IS NOTORIOUSLY DIFFICULT to know what ancient heretics actually taught. Usually the authentic writings have long since been destroyed. We know of them only what their enemies have written about them, often with considerable rhetorical exaggeration. But we can be pretty sure about Pelagianism, the doctrine of Pelagius, a "British Sicilian" contemporary with Augustine. Pelagius was the spokesman for a group of aristocratic Roman ascetics whose model (in their own eyes) was St. Jerome. He taught that it was possible for men, exercising their own free will, to take the first steps toward their own salvation. It was a doctrine actually developed in defense of ascetic life, but it seemed to Augustine to deny the abjectly fallen nature of the human condition. If a man could, without divine initiative, take a step toward salvation, did that not question the absolute character of divine justice?

On the whole Augustine was decidedly against heresy, but he did have one good word to say for it. Wrong ideas powerfully or persuasively expressed had the virtue of requiring for their effective refutation the deepest possible thought from their Catholic opponents. The ideas of Pelagius were not merely well put; they were also sympathetic and attractive. For this reason they reappeared, in one form or another, in various moments of Church history as the irritant grains of sand which goaded the orthodox to the fabrication of their theological pearls. One famous episode came in the middle of the fourteenth century when Thomas Bradwardine, later an archbishop of Canterbury, wrote in nine hundred pages a kind of early draft of the *Augustinus* entitled *De causa Dei contra Pelagianos* (*In Favor of God Against the Pelagians*). Bradwardine's Victorian biographer, Walter Farquar Hook, put it thus: "These abstruse subjects present themselves, from time to time, for discussion in the Church, being designed, probably, by Divine Providence to interest the minds of men, by compelling them to stretch out their necks, as it were, that, if it be possible, they may look over the ramparts, which separate eternity from time."

From the irresistible logic of such doctrines as the total depravity of mankind and the unquestionable justice of God flowed various alarming conclusions such as, for example, the equable insistence that unbaptized babes might sizzle eternally in hell, and do so justly. To return to the admirable Dean Hook: "Many minds have, in all ages, found it difficult to reject Augustinianism, or, as it was subsequently called, Calvinism; for it is against the conclusions that they have revolted, while by the process of argumentation through which the conclusions have been reached, they have been fascinated."

THE TRAGEDY OF JANSENISM, as several historians have called it, naturally involved much more than ideas in conflict. It will forever be linked as well with certain personalities and places. In addition to those already named, a Parisian family named Arnauld played a leading role. Antoine ("the Great") Arnauld (1612–1694) was the most prominent of Jansenist apologetic theologians. His voluminous writings range from highly subtle technical theology to popular spirituality of wide influence. His masterpiece in the latter genre was a book about the frequency with which a Christian should receive the Eucharist. His view was that it should be done infrequently, and only after the most scrupulous self-examination. If one can imagine a world in which such a book could become a best seller among a still fairly small reading public, one has made a giant step toward understanding the Age of Enlightenment.

The Great Arnauld had an elder sister, Jacqueline-Marie-Angélique Arnauld (1591–1661, known to history as "Mère Angélique"), who was a kind of spiritual dynamo. In the old Catholic world the religious life was, for many, and especially for many women, as much a social choice as a spiritual vocation. Many nunneries had the social selectivity of an exclusive country club. They often required dowries, and a family would "settle" a superfluous or inconvenient daughter in a "good house." Life within such houses might be notably unrigorous. The Italian novelists of the fourteenth century, who made the scandalous nun a permanently current type in European literature, were doubtless exaggerating; but the "society nun" was a reality. An epistolary novel in the form of the supposed love letters of a Portuguese nun was one of the great European literary successes of the late seventeenth century.

Angélique was "pre-enrolled" into religion at the age of seven. At the age of ten she found herself the prepubescent "mother superior" of a quite laid-back society of Cistercian nuns at an old convent in the marshes near Paris, called Port-Royal, or Port-Royal des Champs—Port-Royal in the Fields. A few years later a friar's sermon triggered in her a dramatic religious conversion. Religious history is replete with examples of nominally religious people who are made *actually* religious by contemplating their responsibilities in a new light. The situation often becomes sticky, as it did, for example, when Thomas à Becket developed a set of archiepiscopal expectations rather different from those of the king who had sponsored him. Many of the Port-Royal nuns, accustomed by tacit contract to a relaxed mode of monasticism, caused difficulties for the suddenly zealous superior. She persisted, however, and Port-Royal, reformed under her inspiration along strict ascetic lines, became a renowned center of spirituality that acted like a magnet for those who thirsted for the beauty of holiness.

Expanded in numbers, it had to move to larger quarters in Paris (also called Port-Royal), but the old rural house remained, destined to become *the* center of seventeenth-century Jansenism, insofar as ideas have centers. A motto of the ancient Egyptian hermits who in large numbers had taken refuge in the wilds of the Thebaid was "the desert a city." The old medieval nunnery "in the fields" continued in that spirit, becoming the host of a kind of permanent religious retreat in which distinguished "solitaries" (hermits) took up residence. Other spiritual-minded lay people, many of some social distinction, bought or rented property near the abbey in order to be close to its spiritual power.

The story of Port-Royal as magisterially narrated by Sainte-Beuve is one of the masterpieces of nineteenth-century French literature. The place has many other literary connections. It was there that the Great Arnauld and others produced the famous *Logic* and *Grammar* called "Port-Royal," which to this day are recognized as important contributions to philosophy and linguistic theory. Blaise Pascal, though he never took up life as an anchorite at Port-Royal, was a devoted fellow traveler. His famous *Provincial Letters* are undoubtedly the most famous piece of Jansenist literature ever produced. They take their name from the fiction that they are letters directed to the Provincial, the title given by the Jesuits to the head of one of the order's provinces. They are actually a wickedly witty satire on Jesuit moral theology as represented in some of the famous "manuals." Pascal's sister became a professed nun at Port-Royal. Jean Racine, one of the greatest of French dramatists, was among the select alumni of the Port-Royal grammar school. He struggled for much of his life to reconcile its ascetic principles with the worldly values of a man of the theater. After a period of apostasy he returned to the spiritual fold, becoming the historian of the institution.

The reader will need an introduction to one more ecclesiastical character: Pasquier Quesnel. Quesnel, another arch-conservative of strict ascetic habits, was the great vernacular popularizer of Jansenism. He prepared a French-language edition of the New Testament, elaborately annotated with what he called "moral reflections." (In the last quarter of the seventeenth century it enjoyed an extraordinary popularity in many subsequent editions, often under the title *Réflexions morales sur le Nouveau Testament*.) In terms of popular religious literature designed for the laity, it was the age of manuals (literally *hand*books), often prepared by Jesuit authors, that presented doctrine in a cut-and-dried Scholastic fashion and approached the religious life by means of codified systems and practices. Quesnel was an old-fashioned Augustinian exegete who advocated the closest possible reading of the text, in which he typically found a multiplicity of meanings, focusing in good pastoral manner on the "tropological" sense—the one that had to do with the moral life of the individual Christian.

The chief importance of Quesnel is that although "Jansenism" was repeatedly condemned in the late seventeenth century, it was upon Quesnel's book of "evangelical morals" that the definitive papal condemnation eventually fell. The actual *Augustinus* had been condemned by the theological faculty of the Sorbonne in 1649 and also by Pope Innocent X in 1653. But it was the Clementine condemnation of Quesnel that proved definitive. Pope Clement XI, a serious Christian but largely lacking in the political skills demanded by his job, was on this issue easily manipulated by the Jesuits. In 1708, the *Abrégé* (the popular short version of Quesnel's *Réflexions morales*) was blacklisted. But the true crisis of Jansenism came to a head only on September 8, 1713, with the publication of Clement's bull—destined to become one of the most famous and controversial in papal history—beginning *Unigenitus dei filius*. *Unigenitus* condemned one hundred and one propositions extracted from Quesnel.

Most of them had been condemned earlier. At their center were the five central errors concerning grace and the freedom of the will found in Jansen himself. The *Oxford Dictionary of the Christian Church* succinctly summarizes their burden in two propositions: (1) that without a special grace from God, the performance of His commandments is impossible to men; and (2) that the operation of grace is irresistible: and hence, that man is the victim of either a natural or a supernatural determinism, limited only by not being violently coercive. Another way of saying this is that man is "predestined" to damnation or to salvation.

III. The Deacon Pâris

The publication of the bull *Unigenitus* animated a large and long-lasting controversy within the French Church. The geographical "center" of Jansenism, insofar as there was one, was the religious community at Port-Royal. It is with Port-Royal that most of the great names of Jansenism are associated—the theologian Arnauld, the philosopher Blaise Pascal, and many others. Its violent suppression by the Jesuit party was an attempt to put a permanent end to the controversy; but of course it failed to do so. In the decades immediately following the *Unigenitus* there were whole parishes in Paris and elsewhere that might be called "Jansenist," in which the clergy tended to be strictly and ascetically religious and the parishioners disdainful of the easygoing Catholicism of the royal court and the Jesuits. One of these was the parish of Saint-Médard. The immediate object of the cult of the Saint-Médard church-yard was the grave of an obscure deacon, dead at the age of thirty-six, named François de Pâris. François was of a noble family, originally from Champagne. The second estate of the Ancien Régime was itself composed of two classes: the *noblesse de robe* ("nobility of the gown," whose station depended upon their administrative function) and the *noblesse de l'épée* ("nobility of the sword"), the ancient feudal aristocracy. The family de Pâris was gown nobility.

In this family of distinguished lawyers the father assumed that his son, too, would follow a legal calling. Indeed, the young man did study the law, and with a brilliant initial success. But an "irresistible divine grace" had other plans for him, and after overcoming the forceful parental disapproval that is so common a feature of the hagiographic texts, François was at the age of twenty-three at last allowed to follow his vocation of religious life. In addition to the normal clerical studies of philosophy and theology, he undertook an intense private regime of biblical studies, guided by the precepts of Quesnel's *Réflexions*.

François never joined a religious order, but he followed the exam-ple of the saint for whom he had been named in the intense practice of two particular virtues: evangelical poverty and humility. Francis of Assisi had tried to give away his father's property while the father was still living; Francis of Paris at least waited until his father was dead, but he then "gave it all to the poor," leaving himself in the necessity of manual labor (weaving, in particular) to earn his crusts. His Francis-can humility made him feel unworthy of priesthood. He did take the so-called minor orders in 1715, and eventually accepted ordination to the diaconate, normally a stepping stone or even a virtual formality on the path to sacerdotal ordination. But, again like his earlier namesake, he thought himself unworthy of such an exalted station. Needless to say, a reluctance to seek promotion and preferment was not generally characteristic of the French Church of the era.

François de Pâris was a thoroughgoing Jansenist in the style of his extreme personal asceticism, in his associations, and in his opinions. He lamented the suppression of Port-Royal. He denied the "permanence" of the bull *Unigenitus*. This was Jansenist-speak, as it were. The Jansenist could not deny the *fact* of the bull, nor did most of them explicitly challenge the authority of Clement. What they maintained was that so important a theological question as that of divine grace could be settled only by an ecumenical council. No such council had taken place since the Council of Constance in 1415, when a spurious "reunion" of the Catholic West and the Orthodox East had been briefly effected. According to the Jansenists, the Catholic teaching on grace could be determined only by "a future council"—but they knew what the true Catholic teaching was. It was that of Augustine of Hippo, doctor of the Church, in his magnificent anti-Pelagian polemics. So far as the Jansenists were concerned, the theological drift of *Unigenitus* was anything but settled law. The matter was "on appeal"—appeal to the future ecumenical council. The matter was not entirely unlike the situation arising in American political life with regard to certain controversial legislation that hovers uncomfortably in the public consciousness pending its ratification or rejection by the Supreme Court. There was of course a difference, too. So far as the Jesuits were concerned, the Supreme Court had already spoken.

The considerable fame of François de Pâris, however, was not that of a public theological controversialist, even a martyred one. His reputation was that of a *saint* in a time-hallowed tradition of Catholic spirituality. He was a practitioner of heroic asceticism. Here are two examples, both of them reliably evidenced by sound historical documents, despite the fact that they echo the spiritual clichés of medieval hagiographical fiction. As a youth, François de Pâris had by all accounts been a strikingly good-looking fellow. *Item*, it is believed that he intentionally exposed himself to the smallpox in order that his facial beauty might be marred and that, in such a fashion, he be both humbled and, perhaps, insulated from certain worldly temptations. *Item*, it is well documented that he kept the religious fast of Lent with an absolute rigor. That is, he ingested absolutely no food at all for the forty days between Ash Wednesday and Easter eve. This was an austerity not uncommonly reported among Jansenist zealots, but it is made all the more credible in this particular case, as witnesses do allow that he took occasional liquid. Such acts of self-denial were supplemented by numerous works of corporal mercy to folk, most of them poor laborers, in and about the parish of Saint-Médard. Thus even in his lifetime the combination of his notorious Jansenism and his heroic sanctity presented a problem for the guardians of orthodoxy. He would prove a greater problem to them when dead.

The persecution of the dead was something of a Bourbon specialty. At Port-Royal, suppression had been brutal; and warfare against nuns was a policy with a public relations "downside." Among some other unsavory manifestations of orthodox zeal was the disinterment of the dead "saints" from the convent cemetery and the scattering of their anti-Pelagian bones. The idea was to deprive living rigorists of a potentially dangerous site for the observance of an heretical cult. The result, of course, was to create a hundred others, one for every knucklebone or femur that could be scavenged and carried off by adherents of the despised cause. By 1700, relics from the vandalized Port-Royal ossuary were among the revered treasures of many parish churches in France, and in particular the church of Saint-Médard in Paris.

IV. The First Miracles

By the year 1727 the spectacular penances of the Deacon Pâris were already legendary among the Jansenist community. He walked on pilgrimages on painfully lacerated feet. He prayed through the hours that most men slept. He was obviously starving himself to death. Furthermore, he openly stated that the principal circumstance demanding his dramatic penance was the (in his mind) unresolved status of *Unigenitus*, an affront at once to the old Catholic belief and to the prerogatives of the King of France.

Only a full year after the deacon's burial would there be placed above the grave the elaborate and learned Latin encomium composed by the theologian Jandin. It had been commissioned and placed there hurriedly, by admirers rightly fearful that at any moment the authorities might forbid it. But a temporary marker had successfully staked a claim. As the beloved ascetic lay dying in the very shadow of the parish church, his admirers seem to have taken prescient action to anticipate what they feared would be the response of orthodox authority to his death. They wanted at least the foundations for a proper tomb prepared as a fact on the ground, before they could be forbidden to erect one. Among the last sounds grasped by the deacon's fading sense may have been the scraping of the trowels hurriedly preparing a final resting place for his bones.

He died in the night of May 1, 1727. By the time of his funeral on May 3—a funeral widely attended by a broad range of Parisian society, but especially by the common folk among whom he had lived and worked—he was already enjoying an unofficial canonization. On the very day of the funeral there was a wide distribution of those religious souvenirs otherwise called relics: bits of his clothing, chips from the marble of his tomb in the making, various material objects claimed to have been carried on his person or touched by his hand. Paul Valet, a local historian writing in the year 1900, reports that he personally knew of many such relics in private devotional collections at that date.

The miracles at the tomb of the sanctified deacon began at the very funeral service itself. It is important to stress that the early miracles were as normal as miracles can be, bearing in mind that miracles are "physical phenomena for which no satisfactory natural explanation can be found." The most famous episode, that of the Convulsionists, would come only later, and it proved almost as embarrassing to some of the Jansenists as it did ludicrous to the scoffers.

Deacon Pâris's miracles were miracles of healing. Many involved the "healing" of gross physical abnormalities—harelips, clubfeet, palsied limbs—for which psychosomatic explanation might seem implausible. Furthermore, many were "attested to" by competent witnesses, including medical professionals, whose testimony is of the sort that historians normally treat as reliable. We may consider a few examples.

An old woman, Madeleine Beigney (the widow Piquot), a woolspinner, was the deacon's neighbor and acquaintance. She had always admired his sanctity, but from the local chatter about the funeral she learned details of his secret charities that astonished her and encouraged her in a desperate attempt. One of the widow's arms had hung paralyzed and lifeless for twenty years. As the cortège approached the church, the woman knelt down beside its temporary resting place, prayed fervently for the new saint's help, and, as the body appeared, reached up with her undamaged hand and touched its feet. The cure was immediate and, of course, highly public.

Some of the beneficiaries were of a certain social prominence. The daughter of Mossaron, a substantial bureaucrat, the business agent for the Grand Duke of Tuscany, suffered a fit of apoplexy—a term used somewhat ecumenically for strokes and other dramatic neurological disorders. After much unsuccessful medical consultation, she undertook a novena (a program of special intentional prayers of nine days' duration) at the tomb of Deacon Pâris. Her intention was to pray for patience, but again there was a sensational cure. On the very first day she found herself able to kneel, then to make other bodily movements previously impossible for her. She was soon able to return to her house in the rue de Grenelle and mount its challenging staircases with agility. Her grievous impairment had vanished totally.

Most of the recipients of the saint's favors were women. There was a special term for the deeply religious laywomen who played such an important role in the spiritual life of the Church, and especially among the Jansenists. They were called the *dévotes*—of which our "devotee" is a most imperfect memorial—and the cult at the deacon's tomb attracted many. But there were also prominent episodes involving men. One amusing one is the "case" of the Spanish student Alfonso de Palacios. He had lost the sight of his left eye six years before he appears in our history. In a brawl he received a severe blow to the right eye, leaving him totally blind for a period of eight days. (Boys *will* be boys. The great American historian, Prescott, was blinded in the left eye in a food fight in a Harvard refectory.) After that Alfonso's damaged right eye did partially recoup, but in a fashion so debilitated as to leave him incapable of sustained reading. Whether it was sufficient for brawling we are not told.

One deduces Alfonso was not notably pious. His immediate recourse was to the medical profession, who applied various ointments. The quaint names of several have been recorded. Madame Macaire's Mixture (*l'eau de Madame Macaire*) proved partially effective, but he was still badly impaired. Only as a last resort did he undertake a novena at Saint-Médard churchyard. This he did with the encouragement of the famous scholar Charles Rollin. At the same time he continued to consult the most renowned oculists in Paris, whose prescribed bleedings he abandoned in favor of a relic, a piece of the dead deacon's shirt. That bandage seemed to cure the eye completely.

That is, perfect vision was restored to the *right* eye. The left eye remained in the sightlessness in which it had languished for many years. This fact became of polemical importance later. The miraculous healing of the Spanish student's wounded eye is about as well documented as any such thing could be, but it was stoutly contested by such anti-Jansenists as the archbishop of Sens on the following grounds. Surely if God were going to restore a blind man's sight miraculously, he would not restore it in *one eye only*! Here we have a nice echo of the theologians' objections to the operations of Greatrakes the Stroker. If he were really a miracle worker, the miracles would not be partial or intermittent. It could be pointed out, however, that the Spanish student had sought medical relief for his *right* eye. We may presume that the prayers of his novena were directed to the same end. There is on the face of it no reason that the principle of parsimony, which plays such an important role in various philosophical procedures and theological propositions, might not operate in this situation. It is one thing to deny that a miracle has occurred. It is quite another to tell God how He ought to perform His miracles.

We know about these miracles from many sources, but particularly from Louis-Basile Carré de Montgeron, a highly competent lawyer and magistrate for whom the defense of Deacon Pâris's miracles would become a life's work. Several Jansenists—like certain Protestants with whom they shared a good deal in common—report dramatic moments of conversion. The most famous of these was Blaise Pascal, who on November 23, 1654, was overcome with a direct perception of God— "the God of Abraham, the God of Isaac, the God of Jacob, and not the philosophers and men of science." (He was himself, of course, a philosopher and a man of science.) Pascal wrote a brief memorial of his moment of conversion, which he carried on his person, invisibly secured within his clothing, for the rest of his life.

Montgeron had a like moment on September 7, 1731, in the cemetery of Saint-Médard. According to his autobiography, which despite its evocations of hagiographic stereotypes we can have no defensible historical reason to dismiss, he had spent his youth in the pursuit of worldly pleasure and advantage, and without any particular interest in religion. He went to Saint-Médard if not to scoff, certainly not to pray. He was curious as to what might be the cause of the hubbub. But he was in an instant overwhelmed by spiritual intensity and authenticity. Regarding the sudden healing of a gross moral blindness as hardly less miraculous than the restoration of physical sight, he forever after listed himself among those to whom God had shown a special mercy through the intermediation of Deacon Pâris. He memorialized his moment of conversion in a fashion somewhat different from that of Pascal. He took it as his vocation to research, publish, and defend the miracles of the Saint-Médard churchyard. The documentary evidence he collected is invaluable. Furthermore, he plays a role with regard to the activities at Saint-Médard analogous to the role played by Stubbe, and to a certain degree by Robert Boyle himself, with regard to Greatrakes the Stroker. It is quite difficult to dismiss Montgeron's elaborately documented evidence as delusion, and perhaps harder yet to attribute it to bad faith.

V. The Convulsions Begin

The events just described—miracles or "miracles," depending upon one's point of view—are a small sample of the notable occurrences surrounding the origins of the cult of the Deacon Pâris centered on his tomb in the Saint-Médard churchyard. As much for political as for spiritual reasons they excited great interest, attracted investigation by both the reverent and the skeptical, and elicited a considerable pamphlet literature. The contemporary literary controversy surrounding the episode was one of two that marked it, for all its reactionary strangeness, as belonging to the *Age des Lumières*. Paris was a comparatively small city in terms of its internal distances, yet largely populated with the intellectual elites of the day. One could buy and read a pamphlet about the wonders of Saint-Médard churchyard in the morning, and drop by for a personal inspection in the afternoon. This was very different from the process by which medieval holy sites had established themselves. The second point is that much of the discussion was *medical*, as we have seen it was also with the stroking miracles of Valentine Greatrakes.

In retrospect they became known to some Church historians as the "normal" or the "respectable" miracles of the holy François de Pâris. One of the early historians of Convulsionism, the antiquary Paul Valet, insists on a point ever worth remembering. No hint of fraud or mercenary exploitation attended these astonishing histories. Nor, at first, did the Jansenist party make much of an effort to exploit the political dimension.

THE FIRST OF THE CERTIFIED Convulsionists was a pubescent girl of about thirteen, Marie-Elisabeth Giroust, the daughter of a shopkeeper in the parish of Saint-Eustache, across the river and at some distance from Saint-Médard. In 1731, this girl was suddenly visited with some alarming neurological disorder, apparently grand mal epileptic seizures. The drama of her miraculous cure played out over the course of the year punctuated by the official closure of the Saint-Médard grounds. Her parents do not seem to have been unusually religious, and their first recourse was to the medical profession. Contemporary medicine knew little about brain function and lacked the pharmacopia with which epilepsy is often controlled today. A program of bleedings did nothing to improve the girl's seizures, which remained severe and of frequent occurrence. She was by now suffering from dramatic full-body convulsions about five or six times a day. At this point the despairing parents decided to implore the supernatural aid of the new Jansenist saint surrounding whom there was such lively gossip.

A very common Catholic religious practice of the age was the aforementioned novena of petition—a program of prayer extending over nine days, undertaken in the hope of achieving a special grace, often medical in nature. The novena was often undertaken communally—that is, with two or several people praying in concert for the same goal—and it was often performed at a specific shrine, such as a local pilgrimage site, or before a particular devotional image in a church. The site might also be in a private place in the home.

Toward the end of August 1731, it was determined that the young girl and her mother would perform a novena, with the special intention of invoking the help of the Deacon Pâris in the healing of the girl's alarming illness. It is of some interest in light of what followed that since the girl was suffering such frequent convulsions it was deemed inappropriate that she herself should go to the Saint-Médard cemetery. The mother did indeed go there to pray at the deacon's tomb, while Elisabeth herself remained at home to pray.

At first there was no change, but by the end of the first of what would become several novenas, the frequency of the seizures had decreased. The mother determined to continue a regime of orchestrated prayer, though in a church closer to the family home on the Right Bank. In September, the first event recognized as undoubtedly supernatural occurred. The daughter saw a paper packet "trailing over the counter," and picked it up. Precisely at that moment she was struck by a convulsion but one, in the father's view, completely different in its character than those to which he had become accustomed. The seizure now seemed to be ecstasy rather than malady. Removing the package from the girl's hands he discovered it contained a cross-reliquary with some relics of Deacon Pâris within.

Later, while the child slept soundly, the father decided to perform an experiment. He brought the sanctified materials to her bedside. Immediately, while still asleep, she fell into an ecstatic paroxysm, contorting her body finally into a circular shape. When the father removed the holy parcel from the bedside, the girl's body immediately relaxed into a posture of more normal dormition. Later, awake, Marie-Elisabeth had no recollection of her happy convulsions, though she reported an unusual sense of well-being.

In its tantalizing combination of specificity (the shape of the portable reliquary) and vagueness (*where* had the packet come from?), the testimonial documentation of the completion of Marie-Elisabeth's cure continues in the medieval genre of the hagiographical dossier. But it has to be said that, taken together with many other "cases" from the early history of the deacon's shrine, the evidence is quite different in texture from that of medieval legend. The flavor is nearer to that of modern tabloid journalism, which indeed had its clear parallels in the eighteenth century.

It is important to bear in mind that many of the "early" miracles had nothing or little to do with convulsions. They were the only ones to command the universal credence of the "miraculous" party. The episode of the actual Convulsionists followed. Though it is much more famous, the Jansenists themselves were seriously divided over it. In the history of Convulsionism, Marie-Elisabeth Giroust was both a pioneer and a transitional figure. Insofar as any medical condition can be confidently diagnosed across the centuries, she was suddenly attacked by grand mal epilepsy, which for a time was unusually severe. At the time she entered history, her convulsions were the chief evidence of pathology. By the time of her exit, her convulsions were an evidence of the removal of pathology.

A French sociological scholar, Daniel Vidal, subjected the Convulsionists (*Miracles et convulsions jansénistes au xviiie siècle,* 1987) to an elaborate sociological and semiotic analysis, linking them with the slightly earlier but similar phenomena among the persecuted Camisards, or recusant Huguenots of the mountainous hinterlands of the Cévennes in southeastern France. These people were often called "The Tremblers" on account of their frequently physical manifestations of spiritual activity. The term had a similar ironic valance to that of "Holy Roller" still in use today. One chief point of distinction would seem to be this. The "French Prophets" (as the English derisively called the charismatics among the refugee Huguenots) apparently thought of their gyrations as reduplications of Apostolic "signs and wonders" described in the early chapters of the Book of Acts. Yet their experience went far beyond the "speaking in tongues" of the biblical account of Pentecost. According to the sermon preached by the apostle Peter, apparently acting upon the eschatological expectation of having entered the "last days," the words of the prophet Joel are now to be fulfilled: "I will pour my Spirit upon all flesh, and your sons and your daughters will prophesy, and your young men shall see visions, and your old men shall dream dreams. . . ." The Convulsionists of Saint-Médard, on the other hand, seem always to have been focused on the medical.

VI. Political

The episode of the Convulsionists was necessarily *political*. The Jansenist controversy, while not limited to French territory, was primarily a French phenomenon. Though its doctrinal and spiritual strands were unique to its particular moment, Jansenism fit in with a long history of restiveness within French Catholicism. A significant group of the clergy believed that the French Church enjoyed by ancient tradition a certain comparative independence from the authority of Rome. This attitude, called Gallicanism, manifested itself in various ways, and its strength would become apparent in the Revolution at the time of the proclamation of the Civil Constitution of the Clergy when, with comparative ease, it proved possible for many Frenchmen, including many clergy, to embrace a Catholicism independent of the Pope. Many scholars trace the Gallican ideas of some of the Jansenists to the period of the "Great Schism" of the Church in the fourteenth century. The faithful of Europe then witnessed the highly unedifying spectacle of competing claimants to the throne of Peter, one of whom was seated in "French" territory at Avignon. Some of the great French theologians of the period, especially Pierre d'Ailly and Jean Gerson, argued for "conciliarism," a doctrine that held that final authority within the Church could be exercised only by action of an ecumenical council.

In their attitude toward the *Unigenitus*, the Jansenists were "conciliarists": they made their appeal to the decision of a future council. In retrospect we can see that the invocation of conciliarism was a plank in a lost cause. The direction of Church history would be toward augmented, not diminished papal power. The doctrine of plenary papal authority was called "Ultramontanism"—a phrase that derives from the Latin for "across the mountains." The country from which the Pope was across the mountains was of course France. Yet at the time the Gallican tradition considerably complicated the secular politics of the situation. The Jansenists could argue with a certain plausibility that in resisting the *Unigenitus* they were exercising an ancient French exceptionalism that mimicked the independence and autonomy of the King of France. The Jesuits, who were the stout defenders of *Unigenitus*, were the shock troops of the Pope, who at least since the thirteenth century had been attempting to aggrandize his powers at the expense of the French monarchy.

An able historian, B. Robert Kreiser, has written a comprehensive book—*Miracles, Convulsions, and Ecclesiastical Politics in Early Eighteenth-Century Paris* (1978)—about the episode of the Convulsionists, and in it he elegantly unravels its twisted secular and spiritual strands. The history of Christianity teaches that if the compulsion of religious conformity is difficult, the compulsion of religious belief is impossible. Almost any action undertaken with the intention of achieving a particular result has the potential to achieve one very different. The attempts to suppress Jansenism were often sensationally counterproductive. The final "dissolution" of the religious house of Port-Royal des Champs had been particularly brutal. The fate of ancient Shechem, plowed with salt, had hardly been more drastic.

The witticism that the Bourbon monarchs "never forgot anything and never learned anything," dubiously attributed to Talleyrand, is brilliantly exemplified in the suppression of the Holy-Rolling in the Saint-Médard churchyard. It duplicated in miniature the more drastic error of the suppression of Port-Royal itself. Among other humiliations inflicted upon that nursery of theological error was the disinterment of the bones of several of the late saints. Here the intention on the part of the triumphant ecclesiastical party had been "to prove their doctrines orthodox through apostolic blows and knocks," and to raze from the earth sites that might in the future serve as shrines to the adherents of a despised cause. But the scattered bones of the dead Jansenists, or what were at least believed to be those bones, clandestinely gathered or purchased by their admirers, now found a home in the reliquaries of half the parish churches of Paris, and many more beyond in the countryside. One of the remarkable features of the cult of Deacon François de Pâris was its immediate profusion and circulation of relics, many of which feature in the miraculous cures or in their convulsionary testimonies.

The sealing off of the Saint-Médard churchyard turned out to be similarly counterproductive, from the "Jesuit" point of view. It in effect transformed Convulsionism from a phenomenon into what the historian Kreiser calls a movement. For "by forcing the convulsionaries to disperse, the royal ordinance had the unanticipated effect of further spreading the cult and rousing its adherents to even greater heights of religious enthusiasm." The contrived drama of modern political demonstrations is no novelty. The continuing controversy over the bull *Unigenitus* was of such heat as to give birth to its own newspaper, the famous *Nouvelles ecclésiastiques*. Its pages now, in Kreiser's words, "described the pathetic scene among the shocked and troubled people at Saint-Médard. They gathered around the little parish church, consternation and despair visible on nearly every face. Some were moaning or sobbing others stood by in stunned disbelieving silence. . . ."

The dispossessed of Saint-Médard churchyard regrouped into dozens of small enclaves meeting in private homes, in sympathetic parish churches, in the residences and schools of like-minded clergy. To believe in one or more of the five rather arid theological propositions condemned by the *Unigenitus* is at most ardency of a tepid degree. But belief in a miracle one has experienced in one's body, or heard reported from a family member or friend, is likely to have a real heat about it.

There was, furthermore, a sociological factor of some importance. The parishioners of Saint-Médard and several of the other "Jansenist" congregations tended to belong to the more economically vulnerable members of the French population, including a significant number of day laborers. The experience of the Convulsionists provided spiritual justification for an anti-monarchical attitude. It has more than once been suggested that the *convulsionnaires* of 1730 were the spiritual grandparents of the *sans-culottes* of 1790.

The authenticity of the miracles of Saint-Médard was at first virtually an article of Jansenist belief. Before long, however, the promiscuous writhings of the convulsed, which at first glance more closely resembled sexual indulgence than medical treatment, became a cause of acute embarrassment. Several Jansenist theologians distanced themselves from them, and more or less actively connived with the police authorities for their suppression. Even among this group, however, there was a universal defense of the "original" miracles of the tomb, before the more extravagant charisms became the focus of attention.

THE MEMORY OF THE Convulsionists remained vivid throughout the middle and later decades of the eighteenth century, and Voltaire included an article on "Convulsions" in the *Dictionnaire philosophique*. Voltaire attributed to Madame du Maine, who certainly commanded sufficient wit and wickedness to allow us to trust the attribution, some scoffing verses that probably well reflected the Bourbon aristocracy's disdain both for the theology of the Convulsionists and for the social standing of many of their adepts:

> *Un décrotteur à la royale*
> *Du talon gauche estropié,*
> *Obtint pour grace speciale*
> *D'être boiteux de l'autre pied.**

But the subject of the Saint-Médard miracles presented Voltaire with a surfeit of targets, and he could not confidently decide which was most worthy of his scorn. In another article in the *Dictionary* (s.v. "Eloquence") he expressed his alarm at Bishop Masillon's famous sermon "On the Smallness of the Number of Those to Be Saved." Masillon was no Jansenist, but it would be hard to distinguish his view of a Heaven with a population density roughly that of the Gobi Desert from the views of Augustine at his gloomiest. These views were far from agreeable to what René Pomeau called the *philosophes*' "optimistic Deism." But of all the rotten fruits of the Christian religion Voltaire perhaps detested most thoroughly the fanaticism of persecution, and the Jansenists, though perhaps repellent in his eyes, were also a people persecuted. Furthermore, a good rule of thumb for "infidels" of that age seems to have been "When in doubt, blame the Jesuits first." So the better part of Voltaire's brief article is given over to the abuse of the Jansenists' abusers, who are supposed to have acted in spiteful jealousy at the superior reputation of the Saint-Médard miracles to those performed by the early Jesuit wonder-worker, St. Francis Xavier, the Apostle of India.

It is perhaps hardly surprising that the prince of scoffers should scoff at the extravagances of the churchyard of Saint-Médard. What is more

---

* A bootblack born of highest race,
His left foot crippled, sad to tell,
Achieved through a miraculous grace
Lameness in the right as well.

remarkable is that the strange phenomena should gain such widespread credit in the face of the hostility of the Catholic authorities of Bourbon France, who found them hardly more comfortable than Cambridge Platonists had found the strokings of Valentine Greatrakes.

Bibliographical

Though much of the work devoted to the Convulsionists is in French, the single most comprehensive book on the episode is B. Robert Kreiser's excellent *Miracles, Convulsions, and Ecclesiastical Politics in Early Eighteenth-Century Paris* (Princeton, 1978). It has a nearly exhaustive bibliography for the period up to publication. As the title suggests, its principal focus is on broader ecclesiastical politics. Robert Bruce Mullin's *Miracles and the Modern Religious Imagination* (New Haven, 1996) deals with the problem of miracles and the modern consciousness. There are some essays of general background relevance in *Enthusiasm and Enlightenment in Europe, 1650–1850*, ed. Lawrence Klein and Anthony La Vopa (Huntington Library, 1998).

Daniel Vidal, *Miracles et convulsions jansénistes au XVIIIe siècle: Le mal et sa connaissance* (Paris, 1987), is of particular interest for, among other reasons, its statistical method.

For Jansenism, there is an engaging English-language introduction by J. D. Crichton (James Dunlop), *Saints or Sinners: Jansenists and Jansenism in Seventeenth-Century France* (Dublin, 1966). Sainte-Beuve's enduring masterpiece *Port-Royal* is available in several English translations, but it is a major undertaking.

Among the French books I have used are Jacques-François Thomas, *La querelle de l'Unigenitus* (Paris, 1950), and Monique Cottret, *Jansénismes et Lumières: Pour un autre xviiie siècle* (Paris, 1998).

SVFFICIT.

N.
MDLX
XXVI
AVG
XVII

O
MDC

IOH VALENTINVS
ANDREÆ

3   *The Rosy Cross*

O NE OF THE PARADOXES of the Enlightenment, a paradox long observed and variously explained, is the fascination of many of the enlightened with the *occult*. Referring to the group of political mystics founded by Adam Weishaupt in 1776, a French literary historian has noted with at least rhetorical surprise that "The Age of the *Lumières* was also the Age of the *Illuminati*." This implies, at the very least, a considerable elasticity in the word "enlightened." Sir Isaac Newton was among the greatest geniuses of his or any other age. Yet his investment in the mysteries of biblical prophecy was not less lavish than his successful attempt to define the fundamental laws of the physical world. That his *Principia mathematica* might one day become in the minds of his intellectual peers more valuable than the Book of Daniel would have struck him as preposterous.

The young Wordsworth gazing upon Newton's statue in his Cam-

Johann Valentin Andreae (1586-1654) was an erudite Lutheran theologian, the alter ego of the legendary Christian Rosenkreuz, and the probable author of the *Chymische Hochzeit Christiani Rosencreutz anno 1459* (*The Chymical Wedding of Christian Rosenkreutz in 1459*), one of the fundamental texts of Rosicrucianism, first published in 1616. The degree to which he was seriously committed to alchemy is uncertain. In his later years he referred to his early work as a *ludibrium*, a jeu d'esprit.

bridge college chapel famously saw "the marble index of a mind forever voyaging through strange seas of thought alone." Yet so far as many of his stranger interests were concerned, Sir Isaac was far from alone. They might even be said to have been typical of the intellectuals of his age, and of the Enlightenment generally. Hence very little in this book, and practically nothing in this chapter, can advance without a consideration of the concept of the *occult.* This is because so very much Enlightenment thought, including that of many of its most brilliant thinkers, was given over to occult pursuits. The ambition of this chapter is, first, to offer some suggestion of what the occult is, or was, and then to attempt a sketch of the sociology of occultism. For though there were "occultists" everywhere, one distinctive institution of the period, Freemasonry, had a unique historical influence on its social manifestations.

The task of discussing the occult, though needful, is hardly congenial. That is because the occult, both as concept and as word, has fallen on hard times, given over mainly to strange magazines printed on strange paper by strange publishers. The modern fate of "occultism" is a conspicuous example of the kind of sweeping intellectual change that makes the just appreciation of the intellectual life of past times so difficult. What was once considered as the essence of science has now been banished by most scientists.

The word "occult" is the English form of the Latin past participle of a verb meaning "to cover over," "to conceal," "to hide." The word bears no necessary association of motive or purposefulness, that is to say no necessary connection to things hidden by human intention. It meant simply "not visibly apparent." The old usage survives in our language, though rarely. Pathologists routinely search for "occult blood" in human waste. The road sign "Hidden Driveway" refers to an objective fact, not an intentional deception. Hence in the seventeenth and eighteenth centuries the idea of the investigation of the "occult" brought to mind what we usually think of as the "scientific enterprise"— the attempt to discover aspects of Nature previously unknown.

The vocabulary of luminosity self-consciously adopted by so many of the period's seekers after truth, whether as would-be masters or would-be disciples, can be confusing to the scholar intent on making accurate distinctions among cognate schools of thought. Yet one can see how intimate is the connection between occultism and Enlightenment simply from a consideration of the concept of light itself. Enlightenment—*Les Lumières*—penetrated the dark crevices of ignorance and superstition.

One sees also the antiquity of the concept, which characterizes the claims of all the world's great religions, including Christianity. The enlightened, whether they sought to clarify and refine the old religion or to overthrow it altogether, had inherited some of the assumptions on which its foundation rested. *Lux in tenebris lucet*, read the famous Vulgate phrase from the Prologue to the Gospel of John: "The light shines on in the dark, and the darkness has never mastered it." In the recent *Encyclopédie de la Franc-Maçonnerie* (in the article "Illumination"), Eric Saunier has published an English engraving of the early nineteenth century, hardly different in spirit from the Renaissance "emblems" of Alciati, allegorically depicting the three "great lights" of Masonry, to wit, the try square, the compass, and the Sacred Law (the Bible). The more conventional mason's tools (compass and try square) are crossed *ad quadratum*, in the usual allegorical manner, and the opening of the folio Bible across which they rest clearly reveals the selected text: the beginning of the Gospel of John.

The prophetic Isaian text once universally known throughout Christendom and still widely known through Handel's *Messiah*—"The people who dwelt in darkness have seen a great light"—actually played a role in many of the rituals of Masonic initiation. This tradition of early Masonry, which probably should be connected with ancient Christian rituals of the "first fire" of the Paschal Vigil, reenacted in quasi-liturgical form the initiate's passage from darkness to light. It became a standard feature of the ritual of many secret societies of the nineteenth century, and survives today in the Greek letter fraternities and sororities of our colleges and universities.

The term "Illuminism" has been stretched thin over the considerable breadth of seventeenth- and eighteenth-century "spiritual" schools, ranging from that of the independent-minded Lutheran Jakob Boehme (1575–1624) to that of the independent-minded Catholic Karl von Eckharthausen (1752–1803), eventually melding (with Madame Blavatsky and others) in institutional "Theosophy"—a term intentionally invented to join together the old concepts of "practical" and "speculative" or theoretical philosophy famous in Boethius. Among the most brilliant constellation of French "Illuminists" are the often-confused gurus Martines de Pasqually, who died in 1774, and the more famous Louis-Claude de Saint-Martin (1743–1803), "the Unknown Philosopher," the fountainhead of "Martinism," whose eminent disciples were legion in the Revolutionary period and beyond, and who has disciples yet.

I alluded a moment ago to one of the more famous groups calling themselves Illuminati (*Illuminaten* in German, also called "the Illuminati of Bavaria"). The Illuminati were founded by Adam Weishaupt, a disenchanted canon lawyer, in 1776. They formed an actual secret order or society with a complex internal structure that soon led to complicated internal sectarian struggles. Only a few of the "secret" societies of the eighteenth century actually remained sufficiently secret to hide from inquiring historians, but there are aspects of this group's stranger teachings that remain opaque. The German Weishaupt was reacting, as so many French thinkers had earlier, to what he regarded as the obscurantism of the Jesuits, who had by his time long since become a powerful force in educating the youth of Catholic countries. His anti-clericalism had at the very least a seriously radical political potential, which found a place also in several other of the secret societies of German-speaking regions. The secrecy was both an index of their "occult" pursuits and a necessity of their politics. Though Weishaupt himself had a dim view of Freemasonry, his disciple and later antagonist Adolf Franz Knigge (1752–1796) became an enthusiastic Mason who tried to advance Illuminist causes through existing Masonic lodges. It has frequently been assumed that Cagliostro, in his later development, had intimate contact with German Illuminati.

One problem presented to the contemporary student of occultism is the nature of the "scholarship" concerning it. Not surprisingly, perhaps, much of it has been written by occultists themselves—that is, by partisans of esoteric doctrine, including magicians and religious cranks. In France, a good deal of such work was of a high quality. There was a continuous tradition of serious erudition that links, for example, the kabbalist Antoine Fabre d'Olivet (1767–1825) with the occultist "Marc Haven," the nom de plume of Emmanuel Lalande, the revisionist biographer of Cagliostro in the early twentieth century. In England and especially in America the tradition has tended more to the eccentric and the dubious, though with striking exceptions, including such outstanding scholarly books as Frances Yates's *The Occult Philosophy in the Elizabethan Age* (1979). This work indirectly demonstrates many of the frequently overlooked continuities to be found in a good deal of Enlightenment thought. Several of the best studies are "literary"—in effect chapters in the intellectual history of important figures such as de Maistre, Chateaubriand, or Hugo. The most valuable single work on the subject remains the old two-volume study of occult backgrounds of nineteenth-century French Romanticism: Auguste Viatte's *Les sources occultes du Romantisme: Illuminisme, Théosophie*, a gold mine of synthesized information that richly deserves (but has not yet received) an English translation.

It is perhaps a fine historical irony that the precise doctrines and interrelations of so many seekers after light should be clouded in opacity; but some important generalizations do clearly emerge. One of them is the persistence throughout the Enlightenment of what one may call the Spiritual Quest. And here I use the word "Spiritual" in its broad Pauline sense, as the necessarily superior element in a hierarchical relationship of flesh and spirit, matter and spirit, letter and spirit. There *was* a materialist strain in Western thought, though highly attenuated, especially in the Latin tradition. Lucretius was unknown until the Renaissance, and even then not very widely known. He was at any rate a poet. Hobbes is usually called a materialist, and with sufficient reason. In the eighteenth-century Enlightenment, the baron d'Holbach, contributor to the *Encyclopédie* and author of various pseudonymous anti-religious works, published his very ambitious *System of Nature* in a "scientific" spirit comparable to that of contemporary atheist scientists like Richard Dawkins. But it can hardly be too strongly stressed that his attitudes were, in his time, regarded as eccentric in the extreme by men who thought the "scientific" spirit was that of Newton or Kepler.

Within the larger intellectual context of the Enlightenment such materialism was marginal and aberrant. The mainstream of European thought was not materialist but *sacramental*. In the sacramental view, the material and visible world paralleled another that was immaterial and invisible.

Scholars can (and do) engage in heated debate about the precise nature of post-Platonic Platonism (sometimes called Neo-Platonism) in the premodern European scene. They write of the "Platonism" of the theologians of the School of Chartres in the twelfth century. There is the fifteenth-century Florentine Platonic Academy, associated with (among other famous names) that of Marsilio Ficino. The great vernacular literature of the sixteenth and seventeenth centuries often bears the deep impress of one or another form of Platonic thought. In the fourth and fifth centuries St. Augustine found almost everything essential to Christianity in the Platonic doctrines. So proximate were Plato and Christ, he wrote, that all the leading Platonists of his day had been converted to Christianity at the very small expense of making a few adjustments to their philosophical vocabulary. All medieval and Renaissance "revivals" of Plato were explicitly conducted as significant augmentations of orthodox Christian theology—even when some of the less enlightened guardians of orthodoxy might demur. In seventeenth-century England Henry More (1614–1687), friend and intimate of leading members of the Royal Society, was the unofficial leader of the Cambridge Platonists, who exercised a significant influence on their contemporary Anglican theologians.

So far as European cultural history is concerned, the Christian versions of Platonism are the most important. For us the phrase "the invisible world" is likely to sound odd, if not actually creepy, a term from the lexicon of the nineteenth-century table-rappers. Yet there was in Europe for well over a thousand years a universal belief in the "invisible world." The first clause of the Nicene Creed, the fundamental statement of Christian belief, attests that God is the Creator of all things *visible and invisible.* One great medievalist defined the vast task of all of medieval theology as an attempt to bridge the gap between the empirical world of sensory experience and the unseen world of a spiritual realm. St. Thomas Aquinas, whose system eventually became the "official" theology of the Roman Catholic Church, wrote that "there is nothing in the mind that was not previously in the senses."

The entire sacramental system of Catholicism is "Platonic." A sacrament is a *sign*—"an outward and visible sign of an inward and spiritual grace," according to the language of the Anglican catechism. The bread and the wine, real material elements, are likewise spiritual realities.

But perhaps the most pervasive mode of this kind of Platonism was literary in a quite concrete sense. It had to do with the interpretation of the sacred text. St. Paul himself was the first writer to use the word "allegory" in a Christian context. He found an allegory in the history of the offspring of the Patriarch Abraham through his two wives, Sarah and the bondwoman Hagar. He did not discount the historicity of the account in Genesis, but Isaac and Ishmael, the two women's respective sons, were more importantly figures of a future historical reality, that is, the Old Covenant and the New. Paul also found a broad figural meaning in the history of the Exodus. His general word for the hidden or occult meaning of the Scriptures was *spiritual*: "The Letter kills, but the Spirit gives life." Although in medieval Christianity this text was often enough used in anti-Judaic polemic, it in fact reflected a commonplace of the exegesis of the Jewish scholars of late Antiquity. The Judaism of the Levantine diaspora was already heavily Hellenized, meaning that in part it was heavily Platonized. One need only turn to one of the most productive and influential of Hellenized Jewish writers—Philo of Alexandria, a learned contemporary of Jesus—to appreciate the depth of the belief that the words of the Scripture contained hidden or occult meanings.

As regards the development of modern experimental science, the sacramental assumption entailed ambivalent implications. A theologian whose chief interest in birds is to find in the Phoenix, mythical "Arabian bird," an emblem of the self-sacrifice and Resurrection of Jesus Christ, is perhaps unlikely to become a knowledgeable ornithologist. Nor will we find a modern zoologist in the medieval friar and collector of animal *exempla* who perceives a noble ascetic lesson in the action of the beaver. The beaver (*castor*, in Latin), when hotly pursued by his carnivore enemy, escapes by *castor*-ating himself, leaving the detached testicles in the path to distract his pursuers, while he makes his way to safety. (This is an allegory of the ascetic vow of chastity, taken by those who flee the world and "make of themselves eunuchs for the kingdom of God's sake.")

By the seventeenth century most educated people in Europe, and virtually all people in the countries of the Reform, were laughing at the old "monkish" (one of their favorite words) learning. Renaissance thinkers had long scorned and abandoned it. One of the funniest chapters in Rabelais is his parodic card catalogue of the famous monastic library of the great Abbey of Saint-Victor, that nursery of great theologians and mystics. A chief object of satire is the preposterous etymological allegories of such titles as "The Bagpipe of the Prelates" or "The Teeth-chatter of Gum-diddler of Lubberly Lusks." But very few were abandoning the search for analogies between the structures of two worlds, one seen, one occult.

"All men by nature desire to know," writes Aristotle in the famous introduction to the *Metaphysics*. "An indication of this is the delight we take in our senses; for even apart from their usefulness they are loved for themselves; and above all others the sense of sight. For not only with a view to action, but even when we are not going to do anything, we prefer seeing (one might say) to everything else. The reason is that this, most of all the senses, makes us know and brings to light many differences between things." One distinction occurs immediately: that between desiring to know and actually knowing. "It is the peculiar feature of the human mind," says Kant, "to pose questions it is unable to answer." In the gap betwixt reach and grasp lie many of the more shadowy episodes of Enlightenment.

The Rosicrucians

In my youth there used to appear in magazines and journals, and even on the insides of matchbook covers, advertisements, puzzling to me, inviting me to send off for information concerning the Rosicrucians. I didn't know what a Rosicrucian was, of course, but the memorable detail that sticks in my mind is the tagline to the ad: "AMORC—not a religion." I did not then realize that AMORC was an abbreviation, not a magic word, and that it stands for the macaronic phrase "Ancient Mystical Order Rosae Crucis." The Rosicrucians claimed an ancient ancestry, and they flourished in all the intellectual capitals of the Enlightenment. But was there actually such a thing as organized Rosicrucianism? Is it possible for something that does not exist to exercise important influence on the intellectual climate of an age?

On the other hand one can say with confidence that Freemasonry, of which the Mystical Order of Rosicrucians was an ancestor, branch, affiliate, descendant, or parallel—always depending upon which Masonic historian is consulted—certainly existed. It was one of the most impressive social institutions of the eighteenth century, and within its confines historians have plausibly discovered important and even formative influence on such crucial developments as the rise of science, the French Revolution, and the emergence of the modern system of industrial capitalism. European Masonry became significant in the seventeenth century. Its earlier history is somewhat obscure. That fact is of little relevance to our project, however, since for the Enlightenment Masons it was the mythical history that mattered.

The Masons claimed an ancient lineage, one that went back at the very least to King Solomon, the builder of the Jerusalem Temple. Its major metaphors and symbols were taken from architecture and stonemasonry, the defining emblem to this day being a device in which the architect's compass crosses with the stoneworker's try square. Solomon was known for his wisdom, much of which in Masonic lore was connected with the arts of design, stonecutting, building, and the mysteries of the numerical ratios revealed in those arts. As we shall see, some Enlightenment Masons claimed an origin more ancient yet, in the Egyptian architects of the Great Pyramids; but all also acknowledged an important medieval European connection. That was with the Knights Templar, the order of fighting monks brutally suppressed by Clement V and King Philip the Fair in the early fourteenth century. This supposed medieval episode of Freemasonry had particular implications for men of the Enlightenment for whom it prefigured the warfare between enlightened Masonry and the obscurantist Roman Church.

The reason that some consideration of the separate though converging histories of Rosicrucianism and Freemasonry becomes obligatory is their shared role in the transmission of occult ideas and occult practice. Rosicrucianism and Freemasonry were the principal channels for the transmission of numerous ideas and practices that, at least at first blush, might seem at odds with the most fundamental characteristics of the Enlightenment: its exaltation of the Rule of Reason, and the adoption of the scientific spirit.

The secondary literature dealing with Rosicrucianism is now vast, and it cannot be the intention of this chapter to make a review of it. A good deal of the literature will strike the general reader as very odd indeed. To plunge into such a tar pit would be fatal, and even a toe-dip is not without its risks. Fortunately there are a few excellent guides. One of these is a general history by Christopher McIntosh: *The Rosicrucians: The History, Mythology, and Rituals of an Esoteric Order.* The dean of Renaissance esoterica, the late Frances Yates of the Warburg Institute, published her revolutionary *Rosicrucian Enlightenment* in 1972. It includes English translations of the principal Rosicrucian manifestos, which are also available in the older book (1924) of Arthur Edward Waite: *The Brotherhood of the Rosy Cross.* In 1986, the two hundredth birthday of Johann Valentin Andreae (to whom the reader will shortly be introduced) was celebrated with a collection of erudite essays that raised the level of discussion of historic origins to an altogether new height. There have been numerous other serious studies by theologians and literary historians—John Warwick Montgomery and Donald Dickson conspicuous among them.

Whatever may be the remote sources of Rosicrucianism, its actual public origins were textual, to be found in a few remarkable writings associated with the German theologian Johann Valentin Andreae. The two most famous of these bear the titles *Fama Fraternitatis* (*The History of the Brotherhood*) and the *Chymische Hochzeit Christiani Rosenkreuz* (*The Chemical Wedding of Christian Rosecross*). The weasel-phrase "associated with" is required by unresolved scholarly doubts as to the authorship of the *Fama*. In his later life Andreae dismissed Rosicrucianism as a *ludibrium*, a little joke, and that for some has made it seem unlikely that he could have been its founder. But there is another view, for there was in the Renaissance the genre known as *joca seria*, serious jokes. World literature would be the poorer without *The Praise of Folly* or Swift's *Modest Proposal*. Anyone familiar with the role of the Fool in *King Lear* will be able to grasp the concept.

Johann Andreae is a solidly historical personage, but it is his emblematic creature, Rosenkreuz, who first claims our attention. Who was Christianus Rosenkreuz? Among the legendary casualties of the Second Vatican Council were some revered etymological saints— saints, that is, who had a merely lexical as opposed to an historical existence. St. Veronica was a legendary lady who with her handker-chief wiped the sweat from the agonized face of Jesus as he staggered toward crucifixion. A miraculous image of Christ's face was imprinted on the cloth. It was a *vera icona* (true image) of the Saviour and one of the great relics of the Middle Ages; soon enough the woman took the name of the thing: St. Veronica!

According to an ancient legend hardly cleansed of its pagan origins a gigantic dog-headed man once ferried the Christ-child across a river on his shoulder. The Latin verb *fero* means "to carry." Soon enough the giant exchanged his canine for a human head and took a human name: Christopher, that is "the Christ-bearer." At a stroke of the Council's pen, the "protector of travelers" imaged in a million key rings returned to legend. Perhaps nothing better exemplifies the true medievalism of Enlightenment Illuminism than the eponymous founder of Rosicru-cianism, Christian Rosenkreuz, whose imaginary birth may have not taken place in 1378, just as his supposed death at age 106 certainly did not take place in 1484. The two elements of the "surname"—"rose" and "cross"—might invite speculation even without the Christian name. In fact, "Christian Rosencreuz" occupied the same metaphysical space as Spenser's "Red Crosse Knight" in *The Faerie Queene*. "Rose" means both the flower and the color of the flower (rosy), and Rosicrucian symbolism exploited both possibilities to the full. The ambiguity was further enhanced when the German name was translated into Latin. The rosy cross was complemented by the golden cross, gold of course being the productive end of what they called the "Great Work" (*Magnum opus*) of alchemy, which for the Rosicrucians was first a spiritual and only incidentally a material quest.

In another exact parallel with legendary medieval sanctity, the perfectly intact and uncorrupted body of Christian Rosenkreuz (or C::R::C, as he came to be known) was eventually discovered in his seven-sided tomb, along with certain documents destined to fascinate some of the great minds of Europe for the next two centuries.

Johann Andreae himself, though much more "historical," is hardly less mysterious. Beneath the odd Latin genitive form of the surname, which perhaps emblematically suggests the fusion of ancient Latin learning and vernacular Reformed contemporaneity in which he was raised, is the equivalent of the modern English Andrews. Andreae was born in 1586 into a large Lutheran clerical family in Herrenberg, about sixty miles east of Strassburg, in a part of Germany that was the mystical nursery of several of the other figures touched upon in this book.

One can identify certain clear strands of traditional biography. Andreae was in the first place the time-honored "sickly child" of old history books. His physical ailments, which were numerous and severe, encouraged an ascetic spirit on the one hand and on the other a practical interest in medicine, the discovery of natural potions, and the confection of herbal remedies. He became, that is, an amateur chemist, and for a time the ward of two students "trained in both of the medicines"—

meaning the old mechanistic tradition deriving from Galen and what Montgomery calls "the new iatrochemical-alchemical approach of Paracelsus." The single greatest and most enduring influence on Andreae's intellectual development was a certain Mattias Hafenreffer. As a young deacon in the church at Herrenberg, Hafenreffer had actually baptized the infant. Later, as professor of theology and mathematics at Tübingen, he became Andreae's lifelong friend and mentor. Hafenreffer was a theologian of unwavering orthodoxy, but also generous and imaginative.

He represented very clearly what the Protestant theologians of his age meant by the idea of Reform. Though they for the most part rejected the sclerotic Scholasticism of the late Middle Ages, they often continued to use some of its technical theological vocabulary. The specialized meaning of the word "form" (*forma*) was "the essential inhering principle," that which made the thing the thing it was. To *re*-form the Church was nothing other than to return it to first principles and practices, to recover a noble past obscured by the fog of the ages and tarnished with the excrescences of human invention. The Apocalyptic Christ had said: "Behold, I am making all things new." (Rev. 21:5) *Renovatio* was *reformatio*.

The vivifying rediscovery of old wisdom long forgotten, a central ambition of the Renaissance project, was no less a central project of the German Reform. As Warwick Montgomery has convincingly demonstrated, Andreae's Rosicrucian "vision," for all its hermetic ideas and iconography, was radically grounded not merely in his Christian orthodoxy but in his sense of Christian mission. This is a fundamental truth, but one that has not always been fully appreciated by historians of the Enlightenment.

Two apparent features of Andreae's mind-set may help us understand the superficial strangeness of his literary production, a strangeness that may occlude his most fundamental purposes. One of them is broadly historical, the other more personal, and based in literary sensibility. Well before Andreae's time, the Reformation in Germany had proved to be a very rough ride. Some historians have gone so far as to speak of a "spiritual crisis" following upon the age of the great Lutheran founders. Too often the movement claiming to restore purity in the Church had brought with it the death and destruction of sectarian warfare. One of the leading scholars of the "Tübingen circle" of visionary and utopian thinkers of which Andreae was a member attributes their activities at least as much to near despair as to idealism. There is in Andreae's work, and in that of many of his associates, a conscious renovation of the early reforming spirit.

This aspect of his thought is characteristic of all his writings, but it finds its most explicit (and therefore most easily grasped) statement in the book called the *Christianapolis*, an imaginary invocation of an ideal or utopian Christian community. It is not accidental that the utopian mode is characteristic of the Age of Religious Reform. More's *Utopia* dates from 1516, Campanella's *City of the Sun* from the turn of the seventeenth century.

The recurrent persona in Andreae's works is a pilgrim, one who has "wandered as a stranger on the earth, suffering much in patience from tyranny, sophistry, and hypocrisy." The pilgrim of his utopian vision has an odd name of the sort beloved of the erudite humanists: Cosmoxenus Christianus, "Christian the World-Stranger." He is clearly enough a version of the Pauline pilgrim who has on earth "no continuing city," of whom the Christian of John Bunyan's *Pilgrim's Progress* is only the most famous among hundreds. We learn that the island-city of the heart's desire was founded anciently by an exile like himself. The exile was *religion*—a word here used in its old Christian-Latin technical sense to mean the formal "religious life," a "religious order," the spiritual life as organized by vow around an ascetic community. Once again we see articulate the connection between the esoteric brotherhoods of the Enlightenment period and the old orders of Catholic monasticism banished by the Protestants.

The allegory of Andreae's *Christianapolis* is for the most part no less dreary or "medieval" than its genre, but there is something surprising and felicitous at its core. This is the city's creed, spelled out in the traditional twelve articles legendarily supplied, one clause each, by the twelve Apostles. It is a most generous statement. "One particularly interesting aspect of the creed of Christianapolis," writes Andreae's biographer, Montgomery, "is its *de facto* ecumenicity." The Rosicrucian manifestos would radiate a similar spirit.

A second point was Andreae's ambiguous and nuanced response to the old learning of the Middle Ages. We are so used to hearing that the Renaissance "rejected" the Middle Ages that we may be unprepared for all the important ways in which the Renaissance kept the Middle Ages alive. Andreae was an accommodationist, not a rejectionist. He was a writer of theological or philosophical romances. The first English translator of *The Chemical Wedding* grasped this fact perfectly in the title he gave to the work: *The Hermetic Romance*. Thus the literary historians may have something to teach us, no less than the theologians and philosophers.

THE ENGLISH LITERARY SCHOLAR W. P. Ker once made a fascinating contrast between the great humanist poets and the great humanist reformers. We are tempted to exaggerate the rejection of the old learning by the new learners of the Renaissance. It is true that the humanist rejection of the late medieval academic cant of the dogmatic theologians could be brutal. One of the masterpieces of early German humanism is the satirical collection of imaginary letters called the *Epistolae obscurorum virorum* or *Letters from Obscure Men* (1515–19). This work grew out of a controversy in which the humanist scholar Reuchlin had become embroiled precisely about the value of old books, and it is relevant to the esoteric investigations of the Rosicrucians. Reuchlin had developed a knowledgeable interest in the

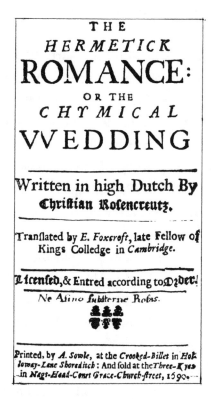

THE
HERMETICK
ROMANCE:
OR THE
CHYMICAL
WEDDING

Written in high Dutch By
Chriſtian Roſencreutz.

Tranſlated by *E. Foxcroft*, late Fellow of
Kings Colledge in *Cambridge*.

Licenſed,& Entred according to Order.

Ne Aſino ſubſterne Roſas.

Printed, by *A. Sowle*, at the *Crooked-Billet* in *Hol-loway-Lane Shoreditch*: And ſold at the *Three-Kyes*
in *Negt-Head-Court Grace-Church-ſtreet*, 1590.

The first English translation of *The Chemical Wedding* appeared in London in 1690. The translator was Ezekiel Foxcroft, a meritocratic Etonian and scholar of King's College, Cambridge, and a man known to Sir Isaac Newton. He was a friend of More, the Cambridge Platonist, and the author of a testimonial letter endorsing the miracle worker Valentine Greatrakes.

Hebrew language, and had made a special study of the conventions and techniques of Jewish scriptural exegesis, including kabbala. As we shall presently see, this interest was actually already of ancient pedigree in Christian exegetical circles, but it was to become a prominent feature of much esoteric speculation in the Enlightenment period as well. A Dominican convert from Judaism named Johannes Pfefferkorn, now turned ferocious anti-Semite, was advocating with a convert's zeal the burning of the Talmud and other religious books of the Jews. The authors of the imaginary letters circulated among the friars pitilessly mocked both their poverty of thought and the poverty of their Latin. But this was not the only possible attitude, and it was certainly not Andreae's.

"Most great writers begin with some sort of critical opposition to the follies, vanities, pedantries, and dullness of their predecessors and contemporaries," wrote Ker. But for great imaginative giants like Rabelais and Cervantes, such an attitude is but a beginning. "Too much emphasis has been laid on their hostility to the dullness of the past; too little has been made, perhaps of their sympathy with the things they laughed at." Cervantes could not have written his great spoof of romance were he not a great lover of romance. As for Rabelais, he "never escaped, nor wished to escape, out of the comfortable absurdity of the Middle Ages. . . . The reformers and the common humanists rejected it all, or drove their lean and blasted cattle through the medieval fields and brought them out as poor as when they went in." Andreae would not reject all that curious lore. On the contrary, he would recuperate as much as possible.

There are certain obscure books that somehow manage to convey the promise of a deeper intelligibility to be found just beneath an illusory surface. Such was the likely effect made by the *Fama* and the *Confessio* upon a kindly disposed reader in the seventeeth century, as it remains for that reader today. With apparently remarkable ease Andreae seemed to synthesize his orthodox but generous Lutheranism with a rich body of allusive myth and legend, all of it gathered and channeled through the imaginative exegesis of Gospel parables.

The Fama Fraternitatis

The very title *Fama Fraternitatis* begs for some prior comment. We can get a better sense of the meaning of *Fama* by examining a few places in which the word appears in the texts of the most celebrated classical poets whose texts became for the learned men of the Renaissance written authority akin to a second Bible. The word *fama* means something halfway between "rumor" (as personified in Virgil's *Aeneid*) and "the written record" (as in Horace's *Ars poetica*.) In his *Art of Poetry*, Horace advances a general doctrine of artistic decorum or plausibility, beginning with the famous images of centaur and mermaid. "If a painter chose to join a human head to the neck of a horse," he writes, "and to spread feathers of many a hue over limbs picked up now here, now there, so that what is at the top a lovely woman ends below in a black and ugly fish"—who would not laugh at such a grotesque composition? The license of fiction does not extend to implausibility: "Either follow *fama*, or invent something verisimilar" (*aut fama sequere, aut sibi convenientia finge*). Here *fama* pretty clearly means "the poetic tradition." If you present us with an Achilles, he must be true to the Achilles of Homer. Your Medea must be "fierce and unyielding," as in Euripides.

This is not to say that Achilles and Medea are not *fictional* characters. The very essence of classical *fama* is that it mingles truth and falsehood. The most famous personification of *Fama* is in Virgil's *Aeneid*, in which she flies about Libya, spreading the fatal rumor of the incipient affair of Dido and Aeneas: "as constant in her tales of baseless scandal as at time she is the herald of the truth . . . with stories manifold, and facts and falsehoods side by side proclaimed." (iv, 174ff.) From these lines Ovid created a celebrated set piece on "Fama's house" (*Metamorphoses* xii, 39ff.), in which he quotes Virgil's very words. Within her great house, "the fickle vulgar come and go, and a thousand rumors, false mixed with true, wander up to fill the empty ears with conversation." Chaucer, in his time, devoted a whole poem to the conceit: his *House of Fame*.

An accurate sense of Andreae's title might be "An Announcement of the Foundation of the Brotherhood." Its hardly modest ambitions are clarified in the larger German title. This is the announcement of a plan for "the Comprehensive and Thorough-Going Reformation of the

Heinrich Jung Stilling, an eminent oculist turned Christian mystic, was both a product of, and a defector from, the Age of Reason. He was for a time a kind of guru to Julie de Krüdener. This page from his diary for August 1805 displays his own "secret" handwriting, in part derived from kabbala and alchemical notation.

Whole Wide World," addressed to "All the Learned People and the Leaders of Europe." But it is the announcement of a plan already put into motion by a secret brotherhood already long established.

Writers and scholars very frequently bemoan the untranslatability of a word or phrase before facing up to their duty actually to translate it. The macaronic (half Latin, half German) title of this remarkable book, which seems simple enough until you make such an attempt, was *Fama Fraternitatis dess löblichen Ordens des Rosenkreutzes*—the "Fama" of the Praiseworthy Order of the Rosy Cross (or Rose-Cross). Colin Wilson, in his foreword to Christopher McIntosh's very readable historical introduction, *The Rosicrucians*, seems aware of a possible difficulty. He notes that McIntosh "translates 'Fama' as 'declaration,' but my own Latin dictionary defines it as 'common talk . . . a report, rumour, saying, tradition.' So it would be hardly unfair to translate 'Fama' as myth or legend."

In calling themselves a "mystical" order, the Rosicrucians were using the word in an original sense that has become rare. What is mystical is what is hidden, and what is hidden can be found, or at least intelligently searched for. Such was the "mystical" sense of the Scriptures after which the medieval exegetes labored. The quest for Enlightenment differed, therefore, from the appeal to a blind magic. It was a process strictly parallel to the procedures of scientific investigation that on all sides were yielding new discoveries in the realm of Nature. Most Masonic occultists doubtless regarded themselves as men of science. The sciences they pursued were not limited to physics, chemistry, and botany. They included alchemy, necromancy, haruspication, sex magic, and the raising of the dead. There was not much that one might find in ancient Carthage—or southern California in the sixties—that was not being pursued in one Masonic lodge or another in the European Enlightenment.

THE ROLE PLAYED BY the Rosicrucian Masons in eighteenth-century intellectual and political life has been so thoroughly studied that one can find maximal claims that they caused the French Revolution or minimalist retorts that they did little more than distract the revolutionaries. On one point, however, there is a broad agreement: many Enlightenment Rosicrucians embraced some very weird ideas and pursued some bizarre spiritual quests. Pioneering work now half a century old, by the French historian René Le Forestier, has provided us with a great deal of detailed information about occult Freemasonry in France, and as we shall see, the occultists were not limited to France. There is no black hole in all of the Enlightenment that is without its Rosicrucian quarks.

Ordo Rosae Crucis means "the Order of the Rose-Cross" or "of the Rose of the Cross," or "of the Rosy [adjective] Cross," all of which meanings appear in later commentary and iconographic formulation. But the Rose Cross of the *Fama* is a man, the order's eponymous founder, Brother Christian Rosenkreuz, usually indicated, like all the other specifically denominated brothers, by his initials. C.R. was the son of noble parents so reduced in their worldly fortune as to place their young son in a monastery. After learning Latin and Greek "indifferently," C.R. traveled with one of his brethren on pilgrimage to the Holy Land. The mentor died on Cyprus, but C.R. traveled on to Damascus. Feeble health kept him from ever making it to Jerusalem, but he nonetheless greatly improved his time in study. He mastered Arabic, allowing him to translate "the Book M." into Latin. He then sojourned for a spell in Egypt, where his erudition advanced to even greater heights. C.R.'s is a biography to remember when reading Count Cagliostro's autobiographical deposition before the court of the Parlement of Paris.

A good deal of the *Fama* is given over to the development of the brotherhood's protocols within an historical context in which increments of social organization went hand-in-hand with a growth in wisdom. Furthermore, the motivation behind its proclamation is not less remarkable than the document's contents. After all, the public announcement in five languages of the existence and operations of a secret society might seem a paradoxical initiative. The Rosicrucian architects of this mystic field of dreams do not seem to have embraced the hope that if they built it, *they* would come. It was more a case of "If we come, *they* will build it." There was no return address in the printed copies of the *Fama*, nor has any scholarly cryptographer yet found one in the obviously cryptic elements of its text—a failure not explicable on the grounds of any want of trying. The financing of the original "public offering," which cannot have been negligible, remains mysterious; nor do we have much information about the means by which the actual physical sheets were distributed.

One cannot, however, argue with success, especially one so brilliant as the birth of Rosicrucianism. Jesus had said, "Come unto me all ye who are heavy laden, and I will give you rest." That has attracted, through history, a certain crowd. "Come unto us," said the Brothers of the Rosy Cross, "all ye who are enlightened or who seek enlightenment, all ye benign ones who seek to know the secrets of Nature, to master the Book M., and to advance the well-being of your fellow men."

What follows has been called in the history books "the Rosicrucian furore." The excitement throughout Europe was intense. Searchers after truth looked high and low through the great edifices of European erudition for the Brothers of the Rosy Cross. A surprising number found them—in their mirrors.

Rosicrucianism became "a circle whose center is everywhere and whose circumference is nowhere"—or, occasionally, vice versa. This metaphor of transcendental amplitude (usually applied to God, the cosmic order, Communism, or some other grand design) has been attributed to Alain de Lille, Rabelais, Pascal, and Nikolai Bukharin, among others; but it seems to have originated with the thrice-great Hermes himself. It was, accordingly, an excellent fit for the brothers and their shadowy order. And "order" (*ordo*) is indeed one of the self-referential monastic terms used by the Rosicrucians, another being *fraternitas* (brotherhood).

The Rosicrucian manifestos were a kind of religious proclamation. They did not announce that the Kingdom of God was at hand, but the message was not dissimilar. What was at hand, indeed what was already established throughout awakening Europe, were secret communities of a new kind of brotherhood, bound by a common search for the secrets of nature and the secrets of ancient wisdom, and united in a grand altruistic design: the betterment of the human species and its modes of living. Like nascent Christianity, like pre-Lapsarian Communism, like certain episodes of Victorian industrial and scientific optimism, the Rosicrucian movement was animated by a powerful confidence barely touched by the cynicism bred of history. The Rosicrucian non-organization had the genius of being a highly exclusive club, but whose members became members by self-election. If you read the *Fama Fraternitatis* and in it recognized yourself, why then you were already a Rosicrucian. All that needed to be done was to search out like-minded brethren.

The secrecy surrounding Rosicrucianism was only in part stylistic, the logical mode of procedure of men who sought occult knowledge. It was also, in most parts of Europe, a prudential necessity. Those who explicitly sought "the reform of the whole wide world" might easily encounter powerful political opposition of a most dangerous kind. It is in fact true that many of the secret revolutionary societies, including the German Illuminati, had Rosicrucian connections. The gemlike flame of the hermetic idealism of Andreae and his generation could not fail to dim somewhat in the succeeding centuries, but its energy survived in various institutional settings, and in particular in certain Masonic lodges. To them we shall now turn.

Bibliographical

Popular literature concerning Rosicrucianism is not hard to come by. The readable and the reliable present greater challenges. Fortunately the primary sources are readily available, as well as a number of outstanding secondary works.

The original Rosicrucian manifestos are available in English in Paul Allen's excellent *Christian Rosenkreutz Anthology* (latest edition New York, 2008). *The Brotherhood of the Rosy Cross: A History of the Rosicrucians*, by Arthur Edward Waite, one of the greatest of modern esotericists, has been frequently republished (latest edition New York, 1993). Christopher McIntosh, *The Rosicrucians: The History, Mythology, and Rituals of an Esoteric Order* (latest edition San Francisco, 1998), is crisp and scholarly.

An indispensable classic history is Frances Yates's erudite *Rosicrucian Enlightenment* (latest edition New York, 1992), for which her *Occult Philosophy in the Elizabethan Age* (1979), dealing with materials earlier than those that appear in my book, is a most useful supplement.

Readers seeking fuller bibliographical information may consult John Warwick Montgomery, *Cross and Crucible: Johann Valentin Andreae (1586–1654), Phoenix of the Theologians*, 2 vols. (The Hague, 1993).

Books specifically cited or alluded to in this chapter:
Dickson, Donald R. *The Tessera of Antilia: Utopian Brotherhoods and Secret Societies in the Early Seventeenth Century* (Leiden, 1998).
The quotations from W. P. Ker come from an unpublished manuscript cited in Ifor Evans's *W. P. Ker as a Critic of Literature*. W. P. Ker Memorial Lecture No. 12 (Glasgow, 1956).

4 : *The Freemasons*

"I DO NOT PROPOSE to discuss the origin of Freemasonry," wrote Arthur Edward Waite. "That vexatious question has been perpetually debated with singularly unprofitable results." That was in 1887, when in our academic libraries the bibliography of Masonic origins was ten or twenty linear feet shorter than it is today. Nevertheless, only the rashest of scholars would abandon Waite's judicious diffidence without the deepest misgivings.

The principal difficulty concerning Masonic origins is that they are in part actual and historical but deeply obscure, and in part vivid but fanciful and legendary. Both tendencies are of importance to the intellectual history of the Enlightenment period, but as a spurious certainty generally triumphs over honest confusion, it has unfortunately proved easier to synthesize the two strands than to purify or purge them.

As Freemasonry spread across Europe, it gained enemies as well as adherents. There were numerous exposés of its rites and mysteries, and repeated attempts to reveal its "secrets." As early as 1742 the abbé Gabriel-Louis Pérau published the classic of the genre, *L'Ordre des francs-maçons trahi* (*The Order of the Freemasons Exposed*), which was many times republished, translated, and expanded. This etching from a 1771 edition published in Amsterdam claims to show "the layout of a lodge prepared for the reception of an apprentice-companion, such as was published in Paris, though inexactly." Its rendition of Masonic iconography is precise and knowledgeable.

Hence the opinion of Frances Yates: "The origin of Freemasonry is one of the most debated, and debatable, subjects in the whole realm of historical inquiry."

To begin with the sometimes forgotten obvious, Freemasonry did originally have something to do with actual stonemasons, the men who built in stone. We often call them "stonecutters," but that is a term that may fall short of the dignity of men whose capacities could be of a high artistic order. In the Middle Ages the skills of lapidary workers were continuous with those of artists we would think of as architects and sculptors. Medieval illustrations of masons at work often show the stonecutting and the figural carving being conducted as a serial process. The mason's skills might include—in addition to artisanal abilities— mathematical and geometrical knowledge of a high order, a mastery of a modern engineer's knowledge of the strength of materials, and the visionary genius of great architects. One of the medieval Latin terms for the architect was *marmorarius*, the "marble expert." The adjective "free" (with its parallels in Latin and other early vernacular European texts) originally referred to the stone itself, "free" stone being the roughly cut blocks on their way to being prepared as ashlar or stone blanks for the sculptor—stone ready to be put to constructive use.

As Freemasonry evolved and the elaborate web of its allegory grew ever stronger, interpretations of the stone, no less than of the tools used to work them, became increasingly complex. The stones were the Masons themselves. They began as rough blocks fresh from the quarry. Masonic sociability and the quest for illumination razed their rough edges and planed their irregularities as they moved through initiation and up the grades of Masonic advancement. The aim was lapidary perfection, the perfectly pumiced surface, the perfect fit. And here, again, an explicit biblical text is frequently cited, I Peter 2:5: "You your- selves like living stones are being built up as a spiritual house, to be a holy priesthood, to offer spiritual sacrifices acceptable to God through Jesus Christ." The great Temple of Freemasonry, though allegorically betokened by the old stones once worked by Hiram of Tyre, was composed of "living stones."

Stonemasons, like other skilled craftsmen, had developed their own craft guilds in the Middle Ages; like most of the others, too, they claimed for their craft a unique prestige and antiquity. The craft guilds have been viewed as precursors of modern labor unions, with which they did indeed share some similarities of function and even of practice. But the labor union analogy is probably more vexatious than helpful. The old guilds were in some ways like social clubs and in others like trade schools. They were not entirely unlike political parties, or at least political clubs. Most of all, perhaps, did they resemble the old religious confraternities, with which in the Middle Ages they often had intimate relationship. All skilled labor has its "secrets of the trade," as we still say—specialized knowledge that to the uninitiated possesses an arcane or mysterious character. One particular masonic marvel was *stereotomy*: the skill of cutting stones in complex shapes and precise tolerances required by architectural demand. There are to be found on the individual stones in many ancient and medieval buildings distinctive masons' marks. Their purpose was probably practical—identification. They served as a device for the tallying of the work of individual stonecutters on the one hand, and provided a guide to the proper placement of finished stones on the other. But it is at least possible that the marks did indeed in some instances have the "enigmatical," "symbolical," or "mystical" meanings attributed to them from the earliest historians of Freemasonry. The word "trademark," however, should be sufficient to remind us that the masons were not alone. Many trades had their marks—including carpentry and smithing in various metals—that could perhaps be regarded as mysterious or arcane.

Certain other lore of the stonemasons had entered popular literary culture well before the Age of Freemasonry. One popular legend, based in a muddled confusion between four stonemasons who had refused to build a stone idol for the emperor Diocletian and five recusant soldiers who refused incense to Aesculapius, was called the *Quatuor Coronati*–the Four Crowned [Martyrs]. Masonry was sometimes fancifully called the *ars quatuor coronati*–"the craft of the four crowned ones"–and that name was adopted for some famous early lodges.

These ancient and mythical stonemasons enjoyed church dedications and eventually became the patron saints of the construction trades. They then survived the Reformation to show up once again in some of the very earliest Masonic documents. Among the more curious of the early documents is a poem in late Middle English (British Library, MS Reg 17.A.I), perfectly awful from the literary point of view but of priceless historical worth, for it is a virtual anthology of the mystical lore that would later become so important in Freemasonry. The four martyrs

> *were as good masons as on earth shall go,*
> *Gravers, and image-makers they were also,*
> *For they were workmen of the best . . .*

The Scottish historian David Stevenson has offered one of the most plausible accounts of actual Masonic origins. His *Origins of Freemasonry* posits Scotland as the locus of the emergence of the first Masonic lodges. The suggestion is perhaps particularly attractive both because of the importance that Scotland would certainly have for European Masonry generally and for the particular genius of the Scottish Enlightenment. But it is also based in serious documentary evidence that goes beyond parochial pride or patriotism. Three of Stevenson's documents are particularly significant, for they show that so far as we know, Scotland was (1) the first place in which the word "lodge" appears in its modern Masonic sense; (2) the first place in which lodge Masonry was connected "with specific ethical ideas expounded by the use of symbols"; and (3) the first place in which "non-operatives" (meaning men who were not actually stonemasons) sought and received admission to a Masonic lodge.

This third point is of especial significance. The Masonry of the Enlightenment would have little to do with the literal construction of stone buildings. It is from this period that we begin to speak of two kinds of "masons"—practical or *operative* masons on the one hand, *speculative* masons on the other. The fact that philosophically inclined gentlemen were welcomed for membership in the early Scottish lodges suggests, perhaps, that these were already conclaves in which intellectual activity and the scientific spirit were present. For there was indeed a good deal of "science" involved with the stonemason's art. The same poetic "charges" just cited above wax lyrical about the mathematical and geometrical expertise required of its practitioners, and include an encomium of Euclid as master mason.

However, the evidence could just as easily suggest that the guildsmen were looking for and welcomed augmented sources of financial support. If so, the new lodges would once again suggest a parallel with the religious orders of the end of the Middle Ages which, with greater or less degrees of spiritual integrity, sought out a broader social fraternity within the world. There are analogies to be seen in the transformation of the nature and function of the ancient aristocratic ranks as they moved from the old, medieval, feudal world to the world of early modernity.

The transformation in "masonry" was dramatic but not abrupt. In Scotland, operative and speculative Masonry found a shared home in some of the Scottish lodges well into the eighteenth century. That is, they remained societies whose function was the regulation of the stonemason's trade. Subsequently the rise of Freemasonry became the decline of stonemasonry, so that for the purposes of this book it must be the allegorical rather than the utilitarian functions of trowel, square, and chipping adze that will concern us. That throughout Europe a specialized trade guild should develop in a very short space of time into a hugely influential, international source of social, spiritual, and intellectual growth is really rather remarkable.

There is no single or simple explanation of a matter so complex, but one aspect—the relationship of Masonic ideals to traditional Christianity—must be touched upon. Freemasonry emerged in a world of Christian institutions, however shaken or contested they may have become. One central tenet of the Masons, their commitment to toleration, eloquently addressed the cultural exhaustion brought on by the disasters of the Wars of Religion. The "movement," which focused in philosophical fashion on broad ethical principles such as the two commandments of the New Law (love of God, love of neighbor), was essentially ecumenical. Its commitment to tolerance was one of its most conspicuously "enlightened" aspects, and certainly the one that could finally attract to membership such a man as Voltaire.

The benevolent and universalist ideals of Masonry could bridge many broad chasms of the old society. There was a proto-democratic element in an organization that expanded a medieval trade guild by the addition of aristocratic sympathizers. While it plays but a small part in our story, it might be noted in passing that Masonry contributed significantly also to the augmented social and intellectual opportunities afforded to women. Though many lodges coalesced around certain political ideas, the sociability of Freemasonry often trumped party. Elias Ashmole, whose private collection of antiquities would become the core of today's great Ashmolean Museum in Oxford, was a royalist and a churchman. He fought for King Charles and with King Charles was defeated. All civil wars have their particular poignancy. An index of this one is the fact that Ashmole's son-in-law, Colonel Henry Mainwaring, was a prominent Roundhead military man. Yet both son-in-law and father-in-law, the latter in effect the prisoner of the former, were initiated into one of the northern English lodges at the same time.

. . .

THE MOST OBVIOUS CHASM, that which had divided Christendom at the time of the Reformation, was in a certain sense the most easily bridged. Despite the particular status of religion as established by law in any particular European area, the Masonic lodge was often a place in which Catholics and Protestants amicably mixed. William Schaw, who played a key role in the formation of Scottish Masonry, was a Roman Catholic. So was an early master of the Grand Lodge in London. Numerous members of the Jacobite party were committed Masons. It must have been with shock and dismay, therefore, that many Masons would have reacted to the bull of Pope Clement XII (1738), which forbade entry into a lodge upon pain of excommunication.

The Pope's reasoning, which seemed less than inexorable to many of the faithful, was double-pronged. Masonic secrecy showed that the brothers could not possibly be up to any good. Moreover, the fact that so many of them "hated the light" (i.e., were not Catholics) proved that they were carnal sinners of a particularly noxious stamp. In many parts of Europe the bull went unenforced. But of course it was rigorously applied in the papal states in Italy, in Iberia, and in some of the other darker crannies of Christendom. A lodge of Irish Catholic expatriates in Lisbon were astonished to find themselves suddenly in dire need of justification before the Inquisition. Though one hears of many important Catholic Masons in France and Germany throughout the eighteenth century, the bull was the prelude to what in essence became total war in the nineteenth century.

The mutual hostility between papal Catholicism and Freemasonry became so articulate in the European Age of Revolutions and later in the great American immigration that we are likely to regard it as an historical inevitability. If so, the inevitability probably flowed from the British political situation of the seventeenth century. Here the two factors were the religious dimensions of the "Glorious Revolution" of 1688, and the French connections of the Jacobites. Whatever the precise circumstances surrounding Masonry's "Scottish origins" may be, the *English* lodges, and especially the Great Lodge of London, inevitably played a major "missionary" role in the transmission of "Scottish rite" Masonry to the Continent, and especially to France. Among European liberals generally, the "British liberties" secured in their Protestant settlement of 1688 were inspiring goals. To the degree to which Masonry could be thought of as English and Catholicism a threat to British liberties—as in the Gordon Riots of 1780—the clash was inevitable. The maladroit and ineffectual support of the Bourbon monarchy for the lost cause of the Jacobites was a second factor. The research of the French historian André Kervella, who has written extensively on Franco-Scottish Masonic connections in the eighteenth century, has suggested that more accommodating possibilities might have existed among Catholics. Among his books is a biography of Alan Michael Ramsay (1686–1743), better known as the Chevalier Ramsay, a Scottish expatriate in France, a Catholic convert, a pretend aristocrat in the Pretender's nobility, a prolific writer, and a key figure in the Masonry of his age.

What might be called Roman Catholic "Freemason envy" eventually led in the United States to the formation of the Knights of Columbus, a group that was quite successful in America and enjoyed as much international success as its American origins would allow. Yet Freemasonry, with all its elaborate regalia and ceremonial, allowed enlightened Europe to indulge in a certain degree of unacknowledged Catholic nostalgia.

Freemasonry was not a religion, at least not at the creedal level. The single dogmatic assent demanded of its members was a belief in "the Great Architect of the Universe." That was almost universally accepted like any other apparently empirical fact, such as the rising and setting of the sun or the gradual change of the seasons. A point perhaps deserving of repetition is that while dogmatic theology recoiled in broad retreat before the Enlightenment, it was very rarely replaced by dogmatic atheism. Yet for most Masons the experience of Masonry was indeed very much like the experience of Christianity in its social and corporate dimensions.

Religious history has often tended to exaggerate the question of *belief* at the expense of the question of lived social experience. Orthodox Christianity, whether Catholic or Protestant, maintained a belief in the hypostatic union (the doctrine that Jesus Christ was both true man and true God). Surely few ideas are more theoretical or coolly intellectual. Yet commitment to a belief in the hypostatic union had been arrived at in the early Church only at the considerable cost of bitter and sometimes bloody debates, schisms, persecutions, and the shaking of the foundation of the civil state. Nobody could say the hypostatic union was not important. Still, it is difficult to conceive that the felt experience of Old World Christians had much or anything to do with their shared "belief" in a theological conundrum. The essence of their experience was in shared liturgy and shared sacraments, and yet more perhaps in those deeply social pleasures of shared human community that one would instinctively label "secular" did they not happen to take place in or around a church building or at a "religious" festival or pilgrimage.

Many men found exactly the same communal pleasures in Freemasonry. For many Christians among them, it is obvious from contemporary writers, Freemasonry was a kind of annex to or augmentation of their old religious life. For many others, it was a surrogate more or less self-consciously acknowledged. It does not disparage the intellectual importance of eighteenth-century Freemasonry to acknowledge the primacy of its more modest sociability.

. . .

GENERAL ACCOUNTS OF THE EFFECTS of the Protestant Reformation in northern Europe often stress the hostility of the Reformers to many aspects of the old Catholic religion regarded as "vain" (ineffectual), "superstitious," or "idolatrous." Only a part of the hostility was strictly speaking doctrinal in a limited sense, but it was broadly so to the degree that it was founded in a particular view of the sacramental system, which is to say in the relationship between outward forms and inward meanings. One very conspicuous manifestation is the iconoclasm characteristic to one degree or another of all reforming movements. Often it was extreme. In veritable orgies of destruction, religious vandals in parts of the Low Countries destroyed in a few weeks the precious glass and stone images, the pious ornamentation created at large expense by three centuries of Gothic religion. In England, the fury against "idols" was often hardly less violent, and the supposed Elizabethan "settlement" proved actually to be the prelude to protracted Puritan restiveness and a bloody civil war.

A revolution of political form can be imposed by force. A revolution in social forms and practices can be achieved by dictation. Ancient titles of social station might yield to *citoyen* or *tovarish*; the traditional names of the months of the ancient calendar could for a time be changed by decree. But mental and sociological change is often of a different sort. Among recent studies by scholars of the Reformation period in Europe such as Eamon Duffy are several that have modified or challenged some of the older and starker accounts of questions that once seemed happily settled into historical consensus. One particular question has been that of partial or covert continuity of certain features of the old popular piety and pious practice. Old habits of the heart do not surrender easily before even the harshest opposition. Witness the surprisingly feeble achievements of several decades of robust anti-religious propaganda in Bolshevik Russia. Aspects of the old religious system were so deeply embedded in social life as to be in effect indelible.

Two of these are of particular relevance to the history of Freemasonry. One of them was organizational. Though Catholicism was by definition universal in its claims, it had distinct local manifestations in diocesan and parish structures. It also had local centers of divergent spiritual emphasis and practice, and sometimes even of belief, in the religious orders. For many scholars, one of the least accountable aspects of the Reformation was the comparative ease with which the religious orders, which despite conspicuous failures and corruptions had for hundreds of years been the dynamos of pious practice and spiritual vitality, were everywhere cashiered from the Reformed churches. In the light of this reality, one prominent feature of Freemasonry throughout the Protestant North is its numerous parallels, both in terms of structure and in terms of secondary social function, to the old religious houses.

A second aspect relevant to an understanding of the Masons was the ancient and universal habit of and appetite for ritual, ceremony, and spectacle. In the medieval Church, ceremony had of course been everywhere. The supposed etymology of the word "liturgy" is "work of the people," or work undertaken on the people's behalf. Many Reformers believed that in its elaborations it in fact had become yet another idolatrous, man-made barrier between the individual Christian and God. Certainly, Christian ritual had a large element of spectacle. The most fundamental ceremony of the Church, the mass, was a kind of drama to be performed with various levels of elaboration and expansion, often with music. The mass was always the same, yet ever different. At its core was an unchanging canon, or fixed core, which within any given sacramental celebration would be supplemented by "propers"—elements particular to the specific occasion, season, function, or votive intention. Once again the universal and the timeless expressed itself in local and temporal form. The participants in the drama wore special clothing, made artificial and allegorical gestures, moved about in a sacred space that had long since been minutely allegorized as the geography of another, spiritual world.

More or less elaborate ceremony attended every stage of the Christian's life: at the baptismal font, at the church gate (where marriages were performed), at the bier from which the dead body was translated to the grave. And the private ceremonies and rituals were the least part of it. Religious ritual, often of a most splendid and impressive nature, was everywhere in the Old World. There were sumptuous parades through the city streets and town squares; there were also rogation processions through the agricultural fields. In the cities of early modern Europe the observance of one summertime festival, Corpus Christi Day, took on many of the features of a modern county fair or grand industrial exhibition, where wealthy burghers lined the route of procession by laying out for display their finest vestments, jewelry, and household plate.

The sacred and the secular were so thoroughly intertwined that even the most thorough "cleansing" of religious ritual necessarily left a vast body of civic ritual untouched. Sacred space forcibly vacated seldom stayed long unoccupied. This was true even in such a violent revolution as that of the Bolsheviks. They could destroy, deface, or forbid the old sacred spaces of Russian Orthodoxy; but just look at any photograph of a Moscow May Day and you will see the grim iconostasis of the Politburo lineup.

The ritual and ceremonial of Freemasonry provided in the Protestant lands, as among the less devout elements of some of the Catholic ones, a welcome opportunity openly to beautify the pursuit of high moral purpose with the garments of allegory. When Kant enunciated the famous Enlightenment principle—*Sapere aude*, Dare to know!—he made explicit acknowledgment of the audacity of knowledge itself. Yet even an exhortation to audacity could be made in a spirit of inner diffidence that for the most part our own age has ignored, forgotten, or abandoned. The first requirement of the would-be magus was reverence. So also was the first requirement of the Mason in his approach to the "Great Architect."

The face of God was a kind of Gorgon's head, to be viewed if at all only by the indirection of mirrored reflections or the oblique glance. God Himself had told Moses of old: "Thou canst not see my face, for there shall no man see me and live." (Ex 33:20) He gave His prophet but a glimpse of His hinder parts. "And it will come to pass, while my glory passeth by, that I will put thee in a cleft of the rock and will cover thee with my hand while I pass by; and I will take away my hand, and thou shalt see my back parts, but my face shall not be seen." (22–23) The contemporary mind prosecutes its search for the truths of Nature in a manner it believes to be bold and direct. The mind of the Old World found it decorous to conduct the search with the aid of a great deal of what we are likely to think of as mumbo-jumbo.

A "Secret" Society

The first distinctive feature of Freemasonry was its clandestine nature. Membership in the brotherhood was to be a secret, and one to be guarded as closely as circumstances would allow. This aspect of the Masonic project was clearly so important to the Masons that they were willing to pay a steep price for it. Masonic secrecy was at the root not merely of the papal prohibition but of all the other suspicions of conspiracy that have brooded in dark cumulus over the lodges for the last three centuries. The Masons were by no means the first secret society, but they soon became so prominent and influential as to become the paradigm for most others. That is the conclusion of one comparative study of the structure and rites of the literally dozens of secret societies that sprang up with nearly fungal growth throughout the period of the Enlightenment and the Revolutions.

There was in the clandestine protocols a thematic unity binding together the ancient ideas of "the secrets of the trade," a secrecy influenced by economic concern, and ideas of occult, esoteric, or simply "scientific" knowledge available only to the worthy, the industrious, and the instructed. Here there is a perfect congruence with what is usually taken to be the essential project of Enlightenment. These men like the sages of all times sought the pearl of wisdom; and pearls were not to be cast before swine. We may think of Masonic secrecy as an obvious instrument of elite exclusivity, but Masons themselves might regard it as spiritual obligation.

Even in the earliest Scottish documents there are references to what is called the "Mason word," as in password. The Mason word was a secret sign by which a Mason might make known his status to a fellow Mason. This "word" (in fact signs of various kinds) was meant to include the right people and exclude the wrong ones. It might be the deadly *shibboleth* of the twelfth chapter of the Book of Judges. It might be the common English words "bread" and "cheese," fatally unpronounceable by the Flemings of Kent in 1381. It could be simply the identifying "sign" of a particularly cohesive group. Many medieval organizations, including institutions of religious life, had a "word." The Franciscan Rule, for example, prescribed a "Franciscan word." Upon entering any edifice the friar must say *Pax huic domui*—"Peace be unto this house."

The particular feature of the Mason word was its secret nature. By now the Mason word has been betrayed, exposed, revealed, confessed, or videotaped on YouTube with sufficienct frequency to demonstrate that there was no such thing as *the* Mason word. That may have been true from the very beginning. In fact, the word was seldom actually a *word*. It could be any conventional sign (gesture, item of attire, detached emblem, etc.) of semiotic utility. No one who has read his justly famous translation of Rabelais is likely to suppose that Thomas Urquhart of Cromarty was a man easily flummoxed by verbal semiotics. In 1653 in his equally amazing *Logopandecteision*, devoted to his universal-language hobbyhorse, this Scotch warrior-savant recorded a cryptic anecdote of men able to make significant communication the one to another without the use of words or any other visible signs. That this was an eyewitness account of the Mason word in action has been doubted by some who have not found his name inscribed in the records of any of the early Scottish lodges; but even in the unlikely event of a bird of a different feather, this one is quacking very like a duck.

The Mason word was one of many covert or coded signals by which men have sought since time immemorial to communicate privately through the use of a closely guarded semiotic system. During the Depression in the United States, itinerant hobos are supposed to have left signs decipherable only to other itinerant hobos indicating a house at which they might receive a handout. Recent studies in "gay semiotics" have claimed to detail with a possibly alarming specificity the coded meaning of red and blue bandanas, or the placement of visibly worn keychains.

Though it was not the first of secret societies, the Masonic Order soon became by far the largest; and the Mason word is the obvious ancestor of the revelatory gestures and secret handshakes characteristic of the dozens of secret societies that came to birth in the nineteenth century, continuing today in such organizations as the Greek letter fraternities and sororities. Most fraternal grips of the academic Hellenes lack the "fiendish simplicity" of the Masonic word, requiring such complicated feats of youthful digital dexterity as to be unperformable by those elders still capable of remembering them.

Masonic secrecy has been the chief cause of the suspicion and hostility with which the order has often been regarded. Even in early Scotland, it suffered the opprobrium of unfounded accusations of malign conspiracy. For a couple of centuries the Masons and the Jesuits between them maintained a near monopoly on the multitude of supposed conspiracies that crowded the European mind. The Jesuits in their decline gave way to The Jews, often enough aligned with The Masons. Within the last decade there was a public controversy in London concerning the police. The fear was that police officers who were

Masons might be required by their secret oaths of mutual allegiance to aid criminals who happened to be Masons.

But if secrecy brought with it potential liabilities, these were outweighed by its assets. Among them was a partly manufactured solidarity of companionship in a shared and noble cause, as well as a sense of exclusive election that seems to be a universal appetite of human nature. Furthermore, it did provide the Masons with at least one genuine mystery that could be revealed to initiates. Nobody else had this secret knowledge, for they had thought it up themselves. Men like Pasquilly, Saint-Martin, or Cagliostro might speak of "secret doctrines." In actual fact there were no secret doctrines. There was instead the aspiration to seek enlightenment secretly, and for purposes of enunciating this pursuit, then of prosecuting it, they did indeed find secret words, signs, symbols, and rites.

The darkest secret of the Masons was that there was no secret, a truth that Casanova, among several of his equally distinguished brethren, makes explicit. "Those who undertake to become Masons for no other reason than to learn the 'secret' can find themselves mistaken, for you can live fifty years as a master Mason without ever penetrating the secret of the brotherhood," he wrote. "The secret of Masonry is inviolable by its very nature, because the Mason who knows it knows it only by intuition. He didn't learn it from anybody. He discovered it by means of time spent at the lodge, in observing, in reasoning, in deducing . . . The secret will therefore remain always secret."

What Casanova has in mind, surely, is that the essence of Freemasonry is an experiential *process*, a gradual movement toward moral amelioration and toward spiritual and intellectual enlightenment. The process is in the secular sphere the obvious analogue to the old Christian aspiration to "perfection," though Casanova himself takes his analogy not from medieval but from antique asceticism. He likens the thirst of "outsiders" for the Masonic secret to that of the old "profanes" with regard to the ancient Eleusinian Mysteries of the cult of Demeter.

What "profane" originally meant was that person or thing excluded from the *fanum*, the temple. The French Masons soon began to use the word *profane* to denote those who had not yet undergone initiation—the Masonically unbaptized.

The secrecy was at least in a general way consistent with ancient guild practice, which also did offer an actual template for the initiation rites. Although they developed considerably over the course of the eighteenth century, these rites seem from our earliest documents to have been already rather elaborate. The grades or "degrees" of Masonry multiplied, but they were founded in the tripartite divisions of old guild life, and their conception is illuminated by medieval practice. The skilled craftsman began as an apprentice, moved on to become a journeyman, and might hope finally to arrive at the status of master.

The very names have much to teach us. Apprenticeship (from French *apprendre*, "to learn") is an elementary stage of practical tuition. The *apprentice* was a man engaged in "on-the-job training," as we now say. Apprenticeship was ideally an intimate and familial relationship, not simply a temporary union of employer and wage earner. In the very important guild statutes drawn up by William Schaw, the Scottish Master of the King's Works in the latter part of the sixteenth century, no master should have more than three apprentices during the course of a working lifetime. However, once apprenticeship had been completed, usually according to a fixed time period agreed in advance by formal contract, the minimum period being seven years, the guildsman advanced to the status of *journeyman*. That is, he now left the shop of the master under whom he had undertaken training and, formally credentialed by his guild, could seek work in other shops with other masters. There is an ambiguity in the word "journey" that is carried over into "journeyman." A "journey" (day's worth) could be both a unit of travel and a unit of work. Certain trades, among which that of the mason was conspicuous, often demanded a supply of itinerant workmen, just as many of the construction trades still do. A single large undertaking—a cathedral, for instance—might occupy the entirety of a mason's life. Other jobs—the repair of churches or of civic buildings, the building of bridges, and so on—would require considerably less time. The third and highest grade was that of the *master*, though of course by no means did all journeymen achieve it. The word still bore the full force of the Latin *magister*—a teacher, a man so advanced in the art as to be trusted to pass it on to a new generation of apprentices. Our word "masterpiece," which now means any achievement of extraordinary quality, once referred to the actual physical artifact—in wood, paint, stone, precious metal—that gave tangible proof of the workman's having arrived at the acme of his skill.

These were the hierarchical grades of guild organization that provided the template of Masonic organization. But before moving toward the actual Masonic rites, it is useful to recall the ways in which the secular organization of medieval guild life echoed or paralleled certain long-established sacred forms. The first of these was structural: the clerical orders within the Church. There are three major orders of Catholic ministry: *diaconate*, *priesthood*, and *episcopacy*. Though the analogy is not exact, it is still significant. The servile status of the deacon is indicated even in the name. The bishop is the one with the power and authority to ordain the lower orders of ministry.

It was inevitable that this scheme would frequently be related explicitly to the Trinitarian theology of which it was born. In psychological terms, the three stages often took the names of *purgation, illumination*, and *union*. The purgative stage emptied by ascetic practice the carnal distractions of the carnal man. The illuminative stage let light pour into the empty spaces now after such great labors spiritually cleansed. The unitive stage brought the seeker to his final goal, God "in himself." These stages often are described in other terms, one very common trinity being initiation, progression, and perfection.

This is not to say that the craft hierarchy of the old masons was in some simple sense a secular adaptation of the old monastic steps of perfection. Rather, the congruence reflects something more comprehensive, a general pattern of thought that throughout the Middle Ages often blurred distinctions between the sacred and the secular. By the late mendicant period, the fraternal orders had greatly expanded the concept of *membership* in a religious order through the construction of lay sodalities and the issuance of letters of confraternity. It will surprise no one familiar with the nature of the medieval confraternities to find confraternal features in the trade guilds of the Renaissance that demonstrate explicitly Christian, even liturgical elements. As already mentioned, the oldest surviving documents of Scottish Freemasons are a varied group of manuscripts called the *Old Charges*. They pretty well span the period of the transition from operative to speculative Masonry. Typically they contain more or less detailed instructions concerning the organization of actual practitioners of the stonemason's craft. But they also continue the convention, undoubtedly of medieval origin, of prefacing the document with a Trinitarian prayer, a petition for illumination.

The initiation ceremonies of the eighteenth century are known from a rich body of literary and iconographic evidence. They varied widely in elaboration of form, and to a certain extent even in content, throughout the wide areas of Europe through which the Masons rapidly spread. But certain themes and elements, the fundamental ones, are constant. We do not have a fully documented "playbook" for the ceremony of initiation of the early Scottish lodges, but an outline can be easily enough deduced. Initiation required a dramatic *mise-en-scène* of an impressive nature, achieved through staged alternation of light and dark, sound and silence. The candidate, who was led into the chamber of initiation blindfolded or in deep obscurity, was required, often repeatedly, to petition for admission. He was required to identify himself as a sincere and voluntary candidate who aspired to the benefits but also the responsibilities of fraternal membership. He was required to make a formal oath that he would reveal nothing that he had seen or heard within the initiation chamber to anyone outside it.

Everything was made to be as spooky and threatening as possible. One of the earliest surviving catechisms prescribes that the candidate should be "frightened with 1000 ridiculous postures and grimaces." Yet all this was to be done with considerable solemnity.

There were many stage props and considerable dramatic or liturgical action. Elements of the process paralleled the initiatory sacrament of Christian baptism, the chief symbolic elements of which are ceremonial purification and participation in Christ first through death and then through Resurrection. The major liturgical action was a movement from darkness to light, the symbolism of the Easter vigil and, in a much wider sense, the central "comic" plot of Christian art, as in Dante's *Commedia*, which begins with a man lost in a dark wood and ends with him dazzled before the Beatific Vision imagined as a sea of light. This movement was emblematized in the initiation ceremony by the removal of an occluding blindfold or the introduction into a darkened chamber of numerous lights. Light imagery was prominent in many aspects of the initiation ceremony. The candidate was asked whether in truth he sought the "true light," a term loaded with the weight of the distinction between John the Baptist and Jesus Christ in the Prologue to the Gospel of John, the so-called last gospel of the mass. "He [John] was not himself the light; he came to bear witness to the light. The true light which enlightens every man was even then coming into the world." The necessary promise to "seek enlightenment" was often symbolized by bringing the candidate before a huge candle, the size of the Paschal light, in an otherwise empty room.

Rapid Spread of the Scottish Rite

David Stevenson draws attention to the "bewildering speed" with which the transformation of Scottish Masonry from operative to speculative, once begun, was accomplished. The rapid transformation of trade guild to secret benevolent society involved both geographical expansion and demographic and social change in membership. Lodges appeared in profusion throughout the towns of the Lowlands.

In one sense both strands of membership—that is the "operatives" and the "speculatives"—can be said to have increased, and to have done so in a fashion that anticipated those comparatively democratic aspects of Masonry that would prove characteristic on the Continent as well. Stevenson considered the ambiguity of the word "operative." Did it mean only a practicing stonemason, or might it be a more generic term for a craftsman (paralleling Shakespeare's "rude" mechanical)? Certainly the seventeenth century witnessed the appearance in the lodges of the aristocratic element that would be such a marked feature of European Masonry. The lodges welcomed as members "gentlemen masons," who were by no means manual workers of any sort, and often even enjoyed aristocratic patronage. But there is evidence that some skilled laborers who were not workers in stone now became Masons as well. In other words, Scottish Freemasonry was expanding its ancient "proletarian" base even as it was attracting an increasingly genteel membership.

There was another important structural way in which the expansion of Masonry mimicked that of the old religious orders: the system of filiations (from *filia*, "daughter") by which a "mother house" expanded its mission by colonization. The pattern of growth in the religious houses of the later Middle Ages is most clearly illustrated by the Cistercians. This famous order of reformed Benedictines took its popular name from the founding Abbey of Cîteaux in Burgundy. By constitutional statute, Cîteaux remained the "mother" of numerous other abbeys that soon sprang up around it; and it remained the "mother" even when some of them had clearly surpassed it in numbers, prestige, and wealth.

A system of filiation was almost naturally adopted by the Freemasons in their early and rapid expansion. However, schematic, hierarchical subordination never became a permanent feature of Masonry; and soon enough the adjective "free," detached from its original connotations of prepared quarry stone, was taken as applying to the independence of voluntary association within the individual lodges. Yet the somewhat ambiguous and troubled relationship frequently characteristic of the "families" of the old religious life continued in the competition among lodges. At the same time, considerable social and spiritual importance accompanied the prestige of a "mother lodge." Sometimes members from a founding lodge made formal inspections of their "daughter" lodges. These men were in some ways the analogues of the old monastic "visitors," whose role was to invigilate moral laxness and encourage a general uniformity of ceremonial practice.

IT IS OF CONSIDERABLE interest that at the time of the so-called Great Schism in the Church of the fourteenth century, which witnessed a credible rivalry of claimants to the papacy, the religious orders, by their very nature international or extranational, nonetheless adopted the royal policy of the king in whose territory they held their lands. At a time of increasingly assertive national sensibility, nascent Freemasonry likewise had the awkwardness of negotiating the conflict of abstract and universal philosophical aspiration with the more mundane realities of national politics. In England and France there soon appeared claimants to be the "national" lodge. In France, the claimant to national supremacy was the "Grand Orient," which was organized in the early 1770s, but its pretensions were resisted by several of the "mother lodges" of the provinces. The title "Grand" was lavishly applied to individual Masonic officers as well as to whole lodges, but of course there was no pope of Freemasonry with a recognized universal authority. A great deal of the vast body of amateur history that has issued from the lodges for the last century and a half is largely engaged, not to say obsessed, with questions of antiquity, priority of foundation, and various other controversies involving the order's spiritual capital.

But though the lodge "system" evolved with a chaos that severely challenges the social historian, it proved wonderfully apt in fostering Masonry as one of the most significant social and intellectual institutions of the Enlightenment. A new lodge could be established with relative ease. This was particularly true in England, where as early as the sixteenth century a fairly elaborate network of male sociability was already in place. The world that gave birth to the gentleman's club, the coffeehouses, and the gambling hells was one that proved particularly genial to the Masons. Many of the English lodges were in fact groups of like-minded friends who met on a scheduled basis in a reserved room in one of the taverns. Such a lodge could be born one day and perish—usually by amalgamation with another, but sometimes through simple atrophy—another. There are dozens of early European lodges of which we know no more than a name, and that only because of some kind of documentary fluke. It is natural to draw the inference that there were many fugitive lodges that disappeared altogether.

The self-appointed "Grand Lodge" of England was founded in London in 1717 through the amalgamation of four of the public house lodges, made up, for the most part, of actual stonemasons and other construction "operatives," though augmented in the Scottish fashion with some gentlemen. These lodges had previously enjoyed the hospitality of such picturesque hostelries as the Goose-and-Gridiron and the Rummer-and-Grapes. In fact, a kind of jockeying for prestige and authority among a chaos of independent lodges was a feature of Masonry throughout Europe—what might be called "grandness envy." The "Grand Lodge," having successfully achieved a status of *primus inter pares* by mere proclamation, actually did very quickly acquire the wealth and prestige of universal recognition. The Grand Lodge of England flourished under the leadership of two non-comforming foreigners, the Scots Presbyterian divine James Anderson and the émigré

Huguenot pastor Jean-Théophile (John Theophilus) Desaguliers. These men had considerable influence in constructing what was almost a formal missionary project of spreading their Freemasonry in France.

Just as the coffeehouses often became associated with a particular political tendency or party, or with a specialized intellectual interest or enthusiasm (mathematics, or chess, for example), so also did the small lodges frequently acquire an articulate "personality." Many lodges were founded on specific intellectual principles in place a priori. In others they developed naturally from the mental congruence of the founders.

The question of the relation between politics and Masonry has been endlessly debated, especially as regards the history of the French Revolution. There is no doubt that Masonry was among the great circulatory systems of progressive and radical ideas in the eighteenth century, for like the academies it had been constructed as an arena of thought. But if Jean-Paul Marat was a Mason, so also were Edmund Burke and Joseph de Maistre, the most profound of the philosophical enemies of the Revolution in Britain and in France respectively.

Individual lodges fostered actual personality as well. Since anyone with money, influence, or charisma might be able to found a lodge, Masonic organization offered certain attractive possibilities to a man of ambition, whether that ambition was sacred or profane. There are numerous examples of "serial" founders. Count Cagliostro was one such. He went farther than most by also introducing his own elaborate ceremonial rite: the Egyptian.

The eighteenth century witnessed throughout many parts of Europe a rapid rise in the frequency of business and cultural travel. (It would be a stretch to use the word "recreational" of even the best-sprung wheeled vehicles of the day.) Bankers, diplomats, lawyers, and whole army regiments moved about with a new vigor. No English gentleman could pretend to call himself educated without having completed the Grand Tour. In this world the rapid filiations from mother lodges provided obvious channels for the transmission and spread of ideas as in earlier centuries the hospitality of religious houses and the itinerant academies had once done. Indeed, the lodges were in part consciously intended to serve such a purpose, to serve as a spiritual conduit no less than as intellectual safe houses. The emissaries who had been sent out from the Great Lodge of London were in fact proto-missionaries, and their philosophical zeal was that of all apostles and missionaries.

Just as a great talker like Ben Jonson or Samuel Johnson might bring eminence by his presence to a London tavern or coffeehouse, so an eminent philosopher, mathematician, musician, or chess player might bring fame to his lodge. One famous example was the "mystic" Jean-Baptiste Willermoz (1730–1824), whose voluminous correspondence brought a reflected glory to the Freemasons of Lyon among whom he lived for decades. The historian René le Forestier devoted three thick and erudite volumes to the role played by Masons like Willermoz and his circle in the formulation and transmission of occult ideas.

Numerous individual lodges have distinguished histories of their own. One such was the Parisian lodge called the *Neuf Soeurs*—the "Nine Sisters," referring to the Nine Muses. The name had been chosen to suggest the elevated artistic and intellectual tone of the conclave. It played a certain role in American history, as it had an influential role in garnering French support for the American revolutionaries. The internationalism of French Freemasonry is illustrated by the fact that both Benjamin Franklin and John Paul Jones were admitted to the *Neuf Soeurs* lodge, and Franklin became for a time its master.

Allegories of a Secular Religion

Already in the most ancient Scottish Masonic documents—the so-called *Old Charges*—we find that Masonic "teaching" advances through an allegorical understanding of the actual tools of the trade. The Masonic emblem par excellence was and is the heraldic device in which the concavity of the try square intersects with that of the opened compass; but every other conceivable mason's tool would be allegorized as well. Once again, incidentally, the habit parallels that of the old ecclesiastical life, in which all the priestly vestments and church furniture had by the end of the Middle Ages arrived at conventionally accepted allegorical meanings. Stone subjected to geometry was the essence of the art. Anyone who has ever examined a dollar bill knows the triangulated all-seeing eye placed above the stone pyramid. This is a secular version of the Masonic emblem in which the divine implication was made explicit in the letter *G*—for God, of course.

The world would little note or long remember another amateur encyclopedia of Masonic iconography, but one point not always made in the dozens already extant, namely, the obvious connections between "Masonic mysticism" and medieval scriptural exegesis, is worth both noting and remembering. Many of the early Masonic manuscripts speak of the "three pillars" of the lodge. These are the *compass*, the *square*, and the *Bible*. They often appear also in pictorial form. Neither the compass nor the try square is an actual biblical verbal image, though both had made their appearance in biblical iconography, in depictions of the Creation, where Christ (the Creation having been, following the Johannine prologue, accomplished by the Son) works with one or the other in laying out the grand design. In the eighteenth century, William Blake famously called the Bible "the Great Code of Art." What he meant by that was that the Bible was the iconographical or symbolic encyclopedia of European painting and poetry. The Bible was likewise the great code of Masonic art.

In the most general sense the meaning of the tripartite emblem is the ordering of the works of man within the divine economy. The Bible, which is the basis upon which man's work is to be erected, is the revelation of the Word of God. It is of course supreme. The compass "belongs" to the master of the lodge, who is charged with the general supervision of its moral geography. The square "belongs" to the individual Mason, and its allegory speaks of the need to delimit and regulate his deportment with regard to other brethren. As in many early etymological allegories, much could be and was made of the derivatives of Latin *rectus* ("straight," "upright,") and *regula* ("straight edge," "ruler"): erect, correct, rectitude, regulate, etc.

The allegorization of the mason's trade among the old "operatives" is more remarkable for its comprehensive nature than for its novelty. Medieval biblical exegetes had for centuries lavished their attentions on the mystical meaning of the architecture of King Solomon's palace, and more important yet, his Temple: its mathematical proportions, its furniture, and its decorations. The exegetical tradition, so long established and so richly documented, proved to be a gold mine for the "speculatives." A text of cardinal importance was the seventh chapter of the first Book of Kings, which provided an historical account of the construction and an inventory of the Temple's contents. This scriptural site became the source of much Masonic legend and symbolic iconography.

The account of the stonework is quite detailed, and it emphasizes not only the preciousness of the stone used but also the care of its preparation and the expertise of its placement. It almost reads like an account written by a stonemason for other stonemasons. It also celebrates by name a particular artisan: Hiram of Tyre. "Now King Solomon invited and received Hiram from Tyre . . . he was full of skill, intelligence, and knowledge in working bronze. He came to King Solomon, and did all his work." (I Kings 7:13–14) The exegetical legerdemain by which an expert in molten metals is silently transformed into a stonemason can be easily imagined. In fact this Hiram became for the Masons the legendary founder of all useful trades, whether artisanal or metaphysical.

Every aspect of Hiram's wonderful manufacture for Solomon's sacred compound is expounded at some length in one or another Masonic commentary, but the "two pillars" had a special philosophical status. Outside the Temple gate, Hiram erected two pillars. Most biblical archaeologists assume that they were free-standing and decorative rather than structural. "And he set up the pillars at the porch of the temple: and he set up the right pillar, and called the name thereof Jachin: and he set up the left pillar, and called the name thereof Boas." (7:21) These became the "J and B" in the Masonic lodges of the eighteenth century, sometimes literally (as architectural features) but always spiritually or emblematically. To the diversity of exertion that the medieval exegetes had devoted to the theme, the "mystical" Masons added several rich binaries. The distinction between "operative" and "speculative," whether expressed in those exact words or in others, already echoed one sacred binary: that of the active and contemplative lives, the *vita activa* and the *vita contemplativa*.

There was another correspondence, this one of a famous literary nature. Throughout the Middle Ages and the Renaissance the most widely read and widely revered philosophical legacy of late Antiquity was the *Consolation of Philosophy* of Boethius. This was in fact a Christian work, but one in which its author intentionally suppressed "theology" (that is, biblical text and doctrine) in favor of "philosophy" (ethical doctrine founded in human reason and frequently expressed in poetic myth, such as that of Orpheus and Eurydice). Philosophy is personified as a great lady (*Domina Philosophia*, or "Lady" Philosophy), whose dignity and authority shines forth from her remarkable physical appearance. Her garment is marked with two Greek letters: Π and θ. These are abbreviations for the Greek words for "practical" and "theoretical," the two branches of philosophy—applied and pure, so to speak.

Freemasonry as a System of Communication

One frequently reads in the pages of intellectual history that around this or that date certain ideas "were in the air." It is a remarkable historical fact that some ideas of striking originality and even revolutionary potential have moved from proposal to widespread acceptance with astonishing speed. But they do not strictly speaking move through the air, except, that is, as the sound waves of human speech. There were two principal modes of communicating ideas in the Enlightenment period: through the printed word and through the spoken word. Like most other cultivated people of the age, the Masons did a very great deal of reading and writing, but they also did a remarkable amount of talking, cultural and political schmooze being a principal feature of their sociability.

Since there were so many Masons among the cultivated population, it is only natural that Masons by mere demographic necessity played a major role in the multiplex diffusion of opinion and erudition. But of course the Masons did not invent the learned press, nor in general did the Masons who contributed to it do so *because* they were Masons. Another major conduit for the written exchange of ideas, private correspondence, was perhaps a slightly different matter. Voluminous private communication is characteristic of many of the leading intellectual figures of the Enlightenment, some of whom (like Voltaire) have left an epistolary corpus staggering in its size. It can be said that European Masons participated in this cultural habit with a particular zeal, and that the organization of some of the lodges encouraged it.

It has already been noted that among the institutional and material developments favorable to the aims of the Enlightenment we must pay some attention to improvements in vehicular traffic and road maintenance. These developments were not surprisingly connected to a major expansion of the postal service. By the year 1700, a person in many parts of Europe could post a letter to someone in many other parts—certainly from capital city to capital city—with much higher hopes of its reaching its destination than in a Hardy novel. Hence the use of the word "post" in several European languages referring to rapid or regularly scheduled travel.

The mention of a few great names is sufficient to remind us of the epistolary contribution to our knowledge of the European cultures of the seventeenth and eighteenth centuries. The letters of Madame de Sévigné (1626–1696) have fascinated a readership of three centuries. It is nearly impossible to imagine the contours of polite society in eighteenth-century Britain without the ten fat volumes of the letters of Horace Walpole (1717–1797). The epistolary novel now may seem to us a form of distracting artificiality, but no aspect of the remarkable realism of *Les liaisons dangereuses* or of *Pamela* is truer to its times.

Pierre-Yves Beaurepaire, a prominent modern French scholar of Freemasonry, has done pioneering work on the nature and role played by networks of epistolary exchange in the rapid transmission of new or controversial ideas. From a prominent correspondent writing from his private house or his communal lodge, letters could go out in all directions like radio waves, circles within concentric circles. Then each node might become its own center. The image often used even at the time was that of the spider's web. The "system" could approach the multiplying leverage of our recent so-called chain letters. A fascinating historical project currently underway involves the detailed study of the epistolary spiderwebs. One special study has examined the correspondence received by the Swiss physiologist and naturalist Albrecht von Haller (1708–1777), which even in its extensiveness can be but a part of a much larger whole. This correspondence comprised 14,207 letters sent from 446 posting stations throughout Europe.

The seventeenth-century coffeehouses often had available for their readers copies of the current press, just as today one will hardly find a European café that does not advertise internet access. This amenity was provided by many Masonic lodges of reasonably fixed abode, which also often went a step further by subscribing to the learned periodical press, most of which consisted in one way or another of letters from the people in the know. The term "newspaper correspondent" has been ossified in our tongue.

One magazine of cardinal importance was the *Journal des Savants*, which from its early beginning (1665) pursued the capacious ambition of offering a comprehensive review of *all* the serious books published throughout Europe. The encyclopedic knowledge which was at least a supposed possibility for the polymath geniuses of the Renaissance might no longer be available even to the most voracious intellectual ambition; but a man who read the *Journal des Savants* on a regular basis could be the Aristotle or Athanasius Kircher of his age. In a cognate development, the radical politics of the Revolutionary age were kept simmering if not boiling by the numerous Correspondence Societies.

The stereotype of the stuffy London gentleman's club with its rack of newspapers clamped into hardwood rods, and its desks supplied with piles of crested, creamy writing paper, is a vestigial memorial to the early Masonic lodges. "The club" was often the place one wrote his letters, and probably even oftener the place he read them. I have already mentioned the mystic Jean-Baptiste Willermoz, templarist of Lyon, who wrote letters rather than books.

Even more frequently than they wrote letters, the Masons talked— and talked. When we speak of historical figures as the center of a "circle" of influence or intellectual exchange, we are speaking first of all of small groups of people meeting in frequent informal contact. It is precisely the goal of club sociability to create the environment in which such circles can form and flourish. They did so with a particular luxuriance in the Masonic lodges of England and France.

By the middle of the eighteenth century a Masonic lodge was likely to be performing numerous functions. It was in the first place a center of male sociability, offering at least the opportunity, and very often the stimulus, for serious conversation concerning science, politics, and philosophy. Numerous individual Masons would call themselves Rosicrucians, and the general Rosicrucian ideal of universal reformation through individual self-development resonated with many more. Many lodges were likely to cultivate a cosmopolitan, international outlook, and to host foreigners on a regular basis. Many lodges were Correspondence Societies and kept up-to-date libraries. One common feature of particular relevance to the themes of this book is that it was frequently among Masons and in specific Masonic lodges that men pursued the three principal occult arts: magic, kabbala, and alchemy.

Bibliographical

The general reader approaching the history of Freemasonry is very likely to be overwhelmed. The maxim of Masonic bibliography might well be taken from Dante: *Lasciate ogni speranza . . .* Masonic history has been the amateur vocation of many Masons for at least two centuries, and the bibliography is huge.

One very solid historical study of probable Masonic origins is David Stevenson, *The Origins of Freemasonry: Scotland's Century, 1590–1710* (Cambridge, 1988). Of the older "standard" synoptic histories, I recommend Robert Freke Gould, *The Concise History of Freemasonry* (1903, with later supplements). Jasper Ridley, *The Freemasons* (London, 1999), is lively and readable.

Moving toward the occult side, one should consult the classic trilogy by Manly P. Hall: *The Lost Keys of Freemasonry* (1933), *Freemasonry of the Ancient Egyptians* (1937), and *Masonic Orders of Fraternity* (1950), published together by Penguin Books under the title *The Lost Keys* (New York, 2006). Alexander Horne's *King Solomon's Temple in the Masonic Tradition*, 2nd ed. (London, 1988) is full of curious lore.

Among general French Masonic histories, the first volume of Pierre Chevallier's *Histoire de la franc-maçonnerie française* (Paris, 1974) is engaging. Serious scholarly inquiry into the French occult scene must begin with René Le Forestier's formidable *La franc-maçonnerie templière et occultiste aux xviiie et xixe siècles*, 2 vols. (Milan, 2003), and *La franc-maçonnerie occultiste aux xviiie siècle et l'ordre des Élus Coens* (Paris, 1987).

The French scholars who have written most interestingly on Masonic "sociability" include Pierre-Yves Beaurepaire in *Espace des franc-maçons: Une sociabilité européene au xviiie siècle* (Paris, 2003) and *République universelle des franc-maçons: De Newton à Metternich* (Paris, 1999), and André Kervella in *Réseaux maçonniques et mondains au siècle des Lumières* (Paris, 2008).

Concerning the intellectual exchange among Masons, Beaurepaire has also written *Réseaux de correspondance à l'age classique: (xvie–xviiie siècles)* and edited *La plume et la toile: Pouvoirs et réseaux de correspondance dans l'Europe des Lumières* (Artois, 2002).

Books specifically cited or alluded to in this chapter:
The Yates quotation is from her *Rosicrucian Enlightenment* (1972); that from Waite is from his *Real History of the Rosicrucians* (1887).

FIGURA CABALISTICA.

Der rechte Grund von der Wunderzahl Gottes,

I. 2. 3. 4.
ELOHIM.

O Arcana Arcanorum.

Der Einig Ewige Gott offenbahret sich in H. Dreyfaltigkeit.

Drey find   die da zeugen im Himmel   Drey find
der V. W. HG.   die da zeugen auf Erden
                       der G. W. B.

und die Drey find Eins und beysammen. I Joh. 5. v. 7. 8.

Nach der Ewigkeit Himmlisch und nach der Zeit Creatürl. Natürlich.

Das ist

Im Himmel und auf Erden

das beschlossene Rosen-Creutz   davon die Welt zu sagen weiß,

augenscheinlich offenbahr, und das Geheimniß aller Geheimnisse im Himmel und auf Erden.

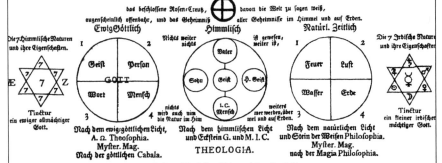

Die 7 Himmlische Naturen und ihre Eigenschaften.

Ewig-Göttlich   **Himmlisch**   **Natürl. Zeitlich**

Die 7 Irdische Naturen und ihre Eigenschaften.

1	2
Geist	Person
GOTT	
Wort	Mensch
3	4

	1	2
	Vater	
Sohn	Geist	H. Geist
	I. C. Mensch	
	3	4

1	2
Feuer	Luft
Wasser	Erde
3	4

Tinctur
ein ewiger allmächtiger Gott.

Nach dem ewig-göttlichen Licht,
A. Ω. Theosophia.
Myster. Mag.
Nach der göttlichen Cabala.

Nach dem himmlischen Licht
und Eckstein G. und M. I. C.
THEOLOGIA.

Nach dem natürlichen Licht
und Stein der Weisen Philosophia.
Myster. Mag.
nach der Magia Philosophia.

Tinctur
ein kleiner irdischer mächtiger Gott.

Erklärung dieser heiligen Figur nach dem A und O.

       1.   2.   3.

Ein Gott { Geist, Person, Wort, 3 Ewige geistliche himmlische Personen — in einem Wesen
Vatr, Sohn, h. Geist, 3 himmlische zeitliche Personen — in einem Wesen
Gott, Christus, Mensch, 3 himmlische und 3 irdische Personen — in I. C. dem Einigen Menschen }

       1.   2.   3.

der gelitten und gestorben ist für alle Menschen. I Tim. 2. Act. 3 & 20. I Cor. 2. Col. 2. Joh. 14. I Joh. 5.

Der Einig und Drey Ewige Gott ist eine Fürbildung der ganzen Natur in allen seinen Werken und Geschöpfen, in

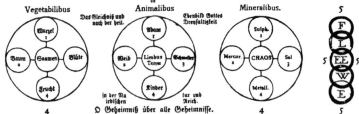

Vegetabilibus.	Animalibus.	Mineralibus.
Das Gleichniß und nach der heil.	Ebenbild Gottes Dreyfaltigkeit	

	Wurzel 1	
Baum 2	Saamen	Blüte 3
	Frucht 4	

	Adam 1	
Weib 2	Limbus Terræ	Schwester 3
	Kinder 4	

	Sulph. 1	
Mercur. 2	CHAOS	Sal 3
	Metall. 4	

in der Na   tur und
irdischen   Reich.

O Geheimniß über alle Geheimnisse.

Wer Jesum Christum recht erkennt, der hat seine Zeit wohl angewendet.

Die geheime Wunderzahl 1. 2. 3. 4. h. e. das rechte Rosen ⊕ Creutz und die Offenbahrung und wahre Erkenntniß Jesu Christi, Gott und Menschen, das ist alle himmlische und irdische Weisheit im Himmel und auf Erden. NB. wie der einige ewige Gott aus und von sich selber gezeuget und gebohren, Drey unterschiedene selbstständige Personen, und ist und bleibet seinem Wesen nach doch nur ein ewiger einiger Gott, geistlich, himmlisch, unsichtbar, in der Ewigkeit nach den drey himmlischen Personen, 1. Geist oder Gott, 2. Wort, 3. Vater, ein Gott, und in der Zeit irdisch, sichtbar, leiblich, ein Mensch und Gott, nach den drey zeitlichen Personen, 1. Geist, 2. Person, 3. Wort, ein Mensch; denn das Wort ward Fleisch h. e. Einigkeit nach Zeit. Gott

5 | *Three Occult Arts*

IT IS IN THE NATURE of the occult that its pursuit will likely be limited to a cognoscenti, a limited group of adepts who think outside the normal boundaries which confine the lives and operations of most of humankind, and within which they carry out their mental no less than their material lives. Yet the occult arts of the Rosicrucians and the Freemasons inevitably seem much weirder to us than they did to our ancestors three centuries past. The Enlightenment world was one of many transitions, but several of the ones that now seem definitely to separate us from so distant a past were as yet far from complete.

In particular, the ambition to encyclopedic knowledge, a desire to "know all things knowable," though it seemed increasingly challenging, was not entirely abandoned. An educated gentleman was meant to know the classical tongues and its literature, but also history, natural

---

The syncretism of Enlightenment esotericism frequently brought together elements of ancient Christian orthodoxy, Jewish kabbala, and alchemical "science." This "Cabbalistic Figure," widely disseminated among German Masons, is meant to explain the mystery of the Trinity according to inner agreement of the "divine light" of Theosophy, the "heavenly light" of Theology, and the "natural light" of Philosophy (alchemy).

science, political economy, and moral philosophy—vast fields all. Neither the specialization of modern learning nor its professionalization in application was as marked then as it is today. Lord Edward Conway, the patron of Greatrakes the Stroker, diligently acquired current learned literature in all fields and from all parts of Europe, and his type continued well into the nineteenth century. What we think of as "science," often including experimental science, was a common pursuit of educated men; works now read mainly in college courses devoted to philosophy and political science found a wide general audience. It is against this background that we must examine the occult arts of magic, kabbala, and alchemy.

Magic

The first of the occult arts is magic, and as usual the first problem is the problem of definition. "Magic," writes Valerie Flint in her wonderful book *The Rise of Magic in Early Modern Europe* (1991), "may be said to be the exercise of a preternatural control over nature by human beings, with the assistance of forces more powerful than they." But the excellent definition of an historian can perhaps be yet improved by the excellent definition of a magician, especially one who was the closest thing to a Renaissance Rosicrucian still extant in the nineteenth century. "Magic is the science of the ancient magi; and the Christian religion, which silenced the counterfeit oracles and put a stop to the illusions of false gods, does, this notwithstanding, revere those mystic kings who came from the East, led by a star, to adore the Savior of the world in His cradle."

Here the author is Eliphas Lévi in his *History of Magic Including a Clear and Precise Exposition of its Procedure, its Rites, and its Mysteries* (1860). "Eliphas Lévi" was the pseudonym, created by pseudo-Hebraic anagram, of Alphonse-Louis Constant. Lévi was not merely the greatest of the academic scholars of the history of magic in his age, but also the most renowned of "practical" magicians. His influence on modern occultism was enormous and, indeed, is still lively. He was vastly learned, but the particular significance of his erudition was perhaps its tenor, which combined profundity and breadth with a rare spirit of indulgent archaism. If ever there was a master of the great library of quaint and curious volumes of forgotten lore, it was he. Born in 1810, he combined the romantic and reactionary aspects of the Catholic revival in France with the living inheritance of the late Enlightenment. His concept of magic was inclusive; his book subordinates beneath its rubric both kabbala and alchemy. But it was founded in the old Rosicrucian sense of *magia*, and he used the old Rosicrucian dialect fluently.

Magia were the arts as practiced by the *Magi* (the biblical wise men of the old Latin text). Magia were thus clearly Christian and Catholic, indeterminate and yet radically legendary. The biblical story of the wise men reeks of Oriental romance. The very names of the Magi (Caspar, Melchior, Balthasar) had to be supplied from the world of romance. The Bible said practically nothing about the Magi. They came from the East. They followed a star. Each carried an obviously symbolic gift. "They are elevated by tradition to the rank of kings, because magical initiation constitutes a true royalty; because also the great art of the magi is characterized by all adepts as the Royal Art, as the Holy Kingdom—Sanctum Regnum. The star which conducted the pilgrims is the same Burning Star which is met with in all initiations. For alchemists it is the sign of the quintessence, for magicians it is the Grand Arcanum, for Kabalists the sacred pentagram."

In this taxonomy—magic, alchemy, kabbala—Lévi follows the lead of many of the eighteenth-century occultists. This chapter, too, will follow their lead, though it must be realized that many scholars, like many of the old magicians about whom they write, use the word "magic" in that most capacious sense aimed at in Flint's definition, as any supposed "exercise of a preternatural control over nature by human beings, with the assistance of forces more powerful then they." In such a scheme alchemy is a subdivision of magic, rather than its parallel, and kabbala more in the order of an ancillary technique.

In his magisterial *Religion and the Decline of Magic* (1971), Keith Thomas surveyed the vast field of "magical" activity in early modern Europe, with special attention to the particularly rich scene in Britain. From the huge domains of the history of magic so broadly conceived, only those few topics most relevant to the Enlightenment period will claim our attention here. In general, however ethereal and mysterious might be the tenets of the magicians of Old Europe, their "practice" was at bottom highly material and usually even monetary in its goals. One can hardly doubt that that has been true in all ages. The desire to have knowledge of the future was the dynamic force behind the ancient oracular system. Obviously one wants to know the future with an eye to material advantage. Shall I follow this course of action? Is the proposed investment wise? Should I engage the enemy in battle or sue for peace?

To take action based on magical knowledge might be seen at the moral level as a kind of supernatural cheating. "What could be more wicked," asks Virgil when his pupil Dante seems taken aback by the harshness of the punishment of diviners, "than to coerce the divine will?" The poet Lucan praises Cato, who refused the easy opportunity of consulting the oracle Jupiter Amnon in advance of the dubious battle that awaited him. The Stoic hero said he already knew everything he needed to know, namely, the justice of his cause. The most famous line of Lucan's poem, applied by his admirers to Robert E. Lee, is

Victrix causa deis placuit sed Victa Catoni:

The victorious cause was pleasing to the gods,
But that of the vanquished to Cato!

A very common form of magic was astrological prediction. In the ancient and medieval worlds only the thinnest of boundaries separated what we would think of as two very distinct enterprises, astronomy (the observation of the heavenly bodies) and astrology (finding predictive portents in the astronomical observations). Even as modern scientific astronomy was making the great strides associated with the names of Copernicus, Galileo, and Kepler, there continued to be a nearly universal belief in the power of astral influence over many aspects of human activity. The concept of the horoscope is so ancient as to lie beyond the boundaries of written history.

It was based in a belief that the entire plan of a man's life was fixed by the positioning of the stars at the moment of his birth. A "horoscope" was the investigation of that hour, *hora* in Latin. A belief in determinative astrology so flagrantly contradicts the fundamental Christian philosophy of the freedom of the will that it may seem surprising that it not merely survived, but thrived, over the long Christian centuries. Spiritualism's heyday was the nineteenth century. It was then that it achieved its own name, its own science ("psychical research"), and its own semi-ecclesiastic institutions. But it had been very much a part of Renaissance magic, and it was widely practiced by eighteenth-century magicians like Cagliostro.

The issue of spirit-raising in Christendom had had a very long history, but its discussion always returned to a classical biblical source: the story of King Saul and the Witch of Endor (I Samuel 28). Upon the death of the prophet Samuel, King Saul had banished from the country "all those that had familiar spirits, and the wizards." The vocabulary in the Latin Vulgate was *magi* (magicians) and *harioli* (soothsayers). The relevance of the biblical Latin is that it was its terminology that dominated the occultist vocabulary. Yet very soon, terrified by the prospect of a Philistine invasion, and despairing lest he had lost the favor of the Almighty, Saul himself sought a medium who could raise up for him the spirit of the dead prophet. So he sent for a woman with a "familiar spirit" (*pythonem* in the Vulgate), and she performed the requested sorcery.

This text was endlessly vexing to medieval commentators. It definitely proved that there was such a thing as spirit-raising, and suggested the possibility of "approved" witches, contesting the Church's claim of monopoly on supernatural apparatus. Hence a good deal of the commentary tradition is in the form of exegetical damage control. The spirit raised was not really that of the prophet Samuel, but a diabolical substitution, and so on. For the Enlightenment wizard, on the other hand, the pythonness of Endor offered a valuable role model of the magical art deployed for the benefit of the Lord's anointed.

The language spoken in the spirit world, as in the Westernizing courts of eastern Europe, was French, as the technical vocabulary of the art will reveal. The word *séance* means "a sitting," as in a particular dinner party or the time of its collation. The Spiritualist use of the term, which has triumphed over all others, refers to the magician's practice of gathering a group around a table, usually in more or less deep darkness, holding hands to create a closed "spirit circle." In these circumstances, the magician attempts to "raise the spirit" of some dead person through vocal communication or even material manifestation.

A common feature of the eighteenth-century *séance* that later somewhat dropped out of fashion was the child medium. Cagliostro's technique, which was common also among other magicians, was to use a young boy of about ten (called a *pupille*) or a girl of about the same age (a *colombe*, or dove) as the actual intermediary of communication between the spirit world and the earthbound *séance*. The "raised" spirit sometimes spoke directly through the child's voice. At other times the magician would interrogate the child, eliciting in reported speech the news from beyond the grave. The purity of virginal youth had here a symbolic element. Skeptics found in it also a practical advantage for a charlatan, who might more easily exploit infantile naïveté.

. . .

THERE WERE VARIOUS FORMS of "mirror magic," sometimes called "speculation" (connected with *speculum*, "mirror," and *specula*, "watchtower"). These survive today in literary form ("Mirror, mirror on the wall . . .") and in the crystal ball of popular magical iconography and common metaphor. Its practice involved the supposed interpretation of ambiguous or distorted images upon a reflective surface, especially the naturally reflective surface of water, but also in artificial mirrors, which technological innovations of the seventeenth and eighteenth centuries greatly improved. Ancient mirrors had generally been flat surfaces of polished metal. Their reflective capacities were comparatively weak, and the images they reflected often dark and imprecise.

In fact it was the imperfection and indeterminacy of mirrored images that was the principal feature of "speculation," which also became a theme in theological and philosophical writings. In a famous image (I Corinthians 13), St. Paul contrasts the imperfect knowledge of God available in the present life to the more complete knowledge in the afterlife. "For now we see as in a glass darkly, but then, face to face." The phrase in the Vulgate was *vidimus nunc per speculum in enigmate*—suggesting both the obscurity of the image, and the desirability of penetrating it.

Some magi of the Enlightenment period did use crystal balls, exploiting the potential of vitreous convexities and concavities to create distorted images inviting enigmatic analysis. At his Masonic *séances* Cagliostro had placed upon the table a shallow basin of water, in effect a miniature reflecting pool.

The idea, apparently, was that the magus could interpret reflections otherwise incoherent, ambiguous, or actually deceptive. For there was an ancient image, used by Augustine among others, to suggest the fallibility of human sensory perception. An oarsman sits in a

boat with his oars secured in the locks atop the gunnels and half submerged in the water. It will appear that the oar bends at the point it
meets the surface of the water. The optical illusion is caused by the
distorting function of the medium through which the submerged part
of the oar is viewed. This image shows up not infrequently in Renaissance Platonic lore. Alciati published an emblem of it, a form of which
appears on the title page of George Chapman's philosophical poem
Ovid's Banquet. The idea behind it is the serious inferiority of sensory
experience as opposed to the intuitions of the "intelligible realm."

Cagliostro on occasion used the polished metallic mirror, for example in his reported session with Madame du Barry. The du Barry
reports that she received the wizard after their mutual friend cardinal
de Rohan had assured her that "the magnetic séances of Mesmer are
not to be compared with the magic of my friend the Count of Cagliostro." Intrigued, she agreed to a meeting. The magician, dressed in one
of his magnificent occult getups and sparkling with diamonds, called
upon the banished royal mistress in her sumptuous exile. He suggested
that the mirror, properly approached, could explain both the past and
the future. Her past, alas, she knew only too well. He warned her that,
though he could facilitate her knowledge of the future, the future itself
he could not alter. Caveat speculator. She does not report what she saw
in the mirror, but it was sufficiently alarming to send her into a faint,
and to make her first interview with the wizard also her last.

So widespread did the occult practice of magic become that many
aristocratic households, and perhaps also some of the Masonic lodges,
kept their own paraphernalia (crystal balls and the like) among the
inventory of their domestic furniture.

One of the commonest forms of magic to appear in the old documents is sorcery. It is almost always regarded as illicit, and frequently
as a capital crime. The trouble is that it has no definite and fixed meaning and can be nearly as indeterminate as the word "witchcraft" itself.
The distant etymological ancestor is the Latin *sors*—election or deci-

sion founded in chance operation such as casting lots, drawing straws, flipping coins, the random selection of lottery tickets, and so on. Such sorcery was very common in the ancient world, and survives today in numerous games of chance. The eighteenth-century sorcerer—and there were plenty of them—was often the person believed to be able to predict or manipulate by occult means the outcome of such ostensibly chance operations. The eighteenth century was the Golden Age of Lotteries. One of the scrapes Cagliostro got into in London came about because of his supposed ability to pick lottery winners.

One form of sorcery became distinctly linguistic, even literary. Bibliomancy was the practice of foretelling the future by the random consultation of an important book: for the Greeks Homer's *Iliad*, for the Romans Virgil's *Aeneid*. The imprisoned Socrates made a Homeric *sors* to discover the time of his execution. The *sors Virgiliana* was quite common among educated Romans and, as the *Aeneid* remained an indispensable text for the study of Latin through the eighteenth century, it was practiced likewise among the Christians, who, however, were more likely to use the Bible. The potential lawfulness of such augury was guaranteed by its frequent appearance in the Hebrew Scriptures, and even by a specific text: "Cast lots, and settle a quarrel; and so keep litigants apart." (Proverbs 18:18) The technique was to approach the book with a question or problem in mind, open its pages at random, and note with eye or finger the first words encountered, which, when properly interpreted, would answer the question or resolve the problem. Since the textual "message" was not in every instance pellucidly clear, there was often a role for the interpretive sorcerer.

Reflections of "biblical lottery" are very common in medieval religious literature, as in Augustine's account of his conversion and the lives of such important saints as Anthony of the Desert and Francis of Assisi. In the eighteenth century, John Wesley, the founder of Methodism, was an avid practitioner of the *sors biblica*, though when he was pondering the desirability of marriage with a particular woman he preferred the clarity afforded by three homemade lots of his own: "yes," "no," and "not now." (It was a no.)

Sorcerers might also "cast spells," a *spell* being a magical formula in written or spoken form. This is a Germanic word, the early English version of which meant something like "narrative" or "proclamation," as remembered in *gospel*, the "good spell." But soon a spell became a prayer or incantation, usually brief, believed to have a particular therapeutic or prophylactic efficacy. In popular culture there were spells for the different circumstances of daily life. One that lived on even after the Protestant Reformation was the "night spell," an amusing form of which ("From ghosties and ghoulies and long leggety beasties and things that go bump in the night, Good Lord, deliver us") was current in Presbyterian Scotland.

A passage in Chaucer shows that he considered the night spell a possibly risible ornament of popular superstition and credulity. But ubiquity and breadth of cultural range were features of the old magic. It was to be found at all cultural levels, from "a cottage of clowns in Botley" to the court of the Virgin Queen, whose official magician, Dr. John Dee, was among the most erudite men in Christendom. On its more learned side premodern sorcery preserved the ancient authority of magical words, signs, and symbols. Here the old Latin word was *character*. It meant a graphic sign or emblem, such as a brand burned into the flesh of a slave or an animal. Though the word has gone off in its own direction in modern English, we still use it in certain circumstances to mean "letter" or graphic shape. In the Old World it meant primarily an occult or magic sign, and once again the casting of characters became a common feature of both popular and learned magic. Some of the early Fathers of the Church rail against it as a common superstition, sometimes diabolical.

. . .

ONE SPECIAL FORM OF MAGIC involved the placement of letters or numbers in surprising puzzle patterns. The "magic square," both alphabetical and mathematical, is very ancient. The crossword construction of the "Sator Arepo" appears in numerous antique monuments, and seems to have been either invented by or adopted by the early Christian community.

S	A	T	O	R
A	R	E	P	O
T	E	N	E	T
O	P	E	R	A
R	O	T	A	S

Various technically possible meanings can be imposed on the sentence *Sator arepo tenet opera rotas*, but none is particularly convincing. *Arepo*, which does not appear elsewhere in the Latin lexicon, must be a personal name, in which case one possibility is "The plowman Arepo holds the wheels in his labors" (referring to the old wheeled plow). It is not unlikely that a specific occult meaning has simply been lost. From the graphic point of view, the construct is remarkable as a sentence of five words that forms a palindrome—meaning that it is the same read backwards or forwards—and is deployed in a geometrical fashion to be read both vertically and horizontally. The "magic" of the square is in the elegance of the five interlocking palindromes and in the Pythagorean mysticism of the number 5 itself. It is of pre-Christian origin, but it soon became popular among the Christians and appears on several early monuments. It proved possible to perform *temurah* (rearrangement of letters or words) upon it to render various far-fetched but grammatically possible sentences of explicitly religious character. Hrabanus Maurus, an erudite monk of the tenth century and an ingenious verbal geometrician, wrote a mind-boggling book in praise of the Cross of Christ, encouraging a vogue for cross words (in a double sense) in which later Christian kabbalists enthusiastically participated.

The "Sator Arepo" is a magic square in letters. Through ingenious effort men were able to find an occult meaning in its words, but the genius of its conception had always been mathematical. The more familiar magic square frankly composed in numbers is probably older. Here a geometrical square is subdivided into three or more ranks of smaller squares (n, where $n>2$). The total number of small squares will naturally be the square of the number of ranks and files into which the larger figure has been divided, i.e., n^2. The complete sequence of the numbers beginning with one and ending with n^2 is distributed among the small squares in such a way that the numbers in every vertical and horizontal column, as well as the two diagonals, add up to the same number. It was this remarkable feature of the construction that caused them to be regarded as magical.

Number theorists have explained the general rules for the construction of magic squares. They differ for constructs with even or odd base numbers, with the even-numbered squares being regarded as the more difficult. The biblical text most frequently cited among the numerologists and kabbalists is Wisdom 11:21—*omnia mensura et numerus et pondere disposuit* ("Thou hast laid out all things in proportion and number and weight"). To penetrate the "secret" of the magic square was to reveal a science that brought the magus into contact with the marvelous harmonies of Creation and, therefore, with the mind of the Creator. The hidden ligatures between letters and numbers so minutely studied beneath the mystical microscope of the kabbala fastened together the nodes of the capacious textile of the material and mental worlds. Such emblems as the "Sator" or the magic square became the insignia of the occult quest itself.

There are numerous visual exemplifications of these assumptions in European art, not counting explicit alchemical iconography, which is an opulent subspecies of its own. One ingenious anagram creates a Latin cross reading "Paternoster" horizontally and vertically with the center on the letter *n*. What remains are two each of the *a* and the *o*, that is, a double alpha and omega to be distributed among the four quadrants defined by the cross. Number magic was a large specialized field on its own. As practiced by European magicians, its syncretistic elements included memories of ancient Pythagorean lore, Jewish kabbala, and Christian allegorical exegesis. There is a famous example in the "background" of Albrecht Dürer's magnificent etching of "Melancholy" in which the numbers from 1 to 16 are distributed among the sixteen partitions in such a fashion as to add up vertically, horizontally, and in the diagonals to 34. The bottom rank—4, 15, 14, 1—has a special significance. Dürer created the masterpiece in the year 1514, when he was forty-one years old. Dan Brown's treatment of Dürer's magic square in *The DaVinci Code*, when compared with the treatment of other aspects of Renaissance occultism in that book, may be regarded as merely a venial sin.

Magical spells could thus be "cast" both in spoken and in written form. Certain articulations were themselves magical. A small library has been written about the origins and significance of the magician's "abracadabra." It is presumably meant to convey an impressive sense of occult learning and esoteric knowledge. That certainly is the origin of *hocus-pocus*, deriving eventually from the words of sacerdotal consecration in the mass: *hoc est corpus meum*. Written spells inevitably wed "magic" to the occult arts of kabbala and alchemy, both of which, and especially the latter, made extensive use of graphic characters of occult significance and, perhaps, of occult power. Here, as we shall see, the influence of the opulent iconography of the alchemical books was particularly important.

The Kabbala

A second field of occult operation was *kabbala*. The Hebrew root of the word *kabbala* means "reception" or "receiving." The specific reference is to the receiving of literary and spiritual teaching transmitted by tradition. But already in the Middle Ages it had acquired its broader and vaguer meaning of occult spiritual doctrine. It has come in common parlance to refer to the entire body of the esoteric lore of Jewish mysticism. The meaning of kabbala or "the kabbala" is sufficiently imprecise, indeed, to invite a good deal of difficulty and confusion into its scholarly discussion. The kabbala remains part of a living mystical element in contemporary Judaism, and there are competing mystical schools claiming unique access to the true meaning of this or that kabbalistic "doctrine." Fortunately, perhaps, such questions are largely irrelevant to what the Enlightenment kabbalists were thinking and doing. This brief account of kabbalistic backgrounds must necessarily be skewed toward this eccentric subject.

Study of kabbala has focused on the vast compilation called the *Zohar*—that is, the *Sefer ha-Zohar,* the *Book of Splendid Radiance*, or the *Book of Illumination*. The *Zohar* is a huge work of scriptural commentary and speculation, compiled by Jews in Spain in the late thirteenth century. Its authorship is not certainly known, and it must in fact be an anthology of the work of several spiritual writers. The name of Rabbi Moses of León, who died around 1305, has sometimes been attached to it.

There can be few of the great books of world literature that are more difficult than the *Zohar.* The vernacular Hebrew (Aramaic) in which it was compiled is full of *cruces* (textual difficulties) that have challenged the most learned of modern philologists. Its principles of organization are less than inexorable. Furthermore, much of it is written in a lyrical mode that often renders its surface yet more strange and enigmatic. There was a principle in ancient and Renaissance pedagogy of the *dificilis per dificilior*—explaining difficult things in a way more difficult yet. The *Zohar* is, as one prominent scholar has put it, "a commentary that demands a commentary." The vast edifice of Jewish mysticism is, in large measure, that second commentary.

All mystical "science" in the Judeo-Christian tradition has as its goal the knowledge of God. A central teaching of kabbala involved a formalized scheme of the various ways of knowing God, through the divine emanations or manifestations in the world. These were called in a Hebrew plural the *sephiroth* (singular, *sephira*), and they were said to be ten in number. They were frequently deployed in an abstract icono-graphic configuration called the "tree" of the *sephiroth*, which vaguely suggested a central trunk with its lateral ramifications. Each of the *sephiroth* was usually indicated by its Hebrew name written within a small circle. At the center of the diagram was *Tiphereth* (Beauty). At the very top was *Kether* (the Crown). The lateral *sephiroth* included such concepts as Intelligence, Wisdom (*Hochma*), Rigor (*Gevura*), Mercy (*Hesed*), Splendor (*Hod*), and Victory (*Netzah*).

The Sephardic *Zohar* was almost certainly compiled in conserva-tive reaction to growing rationalist trends among Iberian Jews, many of whom were readers of Maimonides and others among the "philoso-phers." It is a full-throated defense of divine mystery and a truth far deeper than the categories of Aristotelian logic could penetrate. There are close analogies in the Christian world of the same period, in which many mystics clearly were reacting against what they considered the aridities of Scholasticism. At the same time the *Zohar* inevitably shows some evidence of the peculiarly cosmopolitan intellectual milieu of Spain before the completion of the Catholic Reconquest, a climate in which there was a certain amount of intellectual and even spiritual commerce among the three Abrahamic faiths.

The adoption and pursuit of the kabbala by important Christian thinkers and writers was probably inevitable, and it is to the Christian *Cabbala* (its Latin name) that we now turn, for it was through Christian writers that much cabbalistic lore came into the mainstream of Renaissance and Enlightenment occultism and in particular to some of its Rosicrucian and Masonic adepts. An important feature of medieval Iberian intellectual life had been the ready availability of expert Hebraists. Nicholas of Lyra, the French Franciscan biblical scholar who in the fourteenth century published an enormously influential gloss to the entire sacred text, was one of many Christian scholars who became expert in Hebrew with the help of learned Spanish converts from Judaism. Many of the Christian scholars of the Renaissance took the study of Hebrew to a seriously advanced level. It was inevitable that they would in time encounter the rich traditions of the kabbala. To offer a suggestive example of one of these, it was believed by some of the old Jewish exegetes that Hiram had traced within the floor plan of Solomon's Temple a diagram of the tree of the *sephiroth*, an idea which, when discovered by Masonic occultists, drew the kabbala into the very foyers of their sociability.

ONE OF THE FIRST of the Christian cabbalists was the young polymath genius Pico della Mirandola (1463–1494). It is perhaps not surprising that the Renaissance was full of Renaissance men; but Pico was still in a class by himself. Italian historians used to like to call him "the Prince Charming of the Renaissance." At fourteen, Pico abandoned the humdrum study of canon law for the more serious pursuit of philosophy and languages as he moved about the great intellectual centers of Italy: Bologna, Ferrara, Padua, and Florence, with a necessary sojourn in Paris, still the greatest University of Europe. He sought a perfect knowledge of the three sacred tongues (Latin, Hebrew, and Greek)—"sacred" because it was in those three languages that the Roman authorities had published in placard form the name and pretensions of the crucified Jesus. More unusual for his age was his mastery of Arabic.

At a scholarly congress marking the quincentenary of his death, a scholar offered a paper cataloguing about a hundred and thirty Hebrew books that Pico had owned. At the age of twenty-three he was making a serious study of the kabbala under the tutelage of Flavio Mithridates, alias Raimondo Moncada, a converted Jew. At about the same time he compiled his celebrated nine hundred theses dealing with "everything that can be known"—*de omni scibili*. No small amount of what could be known was, of course, occult. Before he died at thirty-one, he would boast: "I believe I am the first [among Christian scholars] to deal explicitly with the Kabbala."

He was by no means the last. Two learned classicists considerably exceeded the pioneering Pico in the depth of their studies in the kabbala. The first was Johannes Reuchlin (1455–1522), a great reformer of Greek and Latin pedagogy in Germany. His philological approach to biblical studies led him to the Talmud and the *Zohar*. The other was the Augustinian friar Giles of Viterbo, who eventually became a cardinal. The Christian cabbalists found no inconsistency between their theogical anti-Judaism, which could be intense, and their enthusiasm for Hebrew commentary. Young David had decapitated Goliath with the Philistine's own sword. Pico would use Jewish exegesis to refute Judaism. He claimed that the cabbalistic "method" applied to the name "Jesus" actually proved the doctrine of the Incarnation theologically denied by the Jews.

It may tax the credulity to suggest that kabbala had achieved a certain amount of cultural popularity by the end of of the sixteenth century, but there is evidence to suggest it had done so. In 1587 a scholar named John Pistorius published in Basel as a kind of coffee-table book a huge anthology of the *Ars Cabalistica*, which he also called the "recondite theology and philosophy," *reconditus* being a Latin synonym of *occultus*. This collection included several essays in Christian Cabbala by the learned Paul Ricius, some Latin translations of some rabbinic writings thought particularly elegant, the famous book on love by Leo Hebraeus, and Reuchlin's own substantial *De arte cabbalistica*. Reuchlin tried to rationalize the Latin vocabulary of kabbala and, in doing so, seems indirectly to suggest its controversial dimension. *Cabalici* were divinely inspired wise men. Their disciples he called *cabalei*–apprentices of the cabbalistic art. More suspicion hovered over those called the *Cabalistae*, who were the imitators of the *Cabalici*, but perhaps imitators in form only. Ruskin would one day draw a distinction between true and false griffons. Perhaps Reuchlin is here distinguishing between true and false cabbalists.

An important feature of the kabbala was its number lore, a good deal of which had to do with the exegetical practice of *gematria*–another form of the word geometry. In old Hebrew, and also in old Greek, the letters of the alphabet were used also as cardinal numbers, a practice half-remembered in our alphabetical grading systems for academic performance. The first ten letters of the Hebrew alphabet, from *aleph* to *yod*, corresponded to the ten digits of the first decade. The next nine, from *kaph* to *koph*, could represent the decades between 20 and 100. The final three (*resch*, *schin*, and *tau*) could indicate the numbers 200, 300, and 400 respectively.

Since every letter has a numerical "equivalent," every word of the Bible could be reduced to arithmetical form by adding up the numbers corresponding to its letters. Take, for example, the word *kether*, crown, the *sephira* at the top of the diagram of the tree. Its Hebrew letters are *kaph* (20), *tau* (400), and *resch* (200). The geometrical number of *kether*, therefore is 620. We may perhaps think of this, by analogy with the elaborate protocols devised by Wall Street traders to securitize a pool of house mortgages, as a system of sacred derivatives.

If $a = c$ and $b = c$, it must be the case that $a = b$. By this reasoning there was an equality (often of an occult kind) between words and phrases yielding the same numerical derivatives. The ingenuity of the kabbalists in this regard often staggers the modern imagination.

Though the esoteric teachings of the mystic rabbis concerning the emanations of God might well prove controversial in the Christian context, the gematrial method, which long antedated the *Zohar*, had made its way into patristic exegesis. That is, even before the Renaissance and the serious Christian rediscovery of Hebrew and the kabbala, some of the Fathers of the Church had been examining the numbers of the New Testament texts. As mentioned earlier, ancient Greek, too, used the convention of gematria based on its twenty-two-letter alphabet, in which the first letter (*alpha*) had the value of 1 and the last letter (*omega*) had the value of 800.

Ancient Jewish exegesis had forced attention upon the most minute details of the sacred text. It is no easy thing to make a perfect copy of a lengthy manuscript text, such as the text of the Torah. The nearly preternatural purity of the accepted Hebrew text was guaranteed by an elaborate system of mind-numbing scribal "counting" by which it was possible to identify every *letter* of the text by an ordinal number.

One possibly gematrial detail is actually to be found, textually, in the Greek Apocalypse, the final book of the Christian Bible. There the "number of the Beast" is 666—a number we must surely meet again before this book is through. By a kind of "reverse" gematria, eager exegetes have over the centuries been able to find a large number of satisfying verbal equivalences. One of the commonplaces of medieval numerology is that the number 8 is "the number of the Resurrection," an idea that makes its frequent if occult appearance in many places in painting, poetry, and architecture. This fact was "discovered" by numerous exegetical techniques, but the first of them probably was Greek gematria. The Greek name for Jesus bears a gematrial derivative of 888. His "eightness" is confirmed by other convincing resonances, and reflected in numerous musical and architectural constructs, including the typically octagonal baptismal font.

Gematria was the most dynamic way of opening up new interpretive fields in the sacred text, but was not the only way. Two other kabbalistic techniques achieved the same goal. *Temurah* was the system that allowed the rearrangement of the letters of a word to find a new possible meaning—that is, exegesis by anagram. In Hebrew, a language in which the combination of three consonants is a genetic verbal principle, this meant that the rearrangement of radical letters was a fruitful exercise. It creates a kind of linguistic kaleidoscope. In Latin and the European vernacular languages, on the other hand, it usually produces a kind of linguistic short circuit, and it was rarely practiced. A few anagrams, particularly palindromes like ROMA /AMOR, show up in the exegetical literature. *Notarikon*, which takes its name from the kind of shorthand used by stenographers, was a system of syllabic abbreviation or acronym by which word phrases could be shortened and elided. This has been a characteristic development in various modern languages, for example in the Russian of the Soviet period, which produced hundreds of words like *Comintern* (the Communist International). Notarikon is evident especially in Roman monumental inscriptions and continued well into the Christian period. In the alchemical literature long sentences are sometimes abbreviated, not in every instance intelligibly, to the initial letter of each word.

A singular example of this early Christian–Greek gematria was found in the image of the dove. From the earliest times the dove had been used as an emblem of the Holy Spirit, the third person of the Trinity, on account of the Gospel story of the baptism of Jesus, in which it is said that the Spirit alighted on him in the form of a dove. The dove is, indeed, among the earliest items in the visual vocabulary of Christian iconography. The Greek word for dove is περιστερα (*peristera*), with a gematrial derivative of 801. One of Jesus's most famous self-identifications is that in the Book of Revelation: "I am the Alpha and the Omega, the beginning and the end." Hence he is saying, in numerical form, "I am eight hundred and one." Thus was proved by Greek gematria—as Pico della Mirandola would later claim to have proved with the Hebrew letters—the divinity of Jesus Christ. Another

Renaissance occultist, Christopher Columbus, adopted a cabbalistic "mystical signature" for his official documents.

KABBALA WAS, AMONG OTHER THINGS, a dramatic testimony to the dynamic character of ancient scriptural exegesis. Already by the period of Hellenized Judaism rabbinic exegetes—of whom Philo Judaeus is perhaps the most famous and productive—had developed a complex web of allegorical interpretation of the Torah, with a special attention to the *moral* meaning of historical narrative—what the Christians would later call the tropological sense. Thus the story of God's testing of Abraham on Mount Moriah (Genesis 22), when God ordered him to sacrifice his firstborn son, while never ceasing to be sacred history, was *really* about the contemporary conduct of individual moral life. The allegorical tendency in Jewish exegesis was wholly consistent with many contemporary fashions in Greco-Roman religions. As Jerome Carcopino and others have shown us, sophisticated Romans of that age were already interpreting the great myths of their tradition in moral-allegorical ways on their funerary monuments. The overwhelmingly allegorical nature of Christian exegesis of the patristic period was a development rather than an innovation.

Belief in a bottomless profundity of the Torah set in motion a self-sustaining program of perpetual commentary. Kabbalistic texts are already themselves essays in scriptural exegesis, but they invite, indeed may require, exegetical satellites of their own. A distinguished American literary critic some years ago stated quite openly his belief that literary studies, having reached their maturity, could now recognize that works of literature were probably less important than what critics were now able to say about them. It is important to recognize that the kabbalists had a very different view. They thought of their project as one of discovery rather than of invention. They were finding things—*occult things*—in the secret chambers of the divine Word.

It was only natural, therefore, that there should be a comradeship, and often more than that, a collaboration or a conspiracy, between kabbalist and alchemist. Both were seeking to penetrate to the very heart of things.

Alchemy

"Alchemy" is an Arabic loan word, of which there are dozens in English, such as "alembic" and "algebra," and hundreds in Spanish, such as *algodón* (cotton) and *alcahuete* (a go-between), in which the fossilized Arabic article remains as a vivid reminder of an ancient but often forgotten cultural exchange. The Iberian reference is not a mere diversion, since so much of European alchemical lore was of Sephardic transmission. Though for us there is nearly as much difference between an alchemist and a chemist as there is between a hawk and a handsaw, there is actually only an act of linguistic modernization deployed in the service of the dignity of science. Alchemy was once *the* chemistry, and the practitioners of *the* chemistry were among the principal scientists of their ages. No point is more important for understanding a figure like Cagliostro than the prestige of alchemy among the learned men of his age.

Like Freemasonry itself, alchemy was for many an ethical quest based in the allegory of artisanal technique, so that it is not improper to make a distinction between "operational" and "philosophical" alchemy. The origins of operational alchemy are prehistoric; but European alchemy, as it flourished in the Middle Ages and was reborn with even greater enthusiasm in the Renaissance, bears the clear influence of Egyptian, Greek, and Arabic sources. It was founded in certain metaphysical principles of Aristotle, made mystical by the Egyptians, and made scientific by the Arabs. As it flourished in Christendom, it not surprisingly also became Christian. What perhaps *is* surprising is the way it did so. Christian ideas were not superimposed upon ancient alchemy in some superficial way. Instead, for most of its practitioners, alchemy would become the scientific branch of Christian mysticism.

The practical aim of alchemy was the transmutation of metals. The alchemists had no conception of molecules or molecular structures. They did, however, have a practical knowledge of some chemical compounds and metallic alloys. They also believed in an "original matter" (*prima materia*) of which all other matter was a corruption or debasement. The *prima materia* was associated with the chaos or nothingness out of which God had created the world. "The earth was waste and void; and darkness was upon the face of the deep." (Genesis 1:2) This text was parsed minutely. It did not say that God had created *ex nihilo*, out of nothing. It did not say that there was no earth, but that the earth was waste and void. There could be no darkness upon the face of the earth were there no face of the earth. Here was the theological spoor of the *prima materia*.

The art of the alchemist was very different from modern experimental science. "The chemistry," wrote Friar Bacon in his thirteenth-century treatise on alchemy, "is the science that teaches the method of creating a certain medicine or elixir which, when brought together with impure metals, infuses them with perfection at the very moment of contact." The alchemists were not trying to discover the nature of the physical universe. They were trying to rediscover, largely through the study of arcane books and the performance of established rituals, an elite high art transmitted to them in a dark and secretive fashion over long centuries from the ancient philosophers. Their work in the laboratories (workshops) will seem to us less experimentation than performance: the performance of magical or sacramental rites demanding a setting blessed by tradition.

We have literally hundreds of pictorial representations of the alchemist's laboratory, some of which, from the Rosicrucian period, are highly detailed. We also have some well-preserved Renaissance laboratories now housed in museums. Though they vary greatly in elaboration, the basic furniture is constant. There was a furnace or forge upon which a crucible (a vessel so named because of its traditional cruciform shape) could be fired. There was also a free-standing warming oven called an *athanor*, often built in the shape of a tower. Several of the implements came into Latin and the European vernaculars, like the word "alchemy" itself, with the old Arabic article still prefixed. The furnace required various metal bowls and dishes, *alembics* (used in distillation), *aludels* (pear-shaped ceramic or glass vessels used in sublimation), tongs, a hammer, and perhaps above all a bellows to increase the heat produced by the fire. Some of the tools were identical to those used by potters, glassblowers, and masons; most of them were already ancient in the Middle Ages.

The furnace had two chambers, separated by a carefully constructed tight-fitting door called by the wonderful name of the "seal of Hermes"—the distant original of our "hermetically sealed" and "vacuum-packed" processed foods. The complex of retorts and alembics used in the distillation process was called the *pelican*, as the positioning of a long glass "beak" suggested the distinctive shape of that bird. In the moralized nature of the bestiaries, the "pious" pelican was said to feed its young with its own very life blood spouting from its pierced breast. The commonplace interpretation of the "pious pelican" as image of the self-sacrifice of Christ was incoherently, but piously, attached to the alchemist's quest.

An accoutrement of cardinal importance was the *egg*. Allegorical eggs are a dime a dozen in alchemical literature, and the Egg was one of the most striking features of alchemical iconography. This egg was an ovoid receptacle in ceramic, glass, or even crystal, intended to contain the final stage of the Great Work, or *Magnum Opus*. This term referred with a rich ambiguity both to the final metallic transformation of the matter and to the fullness of the ethical self-mastery and self-realization of the alchemist. All of the alchemical apparatus soon took on symbolic meanings. The egg would appear to have been born of symbolism and finally returned to it. Such is the suggestion of A. J. Sheppard, who wrote learnedly on "Egg Symbolism in Alchemy," in which he briefly traces the nearly universal cultural symbolism of the egg as ground of gestation. The "world egg" being the central symbol of ancient Creation myth, the alchemists almost naturally adopted it as the emblem of their attempts to return to the *prima materia*. "For this purpose the apparatus was of no less significance than the materials themselves: the creation analogy was carried a stage further by the employment of a vessel of truly symbolic form—a *vas mirabile*."

Alchemy was founded in a scientific observation concerning the states of matter that is as honored today as it was in ancient Egypt: the observation that the same material can exist in solid, liquid, or gaseous state. It was an observation founded in quotidian empiricism, in seeing the effects of cold weather on a pond or observing the steam rising from a boiling pot. Skilled workers in ceramics and metals exploited it with considerable sophistication. The whole business of alchemy was to explore its implications, which is to say that alchemy was an art of the stovetop and of the furnace. Alchemists were forever at the forge boiling and melting away, always in the hope of effecting an igneous purification or substantial transmutation.

Like everything else in the material world, metal had its hierarchy. Silver was less precious than gold but more precious than copper; all were more precious than iron. The hierarchy is with us still today, with certain modifications. The consummation most devoutly wished by the alchemists was the transformation of "base" metal into gold. That was what they often meant by the Great Art, and it is probably what the popular mind today thinks of when it hears the word "alchemy."

It is precisely in the concept of the Great Art, however, that we shall find an enabling ambiguity of Enlightenment occultism. Probably from very ancient times, from the "alchemy" of the ancient cults of Egypt, the initiation into the science of metals had also an allegorical-moral valence. The project of purification, amelioration, and transformation externally manifested at the forge betokened an inner transformation of the alchemist's spirit. The analogy with the relationship between operative and speculative Masonry will be obvious. C. A. Burland, one of the elegant popularizers of alchemical history, describes the development of Renaissance alchemy precisely in terms of a spiritual return. "The alchemist of medieval times was gone from his cell. His books remained to lead others, but they were used in a way he hardly imagined," he writes. "The true philosophical alchemists thought of them as allegories and, although they performed the actions as a ritual, few of them saw more in the work than an illustration of a theory."

Our old literature is rich with works which play off the contrasts between the literal and the symbolic, or the "carnal" and the "spiritual," to use the terms their authors themselves were comfortable in using. One recurrent image is that of the journey, and especially that self-consciously religious journey that was pilgrimage. Dante's *Divine Comedy* begins with a narrator both literally and figuratively "in the middle of the journey of our life." (The actual, empirical author, Dante Alighieri, born in the year 1265, and allotted as all men are allotted by the Bible a lifespan of seventy years, is in the year 1300, the year in which the poem is set, exactly thirty-five years old.) He is also lost in a dark wood, a real one—real at least for a moment before emerging, like a photographic negative developed in its chemical bath, into a spiritual landscape.

Dante's subject is supernatural, the state of souls after death. Chaucer in the *Canterbury Tales* never entirely leaves the realm of an earthly verisimilitude. His characters are on the road, an actual one, the road leading from South London to the Martyr's shrine at Canterbury. But the great moral force of the work arises precisely from the exploitation of a contrast always implicit and often enough explicit between theory and practice, between a spiritual ideal and a mundane reality. All the great literary epics of the Renaissance have their allegorical levels. Some, like Spenser's *Faerie Queene*, seem to have no other. Alchemy, too, was a journey, and one fully freighted with ambiguous potential.

Chaucer has a whole story about alchemy, but he also has some zingers in couplet form that underscore the ease with which cupidity might be confused with philosophy. We cannot say for certain that Chaucer's medical pilgrim (the Doctour of Phisik) is an actual alchemist. Many alchemists were doctors, and for probably obvious reasons doctors and alchemists frequently collaborated. Chaucer concludes his description of the doctor—a man learned in the medical literature of a millennium, but one whose "reading was but little on the Bible"—with the following couplet:

> *For gold in phisik is a cordial.*
> *Therefore he lovede gold in special.*

A cordial meant a "heart medicine" or remedy. Medieval doctors did use tinctures made from ground gold, and they sought to refine a "potable gold." Paracelsus, perhaps the most famous of alchemist-doctors, in the sixteenth century found in gold an effective treatment for epilepsy. Medicinal gold has not entirely disappeared even from the modern pharmacopia. But of course one knows that Chaucer's doctor loves gold "in special" for reasons other than medicinal. The Rosicrucians had a word of contempt for alchemists whose terminal interest was the material gold. They called them *souffleurs*: puffers, bellows men. One popular image of the carnal alchemist was that of a man with visage burnt or reddened from blowing upon the fire beneath the crucible. "I blowe the fir til that myn herte feynte," says the alchemist's apprentice in Chaucer.

In describing one of his few "ideal" pilgrims, the Clerk of Oxford, that same poet approaches the Great Art directly. The clerk is a studious, intellectual, unworldly fellow, with threadbare cloak and scrawny mount.

But al be that he was a philosophre,
Yet hadde he but litel gold in cofre.

Here there is play on the word "philosopher," which meant both roughly what it means today, a seeker after truth, and an alchemist. The latter meaning was probably the more common at the time. Most intellectuals know that the classic goad—*If you're so smart, why aren't you rich?*—is unanswerable. The indictment of "philosophers" on the charge of cupidity was very broad. They had a reputation for lechery as well as for avarice. It is Faust's weakness that turns a search for all knowledge into the desire to have Helen of Troy in his bed.

Today, "philosophical" alchemy survives in a single linguistic fossil that was at the very center of the old alchemists' quest: the philosophers' stone, *lapis philosophorum* in the Latin. The philosophers' stone was the *summum bonum* of the alchemists, the means by which the Great Work was to be accomplished. Perhaps no concept in the vast lore of alchemy more perfectly exemplifies the marvelous ambiguity of the enterprise. For some alchemists it would be an actual substance, perhaps even an actual stone. For others it was a *spiritual* substance, related by triangulation to the sulphuric sun, the mercurial moon, and Azoth. For yet others the true *lapis philosophorum* was the cosmic Christ, the stone that the builders had rejected, now become the chief cornerstone (Ephesians 2:20). An ancient strain of alchemical theory had held that the Great Work would be a symphony of science and soul. The man who set out to purify the elements of the fallen earth must himself first be purified.

A significant image of medieval alchemy had been that of the "chemical marriage," taken, as we have seen, for the title of one of the important Rosicrucian manifestos. Such nuptial imagery was very ancient, but it can be said to have been endemic both in ancient Greek idealism and in the medieval Christian mind, fed by the Pauline idea of the wedding between Christ and his Church. The allegory of this marriage became standard in the exegesis of the lush language of the epithalamium of the *Song of Songs*, which had indeed in rabbinic exegesis already received spiritual interpretation. The idea that the Song of Songs was "actually" a love duet sung by Christ and the Church was so universally accepted that it appears in the running heads of the Authorized Version of 1611. In the later Middle Ages the poem had been given a Marian interpretation, with the *sponsa* (the female "beloved") now identified as the Blessed Virgin.

These sacral allegories manifestly influenced alchemical iconography, but there was an ancient secular tradition that was also important— namely, the marriage of Mercury and Philology. That is the unlikely title (*De nuptiis Mercurii et philologiae*) of a best-selling work by the fifth-century pagan grammarian Martianus Capella. Martianus's book popularized the idea of the Seven Liberal Arts—an idea that dominated European pedagogy well beyond the Renaissance and can be said to be alive yet. The precise valence of the allegory is difficult to isolate, but it may roughly be said to concern the union of wisdom and eloquence, or abstract knowledge and its written expression. Augustine had made a somewhat similar allegory of the gold and silver liberated from Pharaoh's household by the escaping Hebrews. The gold was the wisdom of the pagans; the silver the eloquence in which it had been expressed.

The alchemical marriage was that between the (male) sun and (female) moon, chemically sulphur and mercury, and the generation from the chaotic *prima materia* (original matter) of the philosophers' stone. A remarkable etching published in a cabbalistic-alchemical handbook in Frankfurt in 1628 includes an image of "Coitus" in which the sun-king propositions the moon-queen in the language of the Song of Songs: "Come, my beloved, let us embrace to generate a son who will be unlike his parents." Her reply is: "Behold, I come to you, and I am most ready to conceive such a son, unlike any in the world."

The study of alchemy has been called "the study of an error" that has small claims upon the historian of science. Yet practical and positive results can flow from radical theoretical error. The consequences of Columbus's discoveries in the American hemisphere are not blunted by his own theory that placed him in Asia. A very great deal of the practical techniques of experimental chemistry, and a good deal of material science, we owe to the old puffers and distillers, condensers and sublimators lost in their wild goose chase of the mind.

Some of the old alchemists seemed to know this even while in mid-chase. In his wonderful poem "Love's Alchemy," Donne despairs of ever plumbing the mystery of love to its depths, but nonetheless finds his accidental consolations:

> O! 'tis imposture all;
> And as no chemic yet th'elixir got,
> But glorifies his pregnant pot,
> If by the way to him befall
> Some odoriferous thing, or medicinal.
> So, lovers dream a rich and long delight,
> But get a winter-seeming summer's night.

A very remarkable work by a very remarkable man is the *Alchymista christianus* (*The Christian Alchemist*) of Pierre-Jean Fabre, published in Toulouse in 1632. Fabre was born into a provincial French Catholic family about 1588 in Castelnaudary in the old compté of Lauragay (now the Aude). Though he developed cosmopolitan interests, he remained a life-long provincial. His center of gravity was never Paris but the small, old cities of the South. He trained in medicine at Montpellier, still among the foremost medical schools of Europe, and maintained intimate intellectual connections with the university circles in Toulouse.

Fabre is important less because he was in many ways exceptional, though he was, than because of the ways in which he was representative of a major strain of amateur erudition in pre-Enlightenment Europe. Fabre tried—and without many visible signs of inner struggle apparently tried with success—to keep abreast of science within the context of a liberal Catholic consciousness. On the other hand there is some evidence of *external* tensions. His overt defense of Paracelsus and the "Empirics" caused him some problems with the theology faculty.

In the Middle Ages and the Renaissance the genre of the spiritual allegory, in which the Christian life could be compared with every imaginable analogue (and a few scarcely imaginable), was tediously rampant.

ALCHYMISTA
CHRISTIANVS·

IN QVO DEVS RERVM AVTHOR omnium, & quamplurima Fidei Christianæ mysteria, per analogias Chymicas & Figuras explicantur, Christianorúmque Orthooxa, doctrina, vita & probitas non ostentanter exchymica arte demonstrantur.

'Auctore PETRO IOANNE FABRO,
Doctoris Medici Philochymici
Monspeliensis.

TOLOSÆ TECTOSAꞮVM,
Apud PETRVM BOSC, Fibliopolam.

M. DC. XXXII.
CVM PRIVILEG. U REGIS.

The title page of the *Alchymista Christianus* (1632). The *Christian Alchemist* was an early attempt by Pierre-Jean Fabre, a learned Provençal physician, to reconcile alchemical science and Catholic theology. The year 1632 was the same year that Galileo was ordered to Rome for ecclesiastic trial.

One had not merely soldiers of faith, but also farmers, tinsmiths, vine-dressers, fishermen, hostlers, cutlers, saddlers, and bricklayers of faith. Fabre's *Christian Alchemist* is decidedly not of this genre. He is a *real* alchemist, who has appointed himself the task of demonstrating that the pursuit of the Great Art and the pursuit of Christian perfection are not merely analogous but identical. He argues, accordingly, that the interpretation of the mystical emblems inherited from the ancient alchemical emblems is strictly analogous to the decipherment of Holy Writ.

While it is not easy to adduce a representative example from a work so large and complex, his treatment of the cross will perhaps serve. "Wise men [*sophi*], and all the ancient magicians and cabalists [*magi, cabalistae*] concealed the mysteries of Nature beneath enigmas, tropes, and figures" of such economy that a single icon might convey as much as could be written in a large book. In support he alludes to the Egyptian hieroglyphs in which, just about that time, the early generation of Egyptomaniacs typified by Athanasius Kircher had discovered their own universal key to all mythologies.

In one sign alone, the ancient astrological sign for Mercury—a cross, atop which has been placed the sun, a circle, and above that the moon, a crescent—Fabre found a summary of the entire created world in its connection with the Creator. The central sun is the origin of that "hot" (in the humors theory) that is the source of all earthly vitality. The geometrical peculiarity of the line of the circle is that it has neither beginning nor end. It is permanent continuity—"just as the natural heat enclosed within the special motion of the world has neither beginning nor end." The moon, for its part, supplies the "moist." "That radical 'moist' is the mother of all things, just as the inner 'hot' is the father."

This, so far as Fabre was concerned, was ancient wisdom as solid as Holy Writ itself. Or perhaps one should say as liquid. Mercury, the anomalous liquid metal, which had been discovered early, had a particular fascination for the early chemists. Later, the medical doctors discovered that its poisonous qualities might be harnessed in the chemotherapeutic treatment of syphilis. In the earliest chemical theology, Mercury was of course identical with Hermes, the "thrice-great" (Trismegistus) god of the wisdom of the Egyptians. Hermes made the somewhat awkward descent from being a god to being an author. It was he to whom our oldest occult writings are ascribed, and from whom they take their name: the *Hermetic Corpus* (*Corpus Hermeticum*). Among his works was the most ancient and influential of alchemical treatises: the *Tabula Smaragdina*, or *Emerald Notebook*. The *Hermetic Corpus* was said to have been transmitted through the prophetess Mary, or Miriam, sister to Moses. The wisdom of Hermes began, as all such books must, with a cosmogony, an account of the Creation of the world. With little effort the Christian occultists were able to see in it a manifesto of pure monotheism. "As all things came into being by the contemplation of One, so all things arose from this One, by a single act of creative adaptation. The Father therof is the Sun. The Mother is the Moon. It was carried in the womb by the wind. The earth is the nurse." Here we have in a slightly variant form an early expression of the four essences: earth, air, fire, and water. Shakespeare repeatedly calls the moon "watery," an idea doubtless as old as the most ancient observations of the operation of the tides.

Medieval plagiarism differed from modern plagiarism in a dramatic way. The modern plagiarist hopes to pass off someone else's work as his own. For the medieval plagiarist, the operation was reversed. He hoped to pass his own work off as someone else's. For if Bede or Caesarius of Arles had written it—above all, if Augustine had written it—it was bound to be read. The actual origins of thrice-great Hermes are shrouded in the mists of Hellenistic Egyptian antiquity. This uncertainty provided an opportunity to his doppelganger, pseudo-Hermes, to publish such theological tractates as the *Book of the Twenty-Four Philosophers*, in which two dozen thinkers come together for a seminar on a single question: "What is God?"

So for Fabre, hermetic and patristic traditions could unite in a single stout cord of "wisdom." That still leaves the base of the sun and the moon—the cross. The whole of the physical and chemical operations of the world—for Fabre still the center of the only known universe—is supported by the cross, to which he then devotes several chapters that are "mystical" and "scientific" in equal measure. There is so much cross-lore in medieval literature that it would be rash to attribute to Fabre an absolute originality here. Many writers found in the cross the fixed staple from which the material world took its stability. One great writer, Bonaventure, in his widely read *Lignum vitae* (*Tree of Life*), found in the shape of the cross the essential geometry of the universe.

That probably was the source of the speculations attributed to Paracelsus in a book of similar title: the *Liber Azoth, sive de ligno et linea vitae*. Paracelsus was perhaps the most famous of all alchemist-physicians, of whom there were very large numbers well into the eighteenth century. Fabre cites this book. "Azoth" was the alchemical name given to a supposed universal medicine, the object of one of the alchemists' perennially fruitless searches. Its "cross connection" was probably unavoidable given the verse of the Apocalypse (22:2) in which it is written of the Tree of Life that "the leaves of the tree were for the healing of the nations." The alchemical design encapsulating this book-length mystery is the majuscule *T* set within a circle and touching its circumference at the three extremes. This is "the great sign of God, which roughly corresponds with the sign of Mercury."

We see once again the nearly direct transmission of medieval exegetical ideas into the occult arts of the Rosicrucians and Masons. For the circled *T* is indeed an ancient mysterious sign. It is in the first place geographical and indeed cartographical, being the form of that most ancient of universal maps called the "T and O." Its allegories were numerous. The *T* could stand for *terra* and the *O* for *oceanus*, so that it was a map of the great world surrounded by the great sea. The watery parts were the perimeter of the enclosing circle and the *T* itself, the Mediterranean—a name that means, of course, "the middle of the Earth." The three landmasses were the three anciently known continents: Asia, Europe, and Africa, each of which had been founded by one of the three sons of Noah: Shem, Japheth, and Ham.

But the capital Roman *T* was also, and especially, a therapeutic form of the cross, the final letter *tau* of the Hebrew alphabet, later transposed to the Greek *tau*, which was in the form of the Roman *T.* This letter had a general meaning of "sign," as the legal "mark" of an illiterate was an *X*, and as we still say, "*X* marks the spot." Already in the Hebrew Scriptures the *tau* had a "kabbalistic" flavor. It was the saving sign, to be made in the blood of the lamb, at the initial Passover. Later (Ezekiel 9) it was the redeeming mark to be placed on the foreheads of those to be spared in the universal slaughter that was to fall upon Jerusalem. The *tau* cross frequently appears in later Christian exegesis and mysticism. It was for its therapeutic powers that it became the insignia of nurses in the medieval world. For the same reason Francis of Assisi appropriated it as his "mystical signature." The Cross was the salvation of the world, and its leaves were "for the healing of the nations."

The indirect testimony of contemporary literature sometimes offers a perspective not to be found in the more obvious primary sources. Two classic works from the earlier periods of English literature give us insight into the ambiguities of alchemy as viewed by those who lived among its practitioners: Geoffrey Chaucer's "Canon's Yeoman's Tale" in the *Canterbury Tales* (about 1380) and Ben Jonson's bitter play *The Alchemist* (first performed in 1610).

At an advanced point in their journey to Canterbury, Chaucer's pilgrims are overtaken from a distance by two men riding hard on their lathered horses. The two are a canon (member of a religious order) and his domestic servant, the yeoman. The canon is an alchemist; the yeoman has been his apprentice or, as he now comes to see it from an altered moral perspective, his accomplice. The tale is an oblique narrative exposure by the yeoman of the fraudulent operations of his master, the canon-alchemist. By the end of his tale the yeoman has decided to abandon his old master and join up with the pilgrimage in progress.

Chaucer is a moralist, and one of the themes he implicitly develops is a contrast between a material and a spiritual alchemy. Through his informal confession, the yeoman has joined in the penitential spirit of which the pilgrim is ostensibly an emblem. In abandoning the attempt to make gold, he has transmuted the base metal of his character into a kind of emblematic gold. Furthermore, the yeoman, long practiced at the forge, deploys a rich technical vocabulary of the equipment, the operations, and the special jargon of the alchemist in a fashion that commands occult authority. The reader (or hearer) will have the sense that this is the real thing. But the subtler interest of the story for the history of alchemy probably lies elsewhere, in the psychology of the alchemist.

He is a cheat and a fraud. Through a mechanical trick he appears to create within his crucible a small fragment of gold with which he can dazzle his victims—dupes or investors, depending on how one views things. Yet Chaucer manages to convey the psychology of a true believer. The canon's motive is more complex than simple greed. One has the sense that he cheats not because he disbelieves in the Great Art, but because he does believe. One aspect of genuine obsession, perhaps, is to subordinate the empirical evidence to the a priori theory. This time it failed. Next time it will succeed . . . *next time.*

The subtlety of Jonson's *Alchemist* is of another sort. The alchemist is indeed named "Subtle"—which means merely cunning and duplicitous—but there is little that is morally nuanced in the play. Another of its major characters is Sir Epicure Mammon. Its subtlety lies rather in the presentation of its characters, all of whom are "bad," though interestingly distributed among categories of folly as well as of active vice. The great vice is cupidity: the love of money is the root of all evil. Jonson does seem aware that all confidence schemes must depend to some degree upon the cupidity of their victims.

In the verse "Argument," or synopsis, preceding the dramatic action, Jonson summarized the crimes of the alchemical conspirators, who have in the temporary absence of its owner commandeered a London house to use as the stage set of their fraudulent activities:

> *Much company they draw, and much abuse*
> *In casting figures, telling fortunes, news,*
> *Selling of flies, flat bawdry, with the stone . . .*

What is interesting here is that alchemy, properly speaking, is but one part of their operation, which includes, in effect, the whole range of the occult arts of the Renaissance. They "cast figures" as magicians

and astrologers. They tell fortunes as clairvoyants. They sell "flies"—
that is, demonic spirits—as sorcerers. And all this is mixed with "flat
bawdry," in the narrow sense the whorehouse they have established
with Doll Common, but in the larger sense the connection everywhere
seen in the moral literature between the illicit search for gold and the
cruder pleasures of sensuality. Subtle boasts that he will make one of
his female dupes

> *feel gold, taste gold, sleep gold:*
> *Nay, we will* concumbere *gold!*

One of the "scientific" problems of alchemy was that its opulent
poetic lexicon and visual library ossified a number of ancient ideas
whose shelf life was finally expiring. We think of modern science as
"advancing" or "building," as one investigator uses the achievement of
a predecessor as a foundation or starting place. Premodern scientists
were much more likely to try to accommodate their activities to
long-established first principles and axioms. Astronomy, even while
rapidly "advancing" in our terms, sought to accommodate its findings
to the Ptolemaic system long after it became difficult to "save the
appearances." So far as the practice of alchemy was concerned, there
were many practical advances in technique, but they were at the theoretical level simply folded into the ancient paradigms. Among the old
tropes few were more venerable than the analogy of macrocosm and
microcosm.

"I am a little world," wrote Donne, "made cunningly of elements . . ."
A more commonplace poet, du Bartas, will put the idea in more commonplace form:

> *For in man's self is Fire, Aire, Earth, and Sea*
> *Man's in a word the World's Epitome,*
> *Or little map . . .*

An advanced thinker like Francis Bacon was discarding this notion, which, as he wrote disapprovingly in his *Advancement of Learning*, implied that "there were to be found in man's body certain correspondences and parallels, which should have respect to all varieties of things, as stars, planets, universals, which are extant in the great world." Yet alchemy was wedded to this notion, even as it strove to transcend it.

Alchemical "anthropology," as transmitted through its iconography, maintained the teaching of man as microcosm, in that both the great world and the small were composed of the four essential elements (essences) of earth, air, fire, and water. Early theories of human nature were singularly lacking in what we would think of as psychology or "personality." The word *personalitas*, had it existed, would have meant the abstract condition of being a personage, and thus roughly equivalent to role, function, or office. The view was mechanistic and indeed chemical. Just as there were four external essences, there were in the human body four fluids (*humores* in Latin): blood, yellow bile, black bile, and phlegm, which in their relation to the admixtures of four qualities (moist, dry, hot, and cold) determined what we would think of as "personality type." The correspondences did not stop there. Each humor related to one of the four seasons of the year and one of four major bodily organs. For example, blood was associated with the essence *air*, the season *spring*, and with the *liver*. Its qualities were *hot* and *moist*. A person in whom this humor reigned was called "sanguine" (from Latin *sanguis*, "blood").

Though we have entirely abandoned the theory of the humors, we still use the adjective "sanguine" to denote an attitude of confidence or self-assurance, just as we use the adjectives "choleric," "melancholic," and "phlegmatic" to denote characteristics or attitudes once associated with them.

The alchemists were in some ways like modern cancer researchers. They were searching for the absolute or fundamental ground of biological life—which for them would necessarily be intimately involved in a complex knowledge of spiritual correspondences. They sought nothing less than the *quintessence* of things—a word manifestly meaning the *fifth essence*, the one that would unlock the mystery of the other four. It is only an intellectual perspective not yet invented in their own age than can deny them the title of scientist. Their science would be avidly pursued throughout the learned circles of Europe, and in particular throughout the complex and far-reaching web of European Masonry.

Alchemical Iconography

One particular feature of the alchemy of the Enlightenment period was its *pictorial* opulence. Alchemical iconography was one of the important conduits of Rosicrucian and Masonic occultism. Western medieval religious art had a distinctly emblematic or symbolical character, and this dimension is prominent also in what is usually taken to be the more "realistic" painting of the Renaissance and Baroque periods. The conventions of Christian iconography as they developed over a millennium became relatively uniform, though so complex that the field of iconographic studies played a significant role in the development of the modern discipline of art history. There were numerous literary sources of Christian iconography, but the *great* source was naturally the Bible. As late as the end of the eighteenth century, as we have seen, the artist-mystic William Blake could still say that the Bible was "the Great Code of Art."

Some secular books also developed more or less elaborate traditions of pictorial illustration. These included certain legal and historical texts. Works of unusually wide diffusion, such as the *Consolation of Philosophy* of Boethius, were lavishly illustrated. A few vernacular poems, such as the thirteenth-century *Roman de la Rose*, have a rich iconographic tradition. But the most opulent body of secular iconography was to be found in scientific texts, among which the alchemical books were preeminent. The illustrations in the alchemical manuscripts often seem very strange. They try to imagine in pictorial terms such notions as the sun-man and the moon-woman. They often include among their decorative elements the signs of the Zodiac, the astral bodies, and the chemical elements derived in many instances from classical ancestors. They frequently introduce mythological figures.

Christian iconography had a signal pedagogic function. It was a very old belief that there were two modes of teaching: *par parole et par peinture*, as Richard de Fourneval put it in the fourteenth century, by word and by picture. Gregory the Great is supposed to have said of the images in the churches that they were the *biblia pauperum*, the Bibles of the illiterate. Alchemy was no art for the unlettered, and from its ancient and medieval origins alchemical iconography heightened rather than attenuated the mysterious doctrines it illustrated. By the height of the Enlightenment, scholars had available an extraordinary body of hermetic images designed to foster and explicate the mysteries of the art. This visual evidence is the subject of an important book by Stanislas Klossowski de Rola: *The Golden Game* (1988).

The efflorescence of alchemical esotericism coincided with the efflorescence of printing. In the incunabulum period, however, very few items from the large manuscript bibliography of alchemy crossed into print. By the end of the sixteenth century the situation had changed dramatically. There was in the first place a new outpouring of more "contemporary" alchemical texts, and many of them were sumptuously illustrated. "By that time," writes Klossowski de Rola, "printing had improved, allowing the reproduction of even the finest line drawings, and copperplate engravings replaced for the most part the coarser woodcuts used previously." Once again, we see technological novelty put to the service of ancient tradition.

The images were called by their inventors "hermetic emblems" and "hierographical figures," among other things. Such names honored two related erudite Renaissance traditions: the enthusiasm for fancifully interpreted Egyptian hieroglyphs on the one hand, and the emblem books on the other. Early Renaissance knowledge of the hieroglyphs derived mainly from the *Hiergolyphica* of Horapollo (Horus Apollo), an alleged Greek translation of an ancient Egyptian work. The history of this text is one that actually satisfies many of the fantasies of scholarship as imaged by Hollywood. It was found on a Greek island early in the fifteenth century by a Florentine monk, who bought it for Cosimo de' Medici. It is a collection of allegories based upon ancient Egyptian images, some real and some imaginary.

Only some of these hieroglyphs were actual elements of the old Egyptian writing system. Most were simply cryptic images, which is roughly the translation of the word "hieroglyph." There was nothing cryptic about the hieroglyphs for literate ancient Egyptians; they would have found Indo-European alphabets "cryptic." Ficino, one of the grandfathers of the Christian Cabbala, praised the hieroglyphs of Horapollo for their capacity to convey in finite imagery nearly infinite flights of thought. He says this, for example, concerning the "dragon"—a monstrous creature circled with its tail in its own mouth. "Our way of thinking about 'time' is complex and shifting. For example: 'time goes quickly'; 'time revolves and ends up where it began'; 'time teaches prudence'; 'time gives and takes away.' This whole range of thought was comprehended in a single firm figure by the Egyptians when they drew a winged serpent with its tail in its mouth."

The "emblem books," most famously exemplified by the sensationally successful *Emblemata* (1522) of the Italian jurist Andrea Alciato, were a literary genre popular throughout Europe. They were in effect a collection of newly minted hieroglyphs in which a small etching, accompanied by a brief moralizing text in Latin, gave a word to the wise.

Many of the cryptic illustrations in the new alchemical literature of the seventeenth century actually did derive from Horapollo, and also from Alciato and his rivals and imitators. One particular feature of the alchemical emblems was their hermetic use of classical mythology. There was already a long tradition in Christian exegesis of spiritualizing mythography—that is, of finding Christian religious meaning in the old pagan texts. The mythographic enterprise, indeed, is one of the signal achievements of medieval humanism. Boethius's *Consolation of Philosophy*, one of the cultural constants linking late Antiquity with the secular asceticism of the Renaissance in an unbroken chain, included famous meters moralizing such classical poetic motifs as the Golden Age and the story of Orpheus and Eurydice. Hercules, already a moral model in antique Stoicism, became in Christian Europe the object of learned philosophical commentary and the model of epic heroism. The baroque *Metamorphoses* of Ovid, which was the Latin world's great mythological encyclopedia, was called without irreverence "the Bible of the poets." So classical mythology offered the alchemists a ready-made high seriousness relatively free of the dangers attendant upon speculation about the sacred text.

One of the finest of the picture books is Michael Maier's *Atalanta fugiens* (1618). Maier, like many alchemists, was a doctor of medicine, who in time became the personal physician to Emperor Rudolf II. It seems to have been Rudolf who converted Maier to occultism rather than the other way around. Maier traveled widely in Europe, and spent some time at the court of James I in England. He was the very model of aristocratic cosmopolitan erudition. The long subtitle of *Atalanta fugiens* begins thus: "New chemical emblems concerning the secrets of Nature, arranged to appeal equally to the eyes and to the intellect . . ."

Atalanta was a kind of Arcadian Artemis. Her father, who would brook no daughters, exposed her as a babe on a mountainside, but she survived, nourished by a bear. Passing over several famous episodes, she later returned to her father's house on condition that she be allowed to remain a virgin, never to marry. When nonetheless harassed by suitors, she and her father agreed to the following plan. Being almost supernaturally fleet of foot, she would compete in a foot race with any suitor brave enough to try. Assuming no man would ever beat her, she agreed, disingenuously, to marry the man who did. Losers, who proved to be numerous, were to be killed.

However, a suitor named Hippomenes, as sage as he was ardent, appeared. He prayed to Venus, who, outraged by any vow of virginity, granted Hippomenes aid. She supplied him with three golden apples. During the race, which Hippomenes was about to lose, he tossed the apples just ahead of Atalanta. Her pauses to pick them up gave Hippomenes the time needed to squeak through to victory. Atalanta reconsidered her position as she contemplated the handsome winner, and she willingly, indeed enthusiastically, agreed to marriage. But Hippomenes made a fatal mistake. Instead of going immediately to the Temple of Venus to thank her for her succor, he took his bride to the Temple of Jupiter to thank *him* for victory. Venus, outraged, so inspired the couple with her erotic influence that they then and there, right in the middle of Zeus' fane, performed the coital act. Even Zeus had some standards, and this he regarded as flagrant *lèse-majesté*. He punished the lovers by transforming them into a pride of lions.

If the myth of Atalanta had not already existed, the alchemists might well have invented it. Here was the allegorical center of the art (gold) playing a complicated and complicating role in their central allegorical institution (marriage). The old Christian moralizers could find a negative "message" in the golden apples. That love of money (*cupiditas* in the Vulgate) had defeated the noble aspirations of votive virginity just as an unbridled sexual desire had incurred its just divine retribution.

The title page illustration to *Atalanta fugiens* presents the history of Atalanta in continuous narration—that is, placing distinct and temporally successive narrative episodes within a single frame. We see the foot race, the amorous foreplay in the temple, the postcoital lover-lions, and a good deal more. The title page declares the book to be "a

new chemical emblem book dealing with the secrets of Nature . . .
accommodated in part to the eye and in part to the intellect. . . ." The
book is among other things a great popularizer and synthesizer that
made the erudite and the arcane widely known among a popular
audience.

There is an analogy of sorts to be drawn with the use of the Tarot
cards, the popularity of which dates from the Renaissance. Early European playing cards varied considerably in design and number before
settling, after a long evolution, into today's generally accepted fifty-
two-card, four-suit deck. There were several different decks used in
different games; the Tarot deck, which also had several different
names, is taken from a once popular French game, *tarot*. Two of its
features were the large number of cards in a set (more than seventy)
and the rich and eclectic iconography of the card faces. Only in the
eighteenth century, at a time when card playing (and especially card
gambling) approached the status of social mania in genteel circles, did
the occult dimension of the Tarot appear. By then the Tarot deck was
old-fashioned if not antique, and its pictorial repertoire increasingly
exotic. The iconography of the Tarot cards was drawn from various
sources, both popular and learned. Among the former were the old
tradesmen's signs, which also featured prominently in the old inn and
public house signs in England. The more learned strain did include a
few time-tested alchemical emblems. Most important, like the images
in the emblem books and the alchemistry manuals to which they are
distantly related, the Tarot cards were of a visual variety and complexity that practically invited a dilated narrative commentary. Such a
commentary, called "reading" the cards, magicians of various genres
were increasingly expert in supplying.

Literary and iconographic evidence alike attest to the very widespread cultural diffusion of alchemical ideas and images throughout
the Enlightenment period. It is true that among many thinkers,
alchemy had a musty and medieval whiff about it. Yet insofar as there

was a "popular" idea of a scientist, it found its expression in the image of a learned man laboring amid his exotic implements with their exotic names. In the year 1700 almost anybody interested in "the advancement of science" was likely to have an interest in alchemy; and even as experimental science developed during the eighteenth century, the alchemical dream remained vivid for many scientists.

Other occult arts demonstrated their vitality. Magic, "the preternatural control over nature by human beings, with the assistance of forces more powerful than they," was perhaps less respectable, yet still widely pursued in a world in which as yet so much of what we today think of as "settled" science was still in mysterious flux. For the literary-minded, indeed for large swaths of the classically educated European intelligensia who sought wisdom from ancient texts, kabbala and its associated exegetical sciences, sacred and secular alike, continued to exercise a fascination. The Rosicrucian manifestos had revealed ancient Eastern wisdom from the tomb of Christian Rosenkreuz. The Freemasons sought the ancient wisdom of Hiram through the portals called Jachim and Boaz. It was only natural that in such circles the old learning would mingle with the new, and even in surprising ways direct its energies.

Bibliographical

A good general introduction to the major topics of this chapter is Antoine Faivre, *Access to Western Esotericism* (trans. of *Accès de l'ésotérisme occidental*) (Paris, 1986).

There are two magisterial scholarly studies of the old magic: Keith Thomas's *Religion and the Decline of Magic* (London, 1971) and Valerie Flint's *The Rise of Magic in Early Medieval Europe* (Princeton, 1991). A work far more in the spirit of the Enlightenment magicians themselves is Eliphas Lévi (A-L Constant), *The History of Magic, Including a Clear and Precise Exposition of its Procedure, its Rites and its Mysteries,* trans., with a preface and notes, by Arthur Edward Waite (London, 1913; many times republished).

From the large literature on alchemy, I suggest the following excellent books: C. A. Burland, *The Arts of the Alchemists* (New York, 1968); Johannes Fabricius, *Alchemy: The Medieval Achemists and Their Royal Art* (Copenhagen, 1976); and P. G. Maxwell Stuart, *The Chemical Choir* (London, 2008). The beautiful book of Stanislas Klossowski de Rola, *The Golden Game: Alchemical Engravings of the Seventeenth Century* (London & New York, 1988), deals with the fascinating iconography of alchemy.

Most of the rich bibliography of kabbala naturally deals with ancient and continuing Jewish spiritual practice. Christian Cabbala, which was at first principally an exegetic aid, took on a life of its own in the Renaissance. The most important work is in French: François Secret, *Kabbalistes chrétiens de la Renaissance* (Paris, 1964), but there is in English Philip Beitchman's *Alchemy of the Word: Cabala of the Renaissance* (Albany, 1998). There are two erudite books by Allison Coudert: *Leibniz and the Kabbalah* (Dordrecht, 1995) and *The Impact of the Kabbalah in the Seventeenth Century: The Life and Thought of Francis Mercury van Helmont (1614–1698)* (Leiden, 1999).

Books specifically cited or alluded to in this chapter:
The citation from Burland is from his *Arts of the Alchemist* (1968).
The Book of Wisdom, relegated to the Apocrypha by Protestants, was very influential in the Middle Ages and Renaissance. The text here cited is from the Latin Vulgate.

COUNT CAGLIOSTRO

6 | *Cagliostro Ascending*

I. Giuseppe Balsamo and Count Cagliostro

If it is a science at all, history is the most provisional of the sciences, an anthology of temporary judgments. For despite the importance of physical climates, of immutable economic laws and class structures, of technological innovations and famines and epidemics, history is very largely concerned with the mysterious *genus* known as *Homo sapiens.* In this terrain it is the novelist and not the historian who may be the true master. "Never," writes Henry James, "say you know the last word about any human heart." To aspire for the penultimate word is sufficiently audacious. The *philosophes* of the Ancien Régime undertook the mighty project of dismantling the fascinating and enchanting castle of ignorance of the European "mentality," accumulated over centuries in its great Gothic subdivisions and baroque elaborations, but like most revolutionaries they were at best only partially successful. Further-

---

Alessandro Cagliostro was a highly controversial character throughout the course of his public career. Among his most ardent followers he could be regarded nearly as a saint. Several of the most widely circulated print portraits, such as this one, borrowed from clichés of sacred iconography to suggest an ethereal and spiritual dimension to the man's character.

more, when their work came in its turn to be reviewed by their ostensible successors, the Victorian sages, the judgments were often no less bemused and severe than that of Voltaire on the Convulsionists of Saint-Médard.

In 1833 Thomas Carlyle, then a rather *young* sage, published two long essays, much celebrated in their era, that painted a distinctly negative picture of the eighteenth century. The first, reprinted in his collected works under the title "Diderot," was ostensibly a book review. The French Enlightenment had no single "poster child," but Denis Diderot (1713–1784), the genius of the great *Encyclopédie*, would have had as good a claim as any man to incarnate its characteristic spirit. In 1821, a scholar named Naigeon had brought out a large edition (22 volumes) of Diderot's works. Ten years later, four more volumes appeared. These were printed from manuscripts left by the dying Diderot to his friend Baron Grimm, another major figure of the French Enlightenment.

The occasion—perhaps the better word would be pretext—of Carlyle's "Diderot" was the appearance of these supplementary volumes. Carlyle's attitude is signaled by his opening sentences. Diderot had not yet been dead for half a century when he wrote them. "The *Acts* of the *Christian Apostles*, on which, as we may say, the world has, now for eighteen centuries, had its foundation, are written in so small a compass, that they can be read in one little hour. The *Acts* of the *French Philosophes*, the importance of which is already fast exhausting itself, lie recorded in whole acres of typography, and would furnish reading for a lifetime."

So little, it would seem, was Thomas Carlyle awestruck by the Age of Reason. But his attitude toward Diderot is not unsympathetic or even unrespectful. He finds him, however, a man severely limited. "What duties were easy for him he did. . . ." His fuller condemnation of the eighteenth century and its principal works is reserved for his essay on Cagliostro, who will be the principal subject of this chapter. Carlyle declares it his intention "to examine the biography of the most perfect scoundrel that in these latter ages has marked the world's history . . . the chief of all such, we have found in the Count Alessandro di Cagliostro, Pupil of the Sage Althotas, Foster-child of the Scherif of Mecca, probable Son of the last King of Trebisond; named also Acharat, and Unfortunate Child of Nature; by profession healer of diseases, abolisher of wrinkles, friend of the poor and impotent, grand-master of the Egyptian Mason-lodge of High Science, Spirit-summoner, Gold-cook, Grand Cophta, Prophet, Priest, and thaumaturgic moralist and swindler; really a Liar of the first Magnitude, thorough-paced in all provinces of lying, what one may call the King of Liars."

This is what English professors usually call "vigorous prose," and we might wish to find the occasional essay by Carlyle in the *New York Review of Books*. But it may tell us more about Thomas Carlyle than it tells us about Cagliostro. A large ocean often separates primary and second sources, between what a person writes and what others write about what a person writes. A reader wishing to test the fairness and justice of Carlyle's portrait of Diderot is not limited to a consultation of half a dozen "definitive" studies and biographies of the last half century. That reader can actually go back to Naigeon's twenty-two volumes, and to the numerous improved editions of various works by more recent scholars. Quite a few have done so, and not many of them have ratified Carlyle's view. But Cagliostro did not leave "acres" of typography. There are few autograph sources to which we can turn. Under these circumstances, the default source has been the secondary source. Most of the "scholarship" on Cagliostro has consisted of interrogations of or contestations of Carlyle. Since Carlyle himself has joined Diderot in cultural oblivion, modern interpreters of Cagliostro have often been battling with two unseen ghosts.

The chiefly significant primary sources that have been used for the life of Cagliostro are the following: (1) a few documents probably written by Cagliostro himself; (2) various dossiers compiled by Louis XVI's police, and especially the lengthy deposition made at the time of the Necklace Affair; (3) some scabrous articles in the journal *Courier de l'Europe* for 1786; (4) an attack by a professional rival, Jacques Casanova; (5) miscellaneous references in contemporary memoirs of the period, especially important for Cagliostro's "Strassburg period"; (6) an itinerary of the Cagliostros' European travel coerced by the authorities from Serafina (his wife), manifestly inaccurate at least in part; and (7) reports of reports made by the Inquisition in Rome and fashioned into propaganda "biography" that might justify throwing the man into a prison from which he would never emerge alive.

Some of the sources of the evidence are themselves clearly suspect. The Paris police would do anything the royal party instructed them to do, and the royal party wanted Cagliostro's scalp. Practically any number of the *Courier de l'Europe*, run largely by blackmailers, will make Rupert Murdoch seem like Louisa May Alcott by comparison. Most historians today regard the Inquisition as a far greater iniquity than any it pretended to expose; and its evidence drawn from confessions produced by torture or the threat of torture are notoriously dubious. Yet the anonymous Inquisitorial biography has perforce been regarded as a document of cardinal importance, especially as it was widely distributed in a French translation, *Vie de Joseph Balsamo* (1791). It paints a picture of a man of the vilest moral character, a pimp, a cheat, a thief, a fraud, a forger, an imposter whose villainies are sordid rather than interesting or engaging. It is nearly impossible to believe that such a man could have commanded the friendship and patronage of so many of the leading men and women of the cities in which he took up residence. Hence, one may wish to entertain doubts concerning the reliability of sources on which we must nevertheless perforce depend.

Thus it is not surprising that room has been found in the documentary interstices for a view of Cagliostro very different from that of Carlyle's King of Liars: a kind of Rousseauian Cagliostro, the friend of humanity, a man of a precociously liberal political spirit, a true seeker after truth and an Enlightenment martyr to a doomed but still potent spirit of reaction. I cannot pretend in this chapter to resolve what is irresolvable, but I do hope to tell Cagliostro's story from a possibly novel perspective. For whether the man was *of* the Enlightenment he was certainly *in* the Enlightenment—that is, made possible by certain circumstances characteristic of the Age of Lights.

Historians beginning with the hack biographer commissioned by the Roman Inquisition are generally settled in the belief that the remarkable man who called himself the count of Cagliostro was actually born to a "good" family of reduced means named Balsamo in Palermo, in Sicily, in 1743. At his baptism he was given the name of Giuseppe (Joseph). Young Giuseppe was a rebellious child—meaning that he kicked against the pricks of the dour religiosity of his guardians, who designed for him a clerical life and sent him off to the pre-seminary of San Rocco. From there, still coerced by family expectations, he went at the age of thirteen to the ancient Sicilian town of Caltagirone, where he became a novice in the hospital of the Benfratelli.

Before proceeding, however, it is necessary to raise a problem not common in modern biography. Biographers may differ in their interpretations of their subjects, but they are usually agreed that they are at least writing about the same person. We have some good documentation for the life of Giuseppe Balsamo. We have some excellent documentation (beginning in the year 1776) for the life of Count Cagliostro. Most standard reference works state as a simple and uncontested fact that Giuseppe Balsamo and Count Cagliostro are one and the same person. A rich literature is founded upon that assumption. Cagliostro's two best biographers, however (Trowbridge in 1911 and Lalande in 1912), point out that there is no definitive evidence to prove it. Count Cagliostro's enemies would have had every reason to slander him, and few slanders would have been more effective in that world than "unmasking" one of the darlings of European esotericism as a Sicilian nobody. Neither writer *denies* the identification, but they see in its too easy acceptance the operation of a persistent historical prejudice that has virtually guaranteed a faulty judgment of Cagliostro. With this rather odd caveat in mind, we can return to young Giuseppe Balsamo.

The picture we get of Italian religious life of that age is far from inspiring. About the time that Balsamo was with the brethren, Edward Gibbon, now very much a *lapsed* Catholic, sat in the Franciscan church of the Ara Coeli in Rome, planning in his mind his great history, the sacred mumble of the friars performing the office seeming to him the perfect emblem of that sad *decline* in Roman magnificence that was Christendom. Much of the greatness of the Old World was made by great monks, the Benedicts and the Bernards. Conversely, much of the greatness of the New World was made by men who shrank from the limitations of religious life—Luther, Erasmus, Rabelais. Young Balsamo was more Rabelaisian than Bernardine.

The order to which he was attached, relatively new, was one of several "hospitallers," for whom the word "hospital" still had its older meaning, more accurately rendered by the modern hospice. The Benfratelli specialized in works of corporal mercy, palliating the suffering of the sick and burying the dead. Though Giuseppe Balsamo soon enough revolted against religious life, one aspect of his education with the hospitallers may have been particularly significant. The brothers had a small apothecary's "laboratory" in which they prepared remedies, potions, and palliatives. The Inquisition biographer claimed that in it Balsamo appears to have learned some rudiments of what we would today call chemistry. The old literature—the Faust legend, *Romeo and Juliet, Friar Bacon and Friar Bungay*, among many others—preserves for us the literary ancestor of the mad scientist, and he was usually a friar.

We can see at the very least certain stylistic affinities between the old polymath friar and the Enlightenment scientist, even if we shrink before the rashness of claiming a lineal descent. In his heyday, the twin aspects of Count Cagliostro's fame were medicine and alchemy. He traveled with his own portable beakers and retorts, and sometimes set up an elaborate laboratory in his rented rooms. It is at least possible that he thought of himself as being as much a friar as a magician.

But the juvenile delinquent, chaffing beneath the yoke of an uncongenial asceticism, several times ran away from the monastery. Such flight was always unsuccessful, for in truth he had nowhere to go. His family would not take him in, and he was as yet too young to undertake the bold international travel that defined his later career. Each time after a brief and unsatisfactory period of liberty, he was forced to return to the Benfratelli, who inflicted upon him the severe corporal punishment that was in that age the expected recompense of youthful rebellion. Not surprisingly he tired of these repeated frustrations, and at last devised an audacious plan of securing a definitive release to the great world after which he lusted. If being bad was insufficient, he would be terrible.

The story, of course, comes from the Inquisition biographer, but it is almost too good not to be true. An important feature of religious life in the old Benedictine tradition was the so-called *lectio divina*, or "sacred reading." The *lectio divina* was actually a technique for turning Bible-reading into prayer and spiritual meditation, not only in the recitation of the psalms from the Divine Office, but in other circumstances as well. Among the metaphors for the spiritual absorption of the holy text were those of manducation. We speak still of "ruminating" over a book or "digesting" its contents. It was only natural that alimentary and spiritual consumption would be joined together. In many religious houses the communal meals were taken "in silence"—meaning that there was supposed to be no conversation among the diners—while a designated member of the community read aloud from the Holy Scriptures or some edifying religious book.

Among the favorite source material since medieval times was hagiography—the lives of the saints. One classic work of the thirteenth century is called the *Legenda Aurea—The Golden Legend*—where the word "legend" still has its Latin sense of "a thing to be read" rather than a tale of dubious veracity. By the later Middle Ages the lives of some newly canonized saints, such as St. Francis of Assisi, were being written with an eye to the needs of refectory lectors. Once when his appointed stint as lector came around, young Giuseppe Balsamo saw his opportunity and seized it. In reading aloud in the refectory from some hagiographic book or another, he substituted for the names of the sacred personages mentioned in the text the names of the most notorious harlots of Palermo.

This induced a near riot of indignation in the monastic dining hall. Though Caltagirone was nearly two hundred kilometers distant from Palermo, many of the brothers—we need not ask how or why—were very familiar with these names. Here was unprecedented scandal. Here was blasphemy. Here was behavior literally incorrigible; and as correction was impossible, only one remedy remained: expulsion. The fox and the wolf threw the protesting rabbit back into the briar patch.

"Of the difficulties that perpetually beset the biographer of Cagliostro," wrote W. R. H. Trowbridge, one of the best of them, "those caused by his frequent disappearances from sight are the most perplexing." Trowbridge actually had in mind the documentary lacunae of the later 1770s and the decade of the 1780s. These years are indeed punctuated by puzzling gaps, but the greater mystery hovers over the period before real documentation begins, between Balsamo's departure from Sicily and Cagliostro's appearance in London in 1776.

We do not know for certain when Balsamo was born, but there is an official ecclesiastical document claiming to be based in an original baptismal registry attesting to the administration of the sacrament of initiation on June 8, 1743, in the metropolitan church of Palermo. A quarter of a century separates this document from the next one we have: a marriage certificate. On April 20, 1768, Joseph Balsamo married a Roman woman, Laurenza Feliciani, in the church of Santa Maria de Monticelli in Rome, presumably the bride's parish. We know much less of Balsamo's wife Laurenza than we do of Balsamo himself. That means we know very little indeed. And after their wedding, Giuseppe and Laurenza Balsamo disappear from the pages of history.

In alluding to the mysterious decade that separates Balsamo from Cagliostro I have intentionally suppressed one testimony that, if we could believe it, would give a picture of the newly married Italian couple. It is in the *Memoirs* of Jacques Casanova. In the spring of 1769, Casanova spent several weeks in Aix-en-Provence recuperating from illness. One day the talk at his inn's *table d'hôte* was all about two Italians, a young married couple, who had just arrived in Aix as pilgrims, on foot, from the celebrated pilgrimage shrine of St. James of Compostella in Galicia—a hike of about a thousand miles. They had made quite a stir by entering into the town with a lavish distribution of alms among the roadside beggars.

Unlike Casanova they spoke little French, and Casanova appointed himself to check them out. He found two weary travelers resting: a beautiful girl holding a large crucifix, and a rather grumpy young man, a few years older, adjusting the cockleshells of the pilgrim's garb. He sized them up with a glance. The woman radiated nobility, modesty, innocence, sweetness, and decency. The man's "vibes" were rather different: boldness, insolence, derision, and knavery. "His passport, issued in Rome, called him Balsamo," writes Casanova; "she, having never changed her name, was called Serafina Feliciani. The reader will find this same Balsamo become within ten years Cagliostro." The Inquisitorial biographer, too, tells a tale of a pilgrimage to Compostella. According to him, it was a hypocritical ruse devised to exploit opportunities for fraud and extortion.

Casanova wrote a good deal about Cagliostro, but only the foolhardy will take his judgments as objective truth. Rarely will the Pot's testimony concerning the iniquities of the Kettle escape its own interrogation. Casanova was wont to approve of beautiful women and to disapprove of their inconvenient husbands. The truth is that Casanova and Cagliostro, if not exactly peas from the same pod, are siblings of the Enlightenment, international travelers and adventurers whose careers were made possible by the same broad social changes and especially by the structures and conventions of the international Republic of Letters. Both men march across the second half of the European eighteenth century trailing scandal, to be sure, but also admiration. Casanova began as a magician and never entirely abandoned his esoteric pursuits. Casanova's most famous exploit was his highly publicized escape from an odious prison in the Venetian Republic. Cagliostro became famous first as a victim of Bourbon tyranny in the Bastille, and then as an actual martyr of the Roman Inquisition. These were credentials of the highest order among the enlightened enemies of the old order.

It is only later that the Count Alessandro Cagliostro and his wife the Countess Serafina appear. Concerning Serafina we know more that we did of Laurenza. All sources agree that she was a woman of great beauty. Several mention her considerable charm. One legal document attests to the fact, supplied by Serafina herself, that she was unable to read or write in any language—a fact rather amazing in light of the learned pretensions of her husband and of the cultivated circles in which she often traveled. In some of the more salacious anti-Cagliostro propaganda she is presented as a woman of loose morals. In particular she is accused of sleeping around in the furtherance of her husband's schemes. The source here is the Inquisition biographer, who presents her as a reluctant whore pimped out by her vile husband. There is, however, no other evidence to support these slurs. On the other hand there is abundant evidence of the love and harmonious affection shared by the married couple. There is no explanation for the fact that they remained childless, but it would be rash to find portentous significance in a not uncommon medical condition.

Were Giuseppe Balsamo and Count Cagliostro one and the same person? The answer must be an annoying yes and no, with the most important action in their shared history taking place off camera. The key to understanding the problem probably lies in the Masonic concept of *elevation*, or philosophical conversion. The Saul of the streets of Palermo became the Paul of the drawing rooms and lodges of London and Paris. This is the idea implicit in Trowbridge and Lalande, and ably augmented by Paolo Cortesi, a popular scholar of esotericism, in an excellent biography entitled *Cagliostro: Maestro Illuminato o volgare impostore? (Cagliostro: Illuminist Teacher or Simple Fraudster?)*. "Balsamo used folk medicine and magic to sell his amazing pills to imbeciles; Cagliostro was committed to the Rosicrucian mission of succor to the ill. We shall never know who or what caused this extraordinary transformation."

II. Cagliostro Arrives in London

In July 1776, about the same time that events of significance to our national history were transpiring in Philadelphia, Count Alessandro Cagliostro and his wife the Countess Serafina were arriving in London. Indirect evidence suggests that they had sailed to England from Lisbon or Oporto. It is sometimes said that the friendly understanding between England and Portugal is the oldest continuing alliance in Europe, and there was a lively wine trade in the eighteenth century, with many ships going to and fro. What is particularly interesting about Cagliostro's stay in London in 1776–77 is that for a man who has earned the permanent reputation of a polished swindler, he himself was repeatedly swindled by comparative amateurs.

Cagliostro took furnished rooms in a house on Whitcombe Street, on the west side of what is now Leicester Square. In the 1770s, the neighborhood was one that would have to be described as transitional—and the transition was of a declining nature. Leicester Fields—the park that has now become the familiar pedestrian square—had originally been the enclosed garden of magnificent Leicester House, but by the middle of the eighteenth century it was surrounded by private residences, apartments, and boardinghouses, respectable but by no means grand. Many of them housed struggling genteel international transients. Cagliostro's landlady, whose curiosity and gossip would prove unhelpful for her new tenants, was wont to boast of having titled foreigners under her roof.

If in somewhat ambiguous social circumstances, the count and countess were at the very least passing for "quality." Even shoestrings cost something, and the problem of Cagliostro's *money* is troubling for a biographer. He arrived in London with a good deal of it—in specie, letters of credit, and jewels—which were commonly used as quasi-liquid tokens of exchange. When he left London in disgust in November 1777, he claimed to have been taken by the city's rapacious residents for 3,000 guineas—an enormous sum. We have no evidence from the post-Balsamo period of credible accusations against him relating to swindles or large-scale financial fraud. Yet he usually had sufficient means to project for lengthy periods of time a "lifestyle" of genteel respectability, and often enough a certain lavishness. He was obviously generous to a fault, as more than one dismal experience attests. Despite his wide reputation as a healer, a reputation that often inundated him with supplicating patients, he made it a point of honor not to accept money payment for his treatments. Where did his money come from?

Later he did, of course, frequently enjoy the hospitality and patronage of very wealthy people. The cardinal de Rohan was one of the richest men in France. In Mitau he had enjoyed the largesse of the von Medems, whose letters of recommendation proved invaluable to him in Poland and Russia. He arrived in Strassburg in notable splendor, with an elaborately decorated coach and liveried servants. The assumption among the "occult" historians has been that he was being bankrolled, for political purposes, by wealthy members of one of the German secret societies, probably the Illuminati of Adam Weishaupt, which had also been founded in 1776.

But his sources of support in London are by no means clear. What seems certain is that in his financial dealings as in other parts of his mysterious career, Cagliostro was enabled by important developments in international banking characteristic of his period and, indeed, intellectually and thematically related to the "internationalism" of the Enlightenment.

One of the count's first moves, news of which was instantly published in the neighborhood, was to establish within his rented quarters an alchemical laboratory, and display within it his impressive beakers and retorts. At this point Cagliostro spoke practically no English and the countess none at all. They soon became friends with one of their fellow lodgers, a multilingual Portuguese woman of the familiar eighteenth-century category "distressed gentlewoman," who became the countess's companion and translator. Cagliostro's boardinghouse seems to have offered shelter to as many protagonists of the humbler sort of life's tragedies as any in Balzac or Henry James.

Madame Blavery (the Portuguese lady) boasted widely among the dubious diaspora of her acquaintance of her friendship with the Cagliostros, advertised their characteristic generosity, and apparently considerably exaggerated the means by which they exercised it. She had an Italian friend, Vitellini (an ex-Jesuit of mysterious exness), who spread the rumors among his own yet more dubious friends. "Thus by the indiscretion of Vitellini," writes Trowbridge, "Cagliostro was soon besieged by a crowd of shady people whose intentions were so apparent that he was obliged in the end to refuse to receive them when they called." It was in this context that Cagliostro encountered the threat, by no means the first nor the last, of blackmail.

Blackmail was altogether more common in Cagliostro's world than in ours. Blackmail today, which appears in detective fiction more frequently than in actual life, is a form of extortion in which Party A threatens Party B to reveal to the police or an unsuspecting spouse information concerning Party B so potentially injurious to him that he will be willing to pay to have it suppressed. This concept of blackmail assumes some actual information of a compromising nature. The eighteenth-century sense was somewhat more elastic. In general the blackmailer threatened publication of certain claims, presumed to be scandalous, in a book or journal of potentially wide circulation. The scandalous material might be true, partially true, or not true at all. It might be put in a fictional form that so very thinly disguised the objects of attack as to leave their identities obvious to anyone in the know.

The word "libel" originally meant just "a writing" or "a little book" as the *libretto* of an opera still does. It took on its negative and legal meanings only with the expansion of printing in the seventeenth century. In fact eighteenth-century "literary" blackmail, of which Robert Darnton has written so engagingly, was one of the undersides of the expanding "print culture" which was also one of the great enablers of the Enlightenment. It depended for its success on a robust gutter press and an ever-expanding reading public insatiable in its appetite for scandal. Both conditions existed in Paris and London. This form of blackmail might be regarded as a quasi-literary form of the protection rackets that later became a staple industry among organized criminals. As we shall see, furthermore, London was the place of publication of one of the more irresponsible French-language international "tabloids," the *Courier de l'Europe*, edited by the notorious Théveneau de Morande.

An Italian named Pergolezzi threatened to publish a libel denouncing Cagliostro as a fraud and an imposter. Specifically, he threatened to expose the count's ignorance of the science he pretended to practice, and to advertise the actual tenuousness of the financial resources that had made him in the eyes of many a great man. Since according to a French document conveniently discovered years later, Cagliostro in his Balsamo days had been an apprentice in Pergolezzi's workshop in Italy, the threat is very remarkable for what it does *not* threaten: namely, to expose Count Cagliostro as Giuseppe Balsamo. As Trowbridge pointed out, none of the many enemies of the man ever came forward to claim that they knew him both as Balsamo *and* as Cagliostro. Furthermore, as Cagliostro did not respond to the threat, and as Pergolezzi did nothing further, we must conclude it was a kind of trial balloon. There would be worse to come.

It is not possible in short compass to give an account of all the scrapes the count and countess got into in London; but the supposedly ruthless Italian adventurers were much more in the category of "harmless as doves" than "wise as serpents." His early difficulties with his fellow lodgers in Whitcombe Street began with a "Captain Scott," who soon enough by self-elevation became "Lord Scott," and who for a time sponged off the Cagliostros with great success. He began by pretending to have lost some of Cagliostro's Portuguese money, which he had offered to negotiate for sterling, before moving on to bolder extortions. When finally chased away by the exasperated Cagliostro, his "wife"—"Lady Scott"—pretending to have been deserted by his lordship and left in the lurch, continued to mulct with success. Eventually she discarded her pretense and reclaimed what might have been a real name (Miss Fry), under which she sued him for money he did not owe her, throwing in a charge of witchcraft for good measure.

Cagliostro's more serious difficulties with these people arose from one of his redundant mystical powers—that is, one which he appeared to regard as a distraction to be avoided in the pursuit of alchemy. He had found in some old manuscript an algorithm or formula or perhaps simply a charm that, he discovered, allowed him to predict the winning numbers in lotteries. (Lotteries were all the rage at the time.) One hardly knows what to say about an occult gift that was a source of embarrassment to him rather than a stimulus to economic enterprise. Captain Scott and his friends by no means shared his embarrassment, and they went to great lengths, including outright theft, to get their hands on the manuscript. One of the highly disconcerting features of the "historical problem" of Cagliostro is the copious evidence that many contemporaries who hardly fit the profile of credulous dupes clearly believed in his occult powers.

As the months went by, things went from bad to worse. His life took on the contours of a picaresque novel, but in it his role was that of prey, not predator. He was gulled, abused, defrauded, deceived, lied to, and eventually confined in a debtors' prison. He had come to London from the Continent, as so many had before him, in search of "liberty."

A good deal of the count's miserable experience in this London sojourn can be attributed to linguistic difficulties. The systematic study of modern foreign languages, with the partial exception of French, was rarely a part of the old educational system. Indeed, the old meaning of the word "literate"—indicating a capacity to read and write the *Latin* language—survived well into the eighteenth century. Whatever education the young Balsamo/Cagliostro had received in Italy would have been based in the ancient tongue, in which most of his alchemical sources would also have been written, as well as much even contemporary medical literature. (Casanova's claim that Cagliostro could read no language seems to be absurd.) International travelers often learned the languages of their adopted homelands, to the extent they did learn them, by immersion in the culture. Standards were rather low. In England it was socially acceptable for an approved visitor speaking execrable English to mingle even in the best society.

What is acceptable, however, is not always prudent or advantageous. Many of Cagliostro's difficulties in London were initiated or exacerbated by his poor command of the native language. He more than once put his signature to a paper he clearly had not read or understood. Trouble also came to him through his dependence upon interpreters, such as the multilingual Portuguese Madame Blavery, who had early befriended Serafina. French he seems to have eventually mastered to an acceptably proficient degree, and this allowed him to travel in Masonic circles in such places as Courland (the Baltic region), Poland, and Russia without ever having to use the local languages at all.

CAGLIOSTRO.

Pour savoir ce qu'il est il faudroit être lui même.

It is difficult to discern a wizard in this popular image of a domesticated Count Cagliostro.

His time in London was of course not merely a series of disasters and persecutions. His declared intention was to concentrate on his chemical investigations, and he did spend many hours in his laboratory. These efforts did not exclude a healing ministry of a quasi-mesmeric character—though unlike Mesmer himself, Cagliostro did not undertake to heal in public, treating his "gift" as medical procedure rather than prodigy to be exhibited. He also yielded to the importunities of many for various kinds of "spiritual consultations," which were in effect *séances* as they would more fully develop in the next century. There is a very clear lineal descent from Cagliostro to Madame Helena

Blavatsky a hundred years later. Indeed, Blavatsky wrote an essay on Cagliostro, in which she expressed a qualified admiration. According to her, all Cagliostro's problems derived from a single cause: his disastrous marriage to Serafina. This is an idea that reappears in various mutations throughout the pro-Cagliostro literature.

As his *séances* were to become famous throughout Europe, we may say a word of their London origins. The word *séance*, "a sitting" as in the gathering of a group or committee for consequential business, suggests the French origin of the institution, and French was the language normally employed. The meetings often began with a secular prayer for guidance or enlightenment directed to "the Great Architect of the Universe," the standard Masonic appellation for God, which had become general in such circles. Cagliostro often followed the French convention, also, of using children as the intermediaries of spiritual communication. The idea of childish innocence is of nearly universal cultural appearance. Jesus in a famous saying had demanded that little children be allowed to approach him, "for of such is the kingdom of God." The notion that children are closer to some primal state of innocent felicity, only later to be ruined by the sophistications and corruptions of the world, is the subject of a famous Romantic poem, Wordsworth's "Ode: Intimations of Immortality":

> *But trailing clouds of glory do we come*
> *From God, who is our home:*
> *Heaven lies about us in our infancy!*
> *Shades of the prison-house begin to close*
> *Upon the growing Boy . . .*

The terminology of these child mediums (as we have seen) was appropriately tender: if male, *pupille*; if female, *colombe*. The frankness and freshness of infantile innocence was supposed to disarm the wariness of skeptics, but of course from another perspective it might just as well increase it.

Cagliostro's formal initiation into the Masonic Order took place during this period in London, but its actual details have been clouded by Masonic legend, one particularly fascinating detail being the suggestion that his sponsor was the famous comte de Saint-Germain. The blackmailer Morande, who does not make that claim, reports that the initiation occurred at the Esperance Lodge, which held its meetings at the King's Head in Gerard Street. This part is probably true, as it seems to be corroborated by the fact that the proprietor of the King's Head, a man named O'Reilly, later befriended Cagliostro during his worst difficulties, and secured his release from jail.

As no other opportunity will occur to introduce the sire de Saint-Germain—whether or not he had any actual part in Cagliostro's Freemasonry—I must grasp this one. Auguste Viatte, whose *Sources occultes du Romantisme* remains after fifty years an indispensable guide, regarded Saint-Germain as the period's most successful type of the occultist-adventurer. He was more successful than Cagliostro precisely in the fact that his *incognito* was never penetrated, his true identity never revealed. In the murky world of shadows in which he lived and operated, his strange teachings could more easily pass for light. For Saint-Germain there was no family Balsamo, and no mean streets of Palermo. His mystery remained open-ended. So Pierre Chevallier, the puckish historian of French Freemasonry, could summarize it thus: "Some believed that he was the son of the widow of King Carlos II of Spain, Marie of Neufbourg; others took him for a Portuguese Jew." Of course Cagliostro himself was also for some a "Portuguese Jew," for in all cases of uncertain identity in this period, whether one option be Venetian renegade, Polish *hasid*, Swedenborgian, radical Illuminatus, or defrocked Carthusian, the other will undoubtedly be "Portuguese Jew."

III. Egypt

A strictly linear and chronological presentation of Cagliostro's biography would be insufficient, for the man was an anthology of themes as well as an actor in a succession of events. In London he had dabbled in alchemy and practiced unconventional medicine—though less unconventional then than it would be now. He had held *séances* through which he claimed to be in touch with a spirit world and unseen realities. But nothing in his London career could have invited the venom of Carlyle toward a "Pupil of the Sage Althotas, Foster-child of the Scherif of Mecca, probable Son of the last King of Trebisond; named also Acharat, and Unfortunate Child of Nature . . ." All that was to come later, and it was all connected with Caglistro's commerce with Freemasonry—what he took from it, what he gave back to it. We must pause to consider some of its implications.

In an earlier chapter I sought to suggest that one of the mental discontinuities between the Old and New Worlds was a shift in the general attitude toward *change*, which might be regarded from the pessimistic point of view as a manifestation of morbid *mutability*, or from the optimistic as *progress*. Naturally, such a large shift in perception would have implications for the idea of learning itself. In fact an uneasy debate between old and new learning was a feature of Enlightenment thought, and the debate is not yet definitively resolved even today.

As enshrined in the mission statements of many of our leading academies, the principal aims of learning have been two: the preservation of old knowledge and the discovery of new. There are different ways of imagining the relationship between the two, old knowledge and new knowledge. We often think of a "march" of science, a linear advance or progression, as from water power to steampower to the power of the internal combustion engine. This mode of thinking might be called the evolutionary theory. Alternatively, there is the popular notion of the "scientific revolution," in which an idea or complex of ideas long regarded as settled is discredited, overthrown, discarded, and displaced by another. Human beings must have gazed with wonder at the night sky and pondered the rising and the setting of the sun for as long as there has been sentient human life. The complex astronomical description published by Ptolemy in the second century, a system based in close observation, mathematical calculation, and logical deduction, satisfied scientific minds in Europe for more than a millennium. Then in a relatively short period of time the work of a relatively few men—Copernicus, Galileo, and Kepler chief among them—rendered the Ptolemaic system obsolete and quaint.

We continue, however, to speak of the "rising" and the "setting" of the sun in obeisance to the weight of a timeless habit and our common experience. In the Old World there was a quite different way of imagining the relationship between the old learning and the new, and we find it enshrined in an ancient Latin poem that up through the eighteenth century was among the most famous in the Western literary canon: Boethius' meter on the Golden Age. In that poem most of what we usually think of as social "progress"—the movement from agrarian subsistence to a complex international money economy—is seen as a falling away from a primal innocence and moral purity. It was for that reason that medieval and Renaissance mythographers so easily saw in the myth of the Golden Age a poetic parallel to the scriptural account of the fall of man and the primal sin that "brought death into the world, and all our woes."

The various and perhaps competing "rites" of eighteenth-century Masonry present a challenge to their historian, for it is not always easy to distinguish clearly between essence and ornament. The distinction in Masonic rites was perhaps more similar to the distinction between religious orders in the Roman Church than to denominations among the Protestants, but it was often of burning interest to the Masons themselves. Cagliostro presented himself not as the inventor of a new rite but as the revealer of one as ancient as the Sphinx. This was the so-called Egyptian rite. Its French foundation was surrounded by flamboyant mumbo-jumbo. He claimed to act upon the urgings of his own private genius, the Grand Copht, of whom he was an incarnation or reincarnation. (The ancient word "Copt," now used only of the remaining indigenous Christians, originally meant "Egyptian.") Cagliostro would later supplement the operations of the originating lodge in the rue de la Soudière in Paris with a private Temple of Isis at which he presided. All this was perhaps a mighty maze—but not without a plan.

The phenomenon of Egyptomania (often called by the French scholars Egyptophilia) must be distinguished from Egyptology, the scientific study of the Egyptian antiquities associated with the name of Champollion, the archaeologist who supervised the scientific side of Napoleon's Egyptian expedition. Yet as the historian Jean Leclant has shown in a delicate essay, the two are on a continuum along which it is not easy to find a definitive division point. European Egyptomania was a Renaissance project continued with distinctive Enlightenment flourishes in the eighteenth century. One can go further and point to its adumbrations in classical antiquity, seized upon by Florentine Christian philosophical mystics such as Ficino and Pico in the fifteenth century. Plutarch and Jamblicus were among the ancient "Egyptologists." The myth of Toth, the legendary god of pharaonic wisdom, informed the famous collection of esoteric writings (the *Corpus Hermeticum*) attributed to Hermes Trismegistus, thrice-great Hermes, his Hellenistic Greek doppelganger.

The Renaissance Egyptophiles had been particularly fascinated by the hieroglyphic writing system. For the very reason that nobody could decipher them, the hieroglyphs were the visible proof that there was something fundamentally true about the idea of a "lost" or "secret" ancient knowledge. There is a parallel here to the rebirth among Christian intellectuals of an interest in the number symbolism of Jewish kabbala, which also became an enthusiasm, often among the same scholars. The early European Egyptophiles did not regard the hieroglyphic system as the written form of a conventional sign system like Greek or Latin, but as a secret or mysterious code requiring an esoteric initiation, and this idea did not vanish entirely even with the discovery of the Rosetta Stone, which was in effect an Egyptian-Greek dictionary. The very name "hieroglyph" (*sacred* carving or inscription) could have been devised only by someone unable to read a hieroglyph. There seems to be a natural tendency to imagine that things said or written in a language one does not understand are likely to be more weighty than they actually are. Those who first called the ancient Germanic graphic system "runes" (secret lore) were illiterates for whom any writing whatsoever must perforce be "secret."

Egyptomania took a great leap forward among the erudite when, in the middle of the seventeenth century, the polymath genius Athanasius Kircher, of the Society of Jesus, published his huge *Oedipus Aegyptiacus* (4 volumes, 1652–54). I do not pretend to have read this book in its entirely, and would be forced to doubt either the veracity or the sanity of anyone claiming to have done so. But its profusion of erudition, information, misinformation, and beautifully erroneous speculation provided Egyptophiles with an inexhaustible sourcebook for more than a century. It was, incidentally, a typically "Enlightenment" encyclopedic undertaking, one of the earlier attempts at a universal field theory of all known philosophical, mythic, and religious systems.

Egyptophilia from early times also contained an important element of architectural enthusiasm, especially with regard to the ruined temples on the Nile and the pyramids in the desert, and it was this element that is naturally most prominent in Freemasonry. The concept of the "mystical" architectural unit is not entirely imaginary. There is plenty of evidence that from very ancient times "secret" or "mystical" Pythagorean numerical conceptions were used in the laying out of important buildings, the most common being the so-called golden section, or division by mean and extreme ratio. The medieval Christian architects continued the "esoteric" architectural ideas in the system called *ad quadratum*, not infrequently adding decorative elements taken from the allegorical interpretations of the Scriptures. By the eighteenth century most Masons believed not merely that "the" Egyptian Pyramid could teach esoteric lore through its mathematical proportions, but that it was an actual repository or library of as yet undiscovered hermetic teachings and that, furthermore, its vast stone mass had in ancient times housed an actual academy of esotericism, in which the happy few were initiated into the secrets of Pharaonic wisdom.

One of the perennially engaging branches of the novel is the story of initiation, in which some young worthy is educated by a wise elder in the secrets of the art or tribe. One artistic convenience for the writer of such a book is that the plot can be pretty perfunctory, since the principal interest for both the writer and the reader is in the body of material taught. There are numerous examples from the period of the Enlightenment, two of the most famous being the *Telemachus* of Archbishop Fénelon and the *Travels of Cyrus* by the Chevalier Ramsay. The two are related, as Ramsay, a Scots Jacobite and an important figure in the early history of Freemasonry in France, was Fénelon's disciple in both a figurative and a literal sense, having been converted to Roman Catholicism by him. (Open warfare between Catholicism and Freemasonry broke out only under Pope Clement XII in 1738, and even then it was not universal.)

Telemachus was of course the son of Ulysses and Penelope, and Fénelon's book is a kind of lost chapter of the *Odyssey* in which the young man is instructed by his sage and venerable tutor, Mentor—with such success as to turn an uncommon Greek personal name into a common English noun. In Ramsay's novel concerning the philosophical training of the great Persian king Cyrus, it is the educational aspect of peregrination that is stressed. The pupil learns not merely through explicit tuition but from the observation of the world's great variety of

"men and morals." Near the end of the century the Catholic Theoso-
phist, alchemist, numerologist, and enthusiastic Egyptophile Karl von
Eckharthausen published his mystic initiation novel, *Kostis Reise von
Morgen gegen Mittag* (*The Journey of Prince Kosti from Morning to Noon*).
Ironic or satirical variations on the basic theme will be found in such
famous books of the eighteenth century as Swift's *Gulliver's Travels*
(1726) and Voltaire's *Candide* (1759). At one level the *Travels of Cyrus* is
a testimony to a concept still current, the virtues of cosmopolitanism,
a concept that took concrete form in the eighteenth century in the
idea of the Grand Tour.

The most relevant of such books for Egyptian Freemasonry, by the
abbé Terrasson, drew heavily on both *Telemachus* and the *Travels of
Cyrus*. Its title is *The Life of Sethos* (1731 in French, 1732 in English).
Sethos is the name of an ancient Egyptian king mentioned in the pages
of Herodotus. It does not hurt that it also looks like a Greek form of the
biblical name Seth, the mysterious "replacement" son sired by Adam in
his one hundred and thirtieth year. To this name, otherwise highly
obscure, the French author was able to attach his vastly popular "history of the education of a prince." It is the old story of the dusty manuscript found floating in a bottle or buried in a chest. This one, in Greek,
was found apparently in some Levantine library. Its curators were so
sensitive as to grant permission for its publication only with the stipula-
tion that the location of the library never be named.

Having essayed such a whopper in his preface, Terrasson is willing
to push his luck no further. Though the story of the manuscript is
truth, the story *within* the manuscript is fiction—exemplary fiction of a
very special kind. The author makes a distinction between history,
which teaches its moral lessons only slowly and presents the nuggets
buried in piles of ore and slag that must be tediously searched, and
moral fiction, in which a reader may find history's concentrated moral
elixir. "We might combine and melt down numbers of the great men in
history before we should find those materials for wonder and imitation

which a judicious author will often produce in but a small part of the life of any single hero."

The education of young Sethos involves plenty of travel, but there is a definite emphasis on "daily life in ancient Egypt." Much of the formal tuition takes place in and around "the" Pyramid, or in the temples of Memphis, and it involves repeated "initiations," formal introductions to mysteries of incremental import. The parallels with the "degrees" of Masonry are obvious; but scholars have been divided as to whether the author of *Sethos* was taking his mysteries from Masonic practice already current, or, on the other hand, that the Masons were constructing their mysteries from the pages of *Sethos*.

Art imitates life, which quickly forecloses on the debt by imitating art. The most absurd document in the Cagliostro dossier, certainly the one that has invited the most complacent ridicule, is the "autobiographical" statement taken down during the criminal investigation at the time of the Affair of the Diamond Necklace. According to that document Cagliostro claimed, among other things, to be as ageless as the Pyramid, to have learned his esoteric arts in the school of an Eastern sage, and to be himself the "Grand Copht." Perhaps anyone making such a statement to the police authorities deserves whatever historical obloquy may come his way; but even historical censoriousness might be tempered by an evaluation of the moral authority of Louis XVI's police.

There have been several dozens of more or less scholarly studies devoted to Cagliostro. Even Carlyle's essay, famous though it became, was far from the first. The most profound, in my view, is the old book of Emmanuel Lalande (1912) entitled *Le Maître Inconnu Cagliostro* (*The Unknown Teacher Cagliostro*) and subtitled "An Historical and Critical Study of the 'High Magic.'" Lalande, who wrote under the pseudonym of Marc Haven, was a Christian cabbalist and esotericist, and one of the principal continuers through the Belle Epoque of the eighteenth-century tradition of "Martinism"—meaning the doctrines and school of the lay mystic Louis-Claude de Saint-Martin (1743–1803). With such a description, however summary, it is probably unnecessary to add that his reputation for eccentricity has been controversial; but there is worse. He was the successor and collaborator of Gérard Encausse (pseudonym Papus), the most important figure in nineteenth-century Martinism, and an anti-Semite of such a stripe as to have invited the charge (false, in actual fact) of having been the forger of the notorious *Protocols of the Elders of Zion.*

Lalande was, however, a considerable scholar, and his *Unknown Teacher,* the fruit of twenty years of laborious primary research, is in a class by itself. In an epilogue that in its poetic spirit strives for that of the old wizard himself, he not so much refutes Carlyle as speaks past or beyond him. What, asks Lalande, are we to make of Cagliostro's bizarre statements? He then answers his own question with an extended quotation, with commentary, from Cagliostro's longer narrative statement to the police: "I do not come from any particular time or place. My spiritual being lives out its eternal existence outside of time and space; and if in my thoughts I plumb the depths of the ages, if I stretch my essence toward a mode of being distant from that you perceive, I become what I desire to be . . . Here I am, a noble traveller. I speak and your soul thrills in recognition of the ancient words. A voice within you, so long silent, responds to mine. . . ."

The advantage gained by presenting the police report in this fashion, rather than as a series of discreet assertions from a legal disposition, is that a reader can recognize Cagliostro's actual literary genre, which is poetic mysticism. A paraphrase yet better, perhaps, is the once famous "Ode" of the now forgotten Victorian poet William O'Shaughnessy:

> *We are the music makers,*
> *And we are the dreamers of dreams,*
> *Wandering by lone sea-breakers,*
> *And sitting by desolate streams;—*

World-losers and world-forsakers,
  On whom the pale moon gleams:
Yet we are the movers and shakers
  Of the world for ever, it seems . . .
In the buried past of the earth,
Built Nineveh with our sighing,
  And Babel itself in our mirth;
And o'erthrew them with prophesying
  To the old of the new world's worth;
For each age is a dream that is dying,
  Or one that is coming to birth.

Cagliostro's fictive autobiography is a kind of self-fashioning that puts him within the literary tradition of eighteenth-century philosophical pseudo-biography and "travel" literature. He is a new yet eternal Telemachus, or Cyrus, or Sethos, both surrogate pupil and surrogate tutor. The Egyptian Sethos is the most important of all. When assigning himself a possible earthly birthplace in his spiritual autobiography, Cagliostro had hesitated between Malta and Medina; yet he never hesitated in claiming an Egyptian source of the "wisdom."

The influential concept of "Orientalism" as a web of scholarly misrepresentations that, either by design or by accident, assert Western cultural superiority and justify the colonial mentality has not considered an important Western tradition that has seen the West as a kind of infantile pupil of Eastern wisdom. The persistence of the trope of "Eastern wisdom," and especially esoteric wisdom, would probably make the subject of a rewarding study. Cagliostro's fantastic testimony of long years spent in Medina studying Eastern science, or in discussing Egyptian philosophy with the mufti, reveal his characteristic *garbo*, but the "trope" itself already had a lengthy history. According to the Rosicrucian *Fama Fraternitatis*, Brother Christian Rosenkreuz had spent three years of study at Damcar and two more at Fez, then capped off the study tour with a brief sojourn in Egypt. "Damcar" is the modern Dhamar in southwest Yemen. Its legendary associations are with the ancient kingdom of Sheba (Saba), whose queen, also called the Queen of the South, famously visited Solomon (I Kings 10:1–10) to search out his wisdom. The extended biblical account has many of the themes so fundamental to the imagination of Freemasonry: desert travel, the gold of Ophir, priceless spices in abundance, "ivory, apes, and peacocks," Solomon, the Temple. Rosenkreuz studied natural philosophy (i.e., "science"), mathematics, and magic. In Egypt he specialized in botany, a subject indispensable to the healer for the preparation of his remedies, elixirs, cordials, and potions.

There was another dimension of "Easternness," namely, its obvious literal associations with Enlightenment. "All light comes from the East, all initiation, from Egypt." Eighteenth-century esotericism, secular and anti-clerical though it often was, nonetheless aligned itself, imaginatively, with various real or imagined reformers of earlier Christian ascetic life. The most obvious general example was that of the Templars. The last Grand Master of the Temple, Jacques de Molay, is a cardinal figure in the legendary history of Masonry. Cagliostro himself maintained a continuing fascination with the Hospitallers of St. John, who after the fall of Rhodes to the Ottoman invaders were making the last stand of medieval military asceticism and the crusading ideal on the island of Malta.

The common ideographic link here is with the restoration of Solomon's Temple in Jerusalem, but there is another. Just as "secular" esoteric knowledge came from the East, so had spiritual esoteric knowledge. The *philosophes* rejected Christianity in its supernatural pretensions and did what they could to undermine its historical support. Many of the esotericists, on the other hand, claimed that they were recovering the "perennial philosophy," the truths of Christianity in its primitive and uncorrupted form. They regarded themselves as reformers, and aligned themselves with the reformers of history. The great reform of monasticism in twelfth-century Europe, centered in France, had imagined itself as a return to the fervor and discipline of the eremites of ancient Egypt, Paul and Anthony, the legendary founders of Christian religious life. In a very famous phrase William of Saint-Thierry, one of the giants of the Cistercian reform, had written of the *orientale lumen*, the ancient wisdom of the religious life of the Egyptians.

Cagliostro seems already in 1777, before his establishment of the first Egyptian rite lodge, to have settled upon this Egyptian myth as the proper vehicle of his own program for the spiritual and intellectual renewal of Christendom, a program that he set out to prosecute with something of the astonishing daring of the authors of the old Rosicrucian manifestos.

IV. The Wheel of Fame

Cagliostro left London in late 1777 in retreat. Whatever his aims had been in the British capital, he had failed. But by the time he arrived in Courland less than eighteen months later, he was a famous man, once again inexplicably financially comfortable, and welcomed, indeed sought after by the rich men and illuminated ones of the Masonic lodges. It is odd that these very months are shrouded with a documentary silence. All Cagliostro himself has said is this: "My fifty guineas, which was all that I possessed on leaving London, took me as far as Brussels, where I found Providence waiting to replenish my purse." He should have used the plural pronoun for now, as always, he traveled with his wife. We must fall back on the highly unreliable testimony of the Inquisition biography, and of other mainly negative notices that appeared from time to time in the gossip of the international press.

He was in Brussels, at The Hague, in Nuremberg. According to his enemies he appeared in Venice under the assumed name of Pellegrini, which as it simply means "Pilgrims" very much fits in with his self-image as waif, as "unfortunate traveler," and as one whose true home is elsewhere than this terrestrial globe. It was apparently in Nuremberg that he for the first time revealed, or perhaps invented, his once famous device. Encountering a fellow Mason—a daily occurrence, of course—he let drop the "Mason word," and responded to the man's request to know his identity by drawing the emblem of the *ourobos*—a serpent circled with its own tail in its mouth:

Mystifications of this sort were very characteristic of the man, who frequently performed gestures or utterances incomprehensible in themselves but hinting at a meaning available to the enlightened. They had a useful purpose beyond the mere drama. They implied, like the old alchemical and Rosicrucian symbols from which they derived, the intimacy of a shared illumination. So far as Masonic mysteries might be concerned, one either got it or one didn't.

The emblem of the *ourobos* says, "In my end is my beginning"—the motto that the doomed Mary Queen of Scots had embroidered in her linen, and that T. S. Eliot, hardly less mysteriously than Cagliostro himself, made the epigraph of "East Coker." The reader knows it has to mean something important—but *what?* The emblem added to the man's fame, which now went before him. Cagliostro's quasi-apostolic tour eastward and northward continued. At some places he was warmly welcomed, in others less warmly; but he hit the Masonic jackpot, so to speak, in the lodge at Mitau. It was a case of the right place at the right time—and with the right people. "As hitherto the cause of Egyptian Masonry does not appear to have derived any material benefit from the great interest he is said to have excited in Leipzig and other places," writes Trowbridge, "it seems reasonable to infer that the lodges he frequented were composed of *bourgeois* or uninfluential persons." The Mitau lodge, on the other hand, was full of occultists of high station, headed by the brothers von Medem, aristocratic children of Enlightenment, whose alchemical and magical enthusiasms went far beyond vulgar curiosity or greed. They were rich patrons in search of a Rosicrucian paladin, and they found him in Cagliostro.

Yet more important for Cagliostro's fortunes was the remarkable daughter of the Count von Medem, Elisa. This beautiful woman, still young, was brilliant, learned, mystical, religious, independent-minded, and bored. She had been so bored by her conventional husband the Count von der Recke, whom she had married as a child in filial duty, that she soon separated from him. She sought enlightenment. In a series of mesmeric healings, clairvoyant predictions, and mysterious *séances*, Cagliostro captured this woman's attention and—at least to a sufficient degree—her credence. It is impossible to see their relationship merely in terms of a fraudster and his dupe, for a dupe Elisa von der Recke was not. But with the wizard's encouragement she came to view his marvelous deeds and occult gifts as the outward, sacramental signs of an inner and spiritual benevolence. He was, as he said, "the friend of mankind." He possessed, as he claimed, an ancient wisdom, that same wisdom of which Augustine had once cried out, "*Sero te amavi . . .*"—"too late have I loved Thee, O Beauty, ancient yet new!" He and he alone brought out the Egyptian in her.

Realpolitik comes in many forms. In order to win the game, one must first play the game. The would-be political reformer cannot exercise power without first achieving it. Cagliostro tried to walk the thin, taut line between the vatic moralism of a proto-Rosicrucian regeneration of the world and the more material aspirations of occult practice. However, he overplayed his hand with the Countess Elisa. One of the most mysterious of Bible passages is the following (Genesis 6:4): "There were giants on the earth in those days, and also afterward, when the sons of God came in to the daughters of men and they bore children to them. Those were the mighty men who were of old, men of renown." In one of his habitual prefatory lectures on Egyptian Masonry, Cagliostro, an early comparative religionist, applied this text both to the demigods of Greek mythology, and to Jesus, born of a union of the Holy Spirit and an earthly woman. He then added, apparently as filler, that *he himself* was the product of such a union.

That would be the parting of the ways. The countess was still too much of a Christian to suffer the implied blasphemy, and she eventually published a book—*Nachricht von des berühmten Cagliostro Aufenthalt in Mitau im Jahre 1779 und dessen magischen Operationen*, or *An Account of the Famous Sojourn of Cagliostro in Mitau and of his Magical Operations*—in which she declared him an imposter. Its negative tone has done much to solidify the historical legend. But the book appeared nearly a decade after the events with which it dealt, and after the Affair of the Diamond Necklace had permanently if unfairly linked the name of Cagliostro with scandal. When Cagliostro moved on, first to St. Petersburg and then to Warsaw—in both of which places he was lauded by some and denounced by others, honored or "unmasked" by a divided public opinion—he had already gained his reputation as the most famous or infamous occult practitioner in Europe. He would be watched by the police wherever he went, but also patronized by the high and mighty.

Cagliostro left Warsaw in late June 1780. The verb preferred by his detractors was that he *fled* the place. He resurfaced in Strassburg about three months later, transported in an imposing, expensive carriage and attended by lackeys. He immediately established himself in upscale digs, where he again deployed the paraphernalia of an alchemist and a medical man. Where had he been during the interim period? "Cagliostro . . . has always been supposed, on grounds that all but amount to proof, to have been at some period in his mysterious career connected with one of the revolutionary secret societies in Germany," writes Trowbridge. "This society has always been *assumed* to be the Illuminés." The chief justification for the assumption is the significant overlap in membership between the Egyptian Masons and the Illuminati. "If this assumption be true—and without it his mode of life in Strassburg is utterly inexplicable—his initiation could only have taken place at this period and, probably, at Frankfort, where [Adolf] Knigge, one of the leaders of the Illuminés, had his head-quarters."

Here was Freemasonry at its most political and conspiratorial; and the "German police-spies" whom Karl Marx would make forever famous in the *Communist Manifesto* were hardly unaware of its potential menace. Cagliostro's subsequent sensational difficulties, first in France, then in England, and finally in the dungeons of the Inquisition, have too seldom been viewed from the political point of view.

Cagliostro's protracted stay in Strassburg may be regarded as the apogee of his career as popular wonder-worker. It was there that the graph of his good fortune reached its most impressive height. We have considerable evidence concerning this protracted stay. One testimony is of particular interest, and refreshing in that it comes not as a libel or a police report but in the memoirs of a particularly knowledgeable and intelligent Alsatian aristocrat, the Baroness d'Oberkirch.

Before turning to it, however, it is necessary to say a word or two about Strassburg itself. Though more a sizable town than a real city, Strassburg in the late eighteenth century was a place of political significance and intellectual vitality, the chief city of the area that was France's culturally fruitful borderland. Alsace was in those days much more genuinely bicultural than it is today: 1780 was not 1870, and the ferocities of national consciousness that dominated the "question" of Alsace and Lorraine in the Franco-Prussian and then again in the Great War had not yet been animated. The region where today Germany, France, and Switzerland meet was both a linguistic and a religious frontier. The French and German languages came together; and Protestantism rubbed up against Catholicism. For travelers from the German-speaking regions, as indeed those from eastern Europe and the land of the czars, Strassburg was the first city "in" France, just as later for the French fugitives of the Revolution, Koblenz would become the first city "in" Germany. As we shall see when we come in another chapter to the remarkable career of Julie de Krüdener, it was a nursery also of mysticism and esoteric philosophies, the sort of place in which a Grand Copht of Egyptian Freemasonry might find himself at home.

Henriette-Louise de Waldner de Freundstein, the future Madame d'Oberkirch, was born in 1754 on her family's ancestral estate at Schweighouse in upper Alsace near Colmar. Both her parents were of the highest Alsatian aristocracy. She was an unusually intelligent and able young woman, and she exploited to the full her excellent education, and the opportunity and encouragement to cultivate her considerable talents in art and music. The family was of the Lutheran confession, and Madame d'Oberkirch was a serious but hardly morose Protestant. A feature of the comparative cosmopolitanism of the Alsatian aristocracy was an almost modern religious pluralism. She was perfectly bilingual in French and German and commanded other languages ancient and modern. She wrote her *Mémoires* in French, which tended to be the literary (and often the conversational) language of the Continental aristocracy from Lisbon to St. Petersburg.

The cardinal de Rohan, a famous conversationalist himself, declared Oberkirch to be among the three most fascinating women of his acquaintance—an acquaintance quite extensive in that category. She indeed fits the profile of a certain kind of "Enlightenment woman."

One recalls the aristocratic philosopher Anne Conway of a hundred years earlier, the woman whose migraines had defeated the therapeutic efforts of Greatrakes the Stroker. The baroness had a wide network of connections within the intelligentsia, and she corresponded with several of the luminaries of her age, including Johann Kaspar Lavater, the poet, mystic, and scientist who was the theoretician of the once popular science of physiognomy. (We must remember that science becomes pseudo-science only by majority vote.)

It was at Saverne near Strassburg, in Rohan's episcopal palace "worthy of a king," that the baroness met the count of Cagliostro, whose arrival interrupted the cardinal's accounts of his recent travels and, in particular, of his idea of raising a monument to the memory of the great French general Turenne, on the battlefield of Sasbach where he had fallen in 1675. Cagliostro's fame had preceded him. Toward the end of November 1780, the baroness had arrived in Strassburg for a short stay. "Upon arriving there," she writes, "we found that all the talk was of a charlatan who had become famous, and who was pursuing with rare skill the high-jinks [*jongleries*] which brought him to play so strange a role."

Oberkirch's testimony has several times been used to disparage Cagliostro. It is certainly far from flattering or credulous. But the word "charlatan" had not yet solidified into a mere reproach. A "charlatan," which had originally meant a street crier, or hawker, by now usually referred to the practitioners of informal or "alternative" medicine—folk doctors or quacks. If one looks closely at the professional medicine to which quackery was "alternative," however, the hierarchical relationship of medicine and quackery may seem less certain than it does today.

One of the problems in assessing Cagliostro is the nature of the evidence. The same problem faces the historian of nineteenth-century Spiritualism, since many of his procedures were similar if not identical to those of the later "mediums." The historians of Spiritualism have been either its apologists or its debunkers. The former have been evangelists and apologists with the enthusiasm of evangelists and the partiality of apologists. The latter have of course scoffed at the very idea of an "impartial" assessment of phenomena for which the only explanation must be fraud or delusion. What is most interesting to me about the baroness's testimony is not that "she saw through Cagliostro," as has been said, but that she recognized amid the *charlatanisme* and the *jongleries* an element of the mysterious, the enigmatic, the inexplicable— and the *beneficent*. "I am going to relate what I saw, quite sincerely," she writes, "leaving it to my readers to judge those things that I was unable to understand."

What she saw primarily was a remarkable display of thaumaturgy differing in degree rather than in kind from that of Greatrakes the Stroker a century earlier. Cagliostro was credited with achieving dozens and perhaps hundreds of "cures" of hard cases. He acted always, as Greatrakes had himself, with an ostentatious denial of the direct financial gain his medical practice easily could have won him. Like Greatrakes, too, his unconventional medicine suffered the obloquy of the medical establishment.

His satisfied patients spanned the entire social spectrum. One interesting, perhaps titillating, aspect of his practice was his supposed expertise in the delicate questions of fertility. In an age in which the continuation of bloodlines still had enormous financial importance, infertility was more often regarded as a social disaster than a personal grief. Among several well-known women who sought consultations at his "fertility clinic" was the Dutch writer Isabelle de Charrière, alias Belle van Zuylen (1740–1805). He also secured a child for the aging Swiss banker Sarazin—and with it the useful "corporate sponsorship" of Egyptian Freemasonry.

In the aristocratic circles of Strassburg, Cagliostro gained the fame usually reserved in that age for military heroes or child musical prodigies. He held astounding *séances*. His one-man free clinic ministered—if we are to believe one contemporary historian who was on the spot—to no fewer than fifteen thousand suffering patients. (That would be upward of fifty a day over the course of a year!) He performed feats of clairvoyance ranging from the humdrum (locating mislaid pieces of property) to the sensational. The empress Maria Theresa, the mother of the French queen, died on November 19, 1780. It is about eight hundred miles from Vienna to Paris. Ordinary carriage travel might be as slow as thirty miles a day, and even the fastest express relay couriers would require upward of a week. Cagliostro, newly arrived in Strassburg, had quite publicly (and daringly) predicted her death to Cardinal Rohan, with whom he had already ingratiated himself. "He even foretold the hour at which she would expire," writes Madame d'Oberkirch. "Monsieur de Rohan told it me in the evening, and it was five days after that the news arrived."

Cagliostro's association with the cardinal de Rohan would soon enough prove disastrous for the enlightened wizard. For the moment it was about to secure his entrée into the very highest circles of Parisian society. For Cardinal Rohan, Grand Almoner of France, bishop of Strassburg, and (to Cagliostro's delight) the titular bishop of Canopus in Egypt, owned, in addition to his lavish Alsatian estate, a great house in the capital. One of the cardinal's cousins and Parisian neighbors, the prince de Soubise, at that moment lay dying in his own *hôtel particulier.* All conventional medicine had failed. Under these circumstances cardinal de Rohan transported the charlatan to Paris in his own carriage, identifying him vaguely only as a "doctor" in order to avoid the hostility of the real doctors already in attendance, who had however by that time given up all hope.

Cagliostro performed a "miracle cure" in the most impressive manner. Ostentatiously taking from his traveling case a small glass flask filled with an unidentified liquid, he banished everyone but the comatose patient from the room. After a mysterious interval he called the cardinal back into the room and made the following pronouncement: "If my prescription is followed" (the prescription being a specific schedule for the administration of drops of the liquid) "in two days Monseigneur will leave his bed and walk about the room. Within a week he will be able to take a drive, and within three to go to Court." All of these things happened exactly as predicted—to the astonished delight of the family de Rohan and the ill-concealed discomfort of the establishment physicians. Everything now seemed propitious for Count Cagliostro's campaign to conquer the French capital as he had conquered Strassburg.

Bibliographical

Some of the problems of the biography of Cagliostro are dealt with directly in the text. The once famous essay of Carlyle has proved the beginning of a long dialogue. There are literally dozens of books about Cagliostro, including many in English. W. R. H. Trowbridge's *Cagliostro: Savant or Scoundrel?* (1911) broke new ground in moving toward a more positive view of its subject. It fell into the public domain and has been republished under various titles. More recent English biographies include Raymond Silva's *Joseph Balsamo alias Cagliostro* (Geneva, 1975) and Iain McCalman's *The Last Alchemist: Count Cagliostro Master of Magic in the Age of Reason* (New York, 2003).

The subtitle of many of Cagliostro's biographies has come in the form of an adversarial binary question: saint or sinner, charlatan or healer, con man or savant? Before Trowbridge (who also used the format but left the answer a mystery), all the answers were negative. In 1912 in Paris, Marc Haven (pseudonym of Emmanuel Lalande) published his life's work, *Le Maître Inconnu Cagliostro*. This book has been the beginning of a major historical revision, exemplified most recently by some of the essays in the scholarly anthology *Presenza di Cagliostro*, ed. Daniela Gallingani (Florence, 1991), and Paolo Cortesi, *Cagliostro: Maestro Illuminato o vulgare impostore?* (Rome, 2004).

Among excellent backgrounds works for materials in this chapter are Frances Mossiker's *The Queen's Necklace* (1961) and the splendid old two volumes of Captain the Honorable D. Bingham's architectural "biography" *The Bastille*, Vols. 11 and 12 of the *Versailles Memoirs* (New York, 1921). See also the bibliographical note at the end the of the following chapter.

Books specifically cited or alluded to in this chapter:

Thomas Carlyle's two classic essays on Cagliostro—he called them "Flights"—first appeared in *Fraser's Magazine* for July and August 1833. My citations come from "Count Cagliostro in Two Flights" in Vol. 3 of Carlyle's *Critical and Miscellaneous Essays* in the Centenary Edition of his *Complete Works* (1899).

7 | *Cagliostro Declining*

A COMPREHENSIVE SKETCH OF Cagliostro's operations in Paris and elsewhere in France, especially at Lyon, would divert us from the disasters that now came upon him, which have accounted for the large historical misunderstanding of the school of Thomas Carlyle. The precipitating crisis was his association—a purely accidental association—with the Affair of the Diamond Necklace. This most fascinating historical episode of the Ancien Régime—part high romance, part moral satire, part true crime story—did far more than ruin Cagliostro. It electrified all of Paris and all of France. It became the gossip of a continent. And it drove another nail into the coffin of the Bourbon monarchy.

My first extensive reading concerning the Affair of the Diamond Necklace was in the book by Frantz Funck-Brentano (*L'affaire du collier,* 1901). Funck-Brentano was an old-fashioned *chartiste,* a graduate of the famous École des Chartes in Paris, the "library school" that has trained several generations of the world's most distinguished archi-

---

The Affair of the Diamond Necklace fascinated all of Europe. Revelations from cardinal de Rohan's trial, far from vindicating Marie-Antoinette as the queen had naively hoped, exacerbated her already bad popular reputation. There were several published sketches of the fabulous necklace.

vists, curators, codicologists, and rare book librarians. He worked for long years at the Arsenal Library, extensively mining in a series of important studies its rich lodes of documentary sources illustrative of the Ancien Régime. A century of cultural change in the academy has left him very much out of fashion. Conservative if not reactionary in his political leanings, he was likewise conservative in literary and historical method, one who believed in letting "the documents themselves tell the story."

But of course documents do not actually tell stories. People who read and interpret documents tell stories, a fact as true for Funck-Brentano as for Thomas Carlyle. *L'affaire du collier* is novelistic in technique and flavor. It is not possible to transform archival documents, even personal letters, into the imaginary conversations that enliven Funck-Brentano's book without imposing interpretations upon them. In any human drama there are people, events, motives. The actual events of this episode are pretty confidently known. Yet ambiguity shimmers over certain aspects of character and therefore necessarily also of motive. The problem is particularly acute as regards Count Cagliostro, but it touches also the principals. Even after I had begun writing this chapter, I came upon Charles Shyer's beautiful film *The Affair of the Necklace* (2001). The principal female "lead" in the historical affair of the diamond necklace was a young woman named Jeanne de La Motte. In the pages of Funck-Brentano, she comes across as something of a Moll Flanders. As interpreted by Shyer and ably impersonated by the beautiful Hilary Swank, she is much nearer to Mattie Ross in *True Grit*—a plucky daughter struggling in a man's world to avenge a wrong inflicted upon a noble, murdered father.

The old documents preserved in historical archives may prove insufficient to satisfy certain generic requirements of a Hollywood costume drama, particularly those relating to horses, to fencing technique, and to human copulation. Even acceding to that reality one must say that Frantz Funck-Brentano and Charles Shyer, while telling radically different stories of the diamond necklace, both tell remarkably plausible and coherent ones. The same may be said of numerous other historical treatments of the episode, including a very readable and substantial book written for a general audience by Frances Mossiker, which incorporate in translation a large number of the surviving primary documents, allowing every reader to become a research scholar.

My interest in this chapter is not the indeterminacy of history, but the role played by Count Cagliostro in one of the greatest confidence swindles ever recorded. The two cannot be entirely separated, however. Cagliostro's association with the affair has been, in the historical record, one of the darkest stains upon his character. That he had some role is certain, but the two chief possibilities—that of engaged conspirator on the one hand, and of innocent bystander on the other—are separated by a large ethical distance. We are wont to appeal to "history" as though it were something fixed and definite like a tombstone, but as history happens it is often kinetic, fast-moving, potential. Quite often in history things might have turned out different. Here an analogy better than the stone monument might be the battlefield or sports arena at the very highest pitch of agonistic contest. In the Affair of the Necklace Cagliostro, already one of history's more mysterious characters, was in interaction with many others of like kind, and all of them moving with the speed and erratic path of soccer players on a pitch.

Historians are not of one mind concerning the larger significance of the affair, but most are inclined to give it some importance as a prelude to the Revolution and its sanguinary episode of the public execution of Queen Marie-Antoinette. The episode reeked of the excess and decadence of the doomed aristocracy and contributed materially to burgeoning popular animosity toward the queen. The queen herself might rightly consider herself a victim.

I. A Strange Alliance

The principals in the Affair of the Necklace, its vixen and its goose, so to speak, were two remarkable specimens of that age, Madame de La Motte and the cardinal de Rohan. The reader needs an introduction to the former, and a fuller account of the latter than has so far been supplied.

i. Jeanne de La Motte Valois

The Valois dynasty of France provided French monarchs from the late Middle Ages through the reign of Henry III, who died in 1589. When the male heirs of the direct line became exhausted, the crown devolved according to the Salic Law to the Bourbon family, which supplied two centuries' worth of royalty, including the various Louises of the Ancien Régime, so well known to us from the history books. There remained, of course, many Valois descendants of varying degrees of obscurity and of propinquity to the old royal line. One such was a penurious farmer in the Aube named Jacques de Saint-Rémy de Valois. Among his children was a daughter Jeanne (born in 1756), who became the central figure in the intrigue under discussion. The family, or at least a part of it that included Jeanne, was later rescued from rural poverty by charitable benefactors, the Boulainvilliers, who removed them to a more genteel home nearer Paris. The family Boulainvilliers had connections with Alsace, and were well acquainted with the bishop of Strassburg.

Though she served her requisite dull time in a convent school, young Jeanne, beautiful and apparently unscrupulous, was wistfully aware that Valois blood flowed through her veins, and she hoped for better days. One day, the marquise de Boulainvilliers was traveling in her coach with Jeanne de Valois when her coachman saw approaching the distinctive and sumptuous conveyance of her friend the bishop of Strassburg, Cardinal Louis de Rohan. The coachmen stopped, and the occupants exchanged pleasantries. The marquise introduced her charge to the bishop. This was the beginning of a connection between the cardinal and the attractive young woman that she exploited in various ways. She interested him in her supposed claims to her family's lost property, now in the possession of the crown, and sought his help in framing legal appeals.

Likewise through the family Boulainvilliers Jeanne met and later married a military man slightly her senior though not manifestly of higher moral character than herself, Marc-Antoine-Nicolas de La Motte, who later styled himself the comte de La Motte. He was probably a count from the same school of accounting as Count Cagliostro himself.

Jeanne de Saint-Rémy, or de Valois, or de Saint-Rémy de Valois, now also the comtesse de La Motte, survived and even to a degree mysteriously prospered in the demimonde of aristocratic social climbers, hangers-on and pretenders, which was no small part of the infirm sociology of the Ancien Régime. The slender means of many of such people, include Jeanne de Valois, was a small royal pension. The type was actually international. Thackeray, not merely a fine novelist but a fine historian of eighteenth-century England, captured in his Barry Lyndon and Chevalier of Balibari the most salient features of universal types. Jeanne Valois de Saint-Rémy de La Motte managed mainly through her persistent hunt for supporters for her legal campaign to insert herself among the spear-bearers in the gaudy pageant that was the court of Versailles. She continued to be in touch with Cardinal Rohan. As he was *persona non grata* at Versailles, it was fairly easy for her to convince him of a fictional familiarity she was forming with the queen. It seemed possible that she might help him, even as he had helped her. This was in the early years of the decade of the 1780s.

ii. Cardinal de Rohan

One of the leading churchmen of France was the cardinal Louis-René-Edouard, bishop of Strassburg and, quite as important, prince de Rohan-Guéménnée (1734–1803). There was no bluer blood in France than that of the family de Rohan, and few men of greater personal wealth than the cardinal. The family motto was a bold one indeed: *Roy ne puis, prince ne daigne, Rohan je suis* ("I cannot be a king; I disdain being a prince; I am a Rohan!"). He was not a man entirely without religious principles—he refused to endorse the Civil Constitution of the Clergy at the time of the Revolution, and retired to a German exile—but they were sufficiently unobstrusive that no one, for example, would have ever suspected him of Jansenism. His distaste for "fanaticism" was almost Anglican, and he exhibited a spirit of toleration which Voltaire himself might have applauded. A prince-bishop and an ecclesiastical statesman of a kind known in all the European countries of the Roman obedience, he was also a notable libertine and a spendthrift.

As he behaved so very foolishly in the Affair of the Necklace, it has been too easy for some historians to conclude that he was a fool. In point of fact, he was rather brilliant. Even in a society whose primary laws were grace and favor, it was no easy thing to be elected to the Académie Française at the age of twenty-seven, or to win among the graybeard immortals the reputation of a fascinating conversationalist. Louis de Rohan was a connoisseur of art and literature. At his great episcopal estate at Saverne, he amassed an important library. Not all aristocratic bibliophiles actually *read* their books, but the cardinal did. One of his special interests was the richly decorated medieval liturgical book. The "Rohan" Book of Hours in the Bibliothèque Nationale is one of the most famous medieval manuscripts in the world, but it was but one of many in his collection.

Above all, so far as our narrative is concerned, cardinal de Rohan participated in several of the intellectual enthusiasms of the Enlightenment. He interested himself in scientific matters. Among the scientific subjects that most engaged the active mind of Louis de Rohan was alchemy. Like many other aristocrats in various parts of Europe, he maintained his own laboratory, and given the fact that he had more money than most, it was rather elaborate. We still speak of our scientists as engaged in "unlocking the secrets of nature," but the image has become a rather tired cliché. Two hundred and fifty years ago, the idea had a real freshness and a vivacity. Today, the word "occult" immediately invokes mumbo-jumbo. If its literal meaning—hidden, concealed—is in general use at all, it is in an unfortunate medical connection with stool samples. But learned men of that age frequently thought of the "scientific quest" as a kind of great philosophical treasure or scavenger hunt prepared in time immemorial by "the Great Architect of the Universe." Hence, for many the scientific quest was a religious quest.

In the early 1770s, the cardinal was sent as the royal ambassador of Louis XV to the court of Maria Theresa in Vienna, which the empress's daughter Marie-Antoinette had recently left to marry the Dauphin of France. He in turn would very soon become King Louis XVI. In Vienna, the cardinal-ambassador cut a very wide swath. The empress Maria Theresa, whose code of personal morality and deportment was in comparison with the ambassadorial prelate's that of a Cistercian nun, was soon offended by his worldly ways. Maria Theresa viewed his popularity with disdain possibly tinged with jealousy. Rather to her disgust he was a great hit with the young emperor, her son, Joseph II, and he conquered most female hearts. "Our women young and old, beautiful and plain, are bewitched by him," the empress wrote to her own ambassador in France. "He is their idol."

Probably without fully realizing it, the gossipy, charming cardinal was walking a fine line, the easiest kind to cross. Soon the diplomat behaved in a way most undiplomatic by becoming a party to unbecoming gossip concerning the young Austrian princess soon to be Queen of France. This was an error potentially fatal to the ambitions of a most ambitious prelate. He was recalled to Paris in disfavor and—in the eyes of Marie-Antoinette—in a just disgrace. There was a very special bond between the two Maries, mother and daughter, that shines through their abundantly preserved correspondence. The young queen neither forgave nor forgot the calumnies to which, at least in her own mind, Cardinal Rohan had subscribed in Vienna. And as the full force of the queen's power and influence became manifest during the early years of the new king's reign, the cardinal surely realized that any hope for future advancement urgently demanded a rapprochement with her. How, precisely, might that be achieved?

Though narratives are sequential, not all events happen in sequence. In the 1770s, a great deal was happening in or involving France. Of continuing importance on the international level was the "rivalry"—often a euphemism for war, hot or cold—with England. French policy hoped through the support of the American revolutionaries to recoup the losses of the French and Indian War. All this, in addition to being largely futile, was very expensive. Meanwhile there was an endemic and festering fiscal instability, a recurrent agricultural crisis, and growing popular discontents. The great historian of the French Revolution, Georges Lefebvre, made the following analogy. The French peasant on the eve of the Revolution, he wrote, was like a man standing in water up to his lower lip. If all remained calm he could survive, barely, but even the smallest wave meant disaster. The appalling excesses and grinding exactions of highly visible aristocrats were not the only cause of popular discontent with the monarchy, but they were a flagrant one. And the apogee of appalling excess was the royal court at Versailles, where *l'Autricienne* (a term of popular contempt roughly equivalent to "the Austrian bitch") played at being a shepherdess in a magnificently costly monument to Romantic rustic simplicity called the Petit Trianon. It had been built by Louis XV for his "old" mistress, then assigned to his "new" mistress.

Popular hostility to the French royals might have seemed unfair to Louis XVI who, as compared with his grandfather Louis XV, was a kind of reformer. His queen having died in 1768, Louis XV had spent the last years of his long and generally feckless reign quite openly besotted with passion for his new mistress, Madame du Barry (born 1743), who vies in the pages of salacious history with his famous old and slightly more discreet mistress, Madame de Pompadour (born 1721). In his reforming zeal the new king had banished his predecessor's mistress from the court.

The defunct king had of course left some loose ends, and one of them was this. Shortly before he died, Louis XV had commissioned from Boehmer & Bassenge, jewelers to the very rich and very famous, a fabulous gift intended for Madame du Barry: a diamond necklace of unprecedented size and cost—a conservative conversion would put it at around $100 million in today's money.

That is not a printing error. The real cost of the diamond necklace was about one half of the real cost of the Louisiana Purchase two decades later. A royal commission once made by a king now dead of a gift intended for a mistress now banished was nothing like a legal contract, and the jeweler Boehmer faced disaster, as did, presumably, many others in his chains of supply and finance. His choices were, in effect, a fire sale—breaking up the necklace and getting what he could from the return or recycling of its sparkling parts—or finding a new buyer. Potential buyers were few. Few but kings can pay a king's ransom. So after overcoming difficulties of diplomacy and protocol, he offered the gems to the new queen, Marie-Antoinette.

Marie-Antoinette has not had what you could call a good press, though it is better today than in the graffiti and subversive libels of the early 1780s, let alone than at the time of her manifestly unjust revolutionary trial. Mark it to the credit side of her ledger, therefore, that she just said no. She never said, "Let them eat cake" to the French peasantry, but she did say no to the jeweler Boehmer. In fact she had done so, repeatedly, over the period of about a decade. The end result could hardly have been worse if she had said yes, however, as the basic elements for the Sting were now in place.

These matters were soon publicized in the manner so much private court business was, in the buzz of drawing-room gossip in which truth and fiction were promiscuously mingled to the detriment of each. It was reported that the queen had demurred reluctantly and under the coercion of the spoilsport number crunchers, and that her heart continued to long for the gems. Boehmer persuaded himself that the queen's apparently final answer was actually temporary or provisional, that hope was still alive. These are the circumstances in which Jeanne de La Motte of the Valois found opportunity and seized it.

The foundation of the confidence scheme was Cardinal Rohan's keen desire to regain the queen's favor, which was far from a secret in court circles. Though we can never know the precise details nor trace in its full complexity the spiderweb of personal relations among all the people involved, Jeanne de La Motte devised a daring and ingenious way to harness the cardinal's wishful thinking. The plan was this. The cardinal must be convinced that the queen's wrath toward him was already much softened and that it might be dissolved entirely, indeed turned to favor, if he would help her achieve her publicly suppressed desire to possess the necklace. The means of doing this would involve a secret, short-term line of credit to the queen. The whole difficulty in clinching a deal with Boehmer was simply a temporary cash flow problem at the Petit Trianon. It would be obviated if Rohan would counter-sign a note guaranteeing payment to Boehmer on a quarterly basis, with the first payment falling due by the Feast of the Assumption, August 15. (It is of later significance, incidentally, that the Feast of the Assumption was the one day of the year that Cardinal Rohan had to be tolerated at Versailles. By ancient custom the Grand Almoner of France was required to celebrate mass in the royal chapel on that day.) In other words the cardinal would with utmost discretion mortgage the better part of his fortune to the jeweler Boehmer, take possession of the necklace, and transport it clandestinely to the queen through the trusted courier, their mutual friend, Jeanne de Valois. The queen would quietly pay off the jeweler according to the agreed-upon contract. For a cost no greater than the effort of signing a piece of paper, Rohan would have purchased the queen's undying friendship. But this plan would develop only organically, in increments, as one step follows upon another.

Jeanne de La Motte persuaded the cardinal to begin a correspondence with the queen for which she, Jeanne, would be the "backchannel" courier. Cardinal Rohan wrote real letters to the queen, who of course never saw them; Jeanne and her confederates wrote forged but convincing answers on purloined or counterfeited royal stationery. Rohan amid eloquent expressions of personal esteem and political loyalty petitioned for forgiveness. The supposed letters of the queen offered tantalizing hope that it might be forthcoming. Jeanne de La Motte at every stage stressed to the cardinal the delicacy of the matter and its potential to explode should the slightest glimmer of light penetrate the curtain of secrecy thrown over it.

An obvious feature of life under the Old Regime was that the titled felt entitled. Less obvious, perhaps, is that it was often true that the wobblier the title, the firmer the sense of entitlement. Jeanne believed that she deserved a place at court, and the will to power proved to be power itself. She prospered in the cardinal's favor. He personally supplemented her small pension, as he lavished small charity on dozens of others. Trowbridge wrote of Rohan that "He possessed all the conspicuous qualities and defects which in the eighteenth century were characteristic of the aristocrat." History has amply recorded the defects. Among the conspicuous qualities was an open-hearted and open-handed generosity, especially to those he thought worthy. Jeanne may have also embezzled one fairly large grant from the Almonry. She was able to pay back, with a certain ostentation, numerous shopkeepers' accounts and small loans she had borrowed from various Versailles acquaintances. The effect was classic. The credit rating of the would-be Valois heiress was dramatically upgraded. Dressmakers practically queued up to gain her custom on tick. People began to believe that she actually was a special intimate of the queen's. She became her own one-woman credit bubble.

Jeanne de La Motte continued to bring reassuring news from the queen. Rohan was, Jeanne assured him, regaining her royal favor. He was eager to believe—*Credere aude*, indeed—but unfortunately, there was absolutely no public hint that the optimistic reports were true. Cognitive dissonance induced in him a spasm of prudence rather than frank suspicion. He mulled things over. A genuine feeling of friendship surely merited some empirical demonstration, however slight? The cardinal longed for a personal audience with Marie-Antoinette, however public or perfunctory. To Jeanne de La Motte he confided his true position. He realized and honored the necessity for strict confidentiality; but he could not be asked to continue his incrementally expensive campaign without first having the opportunity to express his devotion to the queen herself, in person.

As we know from the histories of our own Ponzi schemes, the initial success of fraud often simply raises the stakes for the defrauder both in terms of potential gain and of danger of exposure. Jeanne de La Motte, a former cowherd, had successfully hoodwinked the Grand Almoner of France and an academician into believing a fine cock-and-bull story, but something more was needed. The cardinal was hooked, but he might yet easily struggle free. The payoff would demand yet more daring and more danger to herself. It was at this point that the "Affair of the Necklace" took the quite literally dramatic turn for which it has merited a hundred retellings.

Fabricated letters from the queen had brought the conspirators very near their goal, but to reach it would require something yet more audacious: a fabricated queen! It is not clear how far ahead the far-seeing Jeanne de La Motte had anticipated the chess game she had orchestrated, but her flair for improvisation was as striking as her strategic genius. She faced the formidable challenges of finding an actress to impersonate Marie-Antoinette, and creating the stage conditions in which the actress might impersonate the queen convincingly to a man who was quite familiar with the real thing. She was able to come up with both.

Idling about the Palais Royale one day, the comte La Motte, the willing tool of his more able and imaginative wife, came across a woman who bore a striking resemblance to Queen Marie-Antoinette. She may have in fact profited from that resemblance, for she was a sometime actress from the demimonde of Parisian street carnivals and puppet shows. Her name was Nicole d'Oliva, alias Mme Leguay. She is usually called a prostitute, probably unfairly. The conspirators enlisted Nicole for the starring role of Marie-Antoinette in one brief scene of their devising.

Jeanne de La Motte told the cardinal that the queen would agree to a meeting under the condition that it would be brief and absolutely private; more than private—it must be conducted in absolute secrecy. The venue proposed was a secluded alley of the Park of Versailles known as "the Grove of Venus." The time would be the dark of night. He must wear a disguise: that of a musketeer. This probably sounded more plausible to the cardinal than it does to the modern reader. From the point of view of normal mortals, a confusion of the real and the fantastic was a fundamental aspect of the court at Versailles; the whole operation was, on a permanent basis, at least half theme park. The gardens of Versailles were not a public amusement park, but they were so frequently the site of various kinds of make-believe, plays, pageants, concerts, amorous promenades, Fragonard-style tableaux, and other high jinks among the high-ups that almost nothing in that line would have alarmed the guardians.

The arranged meeting took place—one is tempted to say *the caper went down*—on the night of August 11, 1784. It followed the scenario of the classic snipe hunt. The cardinal in mufti, guided by Jeanne amid hushes and shushes, came to the Grove of Venus. Jeanne then stepped into the blackness behind a bush. Presently a heavily veiled female, very like a queen, emerged from another part of the arboreal darkness, holding something in one hand. This may have been Nicole d'Oliva's greatest and best remunerated role, but it was also one of her more silent ones. The two disguised figures approached each other in the gloom, and the cardinal knelt before his sovereign and kissed her proffered hand. Before much more could happen, the comtesse de La Motte reappeared in simulated alarm, as though the scene was about to be discovered by the Night Watch. She hurried the cardinal off in one direction while the veiled lady quickly retreated in another. Before doing so, however, she had dropped before her genuflecting petitioner the object she had been carrying: a single long-stemmed red rose.

IN HIS LATER LEGAL TESTIMONY the humiliated Rohan was forced to admit that the meeting in the Grove of Venus had not merely convinced him that he had had an interview with the queen, but had "blinded" him to all the increasingly bold machinations of Jeanne de Valois. In the winter of 1784–85 she summoned the cardinal to Paris (he was in Strassburg at the time), which he reached only with difficulty on account of a snowstorm. She had important news for him from the queen, who needed a big favor. She then for the first time raised the matter of guaranteeing the loan for the necklace, a sum enormous even for Bourbons or Rohans.

Cardinal Rohan counter-signed the bill from the jewelers, little realizing that there was no royal signature to counter. Boehmer gave him the jewels. The cardinal gave them to the Valois pretender to deliver to the queen, and they were never seen again—except by the fences and their unscrupulous or unwary clients. The scam, though fantastically successful, was of course a time bomb for the conspirators. Jeanne de La Motte acted with such apparent recklessness because she felt confident that the cardinal, when the truth was finally forced upon him, would choose to be a pauper rather than the universal laughingstock of France.

This theory, at best highly dubious, was never tested. As the time for the first payment neared, the nervousness of the jeweler Boehmer intervened. Jeanne had counted on his going to the cardinal for explanation. He went to the royal couple themselves. Marie-Antoinette knew nothing of any contract, and certainly she had received no necklace. Boehmer took the document to the king. Here was a grotesque, palpable fraud. In the queen's immediate but errant judgment its author must be Cardinal Rohan, and its purpose her humiliation. She already despised the man, and her dim view was largely shared by Breteuil, the royal household minister. Now she wanted to destroy him.

The Affair of the Diamond Necklace was grand larceny on the grand scale. The queen's fatal misperception was that it was a personal insult different in degree rather than in kind from the scabrous calumnies daily served up by the coffeehouse gossips and the gutter press. The essential facts in the case were easily enough discovered even in a preliminary criminal investigation. The Valois woman was a magnificent adventuress. In his desire to ingratiate himself with the queen, Rohan had made himself the laughingstock of a large nation. Yet Marie-Antoinette remained captive to her *idée fixe* that the cardinal was a villain rather than a fool, and that his motive had been to inflict harm and public humiliation upon her. Her insistence on seeking public vindication through a "public" prosecution of Rohan before the Parliament of Paris was a stupendous blunder that achieved precisely the grievous damage to her reputation she sought to erase. Breteuil seems also to have misjudged the situation, and the king, rarely a competent political strategist, fell in with the queen's desire.

When you see the words "Parliament of Paris," do not think of Westminster, let alone the National Convention of the Revolution. The Parliament of Paris was not a popular or representative legislative body, but principally a court of law. It was the most important of numerous regional *parlements*, vestiges of a medieval institution that in the fourteenth century had been a kind of royal advisory cabinet. It was now a legal consistory that might be called France's Supreme Court, in that it did hear appeals of cases from various parts of the complicated judicial system of the Ancien Régime. In some instances, including the criminal trials of peers of the realm like Cardinal Rohan, it was the court of "first instance." It was full of able, ambitious, and sometimes intriguing lawyers, not all of whom were admirers of the queen. In theory, it remained an organ of royal power. In actuality, it aspired to an acknowledged legislative role. The queen was counting on the prestige and dignity of the Parlement to clear her name by condemning Rohan. Instead, it conducted an independent and reasonably fair trial and acquitted him. It likewise acquitted Count Cagliostro.

For the duration of the trial, which lasted nine months, the defendants were incarcerated in the Bastille. For Cagliostro, the imprisonment was an ordeal that left him shaken if not broken. And like so many other things about the man, it has left its ambiguous traces on his historical reception. There were many houses of detention in Paris, but among them the Bastille was unique. Its iconic significance to the republican consciousness is indicated by the fact that it is Bastille Day (July 14) that has been chosen as the national patriotic holiday. Americans chose to commemorate a document, Frenchmen a sanguinary assault on a complex of buildings that had long since become a generally detested emblem of arbitrary power.

II. A Prisoner of Conscience?

We naturally think of a prison as a place of incarceration for convicted criminals doomed to a specific term. This concept, however, was not a part of the justice system of the Ancien Régime. The Bastille was in effect a very large holding pen. Its miscellaneous population might include at any time people arrested "at the King's pleasure," for whom no trial was actually envisioned, arrested suspects awaiting or undergoing trial, and convicted criminals housed for a short period following conviction as they awaited actual punishment—usually some more or less ghastly corporal chastisement ranging from whipping through branding with a hot iron to hanging and dismemberment. (After her conviction, Jeanne de La Motte was whipped and branded with a hot iron with the sign of the thief.)

The Bastille was in many respects quite like the Tower of London or the Castel Sant' Angelo in Rome, the inquisitorial prison where Cagliostro was fated to suffer. Such buildings had been raised as fortifications rather than penitentiaries, and the peculiarities of their architecture reflected the military motive of keeping people out rather than keeping them in. The administrative name of the prison was the Royal *Castle* of the Bastille. The most prominent architectural subdivision of each wing of the complex was the discreet tower, or keep, the original meaning of the word *bastille*. In the Bastille, seven of the eight towers were given over to prisoners. From the prisoners' perspective the effect was that of a group of contiguous but separate apartment buildings.

The Bastille itself was odious in the copious underground literature of subversive tendency that made up such an important part of the capital's journalism. Odious too was the means by which so many unfortunates found their way within its walls. This was the infamous *lettre de cachet* (literally a letter marked with the official seal), one of the principal instruments of Bourbon tyranny. A letter bearing the king's signature, counter-signed by one of his ministers, was a sufficient warrant for the immediate arrest and indefinite detention, without trial and without appeal, of anyone the king wanted to get rid of. Gross abuse could compound the gross injustice, since not all monarchs in need of revenues were chary of actually selling such letters to people who wanted to rid themselves of enemies or inconvenient rivals. Real criminals and desperate characters were often held in the Bastille, but so foul was the institution's reputation as an emblem of the abusive exercise of arbitrary power that detention there could as easily be taken for a badge of honor as one of infamy. After his eventual liberation and removal to London, Cagliostro ably exploited his incipient reputation as a martyr of Enlightenment. He was, after all, quite innocent of any involvement in the criminal conspiracy.

We have good resources for recapturing a sense of "daily life in the Bastille." Rather amazingly, a vast archive of documentary materials has survived, which was gathered together and carefully edited in the nineteenth century. There is also a substantial literature of political propaganda consisting of more or less authentic prison memoirs. Prisoners at the Bastille were required to take an oath that, upon release, they would reveal nothing of their experiences within the forbidding walls. It would be hard to imagine a more effective goad to authorship.

Prison life can hardly be pleasant under the best of circumstances; yet for the most part the accommodations for prisoners in the Bastille were seldom like the medieval dungeon of popular iconography. Circumstances varied considerably, but for those who could accommodate the system of "pay to stay," things were not intolerable. A fair number of prisoners actually lived the life of paying guests or medieval royal hostages. Cardinal de Rohan, for example, despite being the object of continual royal displeasure, didn't have too bad a time. He was buffered by his own resources, which allowed him to cater his own food when desired. On one occasion he gave a dinner party for twenty of his friends.

Many of the memoirs complain of oppressive conditions, poor food, and unhealthy sanitary arrangements, as well as of high-handed and despotic actions on the part of the prison governor (warden) or of turnkeys. There was no *routine* application of torture, though shackles and restraints were used in many eighteenth-century prisons with a frequency we would find unnecessary and cruel. Nonetheless, like many others Cagliostro was grievously abused, even if his torments were largely psychological.

His situation was in fact very grave. His primary association with the plot came from his close friendship with Cardinal Rohan, who remained throughout the special object of Marie-Antoinette's fury. Even without the grosser forms of torture, his treatment during his confinement was both harsh and cruel. Though he potentially faced drastic punishment—indeed, capital punishment if found guilty of *lèse-majesté*—his greatest concern was for his wife Serafina. In fact she herself had been thrown into one of the towers of the Bastille shortly after Cagliostro's own imprisonment. But the prison authorities repeatedly lied to him about this and other matters of deep concern to him. Many of the deceptive or coercive interrogation techniques that reached their point of refinement in the police states of the twentieth century were already in use, and they were used on the hapless count. His incoming mail was intercepted and often confiscated. His outgoing letters often got no further than the turnkey's hands. He had no access to the press.

This last restriction was particularly severe. Rohan and Jeanne de La Motte were the principal defendants, and Cagliostro was actually exposed to the court only sparingly, too sparingly to see the larger shape of things. The trial excited enormous interest in Paris, and although it was by no means "public" in the modern sense, it might as well have been. Leakers and spin doctors kept up a steady flow of information, a good deal of it surprisingly accurate; and the press dwelt with loving detail on all of it. Had Cagliostro been able to see some of these materials, he surely would have grasped that it was the queen rather than the cardinal who was in the greater trouble.

THERE IS ALMOST ALWAYS a political dimension to history—by which I mean to the writing and interpretation of history—so that the historiography of the Affair of the Necklace has remained to a degree controversial on political grounds. Funck-Brentano's book, mentioned earlier, was attacked almost immediately both on the grounds that it was unoriginal (if not plagiarized) and that it was politically reactionary. According to one way of thinking, to exculpate both Marie-Antoinette and the cardinal, as Funck-Brentano had done, was in a certain sense to exculpate the Ancien Régime at the expense of the incipient revolutionary spirit. Nonetheless, after a century or more of study and analysis it remains most probable that the queen had known nothing about any effort to secure the gems on her behalf, and that Cardinal Rohan's humiliating testimony before the tribunal was true in its essential points. Jeanne de La Motte Valois was flagrantly guilty of fraud, and her husband nearly as much so. The theatrical strumpet Nicole d'Oliva probably didn't know all the details of the plot, but she certainly knew it was a scam.

What about Count Cagliostro? Jeanne de La Motte was vehement in her accusation that he was a conspirator, and that has often been the judgment of history as well. Like Rohan he was acquitted by the judges of the Parlement, and his treatment would win for him among political liberals the reputation of a victim of tyranny. In fact, however, his reputation "in society" was now ruined beyond repair. There can be no doubt that it was his association with the Affair of the Necklace that marked the beginning of his sharp decline.

Yet common sense argues for his innocence. He was simply in the right place at the wrong time. For the right place for Cagliostro was ever in the corridors of the wealthy and the influential, in the *salons* of interesting people, amid the votaries of esotericism around the fringes of the Enlightenment and sometimes closer to its core.

It is not, however, an open-and-shut case. Since the time of the Russian Revolution and the emergence of a "science" of revolution such as that attributed to Lenin, the idea has from time to time been advanced that Cagliostro might have been a covert agent of the Illuminati or some other German secret society. According to this theory, he seized the opportunity to involve himself in an agitation that helped speed the advent of the Revolution. Many historians have been tempted to see in these highly public events of 1784–85 a kind of prelude to the more violent events of 1789. That would, of course, have required a clairvoyance beyond the common or garden kind that Cagliostro normally practiced.

The more material motive of the plot had always been money, money to be squeezed from cardinal de Rohan. A plausible conspiratorial role for Cagliostro would have been the exercise of his influence in encouraging Rohan to take the bait. Since it is pretty clear that Jeanne was trying to join the high aristocracy rather than destroy it, the only thing she could have offered the wizard was a part of the swag. But he already had a part of the swag. He was the cardinal's friend, and nothing in the demonstrated character of either man leads us to think it was other than a frank and generous friendship. They were fellow men of science. The cardinal's sumptuous lodgings—both at Saverne in Alsace and (quite as important for Cagliostro) in the magnificent hôtel de Rohan in the rue Vieille du Temple in Paris, were open to Cagliostro with their libraries, their laboratories, and perhaps above all with their contacts.

There is furthermore Cagliostro's explicit testimony to the court. He countered Jeanne de La Motte's charges of collusion by saying that he had suspected her all along, and that he had on several occasions warned the cardinal that she was an adventuress. The cardinal did not accuse Cagliostro, and seems at least indirectly to have confirmed his testimony when he confessed that after a certain point he had become entirely "blinded" to Jeanne's operations.

Cagliostro had conspicuous faults, perhaps, but the lust for money and the lust for women were not among them. In these matters he has to be judged against the "control group" of socially obsessed international aristocracy among whom he moved. He struggled, at times desperately, to maintain an appropriate external manifestation of his station. But he never took a fee for his medical work, beyond actual reimbursement, in a situation in which he could have made a small fortune. And unlike the cardinal, whose sex life does not seem to have been too severely constrained by any inconvenience of his votive chastity, Cagliostro was a happily married man and a loving husband. One of the most poignant aspects of his long incarceration in the Bastille was the obvious sincerity of his deep concern for the unknown fate of Serafina.

III. The Return to London

London was not the only destination of those summarily expelled from France beneath royal displeasure, but it might be said to have been the destination of choice. It was to London that the exiled Cagliostro almost inevitably returned. There was a very large French population in the English capital, including numerous distinguished descendants of the Huguenot diaspora. There were likewise other martyrs to liberty. Of course there were also, inevitably, numerous criminals on the lam. Jeanne de La Motte upon escaping from the prison of the Salpêtrière in 1787 fled there with her branded bosom, as her disreputable husband had fled earlier with a bag full of loose diamonds. As a result, for more or less good reasons, even before the Revolutionary emigration London was crawling with French police agents, informers, spies, *agents provocateurs*, bounty hunters, and adventurers. Cagliostro's London retreat was greatly troubled by one of these shadowy figures, the fascinating and repellent Charles Théveneau de Morande.

Théveneau de Morande was a man of parts, and we must return to him presently—after considering, briefly, the important arena in which the two men contested. That was the court of public opinion, in which most of the pleading, whether for the prosecution or for the defense, was conducted in the public press.

The historian Robert Darnton, perhaps the world's leading authority on broader cultural implications of the print culture of the Enlightenment period, has written with equal grace and erudition about a kind of literary demimonde in which gossip, slander, satire, subversion, and pornography vied with one another in transgression for the favors of an eager public. Of course it was more pleasant to read about others' iniquities than about one's own. We have seen that people could and did write "libels" for the sole purpose of extorting money from victims able to pay *not* to have them published. But they also wrote salacious books that commanded large, often international audiences. Some of the more famous French pornographers of the period, such as the marquis de Sade (1740–1814) and Nicolas-Edme Rétif (1734–1806), are read today in elegant and learnedly annotated editions, practically oozing with redeeming social value.

In London, the vile Théveneau de Morande was probably the king of the yellow journalists. Morande has recently been the subject of a rich and beautifully written biography by the historian Simon Burrows: *A King's Ransom: The Life of Charles Théveneau de Morande, Blackmailer, Scandalmonger, and Master-Spy* (New York, 2010). This fine book, while resting upon deeply researched scholarship, is attractively accessible to a general reader, and I have profited by consulting it. I do have one small qualification. Burrows treats Cagliostro in a conventional and monochromatic Carlylian way simply as "the greatest charlatan of the eighteenth century." In 1771, writing anonymously of course, Morande made a very famous contribution to the literature of scandal: the *Gazetier cuirassé* (*The Armor-Plated Gazetteer, or Scandalous Anecdotes of the Court of France*). This publication, writes Burrows, was the man's "masterpiece. It offered a heady mixture of pithy invective, informational soundbites and political satire, together with scurrilous gossip, innuendo and sexual defamation. It was instantly recognized as a uniquely scandalous, toxic and dangerous pamphlet, and for many years its very title was a term of opprobrium." It was full of insult, defamation, blasphemy, and depravity. It was of course also *seriously* illegal. It sold for a guinea, and it made a bundle.

Théveneau de Morande was the master of many arts, most of them dark, and through the practice of one of them, journalism, he has had a decisive influence on the creation of the Cagliostro legend. For a good deal of what the world has known about Cagliostro, or thought it has known, derives from some articles published in Morande's paper, the *Courier de l'Europe*.

The *Courier de l'Europe* was one of several French-language journals published in London, where, as also in the larger cities of the Netherlands, there was a significant population of French-speaking compositors, inkers, printers, binders, and other artisans of the publishing trade. It identified itself as "Anglo-French" in focus. Though the *Courier* was something of a specialized journal—its specialties being gutter gossip and scandalmongering—it still represented an important Enlightenment phenomenon, that of organized international communication. Enlightenment thinkers sought to eschew the local and the parochial in favor of the universal and the international. The lovely phrase "the Republic of Letters" denoted no earthly nation but rather a spiritual concept beyond geography. In the vast circulatory system of the Republic of Letters there were a thousand conduits of information exchange, some private, some public.

It is a well-known fact that the so-called Correspondence Societies were among the most efficient conduits for the exchange of ideas and the transmission of new information; they played an important role in the development of political and indeed revolutionary ideas throughout the eighteenth century. In many instances they were associated in one way or another with Masonic lodges. Most of the national academies of the Enlightenment had a distinctly international flavor. To this very day—a day of multiple means of electronic communication—learned societies often have their sections of "Corresponding Fellows" in foreign parts. Remember, this was a world in which practically nobody who was anybody spent less than two hours a day conducting private correspondence, and some expended considerably more.

The Enlightenment witnessed also the rise of the modern periodical. Every European capital saw the appearance of more or less "learned" journals, some of which were intentionally designed to popularize specialized knowledge for burgeoning popular audiences. Among the most famous such journals was the *Gentleman's Magazine*, founded in London in the 1730s. This publication appears to have introduced the modern meaning of "magazine" into the English language. Before that, the word meant a warehouse or storehouse, particularly a repository for arms and munitions. Magazines now became storehouses of facts, ideas, and miscellaneous information, periodic and incremental additions to the *Encyclopédie*.

It would be a mistake, however, to imagine that the international press was universally high-minded. Gutenberg is today associated with the printing of an extremely expensive book in Latin; but nearly since the invention of modern printing in the mid-fifteenth century there had always been a "popular" press, specializing in relatively cheap goods such as religious emblems, prayers, and secular broadsheets. The market for such items only increased during the period that the incremental learning of Europe was flooding Enlightenment Europe in its fat quartos and octavos. Often these cheap goods were sold by hawkers in the street—a social fact remembered in the English word "chapbook." Many ballads, broadsheets, and chapbooks were in fact modern "news" of a kind. The Western epic tradition is founded in the poetic memorialization of great deeds. Many of the Border ballads from the medieval twilight began with actual historical personages and events.

Eighteenth-century journalism continued these traditions and expanded them greatly. The genres of the newspaper and the novel (the *nouvelles* of course being "news") not unsurprisingly develop together. The personality columns and suggestive centerfolds of the contemporary popular press carry on, in attenuated form, two great traditions of the Enlightenment: gossip and pornography.

One favorite genre of the eighteenth-century novel is epistolary—that is, composed of an imagined exchange of letters. Very famous early English and French examples would include Richardson's *Pamela* and *Clarissa* and *Les liaisons dangereuses* of Choderlos de Laclos. In a later chapter we shall have occasion to review a once famous episto-lary novel, the *Valérie* of Julie de Krüdener. It is not surprising, there-fore, that one of the most popular genres of popular journalism was likewise the letter, actual or fictive.

In the wake of the Affair of the Necklace, Cagliostro was attacked in a number of such letters. One of them, allegedly referring to events of the year 1780 but published only in 1786, was entitled *Cagliostro demasqué à Varsovie, ou, Relation authentique de ses Opérations alchimiques et magiques faites dans cette capital en 1780 (Cagliostro Unmasked in War-saw, or, a True Account of His Alchemical and Magical Operations Under-taken in that Capital City in 1780).* The demasker was himself of course masked. Authorship is attributed only to "an eyewitness." The eyewit-ness states his high-minded goal of public service in an introductory "Avis" to his readers. "This true account," he writes, "will serve to fill a large lacuna in the history of the swindles of Cagliostro. . . ." Actually, the Warsaw demasker is rather generic in his abuse. According to his pamphlet Cagliostro, having earlier abused the Masons in Courland (the Baltic) and in Russia, next abused the Masons of Warsaw with his pretended "Egyptian rite" and his materializations of the Grand Copht.

The "letter" of the eyewitness engages another frequent convention of the epistolary novel in making direct quotations from other eyewitnesses, and especially from the contemporary journal of "M. M***." According to this true relation within a true relation, Cagliostro held a *séance* on June 10, 1780, at which the Grand Copht, "several thousand years old," appeared. "He was quite fat, dressed in white, with white locks, with a turban on his head"—that is, Cagliostro himself in Pharaonic drag. As the scene became ludicrous as well as unconvincing, the Copht hastily extinguished the candles. When the lights were rekindled, after a certain amount of thumping and bumping, the Copht was gone, replaced by Cagliostro himself. *Cagliostro demasqué* ends with a flourish of Polish patriotism. "Thus Poland has the glory of having exposed this so miraculous fellow, who had created such a sensation as to have gained great respect at Petersburg and at Mitau, and who finally came to have the whole world believing that he was a prodigy of science."

Cagliostro demasqué reveals a common feature of the negative contemporary assessments on which the Carlylian assessment would be based. While it accused the magus of incompetence, it makes no sustained charge of venality. In his alchemical operations he appears to have claimed on more than one occasion that he had created diamonds in the crucible. The principal aim of most confidence schemes is material gain—usually the gain of money itself, sometimes the gain of valuable property that can be exchanged for money. If Cagliostro was a confidence swindler, he was a singularly unsuccessful one, as there is no documented instance in which he profited financially from his transactions, including the sale of his medicinal "packets." On several occasions, on the other hand, the man was himself the victim of swindlers. We recall that his first visit to London was one long swindle which, he claimed, had cost him the enormous sum of 3,000 guineas.

WE HAVE ALREADY NOTED that there is much social history in the sad etymological development of the word "libel." In Latin the generic word for book was *liber*, and its diminutive form was *libellus*—"a little book" or pamphlet. The vernacular form "libel" originally meant any one of a variety of brief written statements of a public character, such as the written form of a legal claim or charge. But already by the seventeenth century it had acquired the special characteristic it retains to this day: a scurrilous or defamatory attack in written form, the verbal equivalent of which was slander. In the eighteenth century the word "libel" would have brought to mind a popular literary genre rather than a category of legal tort.

I write in the wake of a scandal in popular British journalism that led to the demise of the nation's most venerable yellow sheet, the *News of the World*. Journalists for the *News of the World* were discovered to have hacked into the telephones of newsworthy persons on the trail of private information. One sensationally tasteless invasion of privacy involved the hacking of the cell phone of a young girl who had been murdered. The hackers actually erased some of the messages in the dead girl's mailbox in order to make room for new messages which the journalists might be able to ransack. Yet as grotesque as all this is, it hardly approaches the excesses of eighteenth-century journalism. The *News of the World* hackers were at least on a quest for actual information. Their eighteenth-century predecessors would not scruple at simply making up stories out of whole cloth.

Sometimes such stories were whimsical in character and satirical in motive. Swift, in the *Bickerstaff Papers*, attacked the astrologer Partridge in the following ingenious way. He first issued a prediction that Partridge would die on a certain day, and then, when the day arrived, he published an announcement that he had in fact died. Poor Partridge was left in the ridiculous position of having to maintain the claim of his continuing existence against the overwhelming evidence of the journalistic report! Satire depends upon a tacit collusion between author and reader. It is in the nature of satire to try to convince a reader that the exaggerations or even pure inventions heaped upon the victim by the author are excusable in light of the victim's villainy, stupidity, or dullness. But very often the personal attack was simply scurrilous.

Lord George Gordon was one of the more remarkable characters in an age in which "characters" were scattered quite thickly over the British soil. He was a minor member of the Scottish hereditary nobility who as a quite young man, just before the American Revolution, was returned as the member of Parliament for Lugershall in Wiltshire— one of the "rotten" boroughs that were eventually abolished at the time of the Reform Act. Gordon was a man of notable eccentricities, the most vivid of which, in the eyes of his British contemporaries, was his conversion to Orthodox Judaism. As this stage of his career just post-dated his commerce with Count Cagliostro, it need not concern us except, perhaps, as an index of his capacity to follow his convictions with radical courage.

His most famous historical association is that with the so-called "No Popery" Riots in London in June 1780. This series of violent mob actions, written about so grippingly by Dickens in his novel *Barnaby Rudge*, are indeed usually called the Lord Gordon Riots. They came about in the following way. The Roman Catholic population of the United Kingdom, a minority not negligible in their numbers, and significantly augmented by emigration from Ireland and the Continent, had suffered under onerous restrictions since the time of the Glorious Revolution at the end of the seventeenth century. Full "Catholic emancipation" would not come until the nineteenth century. But in 1778 the government introduced a bill to relieve Catholics of certain disabilities, the most important of which (from the government's point of view) was the necessity of swearing a Protestant oath to join the army. The motive for abolition was less Enlightenment tolerance than the recognition of military necessity. England was fighting wars on multiple fronts, including, conspicuously, the American front.

Like several other aspects of British statute law, this one had tolerantly subsided into legal fiction. The religious test for military service, though not quite a dead letter, had by no means been rigorously enforced in the second half of the eighteenth century. Some prominent Catholics regarded English anti-Catholicism as a sleeping dog best left undisturbed. They actually opposed the proposed legislation on the grounds that its potential for mischief was greater than its promise of practical amelioration. Their concerns were prescient.

Anti-Catholic agitators of various stripes and motives opposed the bill. Lord Gordon led successful opposition to a similar initiative for Scotland, and now an English group called the Protestant Association, of which Lord George Gordon was the president and parliamentary spokesman, organized a petition, to which was appended a huge scroll of signatures, to present to the Parliament in Westminster. Gordon marched to Parliament Square at the head of a large (perhaps 50,000) and, for a time reasonably orderly, crowd. But after he had entered the building, serious "disturbances" broke out amid shouts of "No Popery"—which would become the battle cry of the urban warriors.

Within a few days the army suppressed the rioters with considerable loss of life. However, they had by then terrorized the Irish Catholics in Moorfields and destroyed or damaged Catholic churches, including the private chapels of some Continental diplomats. They had torched a major distillery—one of the grimmest scenes in *Barnaby Rudge*, which presents the event as an alcoholic firestorm in a double sense—whose owner was a Catholic. But they also, and more importantly, attacked the prisons. They liberated the prisoners in Newgate and in the Clink. Mobs attacked the Bank of England. They destroyed the private residence of Lord Mansfield, Lord High Justice, and prosecuted many other acts of violence more obviously attributable to political than to religious motive.

Few historical actions, including pitched military battle, are less reliably observable or confidently explained than mob actions. That is true even today, a golden age of photography, closed circuit televisions, and satellite surveillance. In the introduction to his classic study *The Crowd in the French Revolution*, the historian George Rudé points out that the interpretation of the French "mob," which obviously played a crucial role at cardinal moments of the Revolution, such as the storming of the Bastille, has been largely a function of the historians' political points of view. Such also is true of the Gordon Riots, which need to be appreciated within the larger revolutionary context. A flurry of quick trials followed the government's restoration of order, and several of the ringleaders were hanged. But of course ringleadership (like kingpinship) is often in the eye of the beholding magistrature. Lord George Gordon was indicted and tried, with his life in the balance. His trial was a major public event, and his acquittal, which he owed largely to the brilliance of his lawyer, Erskine, was a large defeat for the government.

The outcome, however, was regarded in enlightened circles not as an endorsement of religious bigotry but as a triumph for political liberty. In this respect it is important to grasp that the virulent anti-Catholicism of the "No Popery" movement veiled republican sentiments, or at least a strong criticism of absolute monarchy. Gordon emerged from all this as a hero of the "liberals," just as John Wilkes, who had led troops attacking the rioters at the Bank of England, emerged as one of their apostates.

. . .

IN ACCOUNTING FOR THÉVENEAU'S persecution of Cagliostro, Burrows is inclined to find an explanation in the wizard's bad company. Cagliostro collaborated with the "radical" lawyers Thilorier and Duval d'Eprésmésnil in propagandizing against the Bourbon tyranny, and he kept company with Lord George Gordon.

The *political* dimension of British anti-Catholicism was made more obvious in the Scottish debates that anticipated the London riots of 1780. There was a sizable old Catholic population in Scotland, and Catholicism was the religion of the Stuart pretender. The family's ancient religion—not to mention the fact that James Stuart's brother Henry was a priest who actually rose to become a cardinal—was a terrible impediment to the Jacobite cause. Still, James's proponents looked to British Catholics for military support, and also to the help of an invasion force from Catholic France. In the famous (and for the Jacobites) disastrous Forty-Five—the unsuccessful Jacobite rising in the Highlands named for the year of its occurrence, 1745—the French troop ships never arrived, having been scattered by bad weather. Just how serious the potential French intervention had been is a matter of contention among the historians. But Anglican preachers, and their even more ferociously anti-Catholic Scots Presbyterian brethren, retrospectively saw in the episode the hand of Providence and a reprise of the defeat of the Armada in 1588. Lord Gordon's opposition to the Catholic Relief bill being considered in Scotland had been founded in his equation of Catholicism with Bourbon absolutism. In this respect, anti-Catholicism was a gesture of political liberalism and a presage of the political radicalism of the 1790s. It was thus in a "progressive" spiritual alliance that Cagliostro joined with Gordon and, indeed, with most of the major figures of the Enlightenment. It was Voltaire who came up with the battle cry *Ecrasez l'infâme*, which in England in 1780 found a literal and sanguinary expression.

But Gordon was both a fanatic and a genuine eccentric—as his amazing subsequent conversion to Orthodox Judaism was to prove. It is almost always dangerous to befriend fanaticism, and it can be very inconvenient to befriend eccentricity. Lord Gordon seems to have thought that *anything* he said about the Catholic monarchs of Catholic France would be indulged by British public opinion and by British governmental policy. In such false security he wrote a vile libel against Marie-Antoinette—no worse, to be sure, than many things being surreptitiously published in France but unfortunately for him not surreptitious. The agents of King Louis sued. No powerful protectors arose in Westminster to shield him. On the contrary, there was in some circles undisguised delight that he had for a second time stuck his head into a noose. This time he had to flee, defeated and disgraced, to the Netherlands. Cagliostro had to pretend that he hardly knew the man—a difficult assignment given their notorious friendship and collaboration.

IV. The End of the Story

Cagliostro had a couple of more "occult" episodes in England, but his star had long since waned, and he crossed the Channel back to the Continent in 1787 a defeated man, a "premature anti-fascist" of the Revolution perhaps. The ever loyal Serafina, now ailing, was of course with him. Not daring to set foot on French soil, he traveled by the Netherlandish route toward Switzerland, where in Basel his old patron Sarazin was still alive, and still generous. It was in Basel that he founded the next to last of his Egyptian lodges, though it seems not to have amounted to much. Such luster as he had gained as a martyr to French tyranny had now faded. There were so many more recent and more noble martyrs. He had always had his enemies, and the widely circulated libels of Théveneau de Morande had pushed a shaky reputation over the tipping point.

His final travels are obscure. Why he should leave the comparative prosperity of Sarazin's pension is not known, but one must conjecture that in Basel, too, he had blotted his copybook in some frightful way. So he left Switzerland, heading south, which surely he should have realized meant heading for disaster. "All towns in which he was likely to be known were carefully avoided," writes Trowbridge; "into such as seemed to offer a chance of concealment he crept stealthily." Now he had no fancy carriage, no rich patrons, no packhorses laden with carefully wrapped glass beakers and retorts.

He made his "last stand" in the Tyrolian town of Rovereto, an old *burg* (fortified place) on the northernmost border of the Venetian Republic, later to become the scene of one of Napoleon's victories. It is a testimony to the nearly universal diffusion of certain "occult" gestures of Freemasonry that he was able to found his last "Egyptian" lodge there, which he rather grandiosely declared an affiliate of the "great" lodge of Lyon. Even there his reputation soon caught up with him, and we know about the whole episode mainly through a Latin burlesque of medieval form entitled "The Gospel According to St. Cagliostro." The net effect of his stay in Rovereto was that he suffered an order of expulsion from the Holy Roman emperor Joseph II himself.

Cagliostro now made a succession of desperate moves. He went to Trent, some thirty kilometers from Rovereto, where he sought the patronage of Pietro Virgilio Thun, the prince-bishop. He perhaps hoped to repeat his success with cardinal de Rohan at Strassburg. But the archbishop, while very interested in the possibilities of transmuting gunmetal into gold, would bear no truck with the Masons. Cagliostro and Serafina made formal professions of penance, and sought full reconciliation with the Roman Church. It is impossible to gauge the mood in which Cagliostro undertook this mad act, which involved the formal abjuration of all his Egyptian occultism, but it was clearly done *in extremis*. Its only practical effect was later to compound the Inquisition's charges of sorcery with the serious aggravation of apostasy. Trowbridge and others think that he had hoped to escape north, to Protestant Germany, where numerous Illuminés and Rosicrucians had taken refuge, but the imperial ban now made that course too dangerous.

Cagliostro's recent Italian biographer, Paolo Cortesi, has published a few documents relating to this period. On February 21, 1789, Thun wrote to the apostolic legate in Milan sounding him out as to the possibility that Cagliostro, now officially penitent, might take up residence there without molestation. Nothing appears to have come from that initiative, as we find Thun writing again in similar vein to the ecclesiastical authorities in Rome the following month. (We are now within the semester of the fall of the Bastille.) The libels of Théveneau de Morande had been republished even in the press of Rovereto. So he speaks of Cagliostro as a person notorious—as he had indeed become notorious throughout Europe at the time of the Necklace Affair—but now impoverished and penitent, married to a loyal wife, a distressed Roman citizen pining to make peace with her very aged parents. The bishop's plea on Cagliostro's behalf was based only partly on the grounds of hardship. It was primarily a triumphalist proclamation that Religion had reclaimed a famous practitioner of infidel Philosophy.

So Cagliostro now went to Rome, where we find him arriving on May 27. He and Serafina were penniless, and their hope of survival depended upon achieving obscurity. There is no evidence that they reconnected with Serafina's family, or even tried to do so. Rome was a big city for the age (about 150,000 inhabitants) with a substantial demi-monde of paupers and transients. While such a population might be quite good for offering a kind of social camouflage, it was less promising as an arena for inconspicuous and legitimate economic activity. Furthermore, as Cortesi writes, "If there was in 1789 a city in which a Mason ought not set foot, it was Rome." The same was as true, perhaps more true, for unconvincingly *ex*-Masons.

Cagliostro's only means of earning a living was charlatanism, his strange mixture of street-corner hucksterism and folk medicine. This was not a mode of life designed to escape the notice of the police authorities or, through them, of his unconvinced and unforgiving ecclesiastical enemies. By now there was revolution beyond the Alps. Each week news reached the Papal Curia of yet more outrageous results of Enlightenment. And here in the very seat of Holy Mother Church was a notorious "friend of mankind," an insulter of sacred majesty, and an intimate of Lord George Gordon!

Cortesi calls Cagliostro's persecution by the Roman Inquisition inevitable and predictable. Once it began, in the autumn of 1789, we have no historical sources other than those of the persecuting agencies themselves. What I have called the Inquisition biography is really a prosecutor's indictment in biographical form. Having served its immediate purpose, it has continued to prove mischievous for two centuries in the kangaroo court of history.

The quickest way to expose the maestro's heresies would be the damning testimony of Serafina (now Laurenza Feliciani once again). She was already a nervous wreck by the time the pair had reached Trent; now she was putty in the hands of the inquisitors. She told them whatever they wanted to hear, beginning with her spouse's recidivist "Egyptianism" and his continuing practice of black magic.

After some weeks of harassment the authorities seized Cagliostro just after Christmas 1789, and confiscated his possessions, which unfortunately included his holograph manuscript of the Egyptian rite. What more did they need? They threw him into the holding pens of Castel Sant' Angelo. The "debriefed" Serafina was sent off to enjoy the enforced "hospitality" of the Convent of Santa Appollonia. For Cagliostro, it was *déjà vu* all over again. As he had once languished desperate and incommunicado in the Bastille, he now languished desperate and incommunicado in the fortress of Sant' Angelo. Only after several months did his interrogation begin. It continued, with varying levels of intensity, from the late spring through the autumn. Surely the prosecutors can seldom have had an easier case, since no matter how preposterous the charges might be, there was a good chance they were actually true. The man was, after all, "on record" as having claimed to be as old as Toth, and like Hercules and Jesus Christ the offspring of a mixed marriage—human and divine.

All the charges brought against him boiled down to a single accusation: Freemasonry! But blasphemy, sorcery, black magic, and gross impiety and theological error were insufficient for these ecclesiastical judges who, however obscurantist, did have some political sense of the importance of European public opinion. So they added to the accusations a number of charges of base secular criminality: extortion, forgery, counterfeiting, confidence swindling, and whoremongering, many of which had already long been part of the whisper campaign that supplemented the newspaper articles of Théveneau de Morande, and most of which the European public was willing to believe. All these threads of iniquity joined to form one stout cord of "revolutionary sedition." The once intimate companion of the cardinal de Rohan had been transformed to *sans-culotte*.

Count Cagliostro enjoyed the formality of a competent defender, but the coerced evidence of his wife, whom he never again was allowed to see and whom (after a brief moment of shock) he continued to hold in affection, was regarded as definitive. After a preposterously unjust process, the Inquisition reached its final verdict of guilt on April 7, 1791. The terms of the judgment do not disguise the papal obsession with Freemasonry. The most important clause has to do with the public burning of the manuscript of the Egyptian rite. The anathema against Masonry is comprehensive: "making particular mention of the Egyptian sect and of another vulgarly known as the 'Illuminés' . . . we shall decree that the most grievous corporal punishments reserved for heretics shall be inflicted on all who shall associate, hold communion with, or protect these societies."

The blind bigotry of the churchmen was not redeemed by their unctuous self-congratulation for showing mercy on a recreant who so richly merited death, but was to be allowed to live out his days in perpetual imprisonment. The judgment revolted thinking Europe. Even the French translator of the Inquisition biography—happy enough to honor its slanders—had to express his disgust with the Inquisition. But to condemn the Inquisition was not the same thing as to rehabilitate Cagliostro. Trowbridge cites a revealing article in a journal called the *Feuille Villageoise*: "The Pope ought to have abandoned Cagliostro to the effects of his bad reputation. Instead he has had him shut up and tried by charlatans far more dangerous to society than himself. His sentence is cruel and ridiculous. If all who make dupes of the crowd were punished in this fashion, precedence on the scaffold should certainly be granted to the Roman Inquisitors."

The rest is legend, but not improbable legend. Cagliostro is supposed to have attempted a violent escape from Sant' Angelo. He invited a Capuchin confessor into his cell and asked him to discipline (that is, flagellate) him with his Franciscan's cord. The friar happily undertook this work of charity, but the penitent then leapt up, seized the cord, and attempted to strangle him. The idea was to walk out of the prison disguised in the throttled man's habit. But the friar succeeded in repulsing the attack. The papal authorities now transferred Cagliostro to the dreaded prison of San Leo. This was the Alcatraz or Devil's Island of Roman penitentiaries. No one escaped from the rock of San Leo, where Cagliostro died on August 26, 1795. A little later, intelligence officers among Napoleon's invading forces were shown the cell—really a well-like shaft—in which he is supposed to have died.

Bibliographical

Simon Burrows's *A King's Ransom: The Life of Charles Théveneau de Morande, Blackmailer, Scandalmonger, and Master-Spy* (New York & London, 2010) is a major contribution to the cultural history of the milieu of Cagliostro. It is also uncommonly well written. For Cagliostro's ally in his combat with Théveneau, Lord George Gordon, see Christopher Hibbert's *King Mob: The Story of Lord George Gordon and the London Riots of 1780* (Cleveland, 1958).

Two particularly relevant essays in the collection *Presenza di Cagliostro* (ed. Gallingani) are André Boyer, "Le myth de Cagliostro et sa fortune littéraire en Europe depuis la seconde moitié du xviiie siècle," pp. 153–64, and José A. Ferrer Benimeli, "El proceso en Roma del Conde de Cagliostro," pp. 553–75.

Books specifically cited or alluded to in this chapter:
Citations from W. R. H. Trowbridge come from his *Cagliostro* (1926).
The principal works of Robert Darnton alluded to are:
Mesmerism and the End of the Enlightenment in France (Cambridge, MA, 1968).
The Business of Enlightenment: A Publishing History of the Encyclopédie, 1775–1800 (Cambridge, MA, 1979).
The Literary Underground of the Old Regime (Cambridge, MA, 1982).

Henri Schild sculpt.

JULIE KRUDNER

L'Auteur de Valérie a dans un cadre heureux
Peint un Sentiment vif, pur, noble, et généreux
ce Tableau dût être fidèle,
l'auteur en étoit le modèle.

8 · *Julie de Krüdener* Mondaine

CHATEAUBRIAND, A CELEBRATED acquaintance of Julie de Krüdener, once said of her, after she had become famous or notorious in half of Europe, "I have known Madame de Krüdener *mondaine*, and I have known Madame de Krüdener *dévote*." She was always the same Madame de Krüdener. *Mondaine* means "worldly" and *dévote* "pious." He was instinctively using the language of the autobiographies of famous religious converts who starkly divide their lives into two parts, a before and an after, with the "before" section often treated mainly with an embarrassed silence. We find such distinctions for instance in the writings of St. Augustine, of Francis of Assisi, or (coming somewhat closer to our subject's time and place) of Jeanne de Chantal, George Fox, and John Wesley. That would also be one plausible way of deploying the life of Julie de Krüdener (1764–1824), the subject of this chapter. Such is in fact the pattern that she herself, in some of her later letters, seems to have imposed upon her own life. Yet if we are to understand the continuities of that life as well as its dra-

---

Julie de Krüdener *mondaine*, in one of several extant prints of "the author of the best seller *Valérie*." Here the engraver is Henri Schild. The most famous portrait of the younger Madame de Krüdener was painted by Angelica Kauffmann.

matic discontinuities, if we are to relate the elements of Julie's life to major themes and moods of the Enlightenment period, we must divide its "before" section into at least two movements. These might be variously described: the domestic and the artistic, the training in sentiment and the expression of sentiment, the search for fame and the gaining of fame. For before Julie de Krüdener became notorious as a prophet, she had become famous as a writer.

Fame is, of course, a relative phenomenon and often enough a transitory one. Julie de Krüdener is no longer a famous writer. Indeed, so far has she fallen from literary fame that even some experts in French literature know little more than her name, and some do not know even that. Before attempting a very brief sketch of her life, therefore, we would perhaps do well to call upon the intermediary offices of a contemporary, a onetime friend and confidante, a woman whose literary fame has better endured than has Julie's: Madame de Staël.

In 1810 Madame de Staël, already famous, published her book about Germany: *De l'Allemagne.* We shall hear more about this formidable woman of letters presently; for the moment it is the impact of this book that concerns us. At the beginning of the nineteenth century there was, strictly speaking, no "Germany" to write about. Political unification, and the emergence of a definite sense of "German" nationality, still lay in the future. What existed at this time was a large geographical area of petty states, kingdoms, principalities, and duchies in which various versions of the German language were spoken. In some of them major contributions of the very highest order to "the advancement of learning," as the Enlightenment enterprise often called itself, were abundant. It is impossible to think of eighteenth-century music without German-speaking composers. No more easily can one approach the study of philosophy without invoking Kant and a dozen others. From "Germany" came huge advances in philological study. German-speaking scholars revolutionized biblical and theological studies.

Madame de Staël decked out as the poet and "woman of genius" who is the heroine of her novel *Corinne* (1807), in a painting by Elisabeth Vigée Lebrun. Staged tableaux in which beautiful women were presented as historical or allegorical figures—such as Valérie's presentation as Truth—were all the rage. The visual allusion to Sappho is obvious. The fantastic plot of *Corinne* is the vehicle for a brilliant "travel book" about Italy, and yet another tedious exploration of the conflict between natural authenticity and social artificiality. Julie de Krüdener wavered between being the author and the subject of her own novel.

Under these circumstances, the self-imposed task of Madame de Staël to "introduce" German language literature to the cultivated European literary public may seem a little curious. Certain special cultural realities of the age make it perhaps less so. Great writers of German appeared in force in the second half of the eighteenth century, but the German language itself remained something of an orphan. French remained the language of the courts of the Continent, including the petty courts of Germany. Readers of Tolstoy, a great documenter of the nineteenth-century Russian aristocracy, will recall his French-speaking Russian aristocrats.

This was one paradoxical insularity of "Germany," and to it a second was attached. In England and in France, philosophy seemed to have lost its universalizing ambitions. The project of medieval philosophy, best typified in the *Summa theologica* of St. Thomas but amply exemplified by some dozens of others, had been global and universal. That's what the word *summa* meant. The "modern" philosophers of England and France had turned their backs on philosophical universalizing, but the Germans loved it.

Such, at any rate, were some of the explanations offered by Madame de Staël's large book for the ignorance of German culture encountered everywhere in France. Very few Frenchmen knew German, she claims. Furthermore, while German translates well into other Germanic languages (Scandinavian, English), just as French translates well into other Romance vernaculars, there is a barrier forever fixed by the river Rhine. He who would cross it needed a guide: to wit, Madame de Staël.

As a guide, Madame de Staël was brilliant but perhaps partial. She had her theories. Cultural stereotypes are of course themselves culturally constructed, not eternal truths. Our common views of the stolid, industrious, law-abiding German, no less than of the hot-blooded, passionate, or feckless Mediterranean, are of comparatively recent development. Madame de Staël had other stereotypes. According to her, the culture of the "Latins" had antedated Christianity, and melded with it. For the "German," Christianity had been the vehicle of culture itself. There was, accordingly, a purer strain of idealism in the North, of chivalry in its purest sense. For many enlightened minds of the eighteenth century the word "Gothic" was a term of abuse, on a par with its fellow, "Vandal." Madame de Staël is among the first to use the "Gothic" in a wholly positive way, and to charge it with a penumbra of

Romantic associations, which it has never entirely lost. "*The scene*: a Gothic turret at midnight. Enter *Manfred* alone."

De l'Allemagne had a large influence in forming popular ideas about a supposed cultural divide between North and South, between Protestantism and Catholicism, between the freshness of Nature and the staleness of Artifice. Many of her ideas live on today in howsoever attenuated a form. The "American" theme in Henry James was one manifestation of Madame de Staël's paradigm. The conflict between winners and wasters in the euro zone might be said to be another. The denizens of "the North" were, according to theory, especially conspicuous for a Romantic depth of soul, and for a consciousness of Nature relatively free of the social corruptions of civilization. One of the favorite adjectives of the Romantic School was "hyperborean," a made-up classicism meaning "far northern." Among the "hyperborean" regions that captured the French cultural imagination, the Baltic littoral from Copenhagen to St. Petersburg was especially prominent. One hyperborean from those parts is the principal subject of this chapter: Julie de Krüdener.

Barbara Juliana Vietinghof, better known as Julie de Krüdener, became in time the competitor and ambiguous friend of Madame de Staël. The relationship was fitting, for if Julie had not quite been created in the pages of *De l'Allemagne* she certainly seemed to exemplify its principal arguments to perfection. Julie de Krüdener was a great "character" in an age of great characters, but she is hardly known today. One struggles to find a plausible modern analogue. Think, perhaps, of a combination of Danielle Steele and Mother Teresa.

One of the precepts of *De l'Allemagne* was that for historical reasons not necessarily obvious, the North was much more firmly attached to its medieval roots than were many other parts of Europe. So far as Livonia was concerned, the theory seems convincing. Livonia was the old name of the Baltic provinces of the old Russian Empire—what is now Latvia, with parts of modern Lithuania and Estonia. Julie de Krüdener was born into one of the most ancient and distinguished families of the Livonian aristocracy.

By the standards of much of the rest of Europe, perhaps, this was not all that ancient. Livonia had been one of the last places annexed by Christians from ancient heathendom. Its conquest was still in progress at the dawn of the modern age. Chaucer, writing a description of an ideal Christian knight around the year 1400, says that his Englishman distinguished himself "above alle nacions in Pruce." That is, his exploits distinguished him among the knights of many nationalities in the wars in Prussia. He adds: "In Lettow had he reysed [campaigned] and in Ruce . . ." Lettow is the modern Lithuania, and the rather general references to Prussia and Russia invoke precisely those Baltic borderlands, then so remote and so hotly disputed, that would one day be the Livonia of Julie de Krüdener.

In the later Middle Ages Europe's borderlands increasingly fell under the sway of the military orders, those strange communities of warrior monks called into being by the crusading ideal. These included the Knights Templar and the Hospitallers, primarily associated with the "eastern" fronts, first in the Latin Kingdom of Jerusalem, then in Malta and other Mediterranean islands in which the Christians hoped to hold the line against Islamic expansionism. In the Iberian Peninsula there were several military orders that played important roles in the Reconquest and, later, in creating and preserving its history. In the hyperborean regions, where the challenges were rather different and immensely complicated from the political point of view, the most prominent group was the Order of St. Mary's Hospital in Jerusalem, usually called simply the Teutonic Order or the Teutonic Knights on account of their principal catchment area in the Low German regions eastward from Flanders. By the year 1200 all of these orders were, according to their historian, "rich, famous, and effective."

The Teutonic Knights included a specifically Livonian battalion founded around the beginning of the thirteenth century, the date of the first crusading operations in the Baltic. Its knights were called the "Brothers of the Army of Christ," with the nickname of "Sword-Brothers" or "Sword-Bearers." The last papally endorsed campaign of the Sword-Brothers came in the early sixteenth century, on the very eve of the Protestant Reformation. The generals within the order were usually called masters, and one of the most famous masters of Livonia was Konrad von Vietinghof, who flourished in the last part of the fourteenth century and first part of the fifteenth. Many heroic exploits were attributed to Konrad von Vietinghof, and some of them may have actually occurred. This Vietinghof was the direct ancestor by unbroken father-to-son descent of Julie de Krüdener's father, Otto Hermann, Baron von Vietinghof.

Martin Luther had made a special appeal to the Teutonic Orders. They largely ignored it, but most were unable to resist the more forceful invitations to Protestantism offered a little later by the Peasants' Revolt. The old Teutonic lands, as was true of most of the northern and eastern German-speaking lands, became for the most part Lutheran. The Catholic religious orders were of course suppressed, but the Livonian Knights were transformed rather than abolished. Their legendary importance in the history of Livonia was too great simply to be forgotten, and for a couple of centuries they continued to have a secularized ceremonial existence. By Julie's time these orders bore about as much relationship to their original ideals as does the New Orleans Mardi Gras to the preparations for a holy Lent. The recently re-Catholicized Napoleon suppressed them in 1809. There was no greater social cachet in Livonia than to be a Vietinghof of the Vietinghofen.

The baron Otto, Julie's father, was a distinguished man in his time, distinguished and decidedly "enlightened" as well. In a paradigm of almost Marxist purity, he exemplified the transition from landed aristocrat to capitalist entrepreneur by founding and then maintaining a large and prosperous distillery. He was active in local dramatic and literary affairs. Thus Julie De Krüdener grew up in a "literary ambience." According to E. J. Knapton's excellent biography, "his most dazzling stroke was the erection of a private theater, opened in 1782 with a performance of Lessing's *Emilia Galotti*." He later sold the theater to the town, but under a special arrangement that gave him access to a door connecting his private house with a pair of theater stalls.

SINCE JULIE WOULD EVENTUALLY become famous for her religious ideas, it is necessary to trace some of the currents of her early spiritual formation. In Riga, where her father settled, what might be called the "religious background" was particularly rich. Riga was at that time a city in the czar's empire. The official religion of the place was Russian Orthodoxy, but Orthodoxy there had no real roots and was confined to a small class of colonial bureaucrats. Before its temporary absorption by the Russian Empire, the area had been solidly Lutheran. The Vietinghofs were a Lutheran family. The father, not untypical of his time and social class, seems to have found his principal religious outlet among the Masons. The mother was a zealous and devout Lutheran, Julie herself a nominal one. By the middle of the eighteenth century the ostensible followers of Luther had mostly settled into the doldrums of all state churches. Remember Lecky's description of the theology of the Church of England: "an admirable auxiliary to the police force." This probably gives a not inaccurate sense of aristocratic Livonian Lutheranism as well.

Christianity was the foundation of the state. It was a school of good deportment and citizenship, and an encouragement to the faithful fulfillment of political and familial duty. Civic respectability by no means precluded personal piety, but it did not encourage "fanaticism." Julie de Krüdener's mother was an upright and faithful Christian who sought by word and deed to instill religious principles in her children. Just as in England religious fervor, which found itself unwelcome in the state Church, found an outlet in Methodism, religious fervor in Livonia found its outlet in several more or less extravagant sects of Pietism. Finally, all of the Baltic cities, but perhaps Riga in particular, had important Jewish communities. There were many erudite Talmudists in the town. It is not unlikely that directly or indirectly some of her later apocalypticism found its seeds in their teachings.

Contrasting, perhaps, with a somewhat cosmopolitan religious scene was Livonia's retrograde social system. The unusual cultural complexity of Livonia was the partner of a profound social conservatism, perhaps better called simply backwardness. The Peasants' Revolt had changed the region's religion, but left mainly intact the old oppressive social relations. Serfdom, essentially unchanged from the time of the Middle Ages, was the basis for the region's abundant agricultural production. It was a lucrative system—lucrative for the landowners, that is. Julie de Krüdener's first recorded "progressive" ideas—she was to have many others later on—were those of a proto-abolitionist. It is sobering to recall that the emancipation proclamation of Czar Alexander II antedates that of Abraham Lincoln by two years. De jure slavery had barely been extinguished at the time of Julie's birth, and its de facto offspring was alive and kicking during her formative youth.

A "Good" Marriage

The principal modern biography of Julie de Krüdener was written in 1961 by Francis Ley, her last lineal descendant. Ley, an able amateur historian, had assembled an impressive archive of important papers relating to her, many of them his personal property, and richly distributed throughout his book, which is a source indispensable for anyone desiring to know his curious ancestor. Furthermore, Ley had an impressively broad command of the diary literature of the period, and particularly that of his family and its immediate circle. Even without ties of blood, however, the relationship between an historian and his human subject matter may become blurred by intimacy, and the reader of *Madame de Krüdener et son temps* may from time to time have some qualms on this score. One problem is that Ley appears to regard Julie's novel *Valérie* as a rather simply coded autobiography.

Julie's husband, the baron de Krüdener, was of old Livonian stock, too. His blood was scarcely less blue than Julie's own. The age of modern diplomacy was still in its youth, and the baron was an excellent and enlightened examplar of the highly polished professional civil servants seen in the background of pictorial representations of Tilsit, the Congress of Vienna, or the Versailles Conference. Just as it was an age of mercenary soldiers, it was an age of mercenary diplomats. The baron spent his career working in the service of the Russian emperors.

There is a mystery about this man, or at least about the apparent complaisance with which Julie married him. He was more than twice her age. More important from the point of view of the mores of the age, he was a man with a past. He had already been twice married and twice *divorced*. By his first wife, a Scottish aristocrat from whom he parted after two years, he had a daughter, Sophie, who was destined to become Julie's intimate friend and surrogate sister. He then married another highborn woman from the Baltic states, but their union proved to be shorter still. All this was decidedly irregular; yet on September 20, 1782, the two were married with all the usual displays of aristocratic self-satisfaction.

The baron's first postmarital assignment was in Mitau (now Jelgava), an important town in Latvia where we may recall Count Cagliostro had performed important operations. His task was to help ease the province's annexation into the empire of Catherine the Great. There is evidence that for a couple of years Julie may have been happy in the marriage—or if not happy, at least not broodingly unhappy. There may have been something of the admiration of a Desdemona for an Othello. In a sketch written at the time, Julie speaks of him as "a just and expansive spirit, adorned with a large variety of pleasing and useful skills." One skill of ambiguous usefulness, it would appear, was the ease and frequency with which the baron charmed other women.

She became pregnant quite soon. On January 31, 1784, her beloved son was born. He was named Paul after his godfather, the future Paul I, emperor of all the Russias (1796–1801). Young Paul de Krüdener himself would later become one of Russia's early ministers to the fledgling United States of America, and was to follow a brilliant and important diplomatic career in Europe. These were definitely top-drawer people. The stay in Mitau, however, was brief. The baron was to be reassigned to Venice, and in the autumn of 1784 the little family moved on to St. Petersburg where the baron was to receive his instructions and prepare for the move.

The visit to St. Petersburg, though short, was in certain respects formative. The young bride, still only a girl really, was formally presented at the court of the empress Catherine, already in her lifetime being called by many "the Great." There for the first time she met the Czarevitch Alexander, then a lad of but seven years, who would many years later become her collaborator in the semi-mystical political project known as the "Holy Alliance."

It is not easy to imagine the conditions of travel in which the family was transported, together with a considerable household of their personal domestic property, in two lumbering heavy coaches from the shores of the North Sea to those of the Adriatic. Francis Ley suggests that it was during this trip that Julie "began to become aware of the shortcomings, real or imagined, of her husband." Julie had been a "scribbler" since her youth. We even have some journals from her childhood. More important, perhaps, Ley possessed a diary, to which either he or Julie herself had given the title *Journal of My First Years of Marriage (1782–1786)*, in which we find the first but abundant signs of the extravagant emotionality and self-absorbed interrogation of "inner states" that would become a permanent part of her spiritual personality. This diary also records, often in poignant detail, her growing realization of what Ley calls the "incompatibilities" of her marital situation.

These incompatibilities were both dramatic and banal. They boiled down, as marital incompatibilities so often do, to differences in temperament, then in the quality of the *response* to the differences in temperament. Julie loved the Livonian wilds, stark, cruel, and monotonous as they often might appear to others. The baron was not without an appreciation of Nature, but his tastes favored the conventionally picturesque, such as the Venetian canals, in which Julie took little pleasure. Most of all he admired the splendid architecture of capital cities. Julie delighted in rustic retreats and the open countryside. Soon she was diagnosing her incipient unhappiness as the result of a spiritual loneliness. "My tears flow, my heart is once again oppressed, and I have no one to tell of my sorrows," she wrote in her journal. "I utterly lack the sweet and consoling satisfaction of weeping with a friend. I am all alone here, far from all those to whom I am dear. I am here instead with that one who long has for me taken the place of them all, with a husband I love passionately. But it is not with him that I can speak of my sorrows; he is their cause without wishing to be so. Or rather it is I myself who causes them. They arise from a soul too ardent, from a sensibility too lively, from a heart too loving. . . ." It must seem clear to any reader that the phrase "a husband I love passionately" was probably a literary species of whistling in the dark.

A Diplomat's Restless Wife

Their next assignment, and the last as an actually married couple, was to Copenhagen, where the baron was made the czar's ambassador. This posting was of greater significance than one might at first imagine, for the empress Catherine was at the time trying to line up Scandinavian support for renewed hostilities with Turkey. In her journal for this period Julie becomes quite explicit about her suspicions concerning her husband, whose gallantry toward the wife of the Danish secretary of state, Charlotte von Beulwitz, seemed to her to exceed the requirements of diplomacy.

In the summer of 1787, the baroness gave birth to their second child, a daughter named Juliette (Julie). The delivery was difficult and dangerous. In retrospect its accomplishment appears perhaps to have seemed to Julie de Krüdener the sufficient fulfillment of marital duty. She stayed on with her husband, amid his intermittent professional absences, for two years more. There was no third divorce, although separation does appear to have been seriously discussed. But from this period forward the baron would no longer be *the* significant factor in her emotional life, despite the fact that he continued for a time to be a serious practical convenience. Her own mind was perhaps not yet entirely settled. From time to time in her correspondence she mentions vague hopes of an unspecified reunion. Julie judged herself ill, and she set off on an indefinite voyage of recuperation. We have no means of assessing with accuracy the degree to which the issue of health was pretext or precipitating cause. The parting was to all appearances an amicable one, and it obviously included financial arrangements more or less satisfactory to the husband.

In early 1789, Julie de Krüdener set off. Her eventual goal was some retreat in the South, later to be determined. But there would first be a stop in Paris, where on May 5, Louis XVI convened the first meeting of the Estates-General to be convoked in a couple of centuries. She had her own modest rendezvous with destiny, for 1789, so prominent a punctuation point in the history of France and indeed the world, was for Julie likewise a decisive turning point. This was the year that in retrospect marked the effective end of her married life, and the effective beginning of her life as a writer and a doctor of sentiment.

It is clear that by now Julie had decided that the audience for her shared sentiments could not be a husband so unsuited by his nature for the delicate task. It would be, instead, the world at large, or at least that portion of it that was the reading public. What is much less clear is how, precisely, she intended to gain the public ear. She would require first some education in the world of letters, a goal toward which she set out confidently. She would seek out, to the degree that opportunity would allow it, the counsel and friendship of successful writers much admired. And although her plan took a decade to find its fruition in literary fame of her own, it proved in the end to have been a sound one. As she set out upon it, she cannot possibly have intuited that the decade would be perhaps the most tumultuous in the history of Europe.

She took with her not merely her own two children but the baron's daughter Sophie, who now clearly had become closer to the step-mother than to her natural father, a fact that perhaps says something about the human sympathies of both the baron and the baroness. The destination, though not yet absolutely fixed, was some pleasant place in the South of France where, free of the demands of her husband's diplomatic life, she could rest and recuperate in seclusion. To get there from the North, one must first pass through Paris, where she would stay for a season and take her first steps toward the literary *salons* and the life of a writer. A cohort of the shifting, glittering, peripatetic inter-national aristocracy were always in residence in Paris, including natu-rally some from the Baltic North. One index of the increasing scale of travel in the eighteenth century was the large stock of rental properties generally available in the eighteenth-century European capitals. Julie found friends and relatives to show her about and settle her in. Where she wanted to be settled tells us a good deal about the evolution of her self-image. For she was now more and more thinking of herself as a writer, and among the people she was most eager to meet were other writers. She had read two French authors with especial admiration: Bernardin de Saint-Pierre and the abbé Jean-Jacques Barthélemy. One link between the two aging literary lions was a vision that combined Enlightenment erudition and the genres of Romantic fiction.

Salon Culture on the Eve of the Revolution

One of the great cultural institutions of the Enlightenment was the *salon*, which might be described as a kind of domestic seminar directed by a person—usually a woman—of recognized intellectual ability, social position, and personal charm. The word *salon*, of course, means the sitting room or a parlor, the more public and social space within the domestic environment. (In English, the word "went bad" in "saloon.") Within it the director or directrice held open house at regular hours of a specific day or days of the week. The "friends of the house" had a standing invitation to the *salon*, and frequently a regular clientele would develop.

The *salon* first rose to prominence in France in the seventeenth century. Then it was a species of satellite or colony of the court, serving as a kind of academy of good breeding, in which genteel and amusing conversation might be conducted against a background of elegantly deployed manners and social rituals. It was thus similar in many respects to other forms of more or less regular sociability that developed during this period. Examples would include the coffeehouse, the tea party, the Masonic Lodge, the academic society, and in various parts of Europe religious sodalities and confraternities now considerably transformed from their medieval origins.

Already in the seventeenth century the *salon* was demonstrating some of the important cultural features that characterized the high point of its efflorescence in the following century: the prominence of the women who held the open houses, and the evolution of the *salon* as a particular meeting place of the literati. Women's cultural power in the Old World often found its outlet in a somewhat oblique fashion.

For the long centuries of the European Middle Ages its chief arena was the female religious house, or convent of nuns, which from its very inception established a gender-exclusive atmosphere in which women must perforce take on most offices of leadership. The *salon*, operating within the domestic sphere of the private house, naturally offered women the opportunity to exercise the role of intellectual leadership not easily found elsewhere in the public society.

The doyens of the *salon* of the seventeenth century were sometimes called "the precious ones," the term *précieuses* then being an unironic compliment to intelligence and recognized cultural prestige. Among them were Madame de Rambouillet and Madame de Sablé. The former presided over the famous hôtel de Rambouillet, one of the great domestic centers of learning and culture in Paris. According to all accounts, Madame de Rambouillet was a woman in whom a lightly worn erudition united with attractive human sympathy and great charm. Her actual name had been Catherine de Vivonne, and from it she artfully created by way of anagram the *nom de salon* of "Arthénice," a name without historical precedent or any certain significance, yet suggestive both of a vague classical antiquity and of the romantic Middle Ages. Arthénice presided over conversations of such sparkling wit as to attract most of the famous writers of the capital. These included, among so many other once famous wits and conversationalists, the likes of Corneille, Malesherbes, and La Rochefoucauld. The ecumenical attraction of the *salon* is perhaps suggested by the presence of Saint-Évremond (a notable representative of the freethinking *libertins*) and Bishop Bossuet (certainly the most famous sacred orator of the age).

Madame de Sablé could perhaps be described as the Jansenists' answer to the hôtel de Rambouillet or, perhaps, the Lady Anne Conway of the Gauls. She was a Catholic intellectual of unusually penetrating intelligence, who toward the end of her life became one of the "solitaries" at Port-Royal. La Rochefoucauld was frequently in attendance at her establishment as well as that of Arthénice, and actually seems to have undertaken the composition of his "Maxims" with the help of the company assembled. Madame de Sablé's reputation for rigor of thought is perhaps suggested by the fact that the "Great" Arnauld, the intellectual champion of the Jansenists, consulted her in the composition of his famous "Port-Royal *Logic.*"

The prestige of the female-led *salon* reached its high point in the pre-Revolutionary decades of the eighteenth century. Famous *salonistes* of this period include Madame d'Épinay, the friend of such cultural heavyweights as Diderot and Grimm, Madame de Geoffrin, who on Mondays received painters and on Wednesdays scholars and writers, and Madame de Scudéry, alias "Sappho," a novelist of ability, and certainly of contemporary popularity, who reigned over the Parisian Saturday. Rousseau and Voltaire were lions of the *salon*, as indeed were most of the famous French writers and scholars of the century.

The *salon* survived the Revolution, and continued after a fashion into the nineteenth century. Indeed, it survived in transmogrified form in the political "circles" of postwar Paris (such as that of Sartre and de Beauvoir) and perhaps can be said to survive to this very day, or at least to swell the coffers of the proprietors of the Café des Deux Magots. Nonetheless, *salon* culture was on the wane by the time Julie arrived in the capital in 1789. But the same kind of nostalgic time lag that led American writers of the fifties to search in Paris for the vanished twenties world of Hemingway and Gertrude Stein led Julie de Krüdener to seek her fortune among the *salons* of the capital.

BERNARDIN DE SAINT-PIERRE, with whom Julie was to develop a real intimacy, remains among the major figures of early French Romanticism. One of his books, which had then been very recently published, is *Paul et Virginie*. It was a best seller of the age, and it deserved to be. It is a great novel, and one that transcends its dated sentimentality and Romantic excesses. Paul and Virginie are two children of Nature raised in the wild on the island of Mauritius in the Indian Ocean, at that time a colonial possession of France. The theme of course is the corrupting power of the sophistications of civilization as they war against the innocence and rectitude of Natural Man. One critic has said that the book expresses the Rousseauian ideal better than anything written by Rousseau himself. "Man is born free but everywhere he is in chains."

Those chains are not exhausted by political oppression, which is merely the most hideous manifestation of social falsities of many kinds, one of which is the class system upon which most of world history had been founded since the time of its first recording. One could regard its pastoralism primarily in aesthetic terms, as Marie-Antoinette and her sister shepherdesses cavorting about Versailles seemed to do; but if taken at all seriously *Paul et Virginie* was a book with a serious revolutionary potential. *Paul et Virginie* was in a sense the "social" supplement to Saint-Pierre's earlier *Studies of Nature*, which Julie had also devoured with enthusiasm. Saint-Pierre is usually, and correctly, described as a master of "sentiment," and "sentiment" is sometimes held up in opposition to cold Enlightenment rationality. In fact strong emotion, often called passion, was fervently praised by a number of the most eminent of Enlightenment thinkers, as for example Diderot.

The abbé Barthélemy was one of the great scholars of the age, a classical historian, a numismatist, and an archaeologist. He had been honored in his youth by the Royal Society in London, and Julie got to know him in his early sixties just as he was being inducted into the French Academy. His most famous book was called *The Journey of the Young Anacharsis in Greece in the Middle of the Fourth Century*. This was not exactly a historical novel, but a novel in which the history was not background but foreground.

It is an index of the attractive social texture of the old Republic of Letters that a talented acolyte like Julie de Krüdener could so easily gain access to the literary great ones of the capital; but it is also a testimony to her personal charm and, one must add, determination. Without entirely realizing it she had a ready-made connection with this aging writer. Many years earlier in Rome, her grandfather had done Barthélemy some kind of favor. He remembered it, and greeted her warmly. According to his testimony this geriatric literary superstar received four hundred fan letters a year, mostly from women who warmly appreciated his sentiment. He complained that he was unable to keep up with such a correspondence, but this particular female admirer he received with alacrity. She visited Bernardin at his suburban *salon*, where she met among others Madame de Genlis. She began to see herself destined for the world of the *salon*. Somewhat oddly, perhaps, the woman who as a girl had developed a strong interest in social conditions seemed strangely opaque to the large political drama being played out about her. The Bastille came tumbling down, not without alarums and gory violence. She does not write of this. She writes instead of her "nerves"—her lifelong and increasingly oppressive curse—and of her need to retreat to the calm of the countryside. For her that meant taking up residence for a time in the South, at Montpellier.

She was a nervous traveler in a double sense, for she could not keep still, moving on from Montpellier to Nîmes, and visiting far and wide through the southern countryside. It is from this period that the intensity of her correspondence with Bernardin de Saint-Pierre increases dramatically. One letter of particular note records her proto-Romantic reaction to a visit to the Fontaine de Vaucluse, the site of Petrarch's famous fourteenth-century rustication. Here Julie de Krüdener was predictably overwhelmed with "profound emotions"; and she claims half seriously to have had an actual vision of Petrarch. "There Petrarch appeared to me among those sacred vaults, which saw the birth of his long passion for Laura." Petrarch and Laura, along with Abelard and Héloïse and Dante and Beatrice, were one of the emotional triumvirate of great medieval lovers.

She was now (1790) ready for some passion of her own. Returning to Montpellier, she had an encounter with a dashing military officer, Charles-Louis de Frégeville. The circumstances were dramatic. Frégeville had arrived at the head of a cohort of national guardsmen who had come to deal with a band of insurgent Jacobites. There was immediate "chemistry," absurdly interrupted by an appeal from the not-quite-forgotten husband in Copenhagen.

She made many "last" acts of marital obligation, and she made one now. She returned to Copenhagen briefly, where according to Julie's early historian E. Muhlenbeck, she informed the baron of the irrevocable transfer of affection to Captain Frégeville. Details are lacking, but we soon enough find documentary evidence of repentance. Was it founded in disappointment or in principle? The baron de Krüdener was now at least as much sinned against as sinning, and he seems to have been looking for a way out. At one point he was willing if reluctant to contemplate a third divorce, but he was quite worried about the scandal of Julie's traipsing about Europe with lovers in pursuit. He also seems to have had a firmer sense than did his wife of the significance of the event usually called the French Revolution. He proposed that she take up residence in Livonia, with her lover if desired, but quietly, until their affairs could be finally sorted out.

Affairs of the Heart

Some previous biographers of Julie de Krüdener have rather sensationalized her erotic life. She had a passionate heart, and she wore it on her sleeve. For her the love between a man and woman must be sacramental, the union of the flesh founded in the protocols of the heart and mind. Our own great Enlightenment philosopher, Benjamin Franklin, enunciated as a timeless principle that "Where there's Marriage without Love, there will be Love without Marriage." For Julie one should probably clarify by substituting for "Love" the less ambiguous word "Passion." She had several lovers, by one of whom, a stripling youth who had not yet achieved his majority, she had an illegitimate son long hidden from the inquiries of her biographers. She can reasonably be described as a "victim of love" perhaps not unlike Gustave de Linar, the hero of her novel, his soul in love with love itself. But she was by no means promiscuous or lascivious, or even, by her own standards, immoral. As always, we must assess her behavior against the background of her historical circumstances. For though she entertained many political ideas that we would perhaps regard as "liberal," she was no less a prisoner of her own aristocratic social class than were many other revolutionary-minded liberals faced with the realities of an actual revolution.

I have already alluded to what is probably an impenetrable mystery surrounding the nature of her marriage. There was a conspicuous mismatch between the middle-aged diplomat and the romantic teenager. One anecdote among many culled from her letters and her journal offers dramatic evidence of the hypersensitivity and egocentrism that her critics have found culpable. The child bride had unreasonable (we would say neurotic) worries about the safety of her husband, especially any time he was on horseback. One day when he was away riding and she awaited his scheduled return, a rainstorm began. She fretted for his safety and could not restrain herself from setting off *on foot* to meet him along the road—an act that was from any practical point of view foolish and useless. When they met on the road, the nonplussed husband was so indelicate as to point this out to her. Why had she not stayed snug at home? That's what *he* would have done. This fatal want of emotional extravagance struck her like a knife to the heart.

Soon after she came to the conclusion that hers would forever be a marriage of social convention, very far indeed from the marriage of true minds, she sought to bring to an end de jure a relationship which to her mind had never existed de facto. The only means of achieving this end of course would have been a legal divorce. The baron, however, though he was willing to accommodate many irregularities in his marital life, now backtracked on the idea of a third divorce. He no longer particularly wished to be married to Julie. She had, after all, certain manifest liabilities. She could be quite selective in her participation in social events attendant upon the baron's professional position, events that he was inclined to view as marital duties and she as voluntary favors. Furthermore, she seems to have been quite extravagant from the financial point of view. The fatal error was probably not vulgar materialism, but the unexamined habits of an upbringing of considerable luxury. Not to want to be married, however, is not the same thing as wanting to be divorced. The baron de Krüdener had already been twice divorced—a most extraordinary situation for a man of the eighteenth century, and particularly for one in the public eye. His reluctance to accept Julie's suggestion was undoubtedly founded in prudence, in the perceived necessity of following a life of conventional appearance if not of conventional reality.

Historians have found it too easy to adopt a censorious attitude toward the various members of the shifting Krüdener ménage. But idealism, even idealism of apparently the purest cast, operates not within an ethical vacuum but within a social context. Julie, the baron, and the baroness's lovers were all, in their own view, idealists. The compromises they made they could regard as having been forced upon them by circumstance.

The most dramatic episode in Julie's emotional life must certainly be her giving birth to an illegitimate son. Such an *histoire* naturally had a history, one soon requiring some delineation. The event was, however, the denouement rather than the prelude to the major phase of Julie's emotional liberation. In late 1786, when Baron Krüdener was transferred from the embassy in Venice to that in Copenhagen, he and his wife naturally passed through Lyon in central France. They were received by an official named Jean-Antoine Terray. Terray had a young son, at that time twelve years old, destined for a major role in her future emotional life. For the moment it was decided that Julie would stay for a time in the Midi in the hopes of recovering her fragile health.

For a beautiful young married woman to establish her separate residence, as though she were a widow, was perhaps to offer an invitation of sorts. Certainly it is unlikely that a young wife could fall passionately in love with another man had she not already in some sense given herself the permission to do so. Julie soon attracted a number of interested male admirers.

Her behavior during this period of her life was not, as her more severe biographers would have it, "shameless"; but it was insufficiently governed by prudence. In Julie de Krüdener's entourage there was a young Swiss governess who played a very important role in her life as friend and confidante. So great did their intimacy become that this woman—Mademoiselle Piozet, who after her marriage was called Madame Armand—actually became the surrogate mother to Julie's illegitimate son. There seems to have been very little if anything in her emotional life that she did not share with Madame Armand, who proved to be a wise, efficient, and coolheaded friend, precisely the sort of person helpful in tempering some of Julie's serial enthusiasms without going so far as to quench her spirit. Julie appears to have already shared with her the disappointments and sterilities of her married life. Now Madame Armand became the intermediary of her extramarital emotional life, at times as guardian, at others as go-between.

Still the most socially notable of Julie's admirers was the dashing cavalry officer, the marquis Charles-Louis de Frégeville. This young man—he was actually Julie's junior by a year—had gained a certain local reputation a year or two earlier by protecting the citizens of Montpellier from some hooligans who were disturbing the peace. There was chemistry between these two beautiful young people, leading to the kind of unstable chemical compound usual in such situations. In fact they fell passionately in love. No episode in Julie's life has proved a more convenient Rorschach inkblot for Madame de Krüdener's biographers than has this love affair with Frégeville. Charles Eynard, her Christian apologist, regards it as the terrible if vaguely sketched sin, which is the expected prologue to the later sanctity of most of the saints of the Church. Muhlenbeck, at times an impatient rationalist and to no small degree an unconscious male chauvinist, treats it as the nearly comic absurdity of a vain and frivolous female. Others, more generous in their view, seem to regard it as a necessary and perhaps forgivable manifestation of a superabundance of "passion."

Certainly there is every evidence of passion. She wrote at the time that their weeks together in Montpellier were "the happiest" of her young life. For his part, young Charles-Louis de Frégeville showed every sign of sincerity in the nature of his own abundant devotion. However, there were certain realities, which were bound to impinge upon the lovers' idyll. She began to get importunate letters from her husband in Copenhagen urging her return to that city. Perhaps he had heard something, or guessed. So Julie and her lover decided, no doubt with Julie in the lead, upon a flamboyant demonstration of "honor." They would travel to Copenhagen, where with a frankness as painful to them as to the aggrieved husband, they would make a clean breast of things. And so they set off northwards. According to Muhlenbeck, Frégeville traveled in the disguise of a lackey. I have not found the documentary evidence for this suggestion, though it has ample precedents in the Romance tradition, in which for various practical reasons lovers frequently travel in disguise, usually as pilgrims. One very practical consideration was that of Julie's reputation. To make a clean breast of things before the husband might be noble; to do so before the entire world would be tasteless, not to mention potentially dangerous.

There is some evidence to suggest that by the time they reached Copenhagen, where the military lover hovered about for some weeks, the couple had realized that they were possessed not by any eternal love but by an affair, poignant perhaps, but also unsustainable. Julie confessed everything to the baron, who reacted with distaste and alarm, but with a degree of savoir-faire that fully vindicated his high reputation as an effective diplomat. He resisted not so much the situation as Julie's proposed solution to it: namely, a divorce. This question appears to have been decided in his mind already before it was raised— or raised again, as it was implicit in the establishment of separate residence in 1789. Although his wife's occasional extravagances caused him financial worries, he would be in the long run dependent upon the ample resources that he quite reasonably realized would inevitably come her way. This was neither cynicism nor gross materialism, but rather submission to that genre of fact that tempered the real-life relations between the sexes. So he would agree to separate living arrangements, so long as scandal was avoided. Not surprisingly, he hoped to see the back of Captain de Frégeville. Frégeville, who in fact did go on to achieve an outstanding military career, was feeling an obligation to return to his regiment. He could not love Julie half so much loved he not honor more. He disappeared from the scene. Julie was surprisingly indifferent. Although she did not yet realize it, she had already met the real love of her life.

Hippolyte Terray

Even the subtlest of social observers are sometimes reticent in the face of the great events of their time. One would hardly learn from the pages of America's greatest novelist, Henry James, that he came of age in the midst of a cataclysmic Civil War. The great event of the formative decade of Julie de Krüdener's life was the French Revolution. She was a woman of French language and French literary culture. Many of her most intimate friends, and most of the authors whom she admired and imitated, were French. The Revolution dislocated her life repeatedly, and its entire course was to a large degree determined by its exigencies. Yet there are to be found in her copious correspondence surprisingly few explicit engagements with the Revolution or any of its possible larger meanings.

She had arrived in Paris first in the spring of 1789. The *day* of the attack on the Bastille, July 14, was baby Julie's second birthday. Her mother was surrounded by ominous signs and portents, but if she noted them, she still kept her focus clearly on her literary goals, and thrilled at the chance to sit for a few moments chatting in the pleasant suburban garden of Bernardin de Saint-Pierre. Only two years later, in the spring of 1791, as she passed again through Paris with her lover Frégeville, does she seem to have taken full account of a change in the social atmosphere that had already alarmed most French aristocrats, and sent not a few of them into exile. And although Julie frequently expressed "liberal" ideas and attitudes that showed a degree of spiritual identification with the lower orders, she was by any standard a member of the endangered aristocracy. What she saw in Paris at that time encouraged her in her resolve to move on toward Copenhagen.

Among those who had taken flight, or had been dispatched toward greater safety by their parents, was Claude-Hippolyte Terray. In 1790, now sixteen, this young man whom Julie de Krüdener had met as a child in Lyon was securing a peripatetic university education under the guidance of a tutor-companion, M. Petit. Young Terray had been pursuing his peripatetic education in a nearly indiscriminate fashion, taking up academic residence successively in Edinburgh, London, Hamburg, and Danzig. By early 1793—the year of the high point of the Parisian Terror, we may recall—he had migrated to Leipzig, where there was a growing émigré community. So, as it happened, had Julie de Krüdener. Hippolyte Terray was now nineteen years old, a young man of noble parts, handsome, chivalrous, athletic, yet a lover of poetry and a reader of *La Nouvelle Héloïse* and *Paul et Virginie*.

Julie de Krüdener was nearly thirty, at the height of her physical beauty, disillusioned with her marriage, which had long since lost the sexual and emotional adhesive of its earliest years and been transformed into a close but carefully monitored friendship, hungry for spiritual nutrition, uncertain of her literary vocation, tardily recognizant of the political whirlwind that had swept away the cultural signposts of her intellectual landscape—in short, a woman adrift. Hippolyte had his own rootlessness. Information from or about his parents in Paris was infrequent and unreliable. He learned that they were being detained in one of the revolutionary prisons, the population of which had in September 1792 been reduced by means of mass murder. Aristocratic fantasies of a quick collapse of the Jacobin madness and a return of the old sweet and familiar life had long since been exposed. It is only superficially surprising that these two would claim the solace of a shared bed.

A most revealing letter from Julie de Krüdener was luckily preserved by its publication in the collected works of Bernardin de Saint-Pierre. It is dated from Leipzig, February 23. In it Julie announces the reclamation of a long-lost equanimity: "After fourteen months, during most of which time I was suffering from a nervous condition so frightful that my reason was threatened and my health reduced to a deplorable state, I recently came back to a colder state of mind. The fever which was burning in my blood disappeared; my brain is no longer affected as it previously was; and Hope and Nature have once again descended upon my soul so tormented by bitter ills and by terrible storms." She speaks vaguely of the therapeutic agent as "the love of friends," without going into unnecessary specification.

To her husband, now relegated in her mind to the status of wise, old friend not unlike that of the ancient Saint-Pierre himself, she wrote in a confessional mode so oblique as to be detectable only with the use of powerful optical instruments. "I have carved out for myself a kind of solitary existence . . . I have a house here . . . I go out in a coach and I frequently see M. Petit and M. Terray, and with them I have enjoyed a happiness that will perhaps be the last of my life."

Julie and Hippolyte were together for the better part of the year. She had taken a private house, which allowed the lovers certain opportunities of discretion and even more for indiscretion. Neither of them could have regarded this as merely a casual love affair—or even as an "affair" at all. For Julie, certainly, it was a marriage of true minds, perhaps the only kind of marriage a tormented world might allow, or her rigorous if socially idiosyncratic ethics might approve. Like many other romances born of social upheaval, it was intense and it was doomed.

In the spring of 1794, Hippolyte's worst fears were realized when he received news that his parents had been guillotined in Paris. The charge against them had been aiding and abetting emigration. The French Revolutionary government, like others since, was obsessed with dangers posed by the flight of capital and the possibilities of counter-revolution organized by exiles. Julie's descendant and historian, Francis Ley, indignantly insists that the Terrays were "innocent"; but their son, who was after all living a reasonably comfortable life abroad on the basis of unclarified financial arrangements, may well have felt a tinge of guilt as well as the assault of pure horror.

Suddenly transformed by an act of tribunal terror from transgressive student prince into the head of an old, distinguished family with complicated financial business affairs, Hippolyte saw his relationship with Julie in a changed perspective. He still yearned for the fulfillment of their shared dream: a little cottage in some Swiss glen. But that desire now competed with the more practical concerns of so many of the émigrés: how would he live, and beyond that, how might he hope to salvage at least some of the confiscated family wealth, which was considerable? The next few years were overshadowed by these concerns.

Julie went to Hanover, while Hippolyte went to London, an important center of émigré banking and brainstorming. When Hippolyte was ready to rejoin her in the spring of 1795, Julie took her mother into her confidence. The mother, though conventionally religious, was even more conventionally maternal, and Julie knew she would have her support. Julie wrote to her of her attachment to "a man of merit whose character, whose morals whose tender friendship have not since I first came to know him ceased to confirm for me how I ought to love him. He is well born, he has a very considerable fortune, shares my manner of feeling concerning all the essential things, and has demonstrated to me for a long time (during 9 months) how my happiness is precious to him."

Hippolyte returned, and in the summer of 1795 the couple determined to live together in Switzerland. Young Terray, ever accompanied by his erudite tutor M. Petit, moved on to Lausanne. Julie returned to the paternal home in Livonia. In April 1796, she again wrote to her estranged husband asking for a divorce. This request he deflected as he had deflected all earlier requests, although without strife or unpleasantness. Terray had in the meantime become acquainted with Madame de Staël and the large circle of émigrés within her orbit. The recurrent topic of conversation among them were certain political developments, the most important of which were typified by the purge of 9 Thermidor, which seemed perhaps propitious to the hopes of the exiles for their safe return to their native land.

In 1797, Julie became pregnant and gave birth to a son, probably in February 1798. Precise dates are lacking. In fact, a great deal is lacking in the documentation of this extraordinary episode so rich in its revelations for social history. The principals effaced it from public notice so efficiently that the very fact of it was revealed in print for the first time only after two centuries, on the basis of family documents in the possession of Francis Ley. There is not so much as a mention of Terray in the thoroughly researched biography by Knapton. There is however the record in the archives of the (Roman Catholic) parish church of Saint-Jean-de-Donaueschingen, of the baptism of a male child named Hippolyte, said to be the son of Hippolyte and Barbara Roschak, both from Vevey in the Vaud in the canton of Berne, and both Calvinists by confession. Perhaps the idea was that the priest's delight at bagging a heretic might allow him not to look too closely into the matter.

The unhappy fate of this child, though not directly relevant to the rest of Julie's history, gives us further insight into the social history of those times, in which the sexual morals of the earlier Bourbons often ruled private life, while the rectitude of Geneva determined the possibilities of the public results. Julie turned to her intimate friend Madame Armand, who took the child, now renamed Philippe Hauget, into her household. Ley suggests that the surname was a common one in the locality, and hence unlikely to invite notice.

The child, who proved to be difficult, was not deprived of a certain degree of nurturing love. Madame Arnaud was an extraordinary woman and the finest of friends to Julie de Krüdener. But to be cared for as an adopted son is not the same thing as to be publicly claimed in a society in which so very much depended on the accident of birth. Julie had been raised in an ambiance in which the larger social duties came second to none, including the maternal. Her letters from those early years following his birth are replete with coded expressions of a mother's love, which were, however, destined always to remain covert.

Philippe Hauget, often known by the affectionate nickname of "Lipperet," became in time known to his legitimate Krüdener siblings. A few surviving letters show that his sister Juliette occasionally reached out to him over the years, attempting with as much grace as possible to assure him of her friendly thoughts and best wishes while still avoiding a public proclamation of intimate kinship. Young Paul de Krüdener, always destined for the diplomatic career that he in fact achieved with distinction, was shielded for as long as possible from the guilty knowledge shared by the families' female members. Only in the 1820s did the two meet, and then under carefully controlled conditions designed to shield Paul from any possible embarrassment.

In a period as rapidly shifting as that of the French Revolution, circumstances can change swiftly in a relatively short period of time. In 1793, most French aristocrats could desire nothing more fervently than to escape France and the swishing sound of the guillotine's blade. In 1795, many of those same people could wish for nothing more fervently than the chance to return to France to reclaim their property. Jean-Antoine Terray had had a château near Nogent-sur-Seine. He had a fine town house in Paris.

So Hippolyte Terray, the father of Julie's third child, left. He did not so much abandon his illegitimate son as simply forget about him. The reclamation of his father's property, which was substantial, became for a while a full-time occupation. He continued to proclaim privately noble and honorable intentions to Julie, but she herself was by now moving on. It would be more accurate, perhaps, to say moving back, for she was determined to make a final attempt at reconciliation with her husband. Her motives at this time seem opaque to a distant historical observer, but they clearly included a strain of expiation. The period of intense immersion in literary work, which led to the publication of *Valérie* and of her moment of literary fame, was perhaps in part another means by which she sought some degree of moral recompense for what she now thought of as her *faute*—a term suggesting something both of folly and of sin.

Julie then entered a period of penitence. Her reaction to the situation appears to have been religious, though in no very conventional way. Her sin was in her own eyes less clearly vulgar adultery than a transgression against duty. The lust of the flesh is a comparatively crude and uncomplicated thing when compared, as it almost always was in the literature of the day, with a more refined contest between love and duty.

"I am more and more decided," she writes, "to exist no longer for society but to retire to the bosom of my home. . . ." Thus did she state the concept of a lay asceticism that would yet for some time war against her strongly felt emotional and physical sexuality.

Julie Goes to Geneva

The fruits of her moral epiphany were perhaps peculiar. Her growing sense of the vanity of human wishes was ratified in the sterile and shallow lives of the Berlin émigrés. Julie now felt authorized to pursue her dreams—for her, recurrent dreams. One dream was geographical. The landscape for which she yearned in vacant or in pensive mood was that of the valleys of Switzerland with their magnificent and picturesque scenery, their fast-running, crystalline waters, and their pristine invigorating air, declared by the general European medical consensus to have nearly magical therapeutic properties. When writing to her mother about her plans to pursue her unconventional union with Terray, she could praise her lover in no more telling a way than by saying he shared her geographical enthusiasm: "The fortune of this friend of whom I'm speaking is considerable; it is furthermore independent. He has come up with the idea, which seems so sweet to him, of buying me a nice piece of land in Switzerland. There the climate, nature, the sunshine indispensable to my health, and the thousand advantages smile on me. There I shall be busy, I shall follow my interests, and the requirements of my health, but I could enjoy none of this if I did not have the hope of seeing you frequently."

She would now go to Switzerland, to Geneva, liberated both physically and metaphysically from her marital burden, and there she would pursue her other importunate dream, that of literary celebrity. One of her biographers, Knapton, points to the particular importance of this Swiss sojourn from the point of view of the later historian. Biography is always difficult. It is after all the attempt to represent a human life, and the simplest of human lives lies beyond the powers of artistic representation. But biography is particularly difficult when the chief, or in some instances the only, materials available are the writings of the subject of the biography. By far the most copious materials available for the life of Julie de Krüdener are her own letters and those written to her. The Geneva sojourn was obviously a turning point in her inner life, though one could scarcely tell that from her letters. It was in Geneva that she set herself to writing with a purpose.

For she had come to Geneva, among other reasons, to reacquaint herself with the French literary life she had first experienced a decade earlier at the beginning of the Revolution. At Coppet near Geneva, in its imposing château, Madame de Staël was in residence; and where Madame de Staël was, a certain proportion of the elegant arbiters of literary life was bound also to be. Julie de Krüdener now reentered the "circle" of Madame de Staël, and in doing so she generated a useful body of secondary commentary. For the Coppet period we have not merely her own letters but others *about* her.

Not surprisingly, the witnesses are not in entire agreement. From Julie's own point of view, the Swiss rustication was an unblemished idyll of plain living and high thinking. Those in frequent contact with her at Coppet, on the other hand, suggest a more complex reality. Madame de Staël herself had a complicated relationship with Julie. She liked her, and to a degree admired her; yet she wished no sister too close to the throne, and when Julie became more competitor than votary, she turned cool. For the present, she was for Julie a font of encouragement and an influential friend. Of course Julie did not know everything that Madame de Staël was saying about her. "I found her distinguished," Madame de Staël wrote to one of their mutual friends during this period, "but she tells so many stories of men who have killed themselves for love of her that her conversation gives the impression of being a wager." Madame de Staël could be formidably acerb, but there is other evidence of Julie's fascination with her own fatal powers of attraction; and as she lived in a world in which the thinnest of partitions divided provocative flirtation from commonplace sociability, she would have had many opportunities to explore that ethical borderline. In her most famous novel, the heroine is a *femme fatale* wholly innocent of any knowledge of her own fatality. The author herself seems to have been not merely aware of it, but happy enough to exploit it. How the morality of sentiment may have differed in her own mind from the self-indulgences of ennui enjoyed by the Berlin émigrés was perhaps a fine point of casuistry.

Madame de Staël had planned to return to Paris before the year (1801) was out, and she now did so, encouraging Julie to follow, and promising to be helpful with the publication of her novel in progress. For the situation in the French capital was considerably changed, and from the point of view of Julie's aristocratic friends, changed for the better. Napoleon as first consul had seized power two years earlier. The Revolution was officially over. Large numbers of émigrés had already returned, and more still were returning. Amid all the uncertainties they carried out their heroic search for equilibrium and the desperate hope that things might return to "normal"—meaning, of course, the way they used to be. French literary life would never be exactly as it had been before, but that was not because Madame de Staël and the large group of *littérateurs* whom she typified were not willing to try. There was a spirited attempt, for example, to reanimate the idea of the literary *salon*, which like many other social institutions of the Ancient Régime had been eclipsed by politics. Literary activity in a new century under a new regime could justly be described as feverish. Madame de Staël's own huge book, *Delphine*, was nearly ready for publication.

WE LACK PRECISE EVIDENCE concerning the pace of composition of *Valérie*, but Julie had surely made significant progress on it before she too moved on to Paris. She settled into an apartment no great distance from the present site of the Madeleine in one direction, or from fame in the other. She arrived, preemptively a literary lion. Madame de Staël, as good as her word, offered her introductions to the reigning

Julie de Krüdener tried to cultivate René de Chateaubriand, among the most famous literary figures of the post-Revolutionary period; but he always kept her at arm's length. This famous portrait by Anne-Louis Girodet (1804) elicited the following comment from Napoleon Bonaparte: "He looks like a conspirator who's come down the chimney."

writers of the moment. Chief of these was Réné de Chateaubriand, just then enjoying the truly fantastic popular success of his little novel *Atala*, and preparing for his apotheosis with the publication of the *Génie du christianisme*. *Atala* (though unfinished) has long been recognized as one of the half dozen most important works of early French Romanticism; its natural peers include the likes of Rousseau's *Nouvelle Héloïse* and Saint-Pierre's *Paul et Virginie*, both of them obvious formative influences on Julie de Krüdener. *Atala*, set in the North American wilderness, which Chauteaubriand had in fact visited, is a story about missionaries and Indians in which the heroes are the missionaries. Though the contest would be close, this point of view was perhaps even less politically correct in 1800 than in 2000, as it attacked the Rousseauian idea of the "noble savage" and by extension the politico-theological theory behind it, the idea that human ill derives chiefly from the corrupting influences of human society.

Elsewhere, Chateaubriand's dissection of the old French society was anything but bloodless. He maintained that the French aristocracy, in which he proudly claimed membership with considerable heraldic detail, had gone through three stages: a primacy conspicuous for its ethical superiority; then one lapsed in the lazy habits of its privilege; and finally an "aristocracy of debauch," the aristocracy swept away with the Bastille. What validates his credentials as a conservative to be classed with Burke or de Maistre is his championing of traditional society as a civilizing as opposed to a corrupting force. The great nurse and preceptor of Europe had been the Christian religion, and to the extent that Europe might rescue itself from a self-imposed barbarism, it might be so again. This is the idea that undergirds his great book, part apology, part poetry, part polemic: *Le Génie du christianisme*. The word in its title means both "Genius" and "Spirit," and he audaciously expands the idea of "Christianity" far beyond the ecclesial, let alone the mere doctrinal or theological, to consider sociological, psychological, and aesthetic dimensions.

Such ideas obviously have the sharpest possible relevance for the kind of religious mission that lay in Julie de Krüdener's future. But that vocation was as yet inconceivable. It must lie beyond the publication of *Valérie*. She would have found in Chateaubriand, at least as she thought, a fellow exile, for no banished French aristocrat could outdo Julie in the spirit of peregrination. She undoubtedly hoped that he might light down upon her web as at least temporarily Saint-Pierre had done earlier. The campaign was to a degree successful. Chateaubriand had considerable influence at the *Mercure de France*, and he was influential in arranging the publication of Julie's *Penseés d'une dame étrangère.*

The "thought" or "maxim" was a well-established literary genre in the Old World, and especially in France, the paradise of aphorists. Rapid wit and verbal dexterity had been the coin of the realm both at the Bourbon court and in the literary *salon.* But if it was a familiar and approved form, it was no less one in which previous masters had established a very high competitive bar. Julie's little apothegms would perforce be vying with those of Voltaire and La Rochefoucauld. Even in this company, Julie could hold her own. The measure of the maxim is its brilliance, not its sincerity or spiritual truth; yet some of Julie's *pensées* have a kind of convincing sentimental sweetness about them: "There are women who go through life like springtime breezes, vivifying everything which they touch." She probably thought she knew at least one such woman. Others now seem a little trite: "social friendships are like small diamonds; they glitter, but are valueless." Still others walk up to the edge of banality, then gracefully leap in: "Life resembles the sea, which owes its finest effects to storms." There is nothing about a box of chocolates.

The *Pensées* was judged a very fine work of its kind. And though it was a slim work both in size and content, it demonstrated verve and intelligence. Most of all, it made her a published author. Now she had a public eagerly awaiting *Valérie.*

Julie showed every talent for literary politics—for lining up useful sponsors, importuning positive reviews, and the like. Her self-serving adroitness made a striking impression on her biographer Knapton: "The skill which the imaginative Julie deployed in bringing her wares to the public eye would lead one to believe that her career in the diplomatic world had not been so empty as she usually claimed." As a matter of fact, the training in the schoolroom of great power diplomacy was useful for many aspects of her social life. In a letter to her daughter Juliette she expressed some shockingly worldly wisdom. "In order to succeed it is not sufficient to have wit, genius, or good intentions," she noted; "everything has its hucksterism." In the following months Chateaubriand appears very frequently in her letters, and always amid expressions of admiration or intimations of his supposed admiration for *her*. Chateaubriand himself sought no further intimacy. He was polite, even cordial toward the aspiring authoress, but he kept his counsel. Many years later when she was dead and he was aged, he made a remark that shocked Eynard by its harshness. For it was Chateaubriand who made the remark with which I began this chapter. He had known Julie both in her "worldly phase" and in her "spiritual phase." His conclusion: "She always struck me as icy."

This may have been the sourness of a crusty old man. Such, at least, was Eynard's opinion: "a naïve and saddened judgment from this man whose sad fate it was to be wholly dedicated to the contemplation of his own vast and noble individuality."

As she moved on with her larger book, Julie de Krüdener met a number of other literary notables, including Benjamin Constant. Though her book was not finished, there was a healthy if entirely uninformed chatter about it. It would be like Richardson's great novel *Pamela* and, like its latest competitor, Madame de Staël's *Delphine*, an epistolary novel.

The Epistolary Novel

The epistolary novel is par excellence a feminine form even when, as is not infrequently true, the author is a man. Furthermore, the most authentic subject matter of the epistolary novel is female passion. *Valérie* is a special case. Its author is a woman. Its subject is a man—though one thoroughly "feminized" from the point of view of sentiment. But its heroine, clearly enough, is the woman who is the object of his passion and, almost as clearly, a sentimental surrogate for the author, Julie de

Krüdener. To appreciate what was new in *Valérie* naturally involves some understanding of what was conventional. That involves a brief excursus into the literary history of the epistolary novel.

As a genre, the epistolary novel had in the first place several natural connections with Enlightenment culture. The Enlightenment had invented neither the letter nor the literary letter collection. The literary foundation of the Christian religion was the dossier of the collected letters of St. Paul, which considerably antedate the compilation of the later Gospels. The Fathers of the Church were looking to other ancient models in the compilation of their letter collections. Even before Petrarch's time in the fourteenth century secular writers had reanimated the epistolary spirit of Cicero. But it was in the Enlightenment period that the letter claimed the practical and cultural importance it was to enjoy well into the Victorian age, and which it has definitely lost only with the "communications revolution" of the late nineteenth and the twentieth centuries—telegraph, telephone, increasingly rapid intercontinental travel, radio and television broadcasts, electronic mail.

The Great Age of the European Letter was probably the period between 1600 and 1800. Its Golden Age was the latter half of that period. As we have already seen in relation to the growth of periodical literature, the Age of the Letter had been enabled by its own material revolutions. They have sometimes gone underappreciated or even unobserved because they were primarily developments rather than inventions. These included advances in papermaking that greatly increased paper stocks while lowering its price, improved processes for ink production, the mass production of quill pens and their artificial surrogates, the development of "penmanship" as a common feature of primary education, and the relatively cheap manufacture of elegant writing boxes and portable desks.

Material innovation can very rapidly lead to observable and sometimes dramatic changes in social habit that, once established, may seem instantly inevitable and perhaps eternal. Bizet and Puccini cannot have foreseen the day when a ritualized plea to silence the cellular phone would be the obligatory overture to the overture. Letter writing had always had its important social roles, but in this age it became a very widespread cultural habit.

There was a democratic element—or at least a democratizing one—to all this. It was not just diplomats, bureaucrats, academicians, and political theorists who might spend a measurable part of each day at their correspondence: reading it, answering it, initiating it. A large section of the upper classes of Europe—including many people we would be inclined to describe as "middle class"—became habitual letter writers. One peculiar feature of the letter is its intrinsically *social* character. To be sure, just as there is such a thing as "closet drama"—works in theatrical format never actually intended to be staged in a theater—there is such a thing as the "closet letter." But for the most part letters, whatever else they might be, were intended to be social communication and, as we would say, interactive. The poet sitting comfortably by his fireside or shivering in his garret might send a poem into the world with hope; yet it was hope of a rather abstract and even ethereal kind. The man or woman who sent a letter to a relative or a friend had a much more concrete and practical hope: the hope or rather the confident expectation of a reply. That reply, in turn, carried its own confident expectation.

Many viewers of Ken Burns's justly famous television series on *The Civil War* have been struck by one feature of its documentation—namely, the informal letters written by soldiers on either side of the conflict, and generally addressed to distant family members at home. Many of these men were private soldiers of modest social station and limited formal education, raised on farms in Indiana or Tennessee. What is likely to seem extraordinary to us is that so many of them wrote with such competence, and often enough with elegance and even eloquence. It might be possible to draw from this evidence potentially useful trends for contemporary theorists of American education, but the point here is an historical one. These men were the late inheritors of a culture in which competence in letter writing was among the fundamentals of literacy.

Literacy was quite explicitly recognized as an important form of social capital, and like other forms of capital it sought opportunities for its display. Letter writing was a social art, and just as people eagerly sought instruction in other social arts—dancing, for example, or music or fencing—they sought instruction in letter writing. The second half of the seventeenth century in England saw the publication of a proliferation of letter-writing manuals. These included such titles as *The Wit's Academy* (1677) and *The Young Secretary's Guide* (1687). *The Lover's Secretary*, first published at the beginning of the eighteenth century, enjoyed wide popularity in several later editions. The Latin origin of the word "secretary" suggests "private" or "personal" more exactly than it does "secret." Like many words, it developed in different directions; one strain stressed the private, the other the public. Thus "secretary" soon enough came to mean "official," often enough of high position, as in the secretary of state. A secretary was first a personal confidant, then one who handled the documentary side of personal or business relations. Among its expanded meanings, still occasionally heard, was a piece of furniture especially designed to be written at.

The eighteenth century saw the publication of literally dozens of such manuals in all the languages of Europe. Within this group was a prominent subgenre designed to teach foreigners the conventions of letter writing in French, the language of the international aristocracy.

Such books had always been culturally multitasked, so to speak—that is, asked to do more work than met the eye. In the medieval schools, the teaching of elementary Latin was almost invariably conducted with the use of books intended to instill the spirit of *contemptus mundi* (rejection of worldly values) that was the ideal of the ascetic communities within which the teaching was done. A standard primer, an anthology of elementary texts to be mastered by the young pupils, was called simply the *Octo Auctores Morales*, the *Eight Moral Authors*. Ten-year-olds were meant to acquire an enthusiasm for votive chastity at the same time they picked up the third declension. In the Puritan abecedarium, the mnemonic for "A" was our arch-ancestor Adam: "In Adam's fall we sinned all"—the Calvinist doctrine of the total depravity of man packaged with the first of the vowels.

Of course, foundations are laid out to be built upon. The form of the domestic letter could be turned by literary genius to the purposes of art. Some famous writers of the period are known *primarily* for their letter writing. That is true of Madame de Sévigné in the seventeenth century and Mary Wortley Montagu in the eighteenth. The surviving correspondence of some academic and literary figures must strike us as enormous. Horace Walpole's collected correspondence takes up 10 fat volumes. It is probably only the amazing copiousness of Voltaire's literary production in so many genres that makes us accept with equanimity the fact that the Pléiade edition of his correspondence *up to the year 1760* contains roughly 10,000 pages. (There are about 20,000 surviving letters of Voltaire altogether!)

Most fiction disputes its own fictionality to some degree. There are of course many exceptions in the form of fantasy literature, science fiction, "magical" realism, and so forth. But most fiction is realistic, and what is meant by "realistic fiction" is a narrative that seems as though it *might* be true, that presents experience in a fashion that a reader, perhaps with some effort or Coleridgean voluntary suspension of disbelief, can accept as plausible, possible, or even convincing. The epistolary novel often challenges its fictionality in a particularly aggressive fashion. About a fifth of all eighteenth-century novels were epistolary in form, and many of those included pseudo-editorial comment asserting that the letters were a genuine correspondence among living letter writers, not the made-up invention of a fiction writer. There are several examples in which the truth claims have been sufficient to convince some or even most scholarly readers.

Julie de Krüdener's *Valérie*

The novel *Valérie*, which appeared in 1803, caused something of a European sensation as a history of female passion. It has often been called "autobiographical." That is because the story it tells has a "real-life" narrative germ. But what made *Valérie* a sensation was its commitment to imaginary rather than to real life. Its engagement with earlier sentimental literature—delicacy forbids the use of the word "imitation" in this regard—also played a role. In particular its kinship with Goethe's *Sorrows of Young Werther* (1774, revised edition 1787), one of the first international best sellers of the Age of Sentiment, is particularly apparent. Even so, the autobiographical germ is not without its interest.

Shortly after their marriage, the baron was posted to Venice. This cannot have been regarded as a hardship post. But the city-state, long in decline from its Renaissance splendor, must have seemed to the young hyperborean matron a hotbed of southern decadence and, perhaps, possibility. No problem in assessing the "marital phase" of Julie's life is more opaque than that of her marital arrangements and her attitude to her husband the baron. It is not clear that she ever invested in her marriage the hopes for a passionate relationship. On the other hand, she had such a well developed sense of dutiful propriety that ordinary categories of marital strife were probably for her unthinkable. "You know," she wrote to Madame de Staël shortly after her estranged husband's death in 1802, "that there was nothing in my union with M. de Krüdener than that friendship that rules so many marriages in the great world; but I respected him, I valued him, and I believe that I was never so unhappy as in the first weeks after that terrible loss." Nonetheless it seems to have been at this quite early period of her life that Julie transferred her inner hopes for emotional satisfaction from her preoccupied husband—from whom she would soon separate on amicable terms—to the world of imagination.

So long as he lived, the baron presented also a kind of fixed and necessary obstacle that would allow if it did not compel her to dramatize to the full the conflicts of a great heart. Thus, when she did fall passionately in love with the marquis de Frégeville, the drama of the already estranged husband was hardly less intense than the passion for the lover himself.

The brief period of residence in Venice offered Julie experience that, when dilated within the novel *Valérie*, would make her one of the most celebrated literary women in Europe. The episode was this. A sensitive and impressionable youth of the Russian diplomatic corps, Alexander de Stakiev, developed an extravagant crush on the wife of his boss, the ambassador. His passion, of which Julie de Krüdener was herself entirely ignorant, gnawed at his bosom. The situation hovered between the hopeless and the absurd, quite possibly seasoned by the dangerous. Animated by that kind of extravagant and noble virtue to be found everywhere in the pages of pre-Romantic fiction, young Stakiev felt impelled to withdraw from the situation and return as soon as possible to St. Petersburg. That surely might have been virtue enough, but he supplemented it by writing the baron a letter in which he explained the situation, offering superfluous praise for the virtue of his wife. The baron, a man of the world, was amused; but he made the mistake of actually showing Julie the letter. She of course had been until that very moment entirely unaware of her fatally attractive powers; but now that they had been suggested to her, she inwardly claimed them in earnest. She began to think of herself as a *femme fatale*, and the thinking was the first step toward the being.

The plot of *Valérie* is the imaginary history of what might have happened to young Stakiev had he not sensibly faced the moral necessity of returning to St. Petersburg. The Stakiev of the novel is a young man named Gustave de Linar. Gustave is a Scandinavian—a Swede, to be specific. But while his specific Scandinavian nationality is perhaps immaterial, his hyperborean passion is essential. Gustave is the personal secretary to a middle-aged count, the husband of a beautiful child bride, Valérie. The personality of the count is but thinly developed, but he is kindly and admirable, nearly terminally broad-minded, a noble man in his unexciting way, but not one to make a passionate young girl's heart go pitty-pat. The three are traveling in Italy. Gustave is keeping a journal, mainly in the form of letters sent home to his friend Ernest de G.

Only gradually does Gustave perceive his emotional state, in the discovery of which the novel expends a considerable amount of rhetorical energy. What I mean by "hyperborean passion" is a peculiar form of sentiment, at first geographical. There is something of the young Augustine about Gustave—even before he finds the object of his passion, passion itself is his object. But there is not much else that is Mediterranean in his emotional metabolism. "Ernest, more than ever *it* is in my heart, that secret agitation which now turns my steps toward the steep summits of Koullen, and then to our deserted dunes . . . the loneliness of the seas, their huge silence or their storming rage, the wavering flight of the halcyon bird, the melancholy cry of the bird that loves the frozen regions, the sad, sweet brightness of our northern lights—all this nourishes the indistinct and ravishing restlessness of my youth. . . . Alas! Will I never be loved?"

That this is a convincing representation of male sexual desire, even pre-Romantic or adolescent desire, can be doubted. The theme does, however, find more or less precise echoes in several of the contemporary writers whom Madame de Krüdener imitates, particularly in Goethe, Jean-Paul Richter, and Mme de Staël. One feature of *Valérie* is distinctive, however, distinctive and decisive. The tragic Gustave is in this novel so thoroughly feminized that one hardly notices the book's lack of a more active heroine. For Valérie, the object of Gustave's passion, is hardly that—except to the degree that she must be the source of the images that scintillate in the mirror of Gustave's mind. Two episodes in the novel, regarded as sensational in their day, underscore the theme of subliminal voyeurism that animates the whole work.

The first is "the Dance of the Shawl." This dance, which has nothing to do with the more recently invented American Indian ceremonial dance, was a species of Protestant belly-dancing, if one may make so bold, apparently first performed by Emma Hamilton, Lord Nelson's friend. (Claims advanced on behalf of the empress Josephine, though discredited, nonetheless suggest its artistic prestige.) Lady Hamilton would drape a shawl over her head and hold tight its edges, then strike various poses or "attitudes" as she moved gracefully and rhythmically to a musical accompaniment.

Literature of the period makes clear that what might be called "chamber dance" was widely regarded as a valuable feminine accomplishment, similar to vocal or instrumental competence. Julie herself is reported to have won admirers with her rendition of a Cossack dance, an exoticism in the *salons* of Paris. The shawl-dance, however, took on a particular cachet.

The dance was entirely improvised, having no fixed steps. Indeed, the name "dance" is probably misleading. A better term might be "emotional soliloquy." In the eighteenth letter, the narrator describes a ball given by the Spanish ambassador in Venice, a ball to which the most glittering elements of the expatriate community are invited. The very presence of Valérie so excites the narrator as to cause a dramatic change in his affect noticed by other merrymakers.

Late in the evening, when some guests have already left, a spontaneous movement arises among those remaining that Valérie should perform the shawl-dance. She is supplicated by many, including her husband and "a woman covered with diamonds and rouge." After long demurral born of her native modesty, she at last agrees. A certain Lord Méry takes up the violin. Valérie calls for a shawl in blue muslin, pulls her hair back from her forehead, and puts the shawl over her, allowing its fringes to fall down loosely over the crossed arms. The doors are shut—so that no one might interrupt the performance, which Gustave describes in minute detail, thrilling in its every aspect.

His description, like so much else in the novel, is highly literary. The scene, he says, would appear to have been designed by Correggio, but with an assist from the Immortal Bard. "And when she raised her downcast eyes and her lips formed a smile, one might claim to have seen there such an image as painted by Shakespeare, Patience smiling at Grief upon a monument."

This is actually a sharp literary allusion to an important scene in *Twelfth Night*, in which Viola, in male disguise, obliquely announces her love for, and to, Count Orsino, in the form of a fictive history of an invented "sister" who can love only secretly and from afar. *Did she ever announce her love to its object?* asks the Duke, and Viola replies:

> *A blank, my lord. She never told her love,*
> *But let concealment, like a worm i' the bud,*
> *Feed on her damask cheek: she pined in thought,*
> *And with a green and yellow melancholy*
> *She sat like Patience on a monument,*
> *Smiling at grief. Was not this love indeed?*
> *We men may say more, swear more: but indeed*
> *Our shows are more than will, for still we prove*
> *Much in our vows, but little in our love.*

It is in fact a brilliant use of quotation. For here Gustave has become, as it were, the disguised Viola. It is Valérie who gives voice, but the words are the silenced sentiment of the hapless narrator, the protestation of love that he can never make to its actual object. We have here, in other words, both the sexual and the emotional transformation of the narrator. Shakespeare's Viola is a woman disguised as a man. Madame de Julie de Krüdener gives us a "disguised" woman giving voice to the inner feelings of the male narrator, Gustave de Linar. The beauty, simplicity, and directness of the beshawled Valérie will haunt the narrator till the end of his days.

So haunted is he by his onetime vision of perfection, associated with the expression of a love that cannot otherwise be expressed, that there is a very melodramatic reprise of the shawl-dance at another cardinal moment in the novel.

Valérie, though by the standards of its age a rather short novel, is nonetheless distributed into two volumes. The final epistle of the first volume (number 36) is largely given over to a description of a bizarre incident, which takes place during a time that the Scandinavian secretary has been left alone while Valérie and her husband are temporarily absent from Venice. Returning one early evening from the island of San Giorgio, Gustave hears as he is walking along the Sciavoni a striking female voice singing what he calls an old *romance*—the meaning of the word here being "love song." "My ears were surprised by a ravishing melody." What he hears is a song frequently sung by Valérie, and now apparently sung in Valérie's own voice.

Looking up, Gustave realizes that he is standing before the house of Bianca. She is a young woman, living with her aunt, who plays in this novel the role of the "Venetian prostitute" familiar in many late eighteenth-century books. One suspects that the author here has in mind various pages in Rousseau's *Confessions* in which he relates his encounters with the famously nippleless beauty Zulietta (Julietta), or in which he talks of his visits to the woman he calls the Padoana, whose name was Giustina. Julie de Krüdener, of course, would never descend to Rousseau's level of frankness; and a certain mystery hovers over the person and position of Bianca. The main thing about her from the narrative point of view is that upon reflection Gustave realizes that she has not merely the voice of his beloved but also, strangely, her nearly exact physical shape. A plan begins to form in his mind.

On another day Gustave proposes to Bianca that they make a kind of promenade by gondola. The conveniently geriatric aunt elects to stay quayside and rest. Out on the water, Gustave is soon overcome by the strangeness of this surrogate passion which Bianca inspires in him. She of course notices the strange affect of his physiognomy, the literary lover's pallor traditional since the time of Ovid. It is only natural that she would mistake it as the result of her own presence. She reaches out, takes his hand, and asks him, touchingly, *"N'avete mai amato?"* ("Have you never loved?") This is a question that echoes the one put to himself by himself in the novel's very first epistle. Gustave is overcome by the delicacy of the situation, for he sees that Bianca believes he speaks in an oblique fashion of herself.

The author's narrative response to the difficulty is perhaps maladroit; according to the text, Gustave removes himself to "the extremity of the gondola." Not surprisingly, Bianca finds this behavior odd. *"Siete matto?"* she asks. *"Perche non state qui?"* ("Are you crazy? Why don't you stay here?") Gustave is in fact crazy, as he well knows, crazy with love for Valérie, which now overcomes his incipient scruples at the prospect of misleading the young tart. He asks her to sing a certain romance, the one that he has heard sung by Valérie herself: *"T'amo più che la vita"* ("I love you more than life"). The intoxicating thrill he experiences through this vicarious music encourages him to his final audacity, certainly one of the sentimental highlights of the novel, and a contender even within the rich competition of pre-Romantic literature generally. He asks Bianca whether on another occasion she would be willing to serve his pleasure. She will be astonished at the form his requested gratification is to take. He dresses her in the costume he associates with Valérie, placing over her head a blue shawl especially purchased for the occasion. He then asks her to sing, softly, the desired romance: *"T'amo più che la vita."* Her compliance with his request carries him to the verge of ecstasy.

There is a lengthy literary history on the theme of the artificial, surrogate lover, as in Ovid's famous story of Pygmalion's statue of

Galatea, or in Shakespeare's reprise of the theme in *The Winter's Tale*. Other, more proximate models are to be found elsewhere in the period's fiction. Yet derivative as it is, this scene became, perhaps, the most famous in Julie de Krüdener's book. It was imitated by other authors. At least one romantic song was written about it. It was enacted in amateur dramatics of the drawing room. It has about it a semi-pornographic allure. It is not, however, the kinkiest episode in the novel. That distinction must surely go to Gustave's obsessive interest in the course of Valérie's pregnancy and *accouchement*.

The second volume of *Valérie* is short but action-packed. As it begins, Gustave is already resigned to death. He informs Ernest, his epistolary sounding board, that he must leave the Count's household, and he does so precipitously. He knows, he says, that he will probably write no more letters, but this diagnosis proves to be optimistic. In fact, the concluding section of Julie de Krüdener's book is made up of documents of several sorts. Ernest, much alarmed by what he hears from his distant friend, writes directly to Valérie's husband, the Count, to inform him of his deep worries and to seek counsel. Gustave himself writes directly to Valérie only when it has become obvious that his wasting illness has been caused not by some distant Scandinavian beauty—a white lie in which he has connived—but by herself. There are several letters from the Count himself, who exhibits a greatness of soul unblemished by the slightest annoyance at his young employee's passion for his young wife. In one intriguing section we get episodes from the journal of Gustave's mother in Sweden, beginning with an event that occurred on his second birthday. The burden of all these documents is to recount the inevitable but supremely Romantic depth of a young man overwhelmed by a passion forbidden him by virtue.

One of the odder gestures of pre-Romanticism was what might be called the thematic eroticization of Christian asceticism. In the eighteenth century, this was reflected in the popularity of the legend of "Abelard and Héloïse," taken up by Pope among others. It had been greatly enhanced by some beautiful pages in the *Génie du christianisme* of Réné de Chateaubriand, Julie de Krüdener's ambivalent friend and admirer.

It is not entirely surprising, therefore, that Gustave's last breaths should be taken in a semi-ecclesiastical setting. To escape the physical presence of Valérie he flees westward into Lombardy, described from his Venetian perspective as "the land of the setting sun." In a small village in the shadow of a monastery the hapless lover is overtaken by a fatal malady, vaguely pulmonary in nature, which he realizes is carrying him away. He engages an invalid's room in a hostel. At this point the Count himself intervenes, having had an epistolary alert from Ernest, and he goes to be by his young secretary's bedside.

The protracted death of Gustave, the rhetorical and emotional climax of the novel, was widely appreciated by its readers as a masterpiece of the highest sentiment. Once again, it is explicitly "literary" to a very remarkable degree. Seeing some books on the stand next to Gustave's deathbed, the Count inquires whether Gustave would like to hear something read to him. "Something in English," is the reply; and the Count reaches out for a copy of Thomson's *Seasons*, opening it at random to some lines near the end of "Spring":

> *But happy they! the happiest of their kind!*
> *Whom gentler stars unite, and in one fate*
> *Their hearts, their fortunes, and their beings blend.*
> *'Tis not the coarser tie of human laws,*
> *Unnatural oft, and foreign to the mind,*
> *That binds their peace but harmony itself,*
> *Attuning all their passions into love;*
> *Where friendship full-exerts her softest power,*
> *Perfect esteem enlivened by desire . . .*

The whole scene is imitated after Goethe's Werther, in which the Romantic Scottish author of choice is, however, "Ossian," not James

Thomson. But the lines cited are among the most famous lines in this most famous poem, a poem read in its age by anyone who read poetry at all. The chances of coming upon them in the random opening of a volume today approximate those of winning the Irish Sweepstakes. They include an expression of the highest of Romantic love, *Perfect esteem enlivened by desire*, an ideal unrealized in the marriage of Julie de Krüdener no less than in that of Valérie herself. As for Gustave, the "perfect esteem" without a licit channel of desire proves to be fatal. At the very end Gustave receives the religious ministrations of a French priest, an orphan of the Revolution, who has found asylum in the Ultramontane monastery. In our more ecumenical age the episode is marked by a strain of doubtless unintended levity, for the priest makes heavy weather of the fact that Gustave, whom he has seen at mass, apparently in fervent prayer, is not in fact a Roman Catholic. He is, however, one of the great saints of sentiment and martyrs of love.

The rigid limitation of the epistolary novel inspired imaginative authorial attempts to say things that letters could not credibly say. *Valérie* ends with some supposed pages from the journal of Gustave's mother who, as she viewed the corpse of her beloved son within his coffin, was struck by seeing a ring upon his finger. "He had on one of his fingers a ring decorated, as is our national custom, with his heraldic arms. I wanted to remove it from him. Then, remembering that he was the last shoot of that illustrious House of Linar, I said, 'Stay, go with him into the tomb.' Then my tears flowed. I put the hand back upon the dead body, and I closed the coffin."

THE PUBLICATION OF *VALÉRIE* created a sensation. Overnight, Julie de Krüdener was acknowledged one of the great writers of the age, claiming her rightful place among her inspirers, her friends, and her peers: the Rousseau of *La Nouvelle Héloïse*, Bernardin de Saint-Pierre, Madame de Staël, Réné de Chataubriand. We may call this constellation of writers the birth of Romanticism if we wish. They were also the harvesters of Enlightenment. As for Julie de Krüdener, she had achieved literary fame just in time to realize she wanted something else.

Bibliographical

Julie de Krüdener presents a bibliographical challenge in two respects. The first difficulty lies in the fact that the primary sources for her biography, her abundant correspondence, has not been collected and edited. Any full assessment of her life and work must await that achievement. The second difficulty is that so much of the scholarship devoted to her has been implicitly or explicitly partisan.

To begin with, there is the excellent biography in English by Ernest John Knapton: *The Lady of the Holy Alliance, the Life of Julie de Krüdener* (New York, 1939). Knapton was a literary scholar with a deep knowledge of French and German pre-Romanticism, and he does a very good job of maintaining balance. This work supplanted Clarence Post's *The Life and Letters of Madame de Krudener* (London, 1893); but Post's book is still valuable for its collection of Julie's letters in translation.

Julie's first serious French biographer was Charles Eynard, *Vie de Madame de Krudener,* 2 vols. (Paris, 1849). This remains the most valuable collection of her published writings. But Eynard was a very religious man, writing from the point of view of a hagiographer. For him the most important thing about his subject was her religious conversion, and he made little attempt (beyond condemnation) to deal with her early "worldly" life. One finds a nearly opposite impulse in E. Muhlenbeck's late nineteenth-century *Étude sur les origines de la Sainte-Alliance* (Paris & Strasbourg, n.d.), a rare book that has some information nowhere else available. The author was an Alsatian antiquarian who had contact with several people who had actually known his subject. But Muhlenbeck's secular and anti-clerical spirit made it impossible for him to sympathize with Julie's religious ideas. So, one of her nineteenth-century biographers presented her as saintly, and the other as merely kooky.

The most important work on Julie de Krüdener is undoubtedly Francis Ley's *Madame de Krüdener et son temps 1764–1824* (Paris, 1961). Ley was a direct lineal descendant of Julie, and he had access to papers never before made public. His big book naturally made a significant advance in the knowledge of its subject. For example, Ley was the first to reveal the episode of Julie's illegitimate son (see *La Revue de Paris* [1965]: 130–42)—an episode so well hushed up that it had remarkably escaped all previous scholars and even, apparently, oral family history. Ley accomplished other important work, including the anthology of letters involving Julie's circle awkwardly entitled *Bernardin de Saint-Pierre, Madame de Staël, Chateaubriand, Benjamin Constant, et Madame de Krüdener* (Paris, 1967).

No manuscript of Julie's famous novel *Valérie* has been found, but there is a modern scholarly edition with a good introduction by Michel Mercier (Paris, 1974). See also the bibliographical note to the next chapter.

Rotmeister junior 1820.

9 | *Julie de Krüdener* Dévote

WHILE JULIE HAD BEEN pursuing and gaining fame, she herself had been being pursued, at times unaware, by a spiritual destiny. As her spiritual "development" was not always linear, it is useful to backtrack over certain personal highlights of the years 1800–1804. The appropriate tempo for religious conversions, according to most of the literary classics of the genre, should be the instantaneous, the scriptural model for Christian conversion being literally the blinding flash on the road to Damascus that transformed Saul of Tarsus into Paul the Apostle to the Nations. Augustine, too, the greatest exemplar in secular letters, represents his moment of conversion as happening in one serendipitous moment as he sat beneath a fig tree. Yet even in writing about that decisive instant, after which his life would never be the same, he makes the reader aware of the long and agonizing anterior thought devoted to what exactly it was that he might be converted to. Julie's "religiosity," though often treated as the aftermath of a single grace-filled moment, was obviously a gradual process.

Julie de Krüdener *dévote*, in Pietist garb and pose, in a print dated 1820 and engraved by F. Rosmaster the Younger. This etching, or one similar, became the model for a once popular subject of shell cameos.

The household of her childhood had been both religious and enlightened. Her mother was a serious Protestant who practiced her faith, externally, in the forms approved by the Lutheran churches of the German-speaking states. These included, in addition to regular Sunday worship, daily household prayers for family and an extensive domestic staff. Her father, though a conventional religious conformist, was not conspicuously devout; he seems to have found his principal spiritual nourishment at a Masonic Lodge frequented by men well read in science and philosophy. All around her in Riga lay a rich religious diversity touched upon earlier. So Julie de Krüdener was, and undoubtedly regarded herself to be, a Christian among Christians, within a context in which that was the general or default social expectation. There is no evidence of an unusual early piety. The adjective she used of herself, and that was used of her by some early literary associates, was *mondaine*: worldly, secular.

Historians sometimes have difficulty with the religious dimension of their biographical subjects because they approach religion primarily from the point of view of *belief.* What did they believe, and when? What did they doubt, and why? Questions of agnosticism and atheism in the Enlightenment period—when they were usually classified under the name of "infidelity"—certainly command our interest. No less interesting, however, are the evidences of religion's social roles, both in terms of community formation and as an impetus to social action. Julie's training in the literary school of *sentiment* (feeling) undoubtedly helped prepare her for that inner light and tutelage of the heart that was to become the mystical center of her being.

There is even in her pre-conversion personality a streak of proto-evangelism. This is typified in a letter published by Eynard (I, 94) without date in which she attempts to console Madame Armand, recently taxed with "painful trials" of unspecified character. "Yes, my friend," she writes, "count always on Providence! She exists, she will bless you, you are her dear child. . . . Courage, dear Armand, courage!

Happiness is far from luxury and high station!" Such advice given to the adoptive mother of her own "sin-child" from a woman who even as she wrote it was lusting after the literary fame of the old Parisian *salons*, may strike us as a bit thick, especially as she goes on to a decidedly egocentric encomium of the consolations of religion. "Oh! Thank heaven for having given me religion. Without it my character, which now takes refuge in melancholy, would become black, hateful, perhaps as miserable as those who inspire in me disdain for their levity." In other words: thank God I am not like those Pharisees! This strain in her religious physiognomy, which the hagiographer Eynard regarded as a striking evidence of the egotistic "before" that would be divinely transformed into a self-sacrificial "after," and which her biographical detractors regarded simply as mawkish sentimentality, did later prove to be a foundation on which something new could be built.

At the same time she was discovering what later theologians would come to call the "social gospel." She was particularly fond of the large family estate at Kosse, in Livonia, for as a child she had been introduced to the wonders of Nature and to the attractive aspects of peasant culture. When at a certain point Kosse became her personal property, she immediately interested herself in the conditions of the tenant farmers, and of the local population of agricultural workers generally. She directly confronted the unwavering and to her mind united conservatism of the property-owning classes, whose enmity she soon attracted with various idealistic plans for the amelioration of peasant welfare. Her factual situation was strikingly similar to the fictional one of Dorothea Brooke in George Eliot's *Middlemarch*. The determined resistance by many landowners to any program of social amelioration for agricultural tenants shocked her, and led her to sympathize with those Russian reformers, including especially in her mind the emperor Alexander I, who had become czar in 1801, and who faced the opposition of ignorant, black reaction.

In those years before her dramatic conversion she rarely spoke of

God. Her preferred term, shared by so many in the eighteenth century, was "Providence." We find her writing thus in one of her letters to Jean-Paul (Richter): "I thank Providence for this heart [she speaks of her own] full of confidence. But what else does it do but dream? Where is its energy? Where are the deeds which would raise me in my own estimation?" At this point in her life the "deeds" she had in mind were perhaps the achievement of literary works that might bring her fame. But even then she showed an increasing appetite for those social "good works" that in Catholic countries were the hallmarks of the so-called *dévotes* or deeply religious lay women, the heiresses of the likes of Madame de Chantal, whose inspiration gave birth to a dozen new socially oriented religious orders. In one of her letters she describes what was in effect a slum-crawling expedition with her children in Teplitz, Bohemia. "We stopped in a narrow street and went up to a gloomy and dirty chamber. The woman was seriously ill, and her husband, although evidently strong, seemed to be overwhelmed. I poured a few crowns which we had gathered together into his wife's apron. My children spoke to her in a sympathetic manner, full of compassion. What a charming expression came in their pretty faces!"

Conversion as Rebellion

An aspect of religious conversion seldom considered was its potential for social disruption, even revolution. The old meaning of the word "conversion" was not what it is today. In the centuries of a thoroughly Christianized Europe such a conversion as that of Augustine, a conversion *from* paganism *to* Christianity, was a historical and literary memory. What conversion usually meant even in early modern Europe was the well-considered entry into ascetic life. The *conversus* formally embraced the so-called *contemptus mundi*, a Latin phrase meaning literally the "despite of the world," and figuratively the abandonment of all worldly values. The ascetic vows of religion, which in the Roman Church had long since become at least the ostensible burden of all clerics, formally abjured all gratifications of material wealth, political power, and sexual satisfaction—that is, the engines that drive most of what we call "real life."

Such radical constraints on human behavior often had social implications that went far beyond the individual. In a society in which the maintenance of family property might be a preeminent consideration, the perceived threat to the preservation of familial assets was grave indeed. Religious life offered a useful asylum for many young people otherwise inconvenient to their families. But for an elder son, let alone an only son, to undergo "conversion" was a catastrophe not cheerfully to be accepted. In his *Chronicles*, the early Franciscan historian Salimbene di Adam gives us an anecdote concerning his own acceptance of the Franciscan habit. Members of his family accompanied by armed knights surrounded the little religious house in which he had taken up residence. They demanded his return; the friars refused. There was a standoff, threatening at any moment to descend into bloodshed, as his relatives loudly berated him for betraying family duty, and while the friars shouted out encouraging (not to mention infuriating) scriptural passages, such as: "Anyone who loves father or mother more than me is not worthy of me." Versions of this pattern of family strife, though seldom so poetically exemplified, were very common in Catholic Europe down to the time of the French Revolution.

Religion had its place, and irreligion was a serious threat to society, vigorously repressed. But as episodes of social history in premodern Europe repeatedly demonstrate, religion taken too seriously might be a threat hardly less alarming. Of this truth the historical exemplifications are many and notorious. King Henry appointed his friend Thomas as archbishop of Canterbury in the wholly reasonable expectation that

Thomas would demonstrate his gratitude for preferment by honoring his royal patron's expectations concerning various matters ecclesial. The rest is, as we say, history. Much closer to the materials dealt with in this book is the career of the reforming abbess Mère Angélique Arnauld. She became head of the famous Jansenist religious house of Port-Royal as a child of eleven—a fact that might well suggest the distance that the social reality of "religious life" could stray from its ascetic theory. When Carlyle in his *Past and Present* chose a subject typifying the dynamic pattern of leadership lacking in the England of his day, he found it in the story of a reforming medieval abbot who had taken religion far too seriously for the comfort of his comfortable monks.

Jean-Paul

Some sense of the compartmentalized nature of Julie de Krüdener's life during the final years of the eighteenth century should be clear from the narrative so far. She led an extraordinarily peripatetic life, circling and recircling in wide arcs among the cities from Lausanne to St. Petersburg. Her extensive travels were only partially required by her social exigencies, and whether they were more cause or effect of the compartmentalization would be difficult to say. Lacking a full edition of her collected letters—a scholarly desideratum that might bring fame as well as pleasure to an archivally minded social historian—it is very difficult to get a full, coherent, and sequential command of her physical movements, let alone her intellectual and spiritual ones.

It seems clear that her residence in Berlin brought certain finalities that, if they did nothing else, cleared the path ahead. It is from this time, in the first place, that her letters begin to be filled with an ascetically tinged world-weariness. Berlin was full of deracinated French aristocrats, who tended often to behave in the manner of other expatriate lost generations. She was genuinely shocked by the openness and coarseness of the hedonism, which often scoffed at even the pretense of high ethical justification, and which from the point of view of sensibility was woefully lacking. Though she remained self-absorbed to a fault, she seems to have constructed no mental parallel between her own rootlessness and the frantic anomie she found about her on every side. Indeed, it is the combination of her acute analysis of the moral vacuity of the social scene in Berlin with her own apparent superficiality concerning her own spiritual condition that has given ammunition to her unfriendly biographers. Nonetheless, in retrospect, leaving Berlin would be the first step in a journey that took her far away from her old life.

Also, she did now resolve, finally and definitively, that her marriage with the baron de Krüdener had ended. Unfortunately, she did not at first tell him exactly that in so many words. This time the pretext for continued separation, recognized as such by the baron, was her health. Though not yet forty years old she suffered with rheumatism, and her doctors counseled—as they usually could be relied upon to do—"the waters." One of her favorite watering places was Teplitz, a Bohemian spa now in the Czech Republic, and she determined to return there. At Teplitz she was with old friends, especially the princesses Radziwill and Galinsky. Social frivolity comes in different strengths or proofs, and that of Teplitz seemed to her desirable. It would take one more "delay" to convince the baron of the finality of the truth. She wrote to him saying that her health now required her to remove to Switzerland. The baron's reply to the situation is an impressive monument to a certain species of moral nobility. He accepted the situation. What else could he do? He did allow himself a few words of chiding: "As you had definitively made up your mind to leave my house, why did you not inform me of your intention previous to your departure?" But it was a rhetorical question, not an invitation to a continuing correspondence; and his last known words to her, with which his dignified letter ends, plead that she should believe him "heart and soul your sincere and devoted friend."

. . .

TRUTH, WE KNOW, IS the daughter of time; but time has several less prestigious sisters, including among them literary fame. Some historical phenomena require a certain amplitude of time to work themselves out. When asked what he thought were the chief results of the French Revolution, Zhou Enlai (or any one of a number of people to whom dubious but desirable quotations are attributed) remarked that it was too soon to tell. True literary fame requires staying power, the approbation of two or three generations at the very least. This is why the phrase "once popular" is among the cruelest in the vocabulary of literary history. But the literary supernova, though particularly characteristic of our own age, has existed as long as literary reputation has been recorded. One of the great literary superstars of Julie's time was her nearly exact contemporary Jean-Paul.

This man was a Bavarian, whose real name was Johann Paul Friedrich Richter (1763–1825). He took up its abbreviated French version in obvious homage to the superstardom of his Romantic hero, Jean-Jacques (Rousseau), and in deference to the reigning claims of French literary culture. He was, however, a German who wrote in the German language, and wrote so prolifically that the first edition of his collected works ran to some sixty volumes. His fiction was highly eccentric both in form and content, but its demonstrations of offbeat erudition, philosophical speculation, and often broad comedy attracted an enthusiastic following. He began writing seriously in the 1790s, and his novel *Hesperus* (1795) clinched his fame.

Enlightenment developments in science and philosophy had established in both France and England the prestige of the German language. It was in this context that Madame de Staël had thought it timely to introduce the French province of the Republic of Letters to German literature. Julie de Krüdener had the considerable cultural advantage of having a perfect command of that literature, in which she had read widely. (Her written German was, as she well knew, clumsy and inelegant, as all her writing training had been in French.) Jean-Paul was not exactly a Bernardin de Saint-Pierre, but he was a rising star with interests (the supernatural adumbrations to be found in the world of Nature, for example) of special appeal to Julie's own sensibility. It was only natural that the aspirant would seek out the newly minted master as soon as opportunity presented itself.

The opportunity came in the summer of 1796, during one of her recurrent peripatetic episodes while she was still trying to hold together her relationship with Hippolyte Terray. She had returned for a second sojourn at Leipzig. Jean-Paul had at that time made a romantic flight to the soothing isolation of the countryside not too far from Leipzig in a beautiful place called Hof. This was one of the more widely advertised rustications since Petrarch took up residence at the Fontaine de Vaucluse. There in an elegant peasant's hut Jean-Paul, who had already been accorded the sobriquet "Jean-Paul the incomparable," received a stream of admiring visitors, many of them women, and not a few like Julie de Krüdener, young and beautiful women.

Ernest Knapton, who was the first to realize the thematic significance of Julie's friendship with Jean-Paul, has documented it in detail. Both of them, in differing styles, were outrageous flirts. Jean-Paul was one of those writers who write down nearly everything, and one of the things that had passed through his youthful mind was a burlesque version of the "questions" set for essay competitions and entrance examinations. "Prize question for the Erotic Academy: How far may friendship toward women go, and what is the difference between it and love?" They both had their roles to play. Julie was that kind of woman attracted to ugly men of talent; Jean-Paul was that kind of man attracted to talented women of beauty. This proved to be a satisfactory basis for acquaintanceship and a brief exchange of letters.

Jean-Paul had written almost gushingly to his intimate friend

Christian Otto, describing Julie as a creature semi-divine. The only sublunary analogies he found appropriate came from the field of sacred art. Julie recalled for him the beauty of a Madonna or a *Mater Dolorosa*. To Julie herself, with whom he initiated a correspondence, he was scarcely less extravagant. "You came like a dream, you went like a dream, and I am still living in a dream."

In her reply Julie kept up the beat. "You also will be unforgettable to me, more from what I saw and from what I felt as I looked at you than from what I read on those occasions when I was struck by deep emotion by your works." But of course she *had* read the works, and was not chary of giving her opinion of them; but it was the work that was the man himself that had captivated her.

She wrote in response: "I can never forget those hours when your eyes, the sound of your voice, the indescribable whole of your emotions as revealed through your expression and accent conveyed me to the sweetest of harmonies—I mean, reason combined with emotion."

That final phrase merits a reflective pause. Knapton was concerned to bring out the element of sentiment in Julie de Krüdener especially in the early and literary phases of her life, including conspicuously her pursuit of famous literary figures like Bernardin de Saint-Pierre and Jean-Paul. It was the element of sentimentality, an element impossible to ignore but perhaps not so easy to assess justly, that made him want to stress her Romanticism. The assumption here is that sentiment marks a sharp departure from the central intellectual concerns of the Enlightenment.

A moment's reflection will reveal the inadequacy of a formulation that would banish Rousseau, Diderot, and even Baron Grimm from the fame of Enlightenment. In fact, what Julie de Krüdener says comes strikingly close to Wordsworth's celebrated definition of poetry in the preface to the *Lyrical Ballads*: "I have said that poetry is the spontaneous overflow of powerful feelings: it takes its origin from emotion recollected in tranquillity: the emotion is contemplated till by a species

of reaction the tranquillity gradually disappears, and an emotion, kin-
dred to that which was before the subject of contemplation, is gradually produced, and does itself actually exist in the mind." But very
significantly the word used by Julie de Krüdener is not "tranquillity"; it
is "reason." The difference, which may seem subtle, is not without its
importance. Kant had said that it was the peculiar feature of the
human mind to set itself problems which it was incapable of solving.
For Julie de Krüdener and many others of the "sentimental" school,
emotion was not the enemy of reason, but its partner or handmaiden.

Julie and Jean-Paul met several times more over the next few years,
but there were limits even to his protean energies, the genuinely erotic
elements of which were increasingly monopolized by the pursuit of his
future wife, Caroline Meyer. Julie felt strangely authorized to unburden
herself to him as though he were the most intimate of friends, often
enough with a whiff of ethical blackmail. "I am one of those silent and
obscure souls who love your splendor," she writes, "not because its luster throws light upon them, no! But because it is beneficial for the
general good and for humanity. My soul loves your worth." A man like
Jean-Paul Richter at a time like that could easily be expected to write
a dozen or more letters a day—that in addition to all the "real" writing,
holding court, and frank socializing that might be required of him.
These were obligations that might impose upon him the necessity of a
kind of epistolary triage, and he let the correspondence lapse.

It is probably for this reason that Richter's importance in the formation of Julie de Krüdener's self-image has been insufficiently explored.
He was important to her in many ways, beginning with her literary
scalp-hunting. Their correspondence, intermittent and even perfunctory as it may have been, gave her another scalp for her collection. But
Jean-Paul's handling of religious topics, which he frequently addressed
in picturesque and sentimental fashion, made the search for transcendence an aspect of his appreciation of Nature. This seems to have been
very much on Julie's wavelength. Further, Jean-Paul had had a sober-

ing experience just about the time of his first great "worldly" success with *Hesperus*, of which he frequently spoke. He had had some kind of vision of his own death, which while not exactly like that effected under similar circumstances to Dickens's Scrooge, had dramatically ethicized if not theologized his conception of his literary vocation. Julie de Krüdener would in due course have a similar moment of ethical clarification at which her lifelong yearning for literary fame would be to her as the sounds of lyres and flutes. But before she despises the fame, she must first achieve it.

During these years, as we have already seen, Julie de Krüdener was on the side conducting the great love affair of her life, giving birth to a bastard son and arranging with unhesitating worldly wisdom for his social concealment, and trying—endlessly, as it seemed—to break free from a marriage from which she appeared to have broken free on at least three previous occasions. She moved about the German cities a good deal and had another stay in Lausanne. Her social community seemed usually to center among the French émigrés, some of whom, on account of marriage, business arrangements, or disasters back in France, had more or less happily become permanent expatriates.

An obviously orchestrated silence hovers over the end of the relationship with Hippolyte Terray. It seems to have been effected without undue emotion, and certainly without public displays of any sort. There were still plenty of men in Julie's life, but they tended toward the elderly, the philosophical, and the clerical. Two appear to have been influential in the tolerant and ecumenical structuring of her developing religious vision. During a visit to Munich she had become acquainted with an erudite Catholic priest, the abbé Becker. She greatly admired this man, who became for her a kind of extra-ecclesial guru; but he died, suddenly, while their intellectual intimacy was still in its infancy. The second was Ludwig Ernst von Borowski, whom she encountered at Königsberg. Borowski was one of the most prominent exponents of orthodox Lutheranism around the turn of the nineteenth century. He was also something of a model of the "society cleric" prominent in the realistic fiction of the period. A considerable correspondence between these two friends survives, and from it is apparent that Borowski took Julie to be a woman of marked intellectual ability and unusual spiritual capacity.

For several years Julie had lived with the considerable tension of having a dead marriage and a living husband. Her inner deliberations concerning marital reconciliation, however intermittent or self-deceiving, finally came to an end when her husband died on June 14, 1802. She was by then well along with *Valérie*. When the news reached her, she grieved sincerely for the loss of her "dearest friend." But she must have experienced also a sense of liberation. She was now free to become famous; but there is evidence that she already regarded fame's achievement with a strange ambivalence.

Seeking New Life: The Pietists

In the spring of 1804 Julie de Krüdener, now a woman of forty, returned to the family home in Riga. A great deal had happened since she set out in naïveté or innocence as a young bride of eighteen. She was now a widow, and fatherless. Her mother was still living, indeed living in good health, but beyond purely local and familial topics the two women no longer had much in common. She had been made famous by her book *Valérie*, but the brief glister of her literary celebrity now seemed increasingly dim. Her letters from this period reveal a general spiritual unease falling between ennui and anxiety. She had in effect become a stranger in her own hyperborean land, the supposed landscape of her exquisite sensibility. In point of fact there were important cultural and intellectual resources available in Riga, but they were academic and Masonic. There was nothing in her native capital that to her mind might approach a Parisian literary *salon*. Most of all, perhaps, she suffered from the loneliness she had so poignantly recorded in the diary of her early married life.

In his classic *Varieties of Religious Experience*, William James describes the general feeling of malaise that often was a prelude to dramatic religious conversion. Many converts, famously including St. Augustine in his *Confessions*, actually spoke of this state in the language of pathology. This was also the controlling trope of the *Consolation of Philosophy*, a classic of the early Middle Ages still read by the philosophers of the Enlightenment. That is, the soul on the threshold of conversion often perceives its own sickness and, yet more terrible, its inability to heal itself. Julie cast about in search of purpose and for a time entertained the possibility of a new writing project. She had a somewhat vague idea for a book to be called *The Peoples of the World*, hardly a modest topic, nor one easily achieved. We may doubt that it was ever much more than a pipe dream, but it provided the occasion for her to offer some highly interesting remarks about *Valérie*. The new book would be, she wrote, "the contrary of *Valérie*. I think this work will be extremely moral: the great number of truths that I have collected, and the great number of wealthy people whom I've seen to be unhappy, will give me a thousand inexhaustible topics from which I can draw moral lessons."

As she had always firmly defended the moral nature of her novel, her remarks here may be rather puzzling. One can easily enough attack the artistry of *Valérie* or its implicit social values; but its morality would seem to be unexceptional. Indeed, from the conventional point of view, all the characters in *Valérie* are "moral" to a fault. The most plausible conclusion one can draw from her remark is that she now regarded the very stuff of romantic love, which is to say the central material of European fiction, as a false and "worldly" goal, incapable of providing the happiness so eagerly sought by the soul. "Thou hast made us for thyself, and our heart is restless 'til it find its rest in Thee." She had made an exchange of ethical banalities from "Love makes the world go round" to "Money cannot buy happiness."

There was a precipitating event. One day as she sat or stood at a window facing the public street, idly watching the activity below, a man, an acquaintance of hers, was passing by below. Their eyes met momentarily, and the man tipped his hat or made some other sign of friendly recognition. Within an instant, within a few steps, while she still had her eyes upon the walking figure, the man dropped dead or dying in the street, struck down by a cerebral occlusion or a heart attack. The empirical experience of the impermanence of human life and the possibility of its abrupt annihilation is one that many people have had, though seldom in so stark a form, and the experience is a natural invitation to somber reflection by even the most slow-witted. The world is surely a most unstable or "tikel" place, muses the old carpenter in Chaucer's "Miller's Tale":

> *I saw today a cors yborn to chirche*
> *That now, on Monday last, I saugh hym wirche.*

Julie de Krüdener, impelled by this accidental and catalytic intimacy with mortality, now appears to have directed the laser beam of her exquisite sensibility toward the *novissimi*, the "Last Things" of Christian theology: Death, Judgment, Heaven, Hell.

The carrot and the stick of the old religion were the hope of heaven and the fear of hell. They had been the motivating forces behind medieval religious practice, of which a good deal remained, even in Protestant countries, through the time of the Enlightenment. It is perhaps a testimony to the sweetness of Julie's personality that the religious views she now began to espouse with fervor were positive and optimistic—at least for the moment. The realignment of her ideas had cheerfully centered on the meaning of happiness. She had spent her entire life wanting to be happy; she continued to want to be happy now. So, for her, religious conversion did not mean the adoption of ascetic attitudes that implied the postponement of all gratification to some supposed future state. It meant, instead, a redefinition of happiness itself. Happiness as an abstraction was the quality possessed by happy people. From her new perspective, the glittering world of famous writers and the scintillating *salon*, the goal for which she had yearned and which she had so surprisingly achieved, was not a world of happy people. Happy people were to be found elsewhere, such as in the cottages of peasants or the workshops of modest artisans. This is after all what Rousseau and Bernardin de Saint-Pierre had taught.

Of course very few religious conversions are in fact as instantaneous as presented by those who experience them and who perhaps unconsciously invest them with a narrative drama their personal significance seems to demand. Religion, and religious practice, had never been entirely absent from Julie's life. Yet it is difficult to map out the contours of her spiritual life in the pre-conversion period. Patterns of allusion in her letters give clear evidence of her familiarity with the Bible, and especially with the Gospels. This was probably gained less from systematic Bible-reading than from repeatedly hearing the reading of the assigned pericopes in regularly attended church services. Evidence suggests, however, that Julie's conversion was primarily "social," having been effected through personal contacts with certain individuals who shattered her received sense of human happiness: Pietists.

MUHLENBECK, THE NINETEENTH-CENTURY ANTI-CLERICAL local historian of Alsatian antiquities, began his indispensable (but nearly unfindable) book *A Study of the Origins of the Holy Alliance* with an arresting declaration: "The heroes of this history were all Pietists and Chiliasts." But he says as well that their world is "today" so little known as to require a goodly amount of preliminary explication. As Muhlenbeck wrote around 1870, hardly half a century removed from that world, for us the need for some background is more pressing yet.

We must wait a moment for the chiliasts; but who were the Pietists? Muhlenbeck's own definition of them is hardly dispassionate. They are "the Pharisees of Protestantism, people who live apart from other Christians and are ceaselessly occupied with devotional reading, pious exercises, and complaints against all those who are not of their coterie."

Pietism was not a church, but a movement or a tendency. The elements of the word "religion" (literally, a "re-tying") point to a concept of the recreation of a once broken connection with God. The thirst for direct experience of God had been the motive, at least at a theoretical level, of traditional Christian ascetic life. It animated many of the great Reformers as well. They longed for ecclesial structures that encouraged a direct access to the divine; but in none of the major centers of official Protestantism (German-speaking Lutheranism, French-speaking Calvinism, English-speaking Anglicanism) were the results satisfactory to all the believers. In this context, Pietism might be regarded as a second wave of the Reform within German Protestantism.

It had no generally recognized leader, but historians have been eager to supply it with a "founder"—the Lutheran theologian Philipp Jacob Spener (1635–1705). Spener, a great preacher, enunciated certain principles that became the essence of Pietism. He placed a primary emphasis on the *laity*. Luther himself had insisted on the concept of the "priesthood of all believers." Spener clothed this abstraction with the attractive garments of his erudition. He had very high standards for the clergy, but his ideal was not different from that of all of Christian history, that of George Herbert's "Country Parson," for example. Ministers should be both pious *and* learned; but their function was to teach people to fish, not to give them fish. The essence of Christian life was with the individual laity, in Bible-reading, in prayer, in pious social action. The pastor's teaching and preaching efforts should be directed toward encouraging individual piety and the broadest possible lay participation.

These Pietist principles are perhaps recognizable in Muhlenbeck's definition, but another is not. Spener insisted on a kind of theological pacifism. Far from authorizing attacks on all those who did not agree with him, he insisted that religious discussion—of which there was a very great deal in the world he inherited—should be conducted gently, charitably, and with as little committed polemicism as possible. If this was a rule chiefly honored in the breach it was hardly the first Christian principle of which that could be said.

Pietism was thus a "spiritual" movement within the Lutheran Church, one with a significant "social" dimension. In important respects it closely resembles other such movements within the state-Protestant churches such as Puritanism, and especially Methodism, in England. The question of "separatism" is more complicated. Should Christians live "in the world" or establish separate, self-sufficient communities? This was a controverted question. Partly impelled by positive principle, partly prodded by persecution, various groups of radical Protestants did adopt separatism. That had, after all, been the mode of life of those seeking "Christian perfection" since the time of Anthony of the Desert. The sense of "separatism" as used of the Pietists by the German historians of religion has a different meaning. It refers to those "extremists" who refused to participate in the official state cult or cross the threshold of its temples. There were many Lutherans who sympathized with Pietist ideals and practice. They remained within the state Church, like "low church" Anglicans. The German "separatist" Pietists were the equivalent of the English Dissenters. They left the state Church altogether. Social separation was a different if cognate phenomenon. To this day there are throughout the world scattered "separatist" groups, descendants of the sixteenth-century Anabaptists, bearing the names of their early leaders—Mennonites, Hutterites, Amish. Only at the very end of her life did Julie de Krüdener contemplate the possibility of a separatist community. Her Pietism, which was born of social contact, would be of a social variety.

. . .

THREE REPRESENTATIVE MEETINGS WITH individual Pietists—using that term loosely—illuminate Julie de Krüdener's new religious consciousness as revealed in the self-fashioning of her letters. Her conversion, like so many others, was the prelude to long periods of self-reproach and morbid speculations concerning the "Last Things." But she came to be convinced that God—at first all unknown to her—had begun to take an interest in the minute details of her life.

She needed new shoes. In the aristocratic world of that time, haberdashers and shoemakers gladly made house calls. So she sent for a man to come and take measurements. The reader must know that in tolerant and multicultural Riga there was now a small but vital colony of Moravian artisans, including at least one master cobbler. By purest chance (or Providence's plan) it was this man who came to Julie de Krüdener's mansion. Either out of modesty, preoccupation, or social hauteur, she did not even look at the fellow as he measured her foot. But the shoemaker asked her a question about the proposed shoes, and she was now required to turn her face and engage him in conversation. What she saw shook her to the core. The man seemed to radiate with an inner, joyous peace. This seemed to her a reproach for her own melancholy.

"My friend," she asked, "are you a happy man?"

"Oh, I am the happiest of men!" was his reply.

She said nothing more, and the cobbler departed, measurements in hand, to his last. But Julie de Krüdener spent a restless night, tossing and turning as she pondered the mystery of felicity. First thing in the morning she set off herself for the cobbler's shop, determined to interrogate this poor, humble man who had apparently found the pearl of great price.

More with his life than with his lips this man seemed to preach to her the most eloquent of sermons. The substance of this sermon has not survived, but we can be pretty sure it closely resembled the Methodist sermon of the "preacher woman" Dinah in the second chapter of *Adam Bede*. No one has better or more generously captured the essence of Christian Pietism than the infidel George Eliot. With Julie's admiration of his simple gospel piety the dark shadows melted from her spirit. All once again was light.

If she ever saw her blessed cobbler again, she left no record of it. More enduring—and more annoying to her historians—was Julie de Krüdener's association with Madame Blau, a Livonian widow whom she first met in 1805, and with whom she had a close spiritual association for many years. Madame Blau seems to have been a type who will be familiar to many readers of nineteenth-century fiction, and to a few perhaps from real life. Madame Blau was, as Knapton puts it, "the first of that long line of fanatics who came henceforth into the career of poor Julie with monotonous regularity." In terms of the world, Madame Blau's situation was hardly an enviable one. She had six children, no husband, and only her wits and dexterous needlework to win bread for her table. Furthermore, she suffered from a chronic nervous condition. It is hard enough to define a "nervous condition" today. The further back in history one moves, the harder still it becomes. Madame Blau's nervous condition, like Lady Anne Conway's in the time of Greatrakes the Stroker, involved frequent headaches of such severity as to send her to her bed. What most struck Julie in all this was the woman's preternatural equanimity in the midst of her sufferings, and her unshakable certainty that they were part of an unfathomable divine plan.

"She is the happiest creature I have ever seen in my life. She fervently desires death, but only to be separated from sin. She is persuaded that she will enjoy an unspeakable heavenly bliss with her Savior and her God; yet she submits to Him, and by no means prays to die." Julie, greatly affected, wrote to her friend and co-conspirator Madame Armand: "Oh, my good Armand! Pray, pray as a child! If you are not yet in this blessed state, pray! Ask for that divine grace that God always grants for the love of his Son. You will receive it, you will sense that man cannot be more happy—in this world or the next—without Jesus Christ, without the belief that salvation cannot be granted save by him. . . ."

On May 17, 1807, Julie de Krüdener had an interview with Adam Müller, the peasant-prophet of Meisenbacherhof, near Nussloch, south of Heidelberg. There was a long tradition of humble prophets, women preachers, child evangelists, and other unconventional intermediaries of the divine Word. Through the course of Christian history, God had repeatedly chosen the weak and powerless as the vessels of His revelation. As the Fathers of the Church had said, *Fishermen*, not *Philosophers*! Julie now thought, *Cobblers*, not *Cardinals*. These were the ones that Christ in his earthly ministry had called to be the bearers of his Gospel. At Christmastime of 1805, an angelic apparition had appeared to Adam Müller with a revelation: there would be a great war among Prussia, Russia, and France. However, the spectral messenger had added a curious coda: "Tell no one!" This was a command later breached, but for the moment Müller held his silence.

The messages conveyed to Adam became increasingly political. The next one, about a year later, commissioned him to set off in search of the king, meaning the King of Prussia. The message was conventionally severe: "Repent! Bring your whole realm to repentance! Trust not in the might of your arms or those of your allies. Help will come only from the living God." This injunction was confirmed a fortnight later when he met on the road a grizzled old man carrying, like Moses, the books of the Law. The graybeard opened his Bible and began reading at considerable length from the prophecies of Isaiah. Then he said to Adam: "Go! Repeat what you have heard to the King. Command him, in the name of the eternal God, to do what is written. . . . If he submits to the will of the most-high, the French will be scattered as the flimsy straw is scattered by the wind. . . . If he refuses to submit to the Lord's Commandments, tell him that the scourge of war will join the scourge of plague and the scourge of famine."

Chiliasm: the Mystery of Iniquity

The prophesying of Adam Müller can lead us to a brief consideration of chiliasm—the second topic that, along with Pietism, defined for Muhlenbeck the career of Julie de Krüdener. The word "chiliasm" derives from the Greek word for thousand. It means the same thing as the Latin-derived millennialism. It is a theological belief in the "thousand-year reign" of the returning Christ. Its literary "source" is the final book of the Christian Scriptures, the Revelation to St. John.

Literary decisions have rarely had a large impact on world history, but the decision taken by some early Church Fathers that the Book of Revelation was canonical—that is, a genuine and authoritative part of the divinely revealed Word of God—is perhaps a rare example of one. The Book of Revelation (also called because of its genre the Apocalypse) is an allegorical prose poem that presents itself as a "vision" sent by God "through his angel to his servant John" on the island of Patmos in the Aegean Sea. This John has traditionally been identified as the Apostle John, author of the fourth Gospel and of three short New Testament epistles; but the identification is doubtful. Historical critics of the Bible are inclined to see the book as a response of the Christian community to a crisis of persecution—possibly that of Nero or of Domitian. The book's anti-Roman polemic is unmistakable. It is full of vivid imagery, some of it "recycled" from the older Jewish Apocalyptic tradition (as in the Book of Daniel) and some of it apparently contemporary. Certain themes are fairly easy to identify: the persecution of the faithful by powerful evil forces and the eventual triumph of the faithful in the Second Coming of Jesus Christ.

The Apocalypse is almost certainly a topical if coded "message" to an early Christian community, encouraging its perseverance in specific and very difficult circumstances—namely, a Roman imperial persecution. Its inclusion in the canon had the tendency to make it timeless, of course, so that its "contemporary" meaning has been sought in every century of Christian history. Today, one is perhaps likely to associate it with strange radio transmissions from Del Rio, Texas, or with pamphlets thrust into one's hand in the Forty-Second Street bus station. But at no period in history was it more assiduously studied than in the Enlightenment. Among the most fervid of Apocalyptic speculators was Sir Isaac Newton.

Of the many perplexing images and episodes in the Apocalyptic book, none has proved more arresting than the prophecy of a thousand-year reign of Christ, which will occur immediately before the final battle and defeat of Satan and the advent of the final and eternal Kingdom of Christ (the opening verses of the twentieth chapter). At the beginning of the passage the visionary sees an angel "coming down out of heaven, having the key to the Abyss and holding in his hand a great chain. He seized the dragon, that ancient serpent, and bound him *for a thousand years.*" It is this "thousand" (*kilias* in Greek) that is the root of the word "chiliasm," meaning an historical or theological view based in an interpretation of the Apocalypse, and by extension any attempt to apply Bible prophecy to an interpretation of secular history.

The strange, wild images of the Apocalypse have attracted the attention of deep thinkers in every century. They proved to be the capacious and versatile forms that have supplied the Rorschach inkblots for a hundred historical systems. Their visual realization has provided an iconography of genius from the Iberian Beatus manuscripts to the woodcuts of Albrecht Dürer. In the late twelfth century Joachim of Fiore, perhaps the greatest of all the chiliasts, completed a vast edifice of chiliastic expectation that would haunt the Church for the next five hundred years, and in some ways haunts it still. There is hardly a major Christian thinker of the Renaissance who did not subscribe to some form of Joachimism, and hardly a major thinker between the period of 1400 and 1700 who did not indulge in some form of chiliasm. Columbus was a chiliast, as were many of the early Jesuit missionaries.

Though it is significant that we find millenarian clichés and patterns of thought even in the folk spirituality of a man like Adam Müller, chiliasm was primarily a learned mental habit. One form or another of it attracted many of the greatest minds of Europe. I have mentioned Isaac Newton, but there were literally dozens of others of his stripe. More recent chiliasts are legion, including, among others in the public eye, President Ronald Reagan. As the general "plot" of the Apocalypse involves a titanic struggle of good against evil, chiliastic (millenarian) thinkers have often sought to understand large world conflicts in terms of scriptural prophecy. In particular, chiliastic commentary has often focused on powerful political or military leaders, such as Frederick II, Charles V, Napoleon, Hitler, Stalin, and Franklin Roosevelt. The Protestant Reformation occasioned a certain canonization of chiliastic identifications. Protestant exegetes found it obvious that the whore of Babylon must be the Pope, while Roman Catholics were sure she was a prophetic emblem of Martin Luther.

When Julie de Krüdener had longed to be a writer among famous writers, she followed the obvious pattern of preparation by reading widely and by trying to become a part of the literary scene. Now that her ambition was to become a great Christian soul among other great souls, she followed a similar apprenticeship. There were two great writers among the German Pietists. The first of them was Nikolaus Ludwig, Count von Zinzendorf, who had been born in 1700 and who died in the year of Julie's birth, 1764. The other, still very much alive, was Jung-Stilling. Julie began a program of self-improvement by reading the works of Zinzendorf and by entering into correspondence with Jung-Stilling.

Zinzendorf: A New Guru

Count Zinzendorf, a brilliant polymath, is now generally admitted to be the most important German Reformed theologian between Luther and Schleiermacher. He was a preacher, a poet, a musician, a missionary, and an ecclesiastical diplomat of rare ability. His fame today rests primarily in his claim to be "the father of ecumenicism," but in the eighteenth century he was chiefly known for his connections with Pietism and with the church of the Moravian Brethren. The Moravians (also known as the Bohemians) were a group of radical Protestants in eastern Europe, the heirs of John Hus and others. Zinzendorf was a Lutheran magnate. When some persecuted Moravians sought asylum in Germany, Zinzendorf, greatly impressed by their simple piety and its sad contrast with the tepid formalism of prevailing Lutheran orthodoxy, welcomed them to his own personal property.

They established a religious community called Herrnhut, and Zinzendorf soon ceased to be their landlord or benefactor and became their leader and principal theologian. What most appealed to Zinzendorf was their simplicity, their sincerity (he credited them with what he called "the religion of the heart"), and their tolerant spirit, which attempted to focus on evangelical fundamentals and to discount sectarian dogma. The name of the Moravian Church had originally been *Unitas Fratrum*, the "Unity of the Brothers." This phrase was taken from the *incipit* of the 133rd Psalm: *Ecce quam bonum et quam jucundum habitare fratres in unum* ("Behold how good and how pleasant it is for brethren to dwell together in unity"). Indeed, the Brethren perhaps took to its limit the generalized Protestant phenomenon of the "secularization of asceticism," turning their entire community into a lay monastery.

Zinzendorf is more important in the rise and spread of Pietist ideas through his personality than through his specific doctrines. Nonetheless, he had espoused a number of the Enlightenment intellectual enthusiasms that have concerned us elsewhere in this book. Among his particular interests was the kabbala. He was probably familiar with the very learned book of Budaeus, *An Introduction to the History of the Philosophy of the Hebrews* (1702). And like so many others in his age, he sought to find in the Apocalypse the meaning of contemporary history.

There were two features of Zinzendorf's religion that would have had a particular appeal to Julie. The first was its conciliatory and ecumenical spirit. One of the great achievements of the Enlightenment, as exemplified in a particularly pleasing way by Voltaire, was its relentless battle for religious tolerance. Wars of religion had devastated Germany in the sixteenth century and France in the seventeenth. Religion had been a major factor in the English Civil War. *By their works shall ye know them.* One not unnatural response to the bloody history of Christianity was to abandon religion altogether, at least to the degree that it might be socially possible to do so. Zinzendorf cannot have been the first Christian to perceive that, even leaving the strapado and thumbscrews aside, the spirit of factionalism and sectarianism alone was a terrible obstacle for Christian apologists. He therefore anticipated one major strand of modern ecumenicism in finding that tolerance was the necessary condition of successful evangelization. Thus, although he was an animated "evangelical," he taught that tolerance was itself a fundamental doctrine of Christianity.

A second point was perhaps even more important. The Moravian Brothers appear to have been one of the few Christian groups since the time of Jesus and his disciples to organize themselves not around creed or confession but around *community.* That is, their emphasis was not in the first instance upon correctness of belief but upon correctness of social relations. Their foundational written document is accordingly not a creed but a social compact. The *metaphoric* identification of the entire human race as a single family of brothers and sisters has been fairly easy to achieve; but groups who have attempted to transpose the metaphor into literal reality have usually run into difficulty from people who imagine a very different model of social organization. The radical egalitarianism of the Pietists, as of other "fringe" sects, was an insult and a threat to prevailing social theories of hierarchical stratification. But it was a mind-set that now drew Julie de Krüdener out of the aristocratic coteries, whether social, religious, or artistic, that had been her whole life.

Julie also would have found in Zinzendorf an appealing aesthetic and poetic element. He was a poet of sorts, and promoter of a collection of Pietist hymns by Gerhard Tersteegen, *Das geistliche Blumengartlein* (*The Spiritual Flower Bed*), that later had an influence on the formation of Methodist hymnody in England. But the greatest influence upon her was not surprisingly the greatest of living Pietist writers, Johann Heinrich Jung (pseudonym Jung-Stilling, 1740–1817), whom she now sought out in correspondence. This man became for her a kind of literary and spiritual guru.

Jung-Stilling

Jean-Paul Richter found the path to literary fame by dropping his surname. Johann Heinrich Jung in achieving fame added a second. He had been born into an artisanal family of modest means as Jung. He later added the "Stilling" apparently in allusion to the Psalm verse (35:20) "For civil words they speak not, but against *the peaceful in the land* they fashion treacherous speech. . . ." Luther's German for the italicized phrase is *die Stillen im Lande*. If this is correct, the *Stilling* signaled the pacifist and irenic spirit of Pietism. In Anglophone Protestantism the parallel group was of course the Quakers, with whom indeed the German Pietists had many ties. The family Jung nicely exemplifies the operations of the meritocratic principle that became ever more evident during the Enlightenment. The family métiers had been agriculture, then charcoal burning, but various members began to distinguish themselves in the skilled professions. One became a lawyer, another an expert toolmaker.

Johann Heinrich Jung, who precociously displayed unusual intellectual ability, picked up a scattered but impressive education. Three early influences were decisive. He had learned to read by reading the Bible, a habit approved by his mother and later reinforced by a much-admired Pietist tailor in Solingen to whom he was for a time apprenticed. Next, a student friend introduced him to the esoteric tradition: some medico-alchemical writings of Paracelsus, and the mystical essays of Jakob Boehme. Finally, he read widely on his own in the copious philosophical works of Christian von Wolff. Wolff is now studied chiefly by specialists, but before the arrival of Kant he enjoyed enormous authority not only in Germany but throughout Europe. In his rigorous rationalism, and his apparent confidence that (*pace* Kant) the mind was indeed capable of answering the questions it posed to itself, he was in a sense an Enlightenment philosopher par excellence. Young Jung read deeply in Wolff, and with each page found him less satisfactory, more spiritually arid.

Walking one day around the lanes of Solingen, where he had taken up an apprenticeship with the Pietist tailor, he saw a brilliantly illuminated cloud in the sky. The external sign was accompanied by an inexplicable but dramatic inner sense of contentment. "He began to tremble in all his limbs, and could scarcely refrain from sinking to the ground, and from that time he felt a strong desire to live wholly to the glory of God, and for the welfare of his fellow men." When shortly after, on April 12, 1763, Jung-Stilling felt a confirmation of the first revelation, the statutory experience of Pietist conversion was complete.

Religious conversion was not for him the same as a clerical vocation. He resumed a peripatetic life sufficiently full of engaging experiences and episodes to make his autobiography something of an adventure tale. The man had, in fact, an extraordinary professional career. His was an age that honored all forms of learning, including autodidacticism. It was assumed that any educated person ought to be able to teach what he or she knew. Hence the private tutors and governesses who so thickly populate the pages of eighteenth- and nineteenth-century fiction. That is how he had first become a teacher, and now became one again. He studied that combination of amateur pharmacology and medicine that we saw in the early career of Cagliostro; later he had more formal medical training at Strassburg. He became an oculist. There is no reason to disbelieve his description of a successful operation on a woman's cataracts—an achievement that alone should dispel the charges of mere charlatanism later made against him by his rationalist critics. Periodical essays published while at Strassburg led to his appointment, around his fortieth year, as professor of political economy at the University of Marburg!

But Jung-Stilling's true vocation would be literary. He became one of the most famous German language writers of the century, and the friend of others. Goethe greatly admired him, Herder much less so; but he was in that rank. He commanded a huge "crossover" audience. His first and perhaps his greatest book is his autobiography, to the writing of which he adopted a remarkable attitude. He made the writing of his life a life's work. That is, the autobiography appeared, like a Dickens novel, in serial parts. Just as his life was a work in progress, so also would be its writing. Its publication dates stretch from 1777, when he was thirty-seven years old, to 1817, the year of his death.

The work is remarkable in its form, which is highly novelistic, always speaking of its author in the third person. While there are no grounds for doubting its essential truthfulness, it seems clear that it has undergone a process of "spiritual editing" not unlike that discernible in many great examples of religious autobiography, such as Augustine's *Confessions*. In one sense it becomes less "literary" as it goes along—meaning that the prose becomes increasingly chaste. But even as it does so, its philosophical motives become increasingly intrusive.

There is a positive and a negative motive. The author wants his readers to answer a question: Is the course of a man's life a series of random events, or does it reveal a plan? If so, whose plan? Jung-Stilling's negative motive is to combat the "atrocity" of Wolff's philosophical "determinism," which (in Stilling's view) held that men, like other features of the phenomenal world, developed according to "Nature," which imposed upon them determining form. Jung-Stilling believed that the purpose of life was to discover and to cooperate with the plan that *God* has designed. He wanted to see, and to illustrate, the evidences of God operating in his own life. In his view, this did not encumber the freedom of the human will. Rather, it returned to men and women the agency, which in his understanding the determinism of rationalist philosophers like Wolff had removed.

But it did mean that for most of the time men saw their lives as in a glass, darkly. Life became a kind of cosmic scavenger hunt. Significance was everywhere, but it was often hidden or disguised; it had to be uncovered or discovered. The medieval theologians had an arresting term for the shadowy world of unreality in which we live out our physical lives. It was the *regio dissimilitudinis*, the land of unlikeness. Things are not what they seem to be. The man facing the mirror raises a right hand; the mirrored man facing back raises a *left* hand. It was a world to be deciphered rather than simply perceived, and all of the oblique arts of eighteenth-century esotericism might be needed to decipher it.

The allegorical or emblematic mentality had by no means disappeared in the Enlightenment. Figurative patterns of thought were simply too deeply entrenched in the European psyche to be junked with the rise of empiricism. But allegory can be thought of in at least two ways: as a mode of construction, or as a mode of interpretation. Jung-Stilling's sensibility embraced both tendencies. He read life as a large and continuing allegory, but he also typically advanced his ideas in allegorical mode.

His autobiography was widely read in Germany, German Switzerland, and the Pietist strongholds in Alsace that would later become one of Julie de Krüdener's theaters of operation. It was translated also into most European tongues. An English translation by the seminary theologian Hazelius was widely circulated among the "Pennsylvania

Dutch," who were of course actually the Pennsylvania *Deutsch*, which is to say German-speakers. It has the historical interest of having issued in 1831 from the press of the Evangelical seminary in Gettysburg, the institution that is remembered in the fatal gazetteer of our Civil War as "Seminary Ridge."

His literary output was varied and enormous, but among his most influential works were a number of explicitly theological allegories that made him something of the C. S. Lewis of his age. His Aslan—C. S. Lewis's leonine figure of the cosmic Christ—was called "the Gray Man." Under this title (*Der Graue Mann*) he for several years published a popular religious periodical of frequently esoteric tendency—an achievement hardly less remarkable in his publishing circumstances than in ours. Between 1777 and 1783, he published a theological trilogy of semi-historical novels dealing extensively (and often negatively) with alchemists, Rosicrucian adepts, and other disturbers of the peace of the Church. Indeed, the consistent motive of his literary work was a defense of his version of universalist Christian orthodoxy against the centrifugal tendencies of the "exalted"—by which he meant separatist— religious movements of the day. But he went a long way toward exaltation himself.

This becomes clear from his huge *roman fleuve* entitled *Heimweh*, which appeared 1794–96, and which caused a great stir throughout Europe and not least in the breast of Julie de Krüdener. *Heimweh* means "homesickness" or "nostalgia." Jung-Stilling uses it in the not uncommon theological sense of the natural yearning of the soul for its celestial homeland, or the recuperation of an original innocence or rectitude by man in a fallen or sinful state. It is in this novel that the distinct strain of Jung-Stilling's chiliasm appears full-blown. For if God's operations were decipherable in the lives of obscure persons living in the rural hamlets of the German principalities, how could they not be observable in the stupendous events of European history, and especially the stupendous event of Revolution in France?

Julie de Krüdener had been born in the year following Jung-Stilling's conversion. By the time the two met, she was in her still youthful forties, he in his valetudinarian late sixties. By then she believed that her own life was the perfect vindication of Jung-Stilling's theories about the purpose of life, that it must be an urgent search to discover the operations of God in one's own life. They were to form an intimate spiritual friendship, marked by a father-and-daughter affection, yet tinged with the competitive admiration of old literary lions.

The Lady of the Holy Alliance

It was mentioned earlier, with regard to Cagliostro's stay in Strassburg, that the Alsatian region had a long history of Pietist association. Some of its villages and small towns were virtual seedbeds of occult religion. In one such place, Sainte-Marie-aux-Mines (Markirk by its German name), Julie de Krüdener fell under the spiritual sway of two extravagant mystics: a Pietist Calvinist pastor named Johann Frederick Fontaines and a self-appointed peasant-prophetess named Marie Kümmer. They were an extraordinary pair. Fontaines was a "convert from reason." He had been a Jacobin, or at least a sympathizer with the Revolution's radical tendencies. Knapton reports the "legend" that he had been among the sacrilegious youth who in 1793 had raced their horses through the cathedral of Strassburg. But he soon took up religion of a highly personal kind—that is to say, the Pietist "religion of the heart"—abandoning his religious orthodoxy, as he earlier had his political orthodoxy, in favor of chiliastic meditations and deeply emotional spiritual conferences.

Secular chronology, though at best speculative and approximate, has had a profound influence on Christian Apocalyptic thought. Only quite recently there was huge excitement among what remains of the chiliastic community as midnight approached on December 31, 1999. The turn of the millennium inspired a particular spiritual energy, but the turn of even a commonplace century is not without its excitements. Such was the case in the year 1800. In its anticipation Fontaines had written a strange prophetical book. It is now extremely rare, and I have not been able to consult it. But he concluded that the countdown to the End would begin with the new century, and that the End would arrive at the very latest by 1836.

Marie Kümmer was one of Fontaines's chief disciples, though her rich spiritual history antedated her association with him. Kümmer was a countrywoman of the style of Adam Müller, the peasant-prophet. Julie de Krüdener was as deeply impressed by her as she earlier had been by Madame Blau. Kümmer became now something of a "role model" for Julie. Marie fell into frequent trances; it was rumored that she on occasion levitated. Julie did not equal these spiritual prodigies, but she did join with Marie, and sometimes with Fontaines, in intense sessions of ecstatic prayer.

Marie Kümmer had achieved biblical literacy, and she studied Pastor Fontaines's book about the Last Times with great care. Like Anne Conway's uncle more than a century earlier, she became convinced that the advent of the Kingdom of God must be preceded by the re-establishment of an earthly kingdom of the righteous ones in Zion. She succeeded in convincing a sizable group of followers, and they took off on foot for the Holy Land, actually making it as far as Vienna— about four hundred miles through often difficult terrain. Julie would later imitate this trek with her own pilgrimage into the hinterland of the Crimea; but initially she imitated Marie in a different way, by beginning the public itinerant preaching for which she became famous—and among many of her former associates, infamous.

Such were the circumstances of Julie de Krüdener *dévote*, as she approached the most famous exploit in her life: her supposed role in the formation of the Holy Alliance. The Holy Alliance, proposed by Czar Alexander I and subscribed to by Russia's triumphant allies Prussia and Austria at the Congress of Vienna in 1815, declared that in the future the political policies of Europe's great powers would be conducted on the basis of "Christian principles" ecumenically shared among Roman Catholics, the Orthodox, and Protestants. It was that anodyne clause, which in actuality would hardly revolutionize the practice of power politics in the nineteenth century, that could render a sweeping conservative retrenchment as "holy." Julie was credited with having first suggested to her friend Alexander the idea of a formal political pact founded on "Christian principles." It is at least possible that she in fact did so, but the transmission of a cliché could scarcely claim for her an important role in the political history of the post-Napoleonic settlement. What does seem remarkable is that an increasingly eccentric religious fanatic might still be an intimate familiar of the Czar of all the Russias. It is perhaps unkind to suggest a parallel with Rasputin, whom she anticipated by a century.

For in the first decade of the nineteenth century Julie de Krüdener arrived at a spiritual tipping point. After that the Masonic occultism, the Pietist chiliasm, and her own personal apocalyptic vision seem to have coalesced in the extravagance that has defined her for history. It is not possible to pinpoint a precise time or event, but the Battle of Eylau may well have played a determinative role. On February 7 and 8, 1807, the Grande Armée of the French Empire met a large Russo-Prussian force on snow-covered terrain in a battle unusually sanguinary even for Napoleonic warfare. There were enormous casualties on either side, perhaps twenty or thirty *thousand* altogether. The outcome was nonetheless inconclusive. Marshal Ney, who had saved the French from what seemed at one point likely defeat, said of his Pyrrhic victory: *"Quel massacre! Et sans resultat!"*

Julie de Krüdener was then living at Königsberg, not far distant.

Shortly after the battle many citizens of Königsberg, some good Samaritans and some simply sensation-seekers, drove out to view the battlefield. Julie was among them. The wounded had been mainly cleared away, but there were still corpses promiscuously strewn about, some grotesquely maimed and mangled, the stiff carcasses of horses, shattered gun emplacements, all the detritus left by the great death machine. And everywhere she looked, Julie saw bloody snow. She knew what she was seeing. "For the mystery of iniquity doth already work: only he who now letteth will let, until he be taken out of the way." (II Thessalonians 2:7) The "worker" of the mystery of iniquity was the emperor Napoleon!

Julie de Krüdener was a European aristocrat. Her friends were aristocrats, or the protégées of aristocrats. During most of the years of her wanderings she had been constantly in the company of French émigrés, one of whom was the father of her illegitimate child. Her experience of the Revolution had been entirely negative. As she became increasingly "religious," then traveled more and more among religious people, she began to see the Revolution as so many of them had seen it—in terms of a chiliastic theology of history.

Napoleon Bonaparte was either the continuation of the Revolution, or its personification. None of the other leaders of the Revolution had lasted long enough to attract the attention of millenarian exegetes. Napoleon was different. In him the awful power of the Revolution reached its apex and what, in the first decade of the nineteenth century, appeared to be permanence. France's imperial expansion seemed to its neighbors, including Britain across the Channel, a terrifying threat to everything that had created Christendom and its values. Naturally the anxiety was the highest in those duchies of "Germany" directly abutting upon French national territory. We saw that anxiety in the supernatural "messages" of the peasant-prophet Müller for the Prussian king. But it was felt hardly less acutely in the further tiers of European territories: in

Austria and Moravia, which was the scene of the campaign of 1805, along the Baltic littoral from Danzig to St. Petersburg, in Prussia from Königsberg toward Vilna and the Russian heartland. In these lands many of the "prophets" were of higher social station than Adam Müller.

ART IMITATES LIFE WHICH, as we know, imitates art. The murky pathway to Julie de Krüdener's political chiliasm is somewhat illuminated by the artistry of one of the world's greatest novelists, Leo Tolstoy. Though *War and Peace* was published two generations after the events with which it chiefly deals, it reveals on nearly every page the careful researches of the realistic historical novelist. The opening scene of *War and Peace* is set at an aristocratic *soirée* in St. Petersburg in July 1805. Its opening words are some banter of the party's hostess, Anna Pavlovna Scherer, to her friend Prince Vasili Kuragin: "Well, Prince, so Genoa and Lucca are now just family estates of the Buonapartes. But I warn you, if you don't tell me that this means war, if you still try to defend the infamies and horrors perpetrated by that Antichrist—I really do believe he is Antichrist—I will have nothing more to do with you. . . ."

The identification of Napoleon with the Antichrist was widespread before 1805, and nearly universal by 1812. It is thus not surprising that it had important impact on the most sensational episode of Julie de Krüdener's career. It is true that we do not know precisely at what point she had herself concluded that Napoleon Bonaparte was the Antichrist. Even the French historians who have most deeply studied the sinister myths or "black legend" surrounding Napoleon have identified no single "source" of the chiliastic identification. But its elements—exegetical, esoteric, Rosicrucian—were precisely those easily found among the Masonic lodges of the German cities and the religious meetings of the Pietists. The "legend" is preserved in its most complete form in certain post-Revolutionary writers, and in particular by some of the Catholic clergy and reactionary political critics associated with the program of French "re-Christianization." The most remarkable of these, in terms of his literary production, is the priest Jean Wendel Würtz.

A brilliant bibliographer, André Blavier, has produced for France a reference work of inestimable value entitled *Les fous littéraires*. One can only hope for the early appearance of its analogue for the Anglophone world. It is a bibliography of crackpots—religious, scientific, medical, metaphysical—of whom the French nation produced unusually fascinating specimens throughout the eighteenth and nineteenth centuries. French "prophets" were numerous among them, and some of Blavier's bio-bibliographics are uniquely valuable contributions to the study of the esoteric thought of the period that now concerns us. He has gathered together what is known about Würtz, who after the Revolution became the rector of the principal parish of Lyon.

According to Blavier, Würtz was born in Germany around 1760. Another Jean Wendel Würtz, undoubtedly a relative, was born in the hamlet of Walschbronn on the Moselle in Lorraine in 1784. We may guess that the abbé Würtz conducted his early ministry among the émigrés of nearby Coblenz, at the confluence of the Moselle and the Rhine. He was among the first Catholic clergy restored in Lyon, and the Revolutionary history of that city is undoubtedly relevant to his attitudes. In 1793, Lyon had attempted to "secede" from the Revolution by siding with the defeated Girondins. In a suspect judicial action that almost immediately became for the Jacobins in Paris a *casus belli*, the radical Joseph Chalier was guillotined in Lyon that July. The Convention eventually unleashed upon the city a terrible punishment that included the destruction of important civic buildings and the brutal execution of more than two thousand citizens. Saint-Nizier, the great Gothic church of which Würtz would later become rector, escaped total destruction but not desecration. It was transformed into a flour warehouse, with bakers' boys and carters camping out in the chapels where the sacred sacrifice had been performed of old.

The atrocities perpetrated against the second city of the Republic by the first were not soon forgotten. Napoleon did his best to placate the survivors by ordering the replacement of destroyed buildings. He could not, however, resuscitate the slain burghers, whose families still dominated the city's society and commerce. During the Restoration, the Lyon town fathers continued to cultivate a memory of royalist resistance to the Revolution. For such a "black" city, the reactionary abbé Würtz was an appropriate pastor.

In 1816, Würtz published the first edition of *Les précurseurs de l'Anté-Christ* in Lyon. The book caught on, and went through a number of enlargements and reprintings. It met with considerable favor among a certain audience. That that favor was not quite universal is suggested by a prefatory statement in Würtz's next book, *Superstitions et prestiges des philosophes, ou, Les démonlâtres du siècle des lumières* (Lyon, 1817). Here the author shrugs off the certainty that some people, more to be pitied than censured, would laugh at him.

Les précurseurs de l'Anté-Christ is an interpretation of the final book of the Christian Scriptures. Its purpose is clearly stated in a subtitle: "A Prophetical History of the most notorious Impieties appearing since the establishment of the Church, up to the year 1816, OR, the French Revolution as Predicted by St. John the Evangelist." In it Napoleon Bonaparte, now "chained" like Satan on the island of St. Helena, plays the major role of the "Angel of the Bottomless Pit."

This terrible figure appears in the ninth chapter of the Apocalypse, following the sound of the trumpet of the *fifth* angel. The relevant details are these. The Angel of the Bottomless Pit (the Greek word being *abyss*) is the "king" of a vast army of locusts, which in appearance "were like horses equipped for battle. They have divine leave to torture earth's inhabitants for five months." The angel-king has a name. "His name in Hebrew is Abaddon; and in Greek he is called Apollyon." "Apollyon" means *Exterminans*, the Destroyer or Exterminator.

The mathematics of the exegesis deployed by Würtz may seem

startling to us, but it was familiar to even the most amateur of esoteri-cists in his audience. The biblical "day" often in fact indicates a year. All months should be regarded, for interpretive purposes, as having thirty days. Hence "five months" actually means a hundred and fifty years (5 × 30); but as there are *two* periods of five months (Rev. 9:5 and 9:10), the actual prophecy is one of *three hundred* years. These are the three hundred years between the inception of the Protestant Reforma-tion and the advent of the Exterminator. By the fifth printing Würtz was apologizing for a lapse of memory by which he had originally dated the beginning of Luther's Reformation to 1515 instead of 1516. It is clear why he made the error. In his mind the three-hundred-year period of which John darkly wrote was the age between the unchain-ing of Luther and the chaining of Napoleon; but 1516–1816 (the year of publication of the *Précurseurs*) would serve as well as 1515–1815. As he approaches his explanation of the *Exterminans*, Würtz makes a gener-ous concession to earlier interpreters of the Book of Revelation. They had all to a man interpreted the malign figure in the rather general sense of the heresies with which they were familiar. The eyewitnesses to the enormity of the French Revolution could have no doubt con-cerning the true meaning.

In Würtz's scheme the heresies of Protestantism both prepared for and were superseded by the horrors of "philosophy," by which he means the doctrines of the *philosophes* working through the Masonic lodges. His representative *philosophe*, interestingly, is not Voltaire but the materialist Holbach. Protestants had merely attacked specific Catholic doctrines concerning sacramental theology and church gov-ernance. The *philosophes* had a much more radical program: the destruction of Christianity altogether. Of earlier exegetes Bossuet had come the closest to seeing the full truth, for he had predicted that Protestantism must end in infidelity.

Recent history had removed the veil of mystery that had disguised the figure of Apollyon *Exterminans*. "Who is this Angel from the abyss, that is to say this apostle, this ambassador of the infernal Dragon? Do you not recognize Napoleon? Is he not here designated virtually by his own name [nAPOLEON/APPOLYON]? Is he not perfectly signified by the name 'Exterminator'? Who ever exterminated more men than he?" Würtz is prepared to brook no dissent. It is a specious argument that Napoleon actually *restored* Catholicism in the Concordat, his famous formal treaty with the Pope. Würtz declares that a mere ruse, a stepping stone to the throne. The abbé is aware that the exiled emperor may remain a hero to the simple and the shallow. Let them remember the anarchist cry heard in the very streets of Lyon: "Long live Hell!" (*Vive l'enfer!*) Was that not the very cry with which the deluded veterans greeted their idol upon his escape from Elba?

All doubts will disappear, Würtz thinks, for the reader who considers the thousand-year reign of Christ and the martyrs (Rev. 20). The abbé identifies this as the period of the *French monarchy*, mythically considered, which began with Charlemagne in 800 and ended (approximately) in 1800, either with the execution of Louis XVI in 1793 or the coronation of Napoleon in 1804. But of particular importance is John's invocation of the great war unleashed by Gog and Magog (Rev. 20:8). As this is an image taken from the prophet Ezekiel, he returns to the source. There in the horrifying images of the thirty-eighth and thirty-ninth chapters, he finds what he cannot doubt is a description of Napoleon's disastrous retreat from Moscow, when starving men did indeed eat horses, and even in some instances the flesh of their own dead comrades in arms.

I have not been able to determine whether Tolstoy had read the fantastic books of the abbé Würtz. But there can be no doubt that he was familiar with their genre. Another passage in *War and Peace* deals explicitly with the kind of number mysticism and gematria that were staples of Enlightenment occultism.

In a central chapter of *War and Peace* the novel's hero, Pierre Bezukhov, arrives at the conclusion that the emperor Napoleon is the Antichrist and that he, Bezukhov, has the sacred duty to assassinate him. The first conclusion is child's play. First you must adapt the ancient conventions of kabbalistic gematria to the Latin alphabet in the manner favored by the mystical Freemasons of Lyon, as follows:

a	b	c	d	e	f	g	h	i	k	l	m	n	o	p	q	r	s	t
1	2	3	4	5	6	7	8	9	10	20	30	40	50	60	70	80	90	100

u	v	w	x	y	z
110	120	130	140	150	160

You then write out, in French, the title *L[e] Empereur Napoléon*, cheating ever so slightly by not eliding the *e* of the article. Now add it all up to get 666, the "number of the Beast" (see Revelation 13:18). More important from Pierre's point of view is that in the fifth verse of that same chapter it is written that the beast will be given authority for a period of "forty and two months." Pierre, an erudite fellow, knows that when the Bible speaks of "days" or "months" it actually means *years*. He knows as well that the year is 1812, meaning that Napoleon, born in 1769, must in fact be forty-two years old.

It takes Pierre a little while to figure out his numerological role in the great scheme of things, but he does so after a certain amount of orthographic jiggery-pokery, this time dropping an *e* that *should* be there. It turns out that the phrase *L'Russe Besuhof* (roughly, *duh Russian Bezukhov*) is also a 666. So the beast has come to the end of his allotted time. Forty-two is all you get. History buffs and readers of Tolstoy will know that things didn't quite work out, but that was the theory.

It becomes necessary to dwell on the strange interpretation that Pierre finds in the number 42. According to Douglas Adams in *The Hitchhiker's Guide to the Galaxy*, 42 contains the meaning of "everything." The old exegetes were perhaps less global in their claims, but more specific in their demonstration. For the number 42 has an ancient and distinguished history in both the sacred and the secular esoteric traditions, and of course also in the marriage of the two that was Rosicrucian mysticism. In terms of human age measured in years, 42 is one of the important "climacterics," or seven-year periods, providing the punctuation points of a man's life. The basis of this idea is the heptameral scheme of Creation as recorded in the Book of Genesis and reflected in the structure of the calendrical week.

Certain ideas that now appear to us very strange and contrived seemed to our ancestors almost too obvious to demand comment—though fortunately they did comment on them in such detail that we can often reconstruct them with adequate confidence. Seven was one of the Pythagorean building blocks of the universe, and also of human life, as Shakespeare records in Jaques's famous lines about "the ages of man":

> *All the world's a stage,*
> *And all the men and women merely players:*
> *They have their exits and their entrances;*
> *And one man in his time plays many parts,*
> *His acts being seven ages.*

Less well known, perhaps, though hardly of less theological importance, are the seven ages of world history—or rather, the world's six ages and its eternal postlude. For the Fathers of the Church, and especially and most influentially Augustine, had divided all of human history, the history of salvation, into six ages. The precise points of division varied slightly among the theorists, but all were agreed that the final age, the Sixth Age, was the Age of the Incarnation. It had begun with the fullness of the divine revelation in the person of Jesus Christ. All who lived after Christ were living in the Sixth Age. The final period of cosmic history—final and eternal—would be heralded by the Second Coming. These ideas had been commonplace among the patristic writers and they were commonplace still among the Protestant Pietists of the eighteenth century. The product of the root of the climacteric (7) and the Age of the Incarnation (6) is 42.

It is remarkable that it is but a short step from medieval mystery to Enlightenment Illuminism. Julie de Krüdener turned to the mysteries of numbers. Now 4, 5, and 7—to name but three—all had more or less highly elaborated allegorical significance in ancient philosophy; but it was the conventions of Christian scriptural exegesis that spread number symbolism throughout European culture. All the numbers of the decade—that is to say, 1 through 10—had commonplace theological associations that survive even today in stock phrases and folklore. Most people, however secular, are probably aware that there are four evangelists, seven deadly sins, ten commandments, and so forth. Other references may be deeply arcane. A strange usage of the word "rivals"—the "three, three, the rivals" of the folk round "Green Grow the Rushes—O"—is probably a reference to the Christian Trinity. Here "rival" seems to preserve its ancient Latin etymology of "riverbank" (as in the *rive gauche* of the Seine in Paris) and mean one of several anglers "fishing in the same stream."

One biblical chapter alone has called forth a whole library of numerological exegesis: the thirteenth chapter of the Apocalypse. There in verse 13 we learn that the beast who speaks "great things and blasphemies" has been given the power to "continue for forty and two months." And in the eighteenth and final verse of the chapter we learn "the number of the Beast," which is "the number of a man," and that number is 666. One other Apocalyptic number completes the anthology: 1,260. In the eleventh chapter we are told that the "two witnesses" will testify for 1,260 days; in the twelfth that the woman clothed with the sun will find a safe place in the wilderness for 1,260 days. An uninstructed reader may welcome a little help with these numbers, beginning with the fact, already noted, that for the exegetes the words "days" and "months" are poetic figures meaning years. The periods of duration are therefore related in the following obvious way. It was forty-two generations from Abraham to Christ, but how long was that in years? It was assumed by convention that there are thirty years in a generation. Thirty multiplied by 42 is 1,260. Hence the first covenant, the promises made to Abraham, dated from 1260 BC. Twelve hundred and sixty years later saw the birth of Jesus Christ. Thinking by analogy, quite a few thirteenth-century Christians anticipated some great apocalyptic event in the year 1260.

There are, however, also several instances of rather more complex biblical numbers. In the story of the miraculous catch of fish in the Gospel of John (21:1–14), Peter pulls his net to the shore to find therein 153 big fish. This is an odd number in more senses than one. Many biblical numbers seem to give the sense of "a lot" or "a long time" ("seventy times seven," the number of times you should forgive your enemy, or "forty days and forty nights," the duration of the protracted rainstorm that flooded the earth). The number 153, on the other hand, suggests the quality of a classified statistic. Peter didn't just catch a lot of fish without breaking his net; he caught precisely 153, and they were big ones. Medieval exegetes knew the number could not be accidental, and they went to extraordinary lengths to interpret it. Very often they found in it themes relating to evangelism or conversion, since in another more famous passage Jesus promised his piscatorial followers that they would now become "fishers of men." Scholars have claimed to find traces of such "meanings" in the proportions and certainly the decorations of some medieval ecclesiastical buildings.

There is, however, a distinction to be made between the extraordinary and the fantastic. One will ransack the extraordinary medieval sources in vain without discovering such fantastic Enlightenment arcana as the following. The height of the Great Pyramid of Cheops, as determined by French and British investigators of the Grand Age, is 486.256 feet. The length of its base is 763.81 feet. Now it is child's play to discover that the product of the base multiplied by pi raised to the fourth power divided by the sum of the height and the tenth part of pi renders 152.999999344—and what are 656 billionths among friends?

But 42 is in a class by itself.

Seven and 9 were heavily fraught even before they came under the scrutiny of the rabbis and the patristic exegetes, and they were the two factors of what were called the climacterics. That is, any number into which 7 or 9 could be divided evenly was thought to be of probable arcane significance. The actual product of 9 and 7, 63, was called the "Grand Climacteric"; and it was regarded as a particularly dangerous number. Indeed, it was often the "fatal" number, since a great many people were supposed to have died in their sixty-third or sixty-fourth years, as they probably did in ages in which male life expectancy hovered in the forties. Forty-two, being the product of 7 and 6, was one of the lesser climacterics and, on the whole, a benign one. It will be seen that forty-two lies midway between the climacteric of twenty-one, which emerged as the legal age of majority in European law, and therefore was a kind of beginning, and the Grand Climacteric of sixty-three, which threatened to be an end. Forty-two could therefore be regarded as a number of maturity or completion, and in this conclusion secular and biblical numerologists were in agreement.

The biblical occurrences ranged from the sublime to the whimsical. Of the former are the forty-two "mansions" or stations of the Exodus. That is, if you make up a list of all the places that the Hebrews stopped on their way to the Promised Land, you will find that there are forty-two of them. Since the Exodus is the very type of the pattern of redemption, 42 suggests itself as a number of fulfillment or completion. Among the more whimsical incidents in prophetic history, perhaps, is that of the forty-two bad boys who got eaten up by an unspecified number of bears for the rude discourtesy of calling Elisha "Baldy." But the definitive 42, so to speak, the instance that linked the number with all serious schemes of medieval Christian chronology, will be found at the beginning of the Gospel of Matthew. There one finds a genealogy of Jesus Christ. As it is patrilineal, it begins with the patriarch Abraham and ends with Joseph, the spouse of Jesus' mother. There are forty-two generations between Abraham and Christ, and they are deployed in three groupings of fourteen, fourteen being the first of the complex climacterics.

In its relationship to sacred history, 42 was the number of completion. At the birth of Christ what had first been promised to Abraham before the Law, then confirmed in Moses under the Law, was now fulfilled under grace. It is for this reason, eventually, that so many medieval and Renaissance literary works structure themselves around the number 42. Dante's spiritual autobiography, the *Vita Nuova*, is "naturally" divided into forty-two chapters. In the margins of the unique manuscript of *Beowulf* some early editor has added puzzling divisions in Roman numerals. Nobody knows quite what they are about, but there are forty-two of them.

Barbara Juliana Vietinghof, later Madame la baronne de Krüdener, was born in November 1764. She completed her climacteric year in November 1806. But the numbers sometimes needed a little help, just as Pierre Bezukhov had needed a little help. The phrase *le Empereur Napoléon* might be bad French, but it's great gematria! Likewise he discovered that the French cardinal number 42 (*quarante-deux*) renders the same result. *And* (three exclamation points!!!) Napoleon, born on August 15, 1769, is forty-two years old in 1812, if one regards not the year in which Napoleon completed his forty-second year of life (1811) but the year during which, in popular parlance, he "was" forty-two years old. To make two years of one is perhaps a minor miracle when compared with the loaves and the fishes, and it was within the easy grasp of the mystical imagination. Madame de Krüdener nowhere to my knowledge explicitly addresses the mystical chronology of her vocation as a prophetess, but her definitive abandonment of the role of literary rock star in favor of that of itinerant preacher corresponds nicely to her visit to the corpse-littered battlefield of Eylau (February 1807)—by easy accommodation her climacteric year.

THE LAST YEARS OF Julie de Krüdener's life were tragicomic as she moved about preaching in the German-speaking lands from Switzerland (where she had an unfortunate association with a crazed young woman who crucified herself) to East Prussia. She and her friends were frequently harassed by the police. But to this period of her life belongs, possibly, her greatest triumph. She had much earlier become a friend of Czar Alexander I. The Romanovs even then, a century before Rasputin, showed a weakness for religious counselors of a strange kind. It was allegedly in a *séance* with Madame de Krüdener that the emperor conceived the idea of the Holy Alliance proclaimed at the Congress of Vienna in 1815. This pact, according to which the subscribing states committed themselves to uphold the principles of the Christian religion, was part of the reaction to Napoleon, and an effort to reverse the consequences of the French Revolution in Europe. Julie de Krüdener died in 1824 in an obscure part of the Crimea, where she had gone on her last preaching mission with the apparent aim of establishing a millenarian community. The unknown location of her tomb became the subject of historical legend.

She had been born late in the year 1764, a few weeks after the young Gibbon had the brainwave that would in time become one of the greatest of all works of Enlightenment historiography. "It was Rome, on the fifteenth of October 1764," he writes, "as I sat musing amidst the ruins of the Capitol, while the barefoot friars were singing vespers in the Temple of Jupiter, that the idea of writing the decline and fall of the city first started to my mind." It might at first seem impossible to imagine two sensibilities or intellectual personalities more disparate. Yet each of them was a true inheritor of different legacies of the Age of Lights.

Bibliographical

There are many good books dealing with some of the French literary influences on Julie de Krüdener. These include two of the older biographies, J. Christopher Herold's *Mistress to an Age: A life of Madame de Staël* (Indianapolis, 1958), and André Maurois, *Chateaubriand: Poet, Statesman, Lover* (English trans. New York, 1938). George Painter completed only the first volume of his biography of Chateaubriand, which does not take the story up as far as his dealings with Julie.

Her important German connections are more difficult to get at. There is little in English about Jean-Paul Richter outside the standard encyclopedic sources. Jung-Stilling's autobiography was translated into English, and copies are to be found in the larger libraries. The German version is frequently reprinted in scholarly format. There is a collection of German essays, many of them relevant to this book, in *Zwischen Strassburg und Petersburg: Voträge aus Anlass des 250 Gebutrstag von Johann Heinrich Jung-Stilling*, ed. Peter Wörster (Siegen, 1992). Many of Julie's Pietist gurus (including Zinzendorf) are treated in Carter Lindberg's *The Pietist Theologians: An Introduction to the Theology of the Seventeenth and Eighteenth Centuries* (Malden, MA, 2005).

Chauncey Tinker's golden oldie *The Salon and English Letters* (New York, 1915) is a good English introduction to the idea of the literary *salon*, though more relevant to Madame de Krüdener are such books as Marie Gougy-François, *Les grands salons féminins* (Paris, 1965), or the elegant anthology put out by the Musée Carnavalet in 1928, *Les grands salons littéraires*.

Concerning the Holy Alliance there is a good English-language introduction in W. P. Cresson, *The Holy Alliance: The European Background of the Monroe Doctrine* (Oxford, 1922). More directly relevant to Julie de Krüdener are E. Muhlenbeck, *Etude sur les origines de la Sainte-Alliance*; Francis Ley, *Alexandre Ier et sa Sainte-Alliance* (Paris, 1975); and

Stella Ghervas, *Alexandre Stourdza (1791–1854), un intellectual orthodoxe face à l'Occident* (Geneva, 1999). Stourdza was a Russian diplomat who knew Julie.

Books specifically cited or alluded to in this chapter:

André Blavier, *Les fous littéraires,* 2nd ed. (Paris: Editions des cendres, 2000).

Quotations from Madame de Krüdener's letters are translated from Charles Eynard's two-volume *Vie de Madame de Krudener,* already cited in the bibliography to the last chapter.

Index

Passages marked in **boldface** identify the most important discussions of persons and topics frequently mentioned in the text.